CURRICULUM
An Integrative Introduction

Evelyn J. Sowell
Arizona State University West

Merrill,
an imprint of Prentice Hall
Englewood Cliffs, New Jersey   Columbus, Ohio

Library of Congress Cataloging-in-Publication Data

Sowell, Evelyn J.
     Curriculum : an integrative introduction / Evelyn J. Sowell.
        p.   cm.
     Includes bibliographical references and index.
     ISBN 0-02-413850-9
     1. Curriculum planning. 2. Educational change. 3. Teaching—Aids and devices.
I. Title.
   LB2806.15.S69   1996
   375'.001—dc20   95-42969
                                                             CIP

Editor: Debra A. Stollenwerk
Production Editor: Mary Harlan
Design Coordinator: Jill E. Bonar
Text Designer: EDH
Cover Designer: Proof Positive/Farrowlyne Assoc., Inc.
Production Manager: Pamela D. Bennett
Electronic Text Management: Marilyn Wilson Phelps, Matthew Williams, Karen L. Bretz,
   Tracey Ward
Illustrations: Tracey Ward

This book was set in New Baskerville by Prentice Hall and was printed and bound by R.R.
Donelley & Sons Company. The cover was printed by Phoenix Color Corp.

© 1996 by Prentice-Hall, Inc.
A Simon & Schuster Company
Englewood Cliffs, New Jersey 07632

Printed in the United States of America

10 9 8 7 6 5 4 3 2 1

ISBN: 0-02-413850-9

Prentice-Hall International (UK) Limited, *London*
Prentice-Hall of Australia Pty. Limited, *Sydney*
Prentice-Hall of Canada, Inc., *Toronto*
Prentice-Hall Hispanoamericana, S. A., *Mexico*
Prentice-Hall of India Private Limited, *New Delhi*
Prentice-Hall of Japan, Inc., *Tokyo*
Simon & Schuster Asia Pte. Ltd., *Singapore*
Editora Prentice-Hall do Brasil, Ltda., *Rio de Janeiro*

Preface

· ·

Curriculum is a topic about which educators as well as laypersons have knowledge, because we all attended school. For most of us, everything in and around schools seems somehow related to curriculum. If we're pressed for its exact meaning, we may hesitate in defining it because the boundaries of "curriculum" are not clear. In this text *curriculum* refers to what is taught in schools, a deliberately open definition that promotes consideration of curricula serving different purposes and contexts.

Planned for teachers and nonteaching school staff, this text seeks to bridge curriculum theory and practice by presenting information in practical settings. It's one thing to read and comprehend how curriculum processes work at the level of book knowledge and quite another to put those processes into practice. Practice informs theory, and *use* of theory helps individuals engage in curriculum tasks appropriately.

TEXT ORGANIZATION

Part One introduces several major ideas, including *technical* and *nontechnical approaches,* to curriculum processes. These approaches exist because curriculum personnel have different views of reality. Planners with largely objective views operate on the basis of knowable reality, but those with largely subjective views contend that each person's reality is unique and unknowable to others. Technical approaches, which use objective views of reality, prevail at most public district or school decision-making levels. Nontechnical approaches can be found in some schools and classrooms where acknowledgment of subjective realities is important.

Part Two discusses the bases for curriculum, including these sources—subject matter, society-culture, and learners. The intent of these chapters is to help readers consider and clarify their values about the relative contributions of these sources to school curricula.

Five different conceptions of curriculum with unique purposes of education and organization or design use content from these sources in different combina-

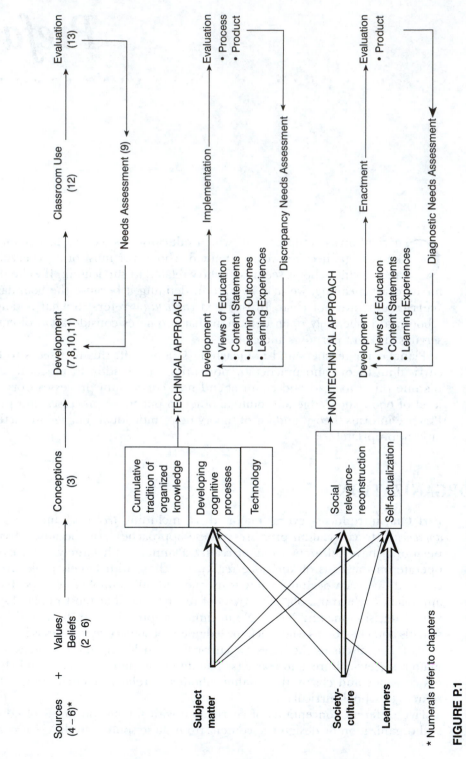

FIGURE P.1

Linkages Between Curriculum Foundations and Processes

* Numerals refer to chapters

iv

tions. To some extent all conceptions use subject matter. But three—the cumulative tradition of organized knowledge, developing cognitive processes, and technology—focus on subject matter. A fourth conception, social relevance-reconstruction, draws its content mainly from society and culture, and the fifth conception, self-actualization, emphasizes learners.

Part Three discusses and illustrates technical and nontechnical curriculum development. Part Four performs the same functions for classroom use and evaluation. Together these parts detail the cyclic nature of curriculum processes. Typically, a curriculum targeted for revision is incompatible with state guidelines, district or school needs, or the desires of the community. After it is revised, the curriculum is used in classrooms where its effects on students and the school community are evaluated. A special context evaluation, called a needs assessment, is sometimes employed to determine which things about a curriculum should be changed.

VISUAL SUMMARY

Figure P.1 displays connections between the curriculum foundations and processes elaborated within this text. These connections provide a rationale for the book title, *Curriculum: An Integrative Introduction*.

ACKNOWLEDGMENTS

Many people deserve thanks for helping to make this book possible. The following individuals offered insightful comments and reviews of the manuscript:

- David G. Blood, Governors State University
- Robert M. Borstad, Northern Illinois University
- Edward W. Holmes, Towson State University
- Cynthia Kruger, University of Massachusetts–Dartmouth
- Marcella L. Kysilka, University of Central Florida
- Michael A. Lorber, Illinois State University
- M. Lee Manning, Old Dominion University
- Albert J. Paulter, Jr., University at Buffalo
- Hampton S. Williams, University of Southern Mississippi

I also appreciate the staff at Prentice Hall/Merrill, especially Debbie Stollenwerk and Mary Harlan, who remained supportive throughout the development and production phases.

My students at Arizona State University West aided this project greatly with their reactions and comments on draft materials. In addition, my colleague Saundra Bryn encouraged me by using the draft manuscript with her students and providing her insights. I also thank the authors and publishers who allowed the reproduction of their materials in this book.

Finally, my family and close friends provided support that made tolerable the long hours and hard work. Thank you very much.

Contents

. . . .

PART TWO
Establishment of Bases for Curriculum Processes

CHAPTER 3
Curriculum Organization

CHAPTER 4
Studies of Subject Matter

CHAPTER 5
Studies of Society and Culture

CHAPTER 6
Studies of Learners

CHAPTER 11

Learning Experiences for Nontechnically Developed Curriculum Projects   217

PART FOUR

Classroom Use and Evaluation of Curriculum Projects   233

CHAPTER 12

Classroom Use of Curriculum Projects   234

CHAPTER 13

Evaluation of Curriculum Projects   256

Epilogue   276

Orientation for Readers

The content for this book was carefully chosen to provide for the development of certain conceptual themes. "Educational change" and "reform" are two themes mentioned frequently in newspapers and newscasts. Have you wondered why there is so much discussion about curriculum reform? Have you thought about why change is difficult? Answers to these questions are discussed in this text. However, the *real* answers lie in the actions that you take with respect to curriculum processes once you understand their operations.

Another theme in this text is "decision making," which suggests the existence of alternatives and choices. Indeed, many curricular alternatives exist, and choices among them are usually based on curriculum developers' beliefs and values. However, because decision making is generally sociopolitical, the beliefs and values incorporated in any particular curriculum may or may not be held by those who use the curriculum in classrooms. Developers and users must make decisions carefully and thoughtfully because living with the consequences of decisions by default or those made in haste can be difficult.

The integration of the conceptual themes of this text, within the context of curriculum foundations and processes, is presented in a comprehensible form that allows your understanding of curriculum to grow incrementally. Major ideas are presented more than once. "Purposes of education," which you will read about in the first chapter, exemplifies this idea. This concept is discussed in detail in Chapter 3 and is mentioned in each subsequent chapter as it pertains to the topic of that chapter. By the end of the book, you will have explored this concept in depth. If, as you study this text, you should wonder how curriculum ideas fit together, reread the Preface. Note that Figure P.1 links major concepts across chapters.

A student who used these chapters in draft form commented, "When I read most textbooks, I complete a chapter and don't look back. I can't do that with this one." That's because these chapters are linked conceptually and you are asked to reflect on what you read. You will see several suggestions to reconsider and think about your reading. These are intended to help you generate your own curriculum knowledge.

Exercises and questions for discussion bear further evidence of this intent. Each chapter contains one or more exercises in which you are asked to reflect on specific content and apply it in practical situations. Some chapter exercises suggest that you analyze or evaluate specific components (e.g., content statements, learning outcomes) of the real world curriculum documents included in Appendix A. Exercises such as these help you think about and prepare your own curriculum projects. Answers to some exercises are included in a separate section to provide feedback on your responses.

Every chapter has questions for discussion that focus on the main points of the chapter. Some questions are open-ended to allow discussants with alternate views to present their ideas. Other questions integrate information from different chapters and require higher-order thinking. Use of these questions can help build your understanding of the major ideas in this text.

Because many people enjoy stories, some information in Chapters 7 through 13 is told as a continuing narrative in which you are asked to role-play an elementary school principal and a high school English teacher. For some readers, this is their real world, but for others it's a convenient way to be involved in thinking about curriculum processes. These narratives, under the heading "Creation of . . . ," are intended to spark your interest in doing curriculum work. The author hopes that you have opportunity to engage in the processes during your study of this text. Enjoy!

If you have recommendations about this text, please forward them using the suggestions form at the back of the book. The author will carefully consider your ideas.

PART ONE

INTRODUCTION TO PROCESSES, PRODUCTS, AND PERSONNEL INVOLVED IN CURRICULUM

Part 1 provides an overview of curriculum processes and products as well as the people who work in curriculum. Chapter 1 discusses several important definitions, then launches the theme of educational change, embodied in curriculum processes. Chapter 2 calls attention to the large numbers of people involved in curriculum and how curriculum decisions result from sociopolitical processes at national, state, and local levels. Educational change and decision-making themes are elaborated in the remaining chapters of the book.

1

OVERVIEW OF CURRICULUM PROCESSES AND PRODUCTS

OUTLINE

Definitions
    Curriculum
    Instruction
    Learning
Levels of curriculum
Relationships between curriculum and instruction
    Nature of possible relationships
    Importance of understanding the relationships
Curriculum processes and products
    Processes
    Products
Curriculum processes as change
    Change defined
    Change applied in curriculum processes

Jackson (1992) notes that the best adjective to describe the state of affairs in curriculum is "confused," due in part to a lack of clear definitions. "What is *curriculum?*" and "To what should this term be applied?" have several answers.

Against this background, *Chapter 1 defines and establishes relationships among major curriculum concepts* as used in this text. These definitions and relationships form the core of communication about curriculum. Of particular importance are the meanings of curriculum processes considered in the context of change. The concepts introduced here are revisited in subsequent chapters where their meanings are broadened.

DEFINITIONS

CURRICULUM

Over the years definitions of *curriculum* have included the following: "1) the cumulative tradition of organized knowledge; 2) modes of thought; 3) race experience; 4) guided experience; 5) a planned learning environment; 6) cognitive/affective content and process; 7) an instructional plan; 8) instructional ends or outcomes; and 9) a technological system of production" (Tanner & Tanner, 1980, p. 36). Because curriculum emphases reflect changing social policies, these definitions are not unusual. Although somewhat disparate, they share generally the idea presented by *Webster's New World Dictionary,* 3rd edition, which provides this meaning for curriculum: "all of the courses, collectively, offered in a school, college, etc., or in a particular subject."

Differences among definitions are not unusual, because some individuals refer to curriculum levels interchangeably or do not distinguish between "curriculum" and "instruction." This text does not insist on an elaborate definition. Instead, you are asked to use the idea that **curriculum**[1] is *what* is taught to students. This broad definition includes both the intended and unintended information, skills, and attitudes that are communicated to students in schools. This definition also permits consideration of curricula based on several content sources and planned for different purposes of education. The interchangeability of terms is explored in the major sections that follow the definitions of instruction and learning.

INSTRUCTION

Instruction is *how* the curriculum is delivered to students. It is the interaction between a teaching agent and one or more individuals intending to learn knowledge that is appropriate for students to learn (Johnson, 1967). Of course, teachers qualify as teaching agents. But agents also include other students, school staff, instructional materials, programmed instruction, computer-assisted instruction, videos, and other technology-based instruction.

---

[1] Terms in bold are included in the glossary.

LEARNING

Usually **learning** is considered "acquired knowledge or skill" as defined in *Webster's New World Dictionary*, 3rd edition. A slightly elaborated classification holds that learning is what students take from classrooms in three classes of outcomes: *knowledge* (facts, concepts, generalizations), *techniques* (processes, skills, abilities), and *values* (norms, attitudes, interests, appreciations, aversions) (Cuban, 1992; Johnson, 1967).

LEVELS OF CURRICULUM

Educators—as well as laypersons—sometimes refer to the different levels of curriculum interchangeably, provoking a situation that can lead to confusion about the meaning of curriculum. As used here, **levels of curriculum** refers to the degree of remoteness from the students for whom the curricula were planned. This section provides information about levels of curriculum based on the account of Goodlad and Su (1992). These levels include societal, institutional, instructional, and experiential curricula.

- The *societal* level is curriculum farthest removed from learners and is designed by the public, including politicians, representatives of special interest groups, administrators at different levels, and professional specialists. Using sociopolitical processes, these groups often decide the goals, the topics to be studied, the time to be spent, and the materials to be used.

- *Institutional* curricula serve schools and derive largely from societal curricula with modifications by local educators and laypeople. This curriculum is commonly organized according to subjects and includes the topics and themes to be studied. Institutional curricula include the district's written documents containing standards, philosophies, lesson plans, and guides. Sometimes this curriculum, also called the *explicit* curriculum, is the target of reform efforts.

- The *instructional* curriculum refers to the one that teachers plan and deliver in schools. Teachers base instructional curricula on what has been determined as necessary or desirable for their school by school authorities. As expected, however, this curriculum takes on the individual teacher's priorities, views of education, and style and is also subject to reform and criticism. An instructional curriculum that is actually used in a classroom often varies from the planned curriculum, however, because of student responses or other unforeseen circumstances.

- Finally, the *experiential* curriculum is the one perceived and experienced by students. What is experienced differs from one student to the next because students have different backgrounds, motivations, and levels of aspirations (to name a few differences). For example, some students form similar purposes for learning experiences to those held by their teachers, but other students hold very different purposes or no purpose at all. Therefore, the experiential curriculum is the one internalized and made personal by learners (Goodlad & Su, 1992).

Educators should be able to distinguish among the levels of curriculum, because failure to do so leads to misinterpretations. Chapter 2 continues the discussion of levels of curriculum in terms of the personnel involved. Now answer the questions in Exercise 1.1 to see if you are beginning to understand these levels.

EXERCISE 1.1

With which level is the curriculum in each of these statements most closely associated? Explain.

1. John Q. Public, a local banker, was reading the morning newspaper when he saw that the agenda for the school board meeting called for plans to discuss a new high school economics curriculum. On seeing this item, he promptly announced to Mrs. Public that he planned to attend the meeting.
2. Ms. Chiu was having dinner with her three school-age children. During dinner Ms. Chiu asked the children to describe something they had learned in school earlier that day.
3. Mrs. Rodriguez was pleased when her grandson Felix, a teacher who lives in a neighboring city, called to ask if he could stay overnight in her home. He indicated that he would be in town attending a districtwide curriculum development workshop where he and his colleagues expect to begin revisions of the social studies curriculum.

RELATIONSHIPS BETWEEN CURRICULUM AND INSTRUCTION

Previous discussion pointed out that the terms *curriculum* and *instruction* are sometimes used interchangeably. This section describes alternative views of the relationships between curriculum and instruction, including one in which the interchange of terms is plausible. The section also explains why knowledge of the distinctions is important.

NATURE OF POSSIBLE RELATIONSHIPS

The definitions for curriculum and instruction suggest that a relationship should exist between "what is taught" and "how it is taught." To suggest that these entities have no relationship defies common sense. That leaves two possibilities: curriculum and instruction could either be disjoint entities with some interrelated functions or not disjoint, sharing several functions. Each possibility is described here.

Curriculum and instruction can be thought of as separate, but interrelated, entities. This means that although curricular functions are separate from those for instruction, the effects of decisions in one entity affect decisions in the other. A number of models have been proposed that show curriculum interrelated with instruction (Hunkins, 1980; Johnson, 1967; Miller & Seller, 1985; Oliva, 1992; Saylor, Alexander, & Lewis, 1981; Taba, 1962; Tyler, 1949). For example, as conceived by Johnson (1967), curriculum and instruction are systematically related; curriculum system decisions feed into an instructional system as shown in Figure 1.1.

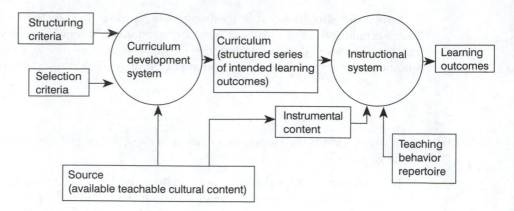

FIGURE 1.1

A Model Showing the Relationship Between Curriculum and Instruction in a Technical Approach

From "Definitions and Models in Curriculum Theory" by M. Johnson, 1967, *Educational Theory, 17*(2), p. 133. Copyright 1967 by *Educational Theory.* Reprinted by permission.

Frequently in this model the curriculum and instructional functions are handled by different sets of people. Curriculum *developers* select and sequence (or structure) content from the available teachable cultural content in the form of intended learning outcomes, two actions that are clearly curricular functions. Based on their repertoires of teaching strategies, *instructional planners/teachers* deliver instruction that enables students to attain actual learning outcomes. As part of this process, teachers choose additional content from the same source (shown in Figure 1.1 as instrumental content) that helps students learn the intended outcomes. For example, teachers who provide vocabulary development instruction often use similes or metaphors as instrumental content to help students learn meanings of new words.

In this model curriculum clearly guides instruction. Although an evaluation system is not shown in Figure 1.1, Johnson's model (1967) requires that observable evidence be gathered in the instructional system. These empirical results are fed back into the curriculum system, setting up potential changes in the curriculum and completing the cycle. Curricular functions are separate from, but related to, instructional functions.

Hunter and Scheirer's (1988) model illustrates the alternate curriculum-instruction relationship, in which the entities are not readily separable. (See Figure 1.2.) In this approach the planner-teacher begins by identifying a general area for study, clearly a curricular function. Then the teacher guides the initial shared experience and assists students in interactions among themselves with the content and teacher.

These interactions make the area of study meaningful through a series of instructional functions such as sharing experiences, observation, recording expressions, questioning, analyzing, and hypothesizing. In the diagram these interactions are noted by double-headed arrows suggesting two-way activity between students and teacher. The planner-teacher may also provide further input and foster closure. Beyond the first step in this particular model, curriculum and instruction are not easily distinguished.

IMPORTANCE OF UNDERSTANDING THE RELATIONSHIPS

How educators view the relationship between curriculum and instruction influences their approach to curriculum processes. Views of the curriculum-instruction relationship can probably be traced to educators' interpretations of reality, which lie along an objective-subjective continuum. Individuals who view the world objectively believe it can be understood and that events proceed in an orderly fashion. Others interpret reality subjectively, believing that individual realities differ significantly and that events are not predictable.

Technical Approach. Those who view curriculum and instruction as separate but related entities typically hold an objective interpretation of reality that is demon-

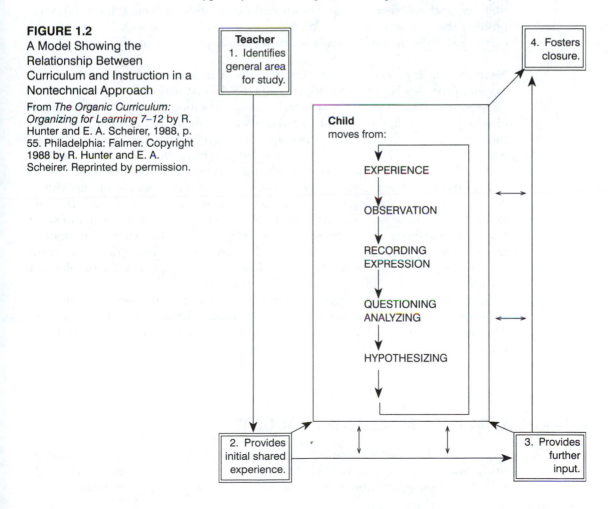

FIGURE 1.2
A Model Showing the Relationship Between Curriculum and Instruction in a Nontechnical Approach

From *The Organic Curriculum: Organizing for Learning 7–12* by R. Hunter and E. A. Scheirer, 1988, p. 55. Philadelphia: Falmer. Copyright 1988 by R. Hunter and E. A. Scheirer. Reprinted by permission.

Teacher
1. Identifies general area for study.

4. Fosters closure.

Child
moves from:

EXPERIENCE

OBSERVATION

RECORDING EXPRESSION

QUESTIONING ANALYZING

HYPOTHESIZING

2. Provides initial shared experience.

3. Provides further input.

strated in a **technical approach** to the curriculum processes. The processes are expected to be rational and systematic. Given their commitment to rationality, these individuals are quite comfortable deciding what the intended outcomes of learning should be for a curriculum.

The technical approach is the traditional way of developing curricula and uses these general procedures. Typically a committee of nonteaching staff (administrators, sometimes curriculum specialists or consultants), teachers, and community members revise a curriculum for a school *district*. Although knowledge from teachers may be included, this approach relies heavily on curriculum knowledge from nonteachers.

The result of this development is a curriculum that is usable in a variety of classroom situations because it is relatively free of concerns about the context in which it will be used (Snyder, Bolin, & Zumwalt, 1992). After the curriculum is planned, teachers are responsible for implementing it in their particular teaching situations.

Nothing within the technical approach itself prevents teachers from assuming important roles in any of the curriculum processes. Teachers *do* assume major responsibilities in school-based approaches, where these are used. Indeed, this text takes the position that teachers should be proactive in curriculum processes. The politics of curriculum decision making, a topic discussed in Chapter 2, are at work here.

Nontechnical Approach.   Other educators use a **nontechnical approach** to curriculum processes because they see curriculum and instruction as not readily separable entities. This approach is favored by educators with a subjective interpretation of reality because it allows them to interact with students and content to develop their own realities. As used here, the nontechnical approach relies heavily on teachers as the major source of curriculum knowledge because they know their students and teaching contexts. They also know why the curriculum needs revision.

A nontechnical approach is often used when the major source of curriculum content is the needs and interests of students or needs of society and culture. Particularly with these sources, curriculum developers do not state their intended learning outcomes at the outset (Klein, 1991b), because what students are expected to learn is not easily predicted. Largely because teachers are the main persons involved in nontechnical approaches, the resulting curricula are planned for specific contexts (Harste & Short, 1988; Paris, 1993).

Technical-nontechnical approaches and objective-subjective interpretations of reality are revisited in the discussion of educational change later in this chapter. The personnel involved in both approaches are described in Chapter 2, and how the approaches are put into operation is described in subsequent chapters.

CURRICULUM PROCESSES AND PRODUCTS

As used here, curriculum processes are the procedures involved in creating, using, and evaluating the curricula represented in various documents or products such as guides, syllabi, and others. This section briefly defines these terms.

PROCESSES

Curriculum processes is a collective term that encompasses all the considerations about which curriculum workers ponder and ultimately make choices in the development, classroom use, and evaluation of a curriculum project. These processes involve changes that some students, teachers, school staff, and community members welcome, but that others resist either actively or passively.

Rarely is a school curriculum developed from scratch, because most "new" curricula represent revisions of those in existence. However, whether generating a brand-new curriculum or revising an existing one, curriculum **development** means recreating or modifying what is taught to students. Development includes a number of decisions whose outcomes aggregate as a curriculum design.

Curriculum designs are based on the primary sources of curriculum content (i.e., subject matter, needs of society-culture, or needs and interests of learners) that make possible the realization of a particular purpose of education. Purposes typically emphasize cultivating cognitive achievement (also known as transmitting the cultural heritage), developing learners to their fullest potentials, or preparing people for living in a changing, unstable world.

In addition to establishing a purpose for the curriculum project, developers also prepare a "views of education" statement outlining the anticipated relationships among teachers, students, and content. The views statement usually shows the relationships of the curriculum to the community beyond the school. Developers then select and organize content so that these relationships can be realized.

Curriculum **classroom use** involves making arrangements for and using curriculum projects in school settings for the purpose of school program development. This term encompasses implementation and enactment used with technical and nontechnical processes, respectively. Sometimes technically developed curricula are tested in a few classrooms before they are put to full use in a district.

Both curriculum development and classroom use involve several considerations that must be managed effectively. Among these are the scope and complexity of the curricular change, communication among all the participants involved, professional development, and resources.

Curriculum **evaluation** encompasses the processes for improving school programs through delineating, obtaining, and providing descriptive and judgmental information about the worth and merit of a curriculum. Evaluation guides decision making, serves needs for accountability, and promotes understanding of the curriculum (Stufflebeam & Shinkfield, 1985). Evaluation of existing curricula for the purpose of determining strengths and weaknesses may occur as the first step in curriculum revision. This evaluation is commonly referred to as **needs assessment**. Typically, revised curricula developed for use in classrooms are also evaluated in at least two ways: whether curricula were actually used in classrooms and how well curricula satisfy their intended purposes.

PRODUCTS

Curriculum products or **projects** result from curriculum development processes and provide the bases for instructional decisions in classrooms. Curriculum projects include curriculum guides, courses of study, syllabi, resource units, lists of goals and objectives, and other documents that deal with the content of schooling.

Curriculum **guides** "usually include details about the topics to be taught, predetermined teaching goals and suggestions for instructional strategies" (Ben-Peretz, 1990, p. 25). Curriculum **guidelines** furnish information about predetermined learning outcomes and are generally less complete than curriculum guides. **Courses of study** or **syllabi** usually specify the content, the learning outcomes, and time allocations for the various topics. Sometimes a rationale for the choices of content is included in syllabi.

Resource units typically include learning outcomes, suggestions for teaching, sources of information, and prepared instructional units. Lists of curriculum goals and objectives, along with their rationales, are another form of project. Try answering Exercise 1.2 as a way of checking your understanding of various curriculum products.

EXERCISE 1.2

Appendix A contains excerpts of curriculum guides, curriculum guidelines, and resource units. Read the introduction to this appendix. Then scan the following projects for the types of information included:

- *Multicultural Social Studies Curriculum K–12* (A1)
- *Wyoming Arts Education Curriculum* (A5)
- *Into Adolescence: Caring for Our Planet and Our Health* (A6)

Answer these questions for each project:

1. Does the project contain goals, suggestions for teaching, or both? Explain.
2. For whom is the project intended? Primarily curriculum developers? Primarily classroom users? Explain.

CURRICULUM PROCESSES AS CHANGE

Educators and laypersons alike agree that social change is ongoing, but many are unsure how to deal with it. As a result, they appear to alternately call for and decry reform in schools. This section defines educational change, then describes and applies different perspectives of curriculum processes as change to technical and nontechnical approaches.

CHANGE DEFINED

Fullan (1991) draws extensively on the literature related to educational innovation for *The New Meaning of Educational Change*, which is the basis for much of the following discussion. Change may occur in response to outside events or because we voluntarily initiate or participate in change as part of a situation where we find dissatisfaction, inconsistency, or intolerability.

Whatever its cause, the meaning of change is rarely clear at its beginning and ambivalence reigns until the change is absorbed and made part of our thinking. "Ultimately the transformation of subjective realities is the essence of change" (Fullan, 1991, p. 36). After change is assimilated, however, a sense of mastery, accomplishment, or professional growth is likely.

Bridges' (1991) distinction between changes and transitions is helpful in understanding the transformation of subjective realities. For him, *change* is external to people and is situational—the new curriculum, the new method of evaluating the curriculum, the new way of supervising teachers as curriculum users. On the other hand, "*[t]ransition* is the psychological process people go through to come to terms with the new situation. Change is external, transition is internal" (Bridges, 1991, p. 3).

Transitions begin with endings, or letting go of things. In curriculum changes, teachers may have to give up their tried-and-true lecture notes or replace their favorite instructional activity. When called to supervise teachers making curriculum changes, administrators may have to relinquish staying in their offices throughout most of the school day or working on budget concerns for hours at a time. Such letting go actions must occur for people to enter the neutral zone. This zone represents "the no-man's-land between the old reality and the new. It's the limbo between the old sense of identity and the new" (Bridges, 1991, p. 5).

The announcement of the new curriculum (or a method of evaluating students or way of teaching)—the change—can happen fairly quickly. But inward transitions take place much more slowly because of inner struggles—of being in limbo. The educator finds it not appropriate to continue with the "old" ways, yet the "new" ways are difficult even to contemplate. It's important to understand the neutral zone. If educators don't expect and understand the neutral zone, they may try to rush through it and be discouraged to learn this is impossible. Or they may be frightened in this no-man's-land and try to escape (Bridges, 1991).

The neutral zone is filled with ambivalence and uncertainty, conditions that occur naturally when people feel lost or overwhelmed with more information than they can handle (Fullan, 1991). Many teachers, for example, work in situations where ambivalence and uncertainty are abundant. Teachers are typically isolated from colleagues, have few opportunities to reflect on what they do, and are required to make many decisions involving many different people and situations—quickly (Lieberman, 1992).

If asked to participate in change, teachers may see no reason to believe in the change or to find out if it is worthwhile. When they feel pressured, teachers may try to escape the neutral zone quickly and "adjust to the 'near occasion' of change, by changing as little as possible—either assimilating or abandoning changes that they were initially willing to try, or fighting or ignoring imposed change" (Fullan, 1991, p. 36).

Such behaviors are normal because the neutral zone produces fright and confusion (Bridges, 1991). However, this is the time that reorientation and redefinition take place. Well-designed professional development activities can spark educators' creativity and bring about their sense of self-renewal. However, educators make new beginnings only by reaching endings and spending time in the neutral zone. Unfortunately, school leaders frequently "try to start with the beginning rather than finishing with it. They pay no attention to endings. They do not acknowledge the existence of the neutral zone, then wonder why people have so much difficulty with change" (Bridges, 1991, p. 6).

Fullan (1991) further characterizes change as multidimensional. For example, at least three dimensions are involved in curriculum implementation: "1) the possible use of new or revised *materials* (direct instructional resources such as curriculum materials or technologies), 2) the possible use of new *teaching approaches* (i.e., new teaching strategies or activities), and 3) the possible alteration of *beliefs* (e.g., pedagogical assumptions and theories underlying particular new policies or programs)" (Fullan, 1991, p. 37). Unless modifications occur in each dimension, true implementation does not take place. To illustrate, teachers could use revised materials without changing their strategies. Or they could alter some strategies without understanding or operating on the beliefs underlying the change. To say the revised curriculum is implemented, teachers must experience change in all three dimensions.

This description affirms that educational change is a complex, time-consuming process. When the change involves more than one person, each must make meaning and resolve ambivalence individually! Consider the sheer numbers of people involved in most curriculum processes and it is clear why true change is difficult to achieve.

CHANGE APPLIED IN CURRICULUM PROCESSES

Depending on their preferred view of reality, those involved in curriculum are likely to pursue the curriculum processes very differently. Not only do they undertake and carry out the curriculum tasks differently, they explain the processes and results of their efforts with different terms.

One perspective on curriculum processes (Leithwood, 1991) that has been tried repeatedly follows a rational-logical process. Based on the idea that events in the world are understandable and predictable, this technical approach says that *developing* a revised curriculum provides a relatively complete solution to a problem in a school or school system. Individuals with this belief assume that the revised curriculum can be *implemented* by teachers and school staff as it was conceived by the developers. Under this perspective implementation is a nonproblematic event in which teachers are expected to quickly understand, value, and carry out the practices required by the revised curriculum.

In fact, one aspect of *evaluation* is judging how faithfully implementors follow the planned curriculum. Of course, evaluators also check to see if the curriculum meets its intended purpose. For individuals who view the curriculum processes as described in this perspective, the change process is both rational and systematic and often involves top-down strategic planning.

Much evidence exists to show that this perspective on change is usually ineffective (Fullan, 1991; Patterson, Purkey, & Parker, 1986). Its proponents believe that changes in programs or procedures, rather than changes in people, lead to improvement. When proponents act on these beliefs, however, they often find that procedural changes do not bring improvement. Sometimes individuals remain unconvinced and try tightening procedures even more. Most of the time these efforts are also unsuccessful. This thinking is characteristic of school personnel who believe in a rational, objective view of reality.

A second perspective takes a different view of change. Patterson, Purkey, and Parker (1986) propose to treat school systems as nonrational social organizations whose logic is nonlinear and complex, but understandable and amenable to influence. "[N]onrational doesn't necessarily mean irrational. Related to organizational life, nonrational behavior usually manifests a weak relationship among goals, structures, activities, and outcomes" (1986, p. 23).

Nonrational systems recognize that competing forces, in and out of these systems, constantly try to make their goals *the* organization's agenda. Decision makers in nonrational systems find ways of handling conflicting goals, such as dealing with them in sequence or moving along multiple fronts toward organizational goals (Patterson, Purkey, & Parker, 1986).

This second perspective fully recognizes schools as nonrational social organizations. Its proponents *develop* a revised curriculum to provide a partial solution to a problem in a school or school system. In a process separate from development, implementors including teachers and school staff collaborate with developers to adapt the revised curriculum to particular contexts where the curriculum is *implemented* with students. The adaptation is expected to provide teachers with ownership of the revised curriculum and enable them to effectively use the curriculum with students. *Evaluation* includes assessing the degree to which the negotiated curriculum is implemented as well as the degree to which its purpose is attained (Leithwood, 1991). Individuals who view the curriculum processes as described in this perspective see change processes as growth in a valued direction brought about by collaboration among the professionals involved.

A third perspective is based on a subjective view of reality. Its proponents are typically teachers characterized as having deep knowledge of their students, of what students need to learn, and of themselves as professionals (Paris, 1993). This group sees curriculum *development* as a mutual construction of content and meaning by teachers and students that varies with alterations among the people. As teachers acquire additional information about subject matter, teaching, students' needs or other pertinent matters, they design curricula that use this information if it benefits students. Because the curriculum is created in the same situation where it is used, the curriculum is said to be *enacted*, rather than implemented (Doyle, 1992; Snyder, Bolin, & Zumwalt, 1992).

Working out and using the curriculum, however, typically involves negotiations among teachers as well as school staff and people in the community. In this perspective, enactment follows development very closely and is handled by the same individuals. *Evaluation* is assessing the degree to which the purpose of education is met. This group also sees change processes as growth in valued directions, similar to the second group. However, the change processes are more individually oriented than those within the second group.

Despite its small chance for success, the first perspective on curriculum processes continues to be tried in school settings. However, this perspective is not discussed further in this text because of its lack of viability. In subsequent discussions the processes described in the second perspective are referred to as the technical approach to development and evaluation. Classroom use in the technical approach is called **implementation**. Processes described in the third perspective are referred to as the nontechnical approach to development and evaluation; classroom use is called **enactment**.

Chapter 2 continues this overview by discussing the nature of curriculum decision making and the personnel involved in curriculum. Of particular importance is the involvement of both school and community personnel.

SUMMARY

This chapter provides information about key concepts in curriculum. Differences in definitions of curriculum and relationships between curriculum and instruction may be either real differences in views or simple interchanges of terminology. Curriculum personnel with an objective view of reality view a world that is knowable with orderly events, but other curriculum people hold that reality is subjective and personal, and that events are not predictable. Differences in interpretations of reality often lead to different approaches to curriculum processes.

Curriculum processes encompass valuing and decision making in developing, using, and evaluating curricula. The output of these processes are products or projects with different designations (e.g., guides, courses of study, and resource units).

Educational change requires that individuals develop their own meanings of social phenomena. Unless they do, there is little likelihood of change. Because people have different interpretations of reality, they describe the curriculum processes and the change processes differently.

QUESTIONS FOR DISCUSSION

1. Ask at least two people associated with schools AND two laypersons, to define *curriculum* and *instruction*. Do their definitions agree with those mentioned at the beginning of this chapter? Explain.
2. Classify the definitions of curriculum in Question 1 according to one of the levels of curriculum described in this chapter. Give reasons for your classifications.
3. Provide at least one original example for each class of learning outcomes described in the Cuban-Johnson definition of learning.
4. Which of the two curriculum-instruction relationships makes more sense to you? Why?
5. Explain why it is important to evaluate curricula.
6. Explain what is meant by the statement "each individual has to make his/her own meaning of educational change." Why is this statement important?
7. Explain the importance of distinguishing among the three perspectives on the curriculum processes described as change.

IMPORTANT IDEAS DISCUSSED
INITIALLY IN THIS CHAPTER

curriculum-instruction-learning
   levels of curriculum
curriculum processes
   technical-nontechnical approaches
   development
   classroom use-enactment
   evaluation
     needs assessment

curriculum products (projects)
   guidelines
   guides
   courses of study (syllabi)
   resource units

2

CURRICULUM DECISION MAKING: ITS NATURE AND PERSONNEL

OUTLINE

Curriculum decision making
    Nature of curriculum decisions
    Arenas for curriculum decision making
Community personnel involvement
    Community-at-large
    Governing boards/site-based groups
Alternative approaches to local curriculum decision making
    District
    School
    Classroom
School personnel involvement
    School staff
    Teachers and students
The case for school-based curriculum decision making

The levels of curriculum introduced in Chapter 1 showed that people other than educators participate in curriculum processes. These individuals include parents/guardians, citizens, taxpayers, and subject-matter specialists. They usually influence curriculum through membership in groups such as professional subject-matter organizations, teacher unions, parent-teacher organizations, and state legislatures.

This chapter surveys the nature of curriculum decisions and the sociopolitical arenas in which community and school personnel make decisions. These people and the groups to which they belong frequently support different expectations for school curricula that reflect differences in their values and beliefs. Despite their differences, however, both groups have expertises that should be pooled in the interests of creating school curricula for students in a democratic society.

Alternative approaches to local curriculum decision making involve school personnel differently, depending on the governance structure. The final section argues for school-based curriculum decision making as a way of effecting change.

CURRICULUM DECISION MAKING

Curriculum decisions are numerous and often difficult, partly because of their interrelationships. Decisions are further complicated by the numbers of people who participate in making them. The discussions that follow briefly describe the nature of curriculum decisions and the arenas in which they are made.

NATURE OF CURRICULUM DECISIONS

Curriculum is broadly described in Chapter 1 as what is taught to students, including planned and unplanned information, skills, and attitudes. This "what" comes from several interrelated sources—subject matter, the needs of society and culture, and the needs and interests of learners. Because of its abundance, all available content cannot be taught. Deciding what can and should be selected is an extremely knotty problem that has different solutions, depending on who poses the problem and who describes the solution.

Decisions must be made about many items in the course of developing and using curricula in classrooms. Klein (1991a) categorizes these decisions as:

- Content
- Purposes, goals, and objectives
- Materials and resources
- Activities and teaching strategies
- Evaluation
- Grouping, time, and space

A brief discussion of these categories follows. Later chapters explore them more fully.

Content comes from the disciplines (e.g., history) or other organized bodies of knowledge (e.g., physical education) and can take several forms, such as facts, concepts, and generalizations.

Goals, objectives, and *purposes* are labels applied to the results of students' participation in purposeful learning activities. Eventual outcomes of learning that result from work in a curriculum over a period of time are commonly called "purposes of education." Goals and objectives are shorter-term learning outcomes with "goals" referring to general learning outcomes and "objectives" to specific learning outcomes. Whereas all curricula have stated purposes, technically developed curricula also have predetermined goals and objectives. These terms are sometimes lumped together as learning outcomes.

Materials and *resources* include "the objects, places, and people used to facilitate the learning process—the tools used with students to assist learning" (Klein, 1991a, p. 33). Textbooks, computers, games, and the talents of various personnel are examples of school and community materials and resources considered in this category.

Activities and *teaching strategies* are the ways in which students become involved in learning the curriculum. Activities can be passive or active, self-directed or teacher-directed, and so on. Teaching strategies describe teachers' roles within activities that help students meet learning outcomes.

Evaluation includes the procedures for determining degrees of student learning—whether by observations, written work, projects, or other methods—as well as methods of analyzing and interpreting results. Program evaluation focuses on determining how well the curriculum works.

Grouping, time, and *space* are all important issues in the use of curricula in classrooms. Grouping refers to the clustering of students for particular experiences either by grade, by experiential background, or by ability levels. Time is a limited resource whose allocations are made by groups outside, as well as inside, the school setting. The wise use of time is necessary in every curriculum. Space refers to the design and use of school and classroom physical work and play areas. The curriculum must be suited to the available space.

In addition to their content, decisions also have a values dimension. People who decide what to teach must contend with concerns about time, money, working conditions and a host of other constraints that can complicate decision making. Ultimately, curriculum decisions are made on the basis of people's values and beliefs (Goodlad & Su, 1992; Tyler, 1949).

As used here, **values** must satisfy the criteria of ideas chosen from alternatives, based on considerations of their consequences, cherished enough to be made public, and acted upon in some way. **Beliefs** refer to ideas accepted as true, but more susceptible to change than values (Raths, Harmin, & Simon, 1978). Though both are reflected in curricula, the question that surfaces immediately is "whose values and beliefs should be accommodated in curriculum decisions?" Answering this question is not easy because the views of many people must be considered.

Because values are important in curriculum matters, additional information about them may be helpful. Figure 2.1 expands the discussion of criteria for determining things that represent values. Figure 2.2 illustrates two applications of the criteria in curriculum situations.

Choices:

1. *Choosing freely.* A choice must be freely selected if it is to be valued.

2. *Choosing from alternatives.* Only when a choice is possible, when there is more than one alternative from which to choose, can a value result.

3. *Choosing after thoughtful consideration of the consequences of each alternative.* Impulsive or thoughtless choices do not lead to values as defined here. Choosers must be aware of the results of each possible choice.

4. *Prizing and cherishing.* Choosers are happy with their values.

Actions:

5. *Affirming.* Choosers are willing to make their values public.

6. *Acting upon choices.* People who talk about something but never do anything about it are dealing with something other than a value. Choosers must act if something is to be considered a value.

7. *Repeating.* Values tend to represent persistent choices that form a pattern.

FIGURE 2.1
Criteria for Determining Values Based on the Work of Raths, Harmin, and Simon (1978)

The discussion of curriculum decision making will continue. But try Exercise 2.1 now to see how well you understand it to this point.

EXERCISE 2.1

1. Identify the category to which each of the following curriculum decisions belongs.
   a. Mr. Ong decided to use the *literature-based readers* with his fifth-graders.
   b. Ms. Blanca outlined a *demonstration* on points, lines, and planes for her high school geometry class.
   c. Dee White planned to schedule physical education classes *in the school gymnasium.*

2. Identify two possible alternatives for each curriculum decision identified in Question 1.

ARENAS FOR CURRICULUM DECISION MAKING

The existence of several curriculum levels shows that practically everybody has ideas about school curricula and seeks to express them. While reasoning suggests that whoever has the expertise should make curriculum decisions, difficulties arise when laypersons and educators do not agree on who has the expertise and authority. The tensions generated by this lack of agreement contribute to the political nature of curriculum decision making.

Let's apply the valuing criteria to some ordinary school situations. Suppose you are an elementary teacher on a curriculum team that is about to undertake revision of the language arts curriculum. You and your colleagues have reviewed the literature and want to develop a program featuring the whole language approach. However, in your state, teachers are required to teach spelling as a discrete subject for 20 minutes daily. Does this situation require values clarification? Probably not. This is *not* a values question because you are not free to choose between teaching spelling as a separate subject and teaching spelling as part of the language arts.

On the other hand, suppose you are part of a high school science curriculum development team that wants to focus on learning outcomes that require problem solving. Does this decision represent a value? Maybe. To answer definitely, we would have to know answers to several questions. Did you freely choose this type of learning outcome? If yes, could you have chosen an alternative? If yes, did you choose problem solving *after* you thought through the consequences of using alternative forms of learning outcomes? Are you happy with choosing problem solving as a learning outcome? If yes, are you willing to share your decision about problem solving with others (perhaps teachers, the principal, parents/guardians of students)? If yes, are you willing to act on your choice in assisting students in working through problem solving procedures? If yes, are you willing to use problem solving again in other suitable situations? Notice that all these questions were answered affirmatively. That's what makes the use of problem solving a value in this situation.

If at any point, you are unable to answer the questions affirmatively, that would cast doubt on whether using problem solving is a value. For example, if you thought of problem solving and decided to use it without considering alternative learning outcomes or without thinking about consequences of each alternative, we would not know if this were a value. Another type of learning outcome might suit just as well. If your answers to questions about choosing are affirmative and you are not happy about your choice or are unable to discuss it with others, then problem solving is probably not a value. Valuing means that we are pleased with choices to the extent of being able to discuss them with others. Should your answers to the prizing questions be affirmative, you would still have to try problem solving with students and consider using it in additional situations in order to declare this a value.

FIGURE 2.2
Illustrations Showing Applications of Valuing Criteria

Conceiving of curriculum processes as change further complicates the situation. But laypersons and educators alike must understand the meaning of change and its ramifications if curricula are to serve children and youth in the 21st century. For change to occur in classrooms, educators (particularly teachers) must be involved in the curriculum processes because the locus of change is in individuals rather than in curricula per se.

As stated previously, curriculum decisions involve values that people express through actions at different levels of a political decision-making hierarchy encompassing national, state, and local levels. These arenas and the decision categories typically affected are described here:

National Level. The U.S. Constitution assigns the primary power for educational matters to state governments who delegate authority for certain decisions to local educational authorities, usually school districts. However, the federal government exerts considerable influence on curriculum decisions through sponsored research, legislation, and Supreme Court rulings, as the following examples show.

From the late 1950s through the 1970s the National Science Foundation used federal dollars for research on mathematics, science, and technology curriculum projects (Elmore & Sykes, 1992) and has continued its influence in recent years through programs for training pre- and inservice teachers in these subject areas. During this era, federal funding pushed evaluation and brought about significant changes in program evaluation (Stufflebeam & Shinkfield, 1985).

The Education for All Handicapped Children Act in 1975 changed school curricula by requiring that handicapped individuals be provided educational opportunities in least-restrictive environments (Elmore & Sykes, 1992). This meant reevaluating and changing public school curricula to mainstream handicapped students into regular classrooms. The Supreme Court decisions banning school-sponsored religious activities deleted curricular activities that had been included on a daily basis in some districts (van Geel, 1991).

These are only four of many actions at the national level that have influenced curriculum decision making. As you reflect on these comments, note that decisions in several categories have been and will continue to be touched by such activities. These examples have affected several categories, particularly content, purposes, evaluation, grouping, and time decisions.

State Level.   Although they use their powers differently, states have major responsibilities for curriculum decisions. Pipho (1991) describes the American system of public education as a crazy quilt because of different degrees of state control. Traditionally, states have boards of education that set policies for public schools in matters such as achievement testing, high school graduation requirements, state subject-specific curriculum guidelines, school evaluation and certification, materials selection processes, teacher certification requirements, and educational information management systems (Tyree, 1993).

Twenty-two states that adopt textbooks for schools generally exert their control through mandates over the curriculum, curriculum guides, content coverage, and testing programs. Interestingly states with textbook depositories tend to have greater control than states where local school districts order their own texts from an approved list (Pipho, 1991).

In the early 1990s, 42 states had some form of minimum competency testing that directly affected district level curricula. Twenty of these states have mandates for high school graduation that have a significant effect on local curricula. "Students failing the test consistently as they move toward high school graduation are usually scheduled into a heavy load of remediation classes in their eleventh- and twelfth-grade years" (Pipho, 1991, p. 70) provided they remain in school. Mandated state tests are usually based on lists of basic/required/essential skills that students are expected to master before graduation. As an example, Appendix A5 provides excerpts from Wyoming's *Arts Education Curriculum* (1992).

Gubernatorial offices and state legislatures through budgeting authority strongly influence the content and purpose of curricula. Both agencies support or curtail certain programs based on a variety of reasons and values. This short survey suggests that decision making at the state level influences, at least broadly, curriculum decisions in all categories.

Local Level.   Ultimately decisions in all the categories are made or remade locally at either the district, school, or classroom level. Although institutional curricula are sometimes developed in schools, many are developed at the district level. Regardless of the level, however, local curricula must comply with federal and state guidelines; otherwise districts risk losing their accreditation or state and federal funds. Additional information about curriculum decision making at the local level is provided later in this chapter, in the sections Alternative Approaches to Local Curriculum Decision Making and School Personnel Involvement.

COMMUNITY PERSONNEL INVOLVEMENT

Community personnel include people *not* associated with particular schools or districts as employees or students. Citizens living in particular school districts as well as people beyond district boundaries are considered community personnel and take part in forming *societal* curricula. Parents and guardians of students in a particular district may also have a voice in its *institutional* curricula as do individuals who serve on district governing boards or site-based management groups.[1] This section surveys community personnel involvement in curriculum matters.

COMMUNITY-AT-LARGE

The community-at-large is composed of individuals and groups who influence curricula, particularly at societal and institutional levels. Their agendas often dictate the purposes, goals, and content of school curricula. For example, since 1975 the Phi Delta Kappa/Gallup polls have sampled public attitudes toward education, including specific items about curriculum. The 1993 poll showed that 48 percent of the public thought that high schools should offer a wide variety of courses, but 51 percent believed high schools should concentrate on basic courses such as English, mathematics, history, and science. One percent did not express an opinion (Elam, Rose, & Gallup, 1993).

These results were largely unchanged in the 1994 poll. This poll also found national support for emphasizing values just as it had in 1987 when the values question was first asked. At least 90 percent or more of the respondents believed that people in communities could agree on a set of basic values, such as "respect for others," "industry or hard work," "persistence," "fairness in dealing with others," and "civility/politeness" that could be taught in the local public schools (Elam, Rose, & Gallup, 1994). Many school districts are likely to continue emphasizing basic subjects and use the poll information as justification if that decision is

---

[1] Site-based management groups usually contain school personnel as well as individuals from the community.

questioned. How the "values" information is used depends largely on political activities at state and local levels.

Government officials and groups also seek to influence curriculum matters. For example, in January 1990 then-President Bush presented six goals for education in the United States that were devised by the National Governors' Association. These goals set lofty intentions for schools by the year 2000. One goal calls for students to demonstrate competency in challenging subject matter including English, mathematics, science, history, and geography. Another calls for U.S. students to be first in the world in science and mathematics achievement (U.S. Department of Education, 1991).

The rationale for these goals was questioned on the grounds of contravening evidence (i.e., the Sandia Report) suppressed by federal officials (Tanner, 1993). The goals themselves have been attacked because they fail to take into account how children acquire knowledge and moral values (Kamii, Clark, & Dominick, 1994). Despite objections, funding for the goals was authorized by national lawmakers in 1994 (Pitch, 1994), again demonstrating the political nature of curriculum decisions. As discussion of the different arenas for decision making shows, government groups sometimes enact legislation or use budget pressures to effect curriculum change.

Professional groups include specialists in any of several disciplines such as the National Council of Teachers of English, curriculum specialists such as those affiliated with the Association for Supervision and Curriculum Development, and groups organized by job functions such as the National Association of Secondary Principals. Some groups put forward position statements or intended to influence curriculum matters. Their intentions are generally advanced, however, by state affiliates working in concert with politicians at that level.

Businesses and industries represent groups concerned about what students learn in schools because they provide jobs and careers for students who leave schools. Civic groups, such as Rotary Clubs, Veterans of Foreign Wars and others, may also evidence interest in school curricula. Even environmental groups, such as the Sierra Club, sometimes seek to influence curriculum decisions (Klein, 1991a). These groups exert their influence in whichever arena they find decision makers willing to listen.

Most parents and guardians are interested particularly in the curricula of schools where their children attend. They attempt to influence the institutional curricula there through participation in parent-school organizations and other contacts with the local school.

The degree to which these groups and individuals actually influence curricula differs, but community groups play a large role in setting priorities for the curriculum. In recent years, for example, topics that communities believed should be handled in schools (e.g., driver education, drug awareness) have been added.

GOVERNING BOARDS/SITE-BASED GROUPS

At one time virtually all school operations were overseen by governing boards composed of citizens elected to serve their local school *districts*. In recent years decentralization has made local *schools*, rather than districts, the primary unit of management and educational improvement in some locations.

For example, beginning with the 1996–97 school year, all schools in Kentucky must have a school-based decision-making format[2] for their operations (van Meter, 1991). However, not all site-based groups have management responsibilities; some simply provide community input to governing boards or school personnel who make decisions based on the input.

Certain responsibilities are required regardless of the managerial approach. Management groups typically schedule public hearings on curriculum matters to provide information to citizens and solicit input from them. Such groups also authorize expenditures for curriculum development, implementation, and evaluation as needed in the district or school. Management groups consider and adopt curriculum proposals that allow their district or school to carry out the purpose of education adopted in that community (Campbell, Carr, & Harris, 1989). Management groups, regardless of their purviews, are expected to influence curriculum matters locally through leadership in districts or schools.

ALTERNATIVE APPROACHES TO
LOCAL CURRICULUM DECISION MAKING

At least three approaches can be conceived for curriculum decision making at local levels. These approaches are described in this section according to their locus, as district, school, or classroom. This information is important because of the significant implications for school personnel participation in curriculum decisions discussed later in the section School Personnel Involvement.

DISTRICT

District-based curriculum decision making is the norm in many locations where boards of education govern schools. Since most states now have mandated assessments, school districts usually use technical approaches to curriculum through an ongoing cycle. One model used by the Horseheads (New York) Central School District is recorded in the *Middle School English Language Arts Curriculum* (1991) in Appendix A3. This cycle has six stages:

1. Overall review and needs assessment
2. Development of philosophy, goals, and objectives
3. Curriculum design and writing
4. Piloting
5. Implementation
6. Evaluation

During stages 1 and 6, district personnel examine the efficacy of existing learning outcomes, activities, materials and resources. Depending on the review and

---

[2] Results are encouraging after two years into a five-year study of school-based decision making in Kentucky. School-based decision making is dramatically changing the roles and relationships among the people as they learn to create shared goals and conditions for reaching them (David, 1994).

needs assessments, a district committee revises learning outcomes, materials, resources, and activities during stages 2 and 3. In the case of the *Middle School English Language Arts* curriculum, a common philosophy and set of program goals were developed for grades 7 and 8, but learning outcomes and learning experiences were developed for the grade levels separately.

Once it is revised, the curriculum may be piloted in a few classrooms (stage 4) by district teachers and evaluated by district personnel. If these trial runs are successful, then the curriculum is implemented in district classrooms at the appropriate grade levels wherever that subject matter is taught (stage 5).

Districts that use a cycle rotate the different curriculum areas such as social studies, music, foreign language, and others through the stages. See Figure 2.3

Program Areas	96–97	97–98	98–99	99–00	00–01	01–02	02–03	03–04	04–05
Art	2	3	4	5	6	1	2	3	4
Business education	4	5	6	1	2	3	4	5	6
Computers	5	6	1	2	3	4	5	6	1
Foreign language	2	3	4	5	6	1	2	3	4
Science	3	4	5	6	1	2	3	4	5
Home economics	5	6	1	2	3	4	5	6	1
Technology–ind. education	3	4	5	6	1	2	3	4	5
Language arts	1	2	3	4	5	6	1	2	3
Mathematics	6	1	2	3	4	5	6	1	2
Music	5	6	1	2	3	4	5	6	1
Drivers education	6	1	2	3	4	5	6	1	2
Health–phy. ed.–drugs	6	1	2	3	4	5	6	1	2
Reading	2	3	4	5	6	1	2	3	4
Social studies	4	5	6	1	2	3	4	5	6
Speech–drama	5	6	1	2	3	4	5	6	1

1. Analysis and review
2. Curriculum revision
3. Text and materials
4. Implementation
5. Monitor and adjust
6. Monitor and adjust

FIGURE 2.3
Cycles for Curriculum Processes
Available from Paradise Valley Unified School District No. 69, Phoenix, AZ. Reprinted by permission.

for an example of how the cycle operates in a K–12 unified school district. Note that each of the 15 program areas is reviewed every six years with one to four program areas subject to review yearly.

Institutional curricula developed under this plan can be used in a variety of situations because the context is not explicitly taken into account. Districts usually provide inservice staff development corresponding to grade levels or clusters of grade levels (e.g., K–3, 5–8) to help teachers implement the new curricula.

But individual teachers usually design the *instructional* curriculum for their students largely on their own, and the school as a whole is not involved. Teachers decide on instructional goals and objectives, materials and resources, activities and teaching strategies, grouping, time, and space, and evaluation of instruction based on the district curriculum. In circumstances determined by the district to be appropriate, teachers and school staff administer the procedures for program evaluation. For information about personnel deployment, see the section School Personnel Involvement.

SCHOOL

District-based curricula can assist developers of school-based curricula, but they are not required. **School-based curriculum decision making** can exist under a district board of education, but it flourishes when site-based management of schools is the norm. School-based curriculum decision making may use the technical approach and cycles or stages.

Two important factors distinguish a school-based curriculum: It is developed by the school administrators and teachers who will use it and it takes into account the context for its use. These differences usually increase the quality of the instructional curriculum because teachers tend to feel ownership of curricula they help to develop.

School-based curriculum decision making may also follow the nontechnical approach, provided teachers within a school, grade, or course level work together in preparing curriculum. These teachers sometimes take ideas from a district-based curriculum document and prepare a curriculum that is tailor-made to particular students and teaching situations.

Where school-based approaches operate, teachers and school staffs have curriculum responsibilities different from their colleagues in district-based situations. Depending on the leadership, school-based curriculum processes may be more visible than those in the district. School Personnel Involvement, the next major section, contains additional information.

CLASSROOM

Neither district- nor school-based curricula are required for classroom-based curricula, but either can provide a useful starting point for classroom-based approaches. **Classroom-based curriculum decision making** may be carried out in schools with site-based management because it is usually developed by individual teachers who want a curriculum especially designed for their students. A nontechnical approach that does not predetermine learning outcomes is compatible with classroom-based decision making. Additional information is provided in the following section, School Personnel Involvement.

Exercise 2.2 provides an opportunity to reconsider the relationships among curriculum levels and local curriculum decision making. An understanding of these relationships is important in the sections that follow.

EXERCISE 2.2

Reconsider the information about curriculum levels and local decision making. Then answer these questions:

1. In many locations, school *districts* translate societal expectations into institutional curricula. Under what circumstances might *schools* serve this function? Explain.
2. Describe any limitations that you see to classroom-based curriculum decision making.

SCHOOL PERSONNEL INVOLVEMENT

School personnel are the people associated with a school or district as employees or students. For this discussion, school staff are nonteaching personnel who, along with teachers and community members, can, and often do, make important contributions to the curriculum processes at the *institutional* level. Teachers and students, of course, are involved with curriculum at *instructional* and *experiential* levels. This section highlights the involvement and expertises of school personnel as they pertain to curriculum.

SCHOOL STAFF

School staff includes the nonteaching certificated personnel in districts and schools. These are administrators (including curriculum and evaluation specialists, as well as other district office and building administrators), resources specialists, counselors, social workers, and health-care providers.

Administrators.   Districts and schools have administrators whose major responsibilities are curriculum matters. In locations where districts manage curriculum operations, specialists (subject matter supervisors or coordinators, research and evaluation personnel, and others) carry many of these responsibilities.

However, where schools manage their own curriculum operations, building administrators are charged with curriculum responsibilities, but have the expertise of district administrators at their disposal. Generally, by whatever title administrators are called, they expect to lead and support other professionals engaged in curriculum development, implementation or enactment, and evaluation.

Depending on their backgrounds, administrators bring expertises to curriculum processes that may be quite different from those of other professionals. Administrators usually have advanced preparation for their positions in areas such as curriculum, evaluation, or general administration. By virtue of their training and experiences, administrators are expected to be aware of the regulations and policies of the state and the local district, know how to plan and set priorities, manage resources, and work with people.

Districts with staff trained in curriculum count on these individuals to know the curriculum processes and state and local curriculum requirements. Sometimes these professionals have extensive subject matter backgrounds in one or more curricular areas. These staff members direct or consult with district- and school-based curriculum committees in the creation or revision of curricula. They help building administrators provide teachers and other school staff with professional development once a curriculum is to be implemented and sometimes serve as **change facilitators** to aid the implementation processes. At other times these individuals provide staff support for governing boards or site-based groups.

Some districts have staff trained in evaluation processes who manage program evaluations. Ideally program evaluation is an ongoing district or school operation. However, at the onset of curriculum development, evaluation specialists frequently conduct a special evaluation of the school-community context to reveal needs that should be addressed in a revised curriculum. Evaluation specialists must work closely with curriculum developers. Once curricula are put into operation, evaluation specialists provide expertise in the evaluation of curricula for both technical and nontechnical approaches.

Site-based management requires that building principals change their roles from managers to instructional leaders (Ambrosie & Haley, 1991; Streshly, 1992). Principals are expected to establish a common vision among teachers and staff, provide a collegial participatory school culture, and focus on instructional improvement and accountability (Streshly, 1992). They are also expected to provide resources (time, money, materials, information, etc.), serve as an instructional resource (conduct classroom observations, talk with teachers about improving instruction, provide support for teachers having difficulty with the program, etc.), communicate (provide regular feedback to teachers, develop programs, etc.), and provide an ethos or satisfying feeling that pervades the school (Ambrosie & Haley, 1991).

Resources Specialists.   Media specialists and librarians serve at either district or school levels. They provide expertise in the curriculum processes through their knowledge of and ability to obtain curriculum materials.

Media specialists understand computer hardware and software. They recommend media sources (e.g., ready-made overhead projector transparencies, interactive video discs) and instruct curriculum developers about the uses of low- and high-technology in classrooms.

Librarians provide information about all forms of print materials. They usually know what resources are available, how to use them, and where to find them if they are not currently available.

Counselors, Social Workers, and Health-Care Providers.   These individuals may also be district- or school-based. Health-care providers include school nurses and school psychologists. Because these staff members frequently work with students individually, they can advise committees on the intricacies of the context for which curricula are prepared. Their specialties include knowledge of students' abilities, interests, and concerns; family backgrounds; and community resources. Sometimes they contribute directly to *instructional* curricula by providing information to students about careers, health, resources, and other matters.

TEACHERS AND STUDENTS

Teachers and students are involved differently in curriculum depending on the approach used. In school- or classroom-based approaches these individuals are active producers; in district-based approaches they are typically consumers.

Teachers have several expertises that can be valuable in curriculum processes. In describing teachers' knowledge bases Shulman (1986, 1987) mentions these seven categories: (1) content knowledge, (2) general pedagogical knowledge, (3) curriculum knowledge, (4) pedagogical content knowledge, (5) knowledge of learners and their characteristics, (6) knowledge of educational contexts, and (7) knowledge of educational philosophies (ends, purposes, and values). Most of these are self-explanatory, but pedagogical content knowledge deserves comment because it is unique to teachers.

Pedagogical content knowledge is "that special amalgam of content and pedagogy that is uniquely the province of teachers, their own special form of professional understanding" (Shulman, 1987, p. 7). It "includes an understanding of what makes the learning of specific topics easy or difficult; the conceptions and preconceptions that students of different ages and backgrounds bring with them to the learning of those most frequently taught topics and lessons" (Shulman, 1986, p. 9).

These definitions show that knowledge of content and how to teach it to others are important. As a result of working with students, teachers learn what kinds of illustrations, analogies, and demonstrations clarify content so it is understandable to students. The development of pedagogical content knowledge involves reorganizing content for teaching based on one's values and beliefs (Shulman, 1986). This element is missing unless teachers participate in curriculum development processes.

Other members of curriculum committees typically hold in common with teachers the remaining types of knowledge. Often, however, knowledge of learners and their characteristics and of educational contexts is conspicuously absent in curriculum documents. When invited to participate in curriculum development, teachers can remind their colleagues of the importance of these considerations.

District.   Although some teachers serve on district-based curriculum committees, most teachers are consumers of an institutional curriculum devised by other people. Their involvement is limited to translating the *institutional* curriculum into one for *instructional* purposes, transforming a curriculum that could be used almost anywhere into one for specific students.

In many cases, teachers make this translation in isolation from other professionals. They impose their own values onto the institutional curriculum, sometimes with less-than-desirable results. For example, Cronin-Jones (1991) reports research on a curriculum project showing that when teacher beliefs contradictory to those underlying a curriculum prevail, they can prevent implementation of a curriculum as it was intended. In this project teachers believed the most important student outcomes were factual knowledge, and taught that way. But the curriculum was intended to teach problem-solving skills, values, and attitudes.

The *instructional* curriculum of teachers undergoes yet another transformation by the students with whom it is used. Students are expected to participate in the learning activities directed by teachers, and choices about their activities may be limited or nonexistent. As students participate, they develop their own *experiential* curricula that can be quite different from the instructional curriculum, because students perceive the events according to their unique backgrounds.

School.   Teachers are very much involved in school-based curriculum decision making. In a *technical* approach teachers and building administrators develop institutional curricula that take into account their school-community contexts and use teacher expertises. When a school-based group needs assistance, it may call district personnel or anyone else it chooses and can afford as consultants.

White (1992) reports a study of districts where decision making had been decentralized in favor of teachers for at least five years. She found that 92 percent of teachers had a lot of involvement in school curriculum decisions and that 90 percent were personally involved.

> School-based curriculum development . . . enabled teachers to recommend new courses, to redesign report cards, to make scheduling changes, to select in-service workshops, and to participate in textbook selection. Teachers reported that their participation on curriculum development committees . . . opened up communication within their own school as well as with teachers and principals from other schools. (White, 1992, p. 73)

In a *nontechnical* approach teachers use their knowledge of teaching, learning, and students to build a curriculum based on students' experiences and needs. Teachers do not predetermine the learning outcomes, because expectations are not uniform for what students will learn. In the school-based mode, teachers work together by grade levels or departments.

Teachers base curricula on either preselected themes, sometimes from district documents, or those suggested by students. Whichever they choose, "[t]eachers . . . get to know children as individuals and, to the extent that is appropriate, recognize their interests and concerns in the definition of work the classes undertake; quite likely, this differentiation will occur in the provision of options to develop core learnings, in adaptations of the class environment and in tailoring teacher assistance to fit children's personalities and levels of accomplishment" (Hunter & Scheirer, 1988, p. 75).

This description shows that students are producers of curriculum decisions under the nontechnical approach. Because they have real choices in the learning

TABLE 2.1
Summary Information Concerning Local Curriculum Decision Making

Locus of decisions	Type of governance	Personnel	Type of curriculum approach
District	Board of education	Administrators (curriculum/subject matter specialists/ building), teachers, community members, consultants	Technical
School	Site-based group* or board of education	Teachers and administrators in a school, as needed— consultants	Technical or nontechnical
Classroom	Site-based group* or board of education	Individual teachers, as needed—consultants	Nontechnical

*Indicates preferred type of governance.

experiences in which they engage, their decisions affect materials, resources, activities, grouping, time, and space. Moreover, in many cases students are expected to reflect on their learning processes as part of their joint efforts with teachers (Short & Burke, 1991). For information about a specific nontechnical approach see the section called The Authoring Cycle in Chapter 12.

Classroom. When decision-making is classroom-based, *individual* teachers are free to use their expertises in a variety of ways. Teachers consult with colleagues or with building or district administrators as they choose, but are not bound to follow curricula devised by others, except that their curricula must promote the purpose of education adopted by the school district. These teachers usually use the nontechnical approach to meet the unique needs of their students.

Table 2.1 summarizes information from the previous section and integrates it with information about school personnel involvement. This table shows relationships among the three approaches to local curriculum decision making, types of governance, personnel, and curriculum approaches.

THE CASE FOR SCHOOL-BASED CURRICULUM DECISION MAKING

Thus far this chapter has described district, school, and classroom-based approaches to local curriculum decision making. Though each approach has advantages, school-based curriculum decision making in one form or another should be included for the reasons that follow:

Teachers, who are expected to be change agents in schools, are heavily involved in school-based decision making. As discussed in Chapter 1, change requires the transformation of *subjective* realities which means that curriculum change occurs only when *people* change. Because teachers are expected to bring about change in schools, reasoning says they must be involved in curriculum decision making.

Both school and classroom approaches involve teachers in decision making to a greater extent than district approaches (see Table 2.1). However, the argument here is for a school approach in one of two forms. One form is the school-based approach described previously where teachers and administrators in a school develop an institutional curriculum without reference to a district curriculum. In the second form teachers and administrators in a school modify a district-developed curriculum so that it meets the needs of their particular school within the district.

As district-based decision making is usually practiced, a district group translates societal expectations, including changes, into institutional curricula. But most teachers, because they are typically not part of these processes, are not affected by those changes. Teachers learn about expected changes by reading the printed district curriculum guidelines or having the changes explained in inservice meetings. In these cases "change" is a second-hand experience because teachers were not involved in the experiences where "changes" developed. This situation is exacerbated where teachers develop instructional curricula in isolation from colleagues (see Figure 2.4a).

Why make a fuss about teachers working in isolation? Curriculum decision making, like teaching and learning, is fundamentally a social undertaking. Making curriculum decisions requires collaboration so that people are able to reflect and develop meanings for decisions.

Although individuals develop their own meanings of change, working with a group through the ambivalence and uncertainty that naturally attend any change activity is stimulating and supportive. Dewey (1938) said it best: "all human experience is ultimately social: it involves contact and communication" (p. 38).

This does not mean that district-based curricula should be abolished. In fact, in most states the authority for local decisions belongs to the district. The argument is that school-based decision making should replace the *individual* efforts of teachers translating an institutional curriculum into one for instruction. Instead teachers within a school should work together under the leadership of a building administrator to plan a school curriculum (see Figure 2.4b).

Even though teachers are very much involved in classroom-based curricula, this approach is not advocated. As typically practiced, these teachers also prepare curricula in isolation. The same argument developed previously applies here that curriculum decisions require collaboration among people.

School-based curriculum decisions accommodate the needs of a particular community and its people. Teachers and school staff know the abilities, needs, and interests of students within a school. They also have contact with parents and guardians and know their expectations. Many districts encompass different contexts—too many to acknowledge in a district-based curriculum. When school-based curriculum development groups meet, they are able to consider special content emphases needed by students in their school and develop a curriculum that takes these

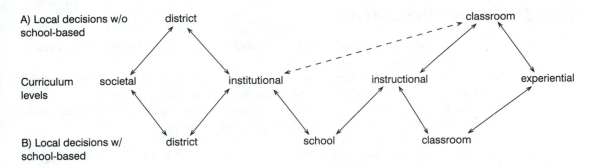

FIGURE 2.4
Relationships Among Curriculum Levels and Local Curriculum Decision-Making
Approaches Without (A) and With (B) School-Based Decisions

needs into account. The collaborative efforts of several professionals facilitate accommodation efforts across a school population.

Finally, *the school-based approach allows for use of both technical and nontechnical curriculum processes*. In many situations schools and districts are obliged to develop curricula with predetermined learning outcomes because of state laws. However, particularly in private schools or community schools, curriculum developers are not bound by these regulations and can use the nontechnical processes. The school-based approach works well with both technical and nontechnical processes.

Regardless of which approach is chosen, the personnel involved in making decisions should be knowledgeable about the processes. This book was written to provide teachers and school staff with the knowledge for engaging in the curriculum processes.

SUMMARY

Curriculum decision making is a sociopolitical process that involves almost everyone. Actions at the national levels, including funding decisions and legislation, influence curriculum even though curriculum matters are supposed to be handled at state and local levels.

The community-at-large shapes societal and institutional curricula by deciding priorities. Whether boards of education or site-based management groups, local governance organizations set the purposes of local curricula. These same organizations dictate to a large extent how school personnel are involved in curriculum decision making.

School-based curriculum decision making is highly favored in this text because it provides the vehicle for change in schools. School-based processes acknowledge that change occurs in people rather than in programs. Change is likely to occur because school personnel including administrators and teachers are involved in creating curricula they administer and deliver to students.

QUESTIONS FOR DISCUSSION

1. Describe original examples of actions at the national level that affect curriculum decisions in your school.
2. Cite instances of businesses or industries in your area that attempt to effect changes in school curricula. To what extent have their attempts been successful?
3. Describe the approach to local curriculum decision making used in your area. To what extent does it take advantage of your expertise?
4. Site-based management of schools requires that building principals change their roles from managers to instructional leaders. Why? Describe the changes that might be difficult or easy for principals who function as managers.
5. School-based curriculum decision making requires teacher participation. What objections might teachers have to such participation? Why might teachers be pleased to participate?
6. Do you think the fact that some teachers serve on district-based curriculum committees make those curricula more credible than they would be without the teachers? Explain.
7. Describe any experiences you have that involved curriculum decision making. How were they similar to or different from those described in this chapter?

IMPORTANT IDEAS DISCUSSED INITIALLY IN THIS CHAPTER

beliefs-values

curriculum decision making
   district-based
   school-based
   classroom-based

change facilitators

pedogogical content knowledge

PART TWO

ESTABLISHMENT OF BASES FOR CURRICULUM PROCESSES

The curriculum processes of development, classroom use, and evaluation are resource hungry! In any school district these processes require vast amounts of time and energy from large numbers of educators. Paying their salaries and purchasing supplies and materials for curriculum activities take large sums of money. It makes sense, therefore, that educators involved in these processes should understand their foundations as part of creating effective and efficient curricula for their constituencies. Part 2 seeks to establish these understandings.

Chapter 3 anchors Part 2 and the remainder of the book through the descriptions of five conceptions of curriculum. Each conception implies a distinct purpose of education, uses one or more content sources, and organizes the results of curriculum decisions in discrete designs. Each conception is tracked from its educational-social-political origin to the present. This chapter also considers content organizational criteria by which planners manage the content in curricula. The final section on curriculum designs describes different ways of organizing content.

Chapters 4, 5, and 6 survey the literature related to subject matter, society and culture, and learners, respectively, as it pertains to curriculum. This information is intended to update and deepen your understanding of these major sources of curriculum content and encourage you to examine your own values and beliefs. A final section in each chapter previews the application of the information in the major curriculum processes.

Specifically, Chapter 4 analyzes subject matter as a source of curriculum content through discussions of several conceptions of knowledge and learning. This information lays the foundation for decisions about the purpose of education and the selection of valid and significant content to help learners meet particular purposes. Chapter 5 provides developers with knowledge about the bases on which to select content consistent with societal and cultural realities.

Chapter 6 discusses views of learner development and knowledge acquisition. This chapter provides foundational information, which developers use to decide if content is learnable and meets the long-term needs and interests of learners. It also lays the foundation for decisions about projected roles for those who deliver the curriculum. Part 3 uses this information in the development of curriculum projects and Part 4 applies this information in classroom use and evaluation of curriculum projects.

3

CURRICULUM ORGANIZATION

OUTLINE

Conceptions of curriculum
>   Cumulative tradition of organized knowledge
>   Social relevance-reconstruction
>   Self-actualization
>   Development of cognitive processes
>   Technology
Considerations in content organization
>   Scope
>   Continuity and sequence
>   Integration
Curriculum organization
>   Subject matter designs
>   Society-culture based designs
>   Learner-based designs
>   Other designs

S everal definitions of curriculum cited in Chapter 1 indicate that educators have different views about the meaning of curriculum. However, curriculum writers generally agree that five conceptions of curriculum capture the essence of contemporary thought on this subject (Brandt, 1988; Eisner & Vallance, 1974; Goodlad & Su, 1992).

A **conception of curriculum** implies a particular purpose of education with appropriate content and organization. Curriculum content originates from the same sources that give rise to the purposes of education—subject matter, needs of society and culture, and needs and interests of learners.

In the United States the conception of curriculum for public schools at the *institutional* level is usually set by the district. This conception usually centers on the cumulative tradition of organized knowledge, popularly known as transmitting the cultural heritage. Many nonpublic schools also use this conception. Although it is congruent with *societal* expectations, other conceptions must be considered because of the expanded role of schools for socializing children and youth at the beginning of the 21st century. History shows that because of changes in social policies, more than one curriculum conception is viable at one time in this country. In recent years schools have offered minicurricula based on conceptions other than transmitting the cultural heritage.

This chapter is intended *to lay a foundation for the ideas to be considered in developing, using, and evaluating curricula.* The chapter begins with a discussion of current conceptions of curriculum and provides the basis for understanding purposes of education and curriculum organization or design. A second section discusses the considerations about curriculum content organization used by developers. The final section describes curriculum designs based on the dominant sources of curriculum content.

CONCEPTIONS OF CURRICULUM

Each source of curriculum content is emphasized in one conception. That is, subject matter is emphasized in the cumulative tradition of organized knowledge; society and culture, in social relevance-reconstruction; and learners, in self-actualization. Two other conceptions are not bound to particular content sources, but are usually associated with subject matter: development of cognitive processes and curriculum as technology. This section describes these conceptions and provides their brief historical backgrounds.

Table 3.1 relates the curriculum conceptions to their corresponding purposes of education and primary sources of content. Table 3.2, found at the end of this section, compares selected major events in the history of the conceptions.

CUMULATIVE TRADITION OF ORGANIZED KNOWLEDGE

Many schools use curricula intended to preserve and transmit the Western culture, the oldest and most fundamental of all the purposes of American education. This conception of curriculum, termed the *cumulative tradition of organized knowledge*

TABLE 3.1
Curriculum Conceptions, Purposes of Education, and Content Sources

Curriculum Conception	Purpose of Education	Primary Source of Content
Cumulative tradition of organized knowledge	To cultivate cognitive achievement and the intellect	Academic disciplines, subject matter
Social relevance-reconstruction	To prepare people for living in an unstable, changing world; to reform society	Needs of society and culture
Self-actualization	To develop individuals to their fullest potentials	Needs and interests of learners
Development of cognitive processes	To develop intellectual processes*	Any source, but usually subject matter
Technology	To make learning systematic and efficient*	Any source, but usually subject matter

*This purpose is a process goal that does not state an educational end.

(Goodlad & Su, 1992; Tanner & Tanner, 1980) or *academic rationalism* (Eisner & Vallance, 1974; Brandt, 1988), holds that schools should transmit the cultural heritage.

In this conception the purpose of education is to **cultivate cognitive achievement and the intellect** by helping students understand knowledge. The academic rationalist believes that through study of the *disciplines* (e.g., mathematics, languages) students learn to think with precision, generality, and power in solving problems in all areas of life. The conception, cumulative tradition of organized knowledge, includes organized knowledge whether disciplined or *undisciplined* (e.g., home economics, computer education).

Background. This conception began with the first schools in colonial America and continues today. In 1647 a Massachusetts state law required the establishment of elementary schools for teaching reading and writing, and Latin grammar (secondary) schools for teaching Latin, Greek, and the Scriptures. After a hundred years, academies began competing with grammar schools. Nearly another hundred years later in 1827, a second Massachusetts law established public high schools that continued the dual curricula of the academy.

Both types of institutions flourished for a while, but the push to equalize educational opportunity for all high school-age students brought problems as more students began to attend. What should be taught at each level? A joint elementary-secondary curriculum was not possible because the high school had been added to a system that already had colleges and elementary schools, each of which had staked out its curricular claims. Not one of the three committees appointed by the National Education Association in the late 1800s to study the question proposed suitable curricular reform (Tanner & Tanner, 1990).

In the early 20th century, different groups of reformers advocating social reconstruction and individual development as curricular purposes attempted to displace academic rationalism, but neither succeeded. (These movements are discussed in later subsections.) Throughout the years, public schools continued to teach subject-based curricula, albeit with variations.

In the midst of experiments with curricula based on sources other than subject matter, the launch of Sputnik I by the former Soviet Union in 1957 triggered a return to basic subject matter curricula. Large quantities of federal funds were targeted to studies of mathematics, science, and foreign languages, while the humanities were pushed aside. These studies resulted in multiple curriculum projects designed largely by academicians, without the benefits of practitioner knowledge. These projects intended to make school curricula rigorous, but most were not implemented successfully. By the early 1990s most projects had been abandoned (Goodlad & Su, 1992).

In the 1970s, growing conservatism in public social policy led to teaching only the essential subjects. When statewide minimum competency testing mushroomed in the 1970s and 1980s, teachers taught to the tests, which resulted in a decline in thinking abilities and writing skills.

A Nation at Risk, produced by the National Commission on Excellence in Education (1983), suggested that the schools were at fault for the decline of America's historic role in dominating the global economy. National studies by Boyer (1983) and Goodlad (1984) showed the need for a coherent curriculum to fulfill the function of general education. More than a decade later subject matter continues to dominate as the primary source of curriculum, with some adjustments for the needs of learners and society-culture. However, needs in general education have not been resolved.

SOCIAL RELEVANCE-RECONSTRUCTION

The *social relevance-reconstruction* conception stresses education in the larger social context where societal needs dominate both subject matter and individual needs. Content comes from societal issues (e.g., AIDS education). Within this conception are two distinct branches, involving both a current and a future orientation.

The "current" orientation is the adaptive approach that calls for personal development in the context of social change. People who advocate this view believe that curriculum should **prepare people for living in an unstable and changing world**. The "futurist" orientation, or the reformist approach, would like schools to intervene actively to shape changes and to **reform society**. Some reformists are idealistic, but others are aggressive in their intentions to see schools deal with change (Brandt, 1988; Eisner & Vallance, 1974).

Background. The social relevance-reconstruction curriculum conception began as part of a two-pronged revolt, with individual development, against the academic rationalist tradition that dominated schools until the early 1900s. As the descriptions show, the history of these conceptions is intertwined.

The reformers wanted high schools to offer a curriculum useful for everyday life because most young people were not going on to college. In 1900 not only were Latin, Greek and foreign languages under attack but also the academic subjects that did not directly serve a social purpose. "For several decades the all-embracing popular term that was coined to counteract arguments of academic discipline was 'social efficiency'" (Butts, 1975–76, p. 5).

Butts (1975–76) describes the social efficiency movement as having two thrusts. One group wished to prepare individuals for their roles in society as it exists, that is, education for social control. This group concentrated on applying management strategies from business models to education that resulted eventually in curriculum as technology. (This conception is discussed later in this section.) The second group wanted to prepare students for social responsibility in a democratic society.

In 1897 Dewey published his pedagogic creed that redefined education and the purpose of schooling. This document clearly suggested that school is primarily a social institution and education a continuing reconstruction of experience (Dewey, 1988). Dewey's views influenced the Commission on the Reorganization of Secondary Education, which published the *Cardinal Principles of Secondary Education* (National Education Association, 1918). With six of the seven principles referring to social concerns, the role of education was broadened considerably (Butts, 1975–76).

The theme of social responsibility was continued by the Educational Policies Commission in its statements through the 1930s and 1940s, but was dropped in the 1950s and 1960s when interest in the academic disciplines revived (Butts, 1975–76). The "current" orientation continued into the 1970s with critics of the status quo calling for relevance in the curriculum. In recent years, schools have added to the curriculum information that society believes young people should have, such as drug awareness information and AIDs education.

The "futurist" branch of this conception also began during the 1920s. Two chief spokespersons were George S. Counts and Harold Rugg, both of whom gave numerous addresses and wrote prodigiously about their views on schools and change. So eloquent was one of Counts' speeches that the Progressive Education Association switched its allegiance to radical social policy away from its previous focus on individual development. During the 1930s Rugg published a social studies curriculum that carried out his ideas about reforming society through schools (Tanner & Tanner, 1990).

Because such radicalism was not tolerated during the World War II era, this movement receded, and in 1955 the Progressive Education Association disbanded. However, the movement was not dead. In 1956 Theodore Brameld published *Toward a Reconstructed Philosophy of Education,* which described how social reconstruction should function. Schools were to help build a new culture in which working people would control all institutions, businesses, and resources. Perhaps most revolutionary of all was the idea that individuals should satisfy their personal needs within societal limits. These ideas did not claim much attention though, because of the renewed interest in academic disciplines.

That legacy was passed on to contemporary critics such as Michael W. Apple, William Pinar, Henry Giroux and others who call attention to injustices related to schooling. Apple and Giroux are described as critical theorists who raise consciousness levels regarding educational issues. Pinar, on the other hand, represents a group of reconceptualists who seek more personal autonomy in the choices of students with respect to their aspirations for learning. These individuals continue to call for schools in which children learn how to live (Eisner, 1992).

SELF-ACTUALIZATION

A *self-actualization* curriculum seeks to provide personally satisfying experiences for individual learners. With an emphasis on student-centeredness, this orientation is toward learner autonomy and growth. Schooling is considered an enabling process with the purpose of **developing individuals to their fullest potentials**. Education is a liberating force, a means of helping individuals discover things for themselves. Schooling is a vital and potentially enriching experience in which subject matter and societal-cultural needs are incorporated as they assist an individual's development (Eisner & Vallance, 1974).

Background.   The 1880s saw the beginning of the child study movement, which sought to change curricula dominated by the disciplines. Led by G. Stanley Hall, members of this reform movement, including many teachers untrained in psychology, studied aspects of children's knowledge and lives. "Child-study as it developed under Hall's leadership was not psychology at all. . . . Hall had grossly misconceived the relationship between a science of psychology and pedagogical practice" (Kliebard, 1992, p. 60). Few of the child-study findings were incorporated into school curricula, but Hall's work led to child-centered, laissez-faire curricula centered at times on the momentary interests of children. Although this situation was clearly not healthy, some schools continued this approach well into the 1920s (Tanner & Tanner, 1990).

Kilpatrick (1918) attempted to rectify some problems of curricula based on student interests by specifying the project as a purposeful act carried out in social surroundings. Kilpatrick saw the purposeful act as the typical unit of life in a democratic society; therefore, he advocated that it become the typical unit of school procedure. Under his plan, children were to pursue projects of their choice, with the teacher merely steering the course. Unfortunately, without a tie to social problem-solving and the progressive improvement of society, this method effected few long-lasting changes in schooling (Tanner & Tanner, 1990).

In 1919 the Progressive Education Association organized and dedicated its efforts to the development of children. This organization sponsored the noteworthy Eight-Year Study which found that students graduating from experimental high schools, where they had not followed the usual college preparatory curriculum, did as well in college as their peers who had followed the traditional plan. Though this finding received little official notice, these results were important because they showed "that schools could develop educational programs that would interest students, meet their needs, and at the same time provide them with the preparation they needed for success in college" (Tanner & Tanner, 1990, p. 235). This legacy is probably the largest contribution of all those made by the PEA.

In 1947 Florence B. Stratemeyer and her associates at Teachers College developed a curriculum design based on continuing life situations (Stratemeyer, 1973). Its purpose was to help children and youth understand and learn how to cope with problems of personal significance. The developers thought that child-selected problems would have intrinsic motivation so that preplanning the curriculum would be unnecessary. However, once the 1950s arrived with their emphases on the disciplines, very little attention was given to this design or any other approach involving individual development.

Years of protests followed in the 1960s and 1970s. Almost everybody, it seemed, had a gripe against the schools. "Free schools, alternative schools, open classrooms became the sesame for escaping the dull routines of the regular class-room, especially as conducted in the public schools" (Butts, 1975–76, p. 9). Some free or alternate schools experimented with humanistic curricula that sometimes used content directly related to student interests. See Figure 3.1 for an excerpt from a humanistic curriculum representative of a self-actualization conception.

The children themselves were the indicated content vehicles. No books, films, or subject disciplines were used. Classroom situations, pupil experiences, and personal experiences contributed to the content. The device through which most of the content filtered was the notion of "glasses," which the participants pretended to wear or, in fact, wore.

Lesson 1. The purpose of this lesson was to show the students (1) that there are different ways of seeing the same situation and (2) that one's state of mind or feel-ing influences one's perceptions.

The teacher held up two pairs of sunglasses, each with different color lenses. He explained that these were very special glasses, that each pair colored the wearer's view of the world with a particular feeling.

Teacher: The first pair of glasses are "suspicious" glasses. When a person wears them, he regards whatever he sees or hears with suspicion. *[The teacher asked for a volunteer to put on the suspicious glasses and tell the class what he saw.]*

Volunteer: *(looking at two children who were talking and laughing, as he put on the glasses):* I wonder if they're talking about me. Are they laughing at me? *[The teacher asked that questions be addressed to the volunteer.]*

Student: Who's your best friend?

Volunteer: Why does he want to know that? Are they going to try to take my friends away?

Teacher: *(holding up second pair of glasses):* I have a second pair of glasses, which are rose-colored. They make whoever wears them see and hear with this feeling: "No matter what anyone says to me, I know they really care for me."
[Teacher asked for and secured the cooperation of another volunteer. Throughout the dialogue that followed the teacher sought to clarify the volunteer's responses by asking: "Are you acting suspicious or just curi-ous?" "Do you really feel that way, or are you exaggerating your reac-tions?" "Do you really think they might be trying to do that to you?"*]*

Teacher: Let's get some reactions from our volunteer . . . .

FIGURE 3.1

Curriculum Illustrative of the Self-Actualization Conception

From *Toward Humanistic Education: A Curriculum of Affect* (pp. 78–79, 89) by G. Weinstein & M. D. Fantini (Eds.), 1970, New York: Praeger. Copyright 1970 by Henry Holt. Reprinted by permission.

In the wake of the social conservatism movement, interest in individual development all but disappeared in the 1980s and early 1990s. Only a few schools and colleges attempt curricula based on individual needs. Programs that exist may be called child- or person-centered instruction. (For examples, see Romey, 1988, and/or Strader & Rinker, 1989.)

DEVELOPMENT OF COGNITIVE PROCESSES

The *development of cognitive processes* curriculum intends to sharpen students' intellectual processes and develop cognitive skills for studying virtually anything. Subject matter is used to **develop intellectual processes** that can be used in areas other than the ones in which the processes were learned. Abilities such as inferring, speculating, deducing, or analyzing are expected to continue long after the content is forgotten (Eisner & Vallance, 1974). The focus is on students' learning processes rather than the broader social context in which learning occurs (Goodlad & Su, 1992). Curriculum as development of cognitive processes is necessarily open-ended and growth oriented.

Background.   The development of this curriculum conception probably came from faculty psychology or mental discipline, which was popular in the 19th century. Faculty psychology assumed that building one's mental faculties, or mental "muscles," enabled that person to apply these cognitive abilities to learning any type of content (Eisner & Vallance, 1974). This view of learning soon gave way to behaviorism which stressed the coupling of stimuli with responses through operant conditioning.

However, behaviorism had to compete with cognitive psychology, a new view of learning begun in the early 1900s by German Gestalt psychologists. Their work clashed with that of behaviorists about the nature of thinking processes. Whereas early behaviorists attributed learning to trial-and-error endeavors, the Gestaltists demonstrated that it came about through thought or understanding (Rock & Palmer, 1990).

During this time, Dewey started testing educational theories that were clearly influenced by the Gestaltists. Dewey theorized that children needed to experience problem solving. He believed that rather than be told they needed to learn content, children should judge, consider, and deliberate about questions of their own making.

Dewey's ideas on reflective thinking were systematized into an educational method and published as *How We Think* in 1910 (revised in 1933). This problem solving approach contains what has come to be known as the scientific method, but Dewey considered the steps as required traits of reflective thinking. During the 1920s and 1930s many progressive teachers used this problem solving approach in classrooms (Tanner & Tanner, 1990) and the ideas continue today in some subject-centered curricula.

During these same years, other curriculum conceptions competed for attention, and emphasis on problem solving ebbed and flowed. In the 1950s and 1960s with the revived interest in academic disciplines, interest was also renewed in the processes. Parker and Rubin (1966) proposed that process is "the highest form of content and the most appropriate base for curriculum change" (p. 1). Some curriculum developers adopted and used the process approach frequently within a subject area.

Also, during this same era, Bruner (1960) helped acquaint Americans with the work of Jean Piaget, the Swiss psychologist, who demonstrated that children play an active role in their own development through direct experiences. Curriculum projects developed in the 1960s and 1970s were very much influenced by Piagetian thought (Tanner & Tanner, 1990). One of those projects was *Science: A Process Approach* (S-APA). Although the content was science, the processes are generalizable to other settings. Figure 3.2 contains a brief statement from the *S-APA Commentary for Teachers* (1970). This curriculum featured hands-on experiences for students and had little written material for children.

INTERPRETING DATA

OBJECTIVES

After you have studied this exercise you should be able to:
1. *DESCRIBE* in a few sentences the information shown on a table of data or graph.
2. *CONSTRUCT* one or more inferences or hypotheses from the information given in a table of data, graph, or picture.
3. *DESCRIBE* certain kinds of data, using the mean, median, and range; *CONSTRUCT* predictions, inferences, or hypotheses from this information.

VOCABULARY

linear	coordinate
nonlinear	mean
relation	median
slope	central tendency
range	variation
equation	photosynthesize

Activity 1 — Interpreting Graphs

Suppose someone gave you a graph which showed the height of a plant at various times after planting. (See Figure 1.) How would you describe the shape of the curve in the graph? You might say: The growth curve shows that the plant sprouted on about the fifth day and then grew in increasing amounts each week thereafter for six weeks. At that time, the plant was about 44 centimeters tall.

This description seems all right, but the term *increasing amounts* is not specific enough. To be more specific, you might describe how much the plant grew between equal intervals. For example, Figure 2 gives the data recorded on the graph in tabular form. The third column shows how much the plant grew each week. Now we see that the amount of growth per week increased from 1.3 centimeters the first week to 13.0 centimeters in the sixth week. If you were a botanist looking at these data, you might next ask questions like the following:

1. Why does the plant grow so slowly at first?
2. Why does the amount of growth during each week get larger and larger?
3. What inferences can be constructed in answer to these two questions?

To answer these questions, let's assume you plant more seeds. At one week intervals, you measure the height of a plant. Then you uproot it, dry it in an oven, and weigh the dry plant.

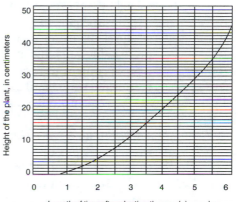

Length of time after planting the seed, in weeks

FIGURE 1

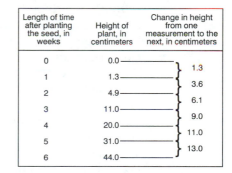

Length of time after planting the seed, in weeks	Height of plant, in centimeters	Change in height from one measurement to the next, in centimeters
0	0.0	
		1.3
1	1.3	
		3.6
2	4.9	
		6.1
3	11.0	
		9.0
4	20.0	
		11.0
5	31.0	
		13.0
6	44.0	

FIGURE 2

FIGURE 3.2

Curriculum Illustrative of the Development of Cognitive Processes Conception

From *Science: A Process Approach: Commentary for Teachers* (pp. 133, 135), 1970, Washington, DC: American Association for the Advancement of Science/Xerox Corporation.

As this history shows, problem solving has been a concern of curriculum developers since the early 1900s and has taken several forms. In 1989 the National Council of Teachers of Mathematics (NCTM) published its *Curriculum and Evaluation Standards for School Mathematics,* in which high priority is given to problem solving. Of interest also is the NCTM's focus on the processes of reasoning, communication, patterning, and others. As with S-APA, although distinct content is used, the emphasis is definitely on the processes.

TECHNOLOGY

Curriculum as *technology* seeks to **make learning systematic and efficient**. Usually this learning is predefined and calls for rather simple outcomes. The focus is on the technology by which knowledge is communicated and learning is facilitated, rather than on the individuality of the learner or the content itself (Goodlad & Su, 1992). Practical problems of efficiently packaging and presenting material for students are solved by curriculum technologists through programmed learning, personalized systems instruction, and certain computer-assisted instructional programs.

Curricula using this approach assume that learning occurs systematically and predictably, and that it can be made more efficient by proper organization. The type of content that can be taught using technology is limited and must be delivered using words and symbols. Typically this content is hierarchical in nature and can be sequenced from simple to complex.

Background.   Curriculum as technology had its beginnings in the early 1900s when Franklin Bobbitt and W. W. Charters sought to bring scientific management to learning. (This is the aspect of social efficiency for social control mentioned under social relevance-reconstruction.) Based on the belief that life activities should become curriculum objectives, these men applied job analysis to curriculum development, an approach that was highly compatible with behavioral psychology and popular during this period. Consequently, Bobbitt and Charters are credited with initiating technical curriculum development.

In 1924 Sidney L. Pressey introduced the first teaching machine, which he claimed provided efficiency in learning because students received immediate knowledge of results. However, the machine was not successful, due in part to the Great Depression of the 1930s (Niemiec & Walberg, 1989).

In the late 1950s B. F. Skinner reintroduced teaching machines and programmed learning. This approach emphasizes the presentation of factual information in small steps, simple tasks to which students respond, and immediate feedback. Skinner envisioned that teaching machines, including a variety of audiovisual aids, might "supplant lectures, demonstrations, and textbooks. . . . They serve one function of the teacher: they present material to the student, and make it so clear and interesting that the student learns" (Skinner, 1968, p. 29). You be the judge of Skinner's claim as you read the example of programmed instruction for a high school physics course in Figure 3.3.

Although simple teaching machines were rather short-lived, the underlying thought continued and manifested itself in computer-assisted instruction (CAI) in

Sentence to be completed	Word to be supplied
1. The important parts of a flashlight are the battery and the bulb. When we "turn on" a flashlight, we close a switch that connects the battery with the _____ .	bulb
2. When we turn on a flashlight, an electric current flows through the fine wire in the _____ and causes it to grow hot.	bulb
3. When the hot wire glows brightly, we say that it gives off or sends out heat and _____ .	light
4. The fine wire in the bulb is called a filament. The bulb "lights up" when the filament is heated by the passage of a(n) _____ current.	electric
5. When a weak battery produces little current, the fine wire, or _____ , does not get very hot.	filament
6. A filament which is *less* hot sends out or gives off _____ light.	less
7. "Emit" means "send out." The amount of light sent out, or "emitted," by a filament depends on how _____ the filament is.	hot
8. The higher the temperature of the filament the _____ the light emitted by it.	brighter, stronger

Note: The machine presents one item at a time. The student completes the item and then uncovers the corresponding word or phrase shown at the right.

FIGURE 3.3
Curriculum Illustrative of the Technology Conception
From *The Technology of Teaching* (p. 45) by B. F. Skinner, 1968. Englewood Cliffs, NJ: Prentice Hall.
Copyright 1958 by *Science*. Reprinted by permission.

major systems at the University of Illinois and at Brigham Young University (Clandinin & Connelly, 1992; Niemiec & Walberg, 1989). Also, during the 1970s and 1980s manufacturers of microcomputer software produced drill-and-practice instructional materials for several subject area curricula. In recent years, however, computer usage has changed so that interactions among teachers and students are facilitated by computer learning environments, such as the World Institute for Computer Assisted Teaching (WICAT) (Niemiec & Walberg, 1989) and computer mediated communications systems (Clandinin & Connelly, 1992). In the 1990s computer usage can no longer be associated strictly with the technology conception.

In the mid-1970s Benjamin Bloom proposed that learning time and quality of instruction are alterable conditions. He believed that adjusting these conditions to the needs of individuals would allow most of them to learn what only some would learn otherwise. This approach, called mastery learning, is conceived as skills to be performed repeatedly. In practice the mastery approach uses the curriculum as technology idea, even though the principles do not require this approach (Tanner & Tanner, 1990). Mastery learning continues to be used in schools.

Table 3.2 summarizes selected events in the history of education related to the conceptions of curriculum. Notice that several curriculum conceptions have competed for attention throughout much of history.

Exercise 3.1 asks you to reflect on the five conceptions of curriculum described in this section in terms of their similarities and differences, and is intended to help you sort out the important ideas. Why not see how well you understood the conceptions by trying this exercise?

EXERCISE 3.1

Reconsider the five conceptions of curriculum, their purposes of education, and their content. Then answer the following questions.

1. Develop a continuum showing the relative positions of the five conceptions based on the degree to which each focuses on needs and interests of learners. Explain.
2. What are the relative positions of the curriculum conceptions as they relate to social concerns of schooling? Explain.
3. How would a continuum of the curriculum conceptions appear that is based on the degree of measurability? Explain.

CONSIDERATIONS IN CONTENT ORGANIZATION

Because huge amounts of content are available for each curriculum conception, developers must choose and organize content carefully. At the school or district level, curriculum developers make these decisions by considering several content factors that include scope, continuity, sequence, and integration.

SCOPE

Scope refers to the breadth of the curriculum at a given time—the horizontal organization of content (Goodlad & Su, 1992). Determining what is required for high school graduation or what is needed to complete second grade are scope questions. Must high school graduates take fine arts as well as mathematics and English to enter college? Must fourth-graders exhibit physical education abilities as well as reading and writing capabilities before they go into fifth grade?

Scope questions operate in less encompassing situations, too. Decisions about which theorems to include in a geometry class or which reading experiences to include in a primary grade classroom are scope considerations.

Scope refers in part to the range of important ideas and concepts included in a curriculum (Taba, 1962). Under no circumstances can all the content in any discipline or subject area be taught in schools, nor should it be. Instead, a few major ideas and concepts representing many others must be made the bases of curriculum content. For example, one social studies generalization says, "People intuitively adapt to their environments." Elementary school learners typically study

TABLE 3.2
Selected Major Events in the History of Curriculum Conceptions

Organized Knowledge	Social Relevance-Reconstruction	Self-Actualization	Cognitive Processes	Technology
1647 MA law—Latin grammar school				
. . .				
1827 MA law—public high school				
1830s McGuffey's readers				
		1880–'90 Hall's child study movement	1890s Demise of faculty psychology	
1893 Committee of 10, college preparation				
1895 Committee of 15, 16 subject elementary curriculum				
1899 Committee College Entrance, affirm academic disciplines	1899 Dewey's *Pedagogic Creed*			
	1900s Social efficiency		1900s Gestalt psychology	
			1910 Dewey's *How We Think*	1912 Scientific management applied to education
	1918 *Seven Cardinal Principles*	1918 Kilpatrick's project method		
	1920s Counts & Rugg reform movement	1919 Progressive Education Assn. (PEA) begun	1920–'30s Progressives use Dewey's problem solving	1924 Pressey's first teaching machine
		1920s Child-centered curricula		

TABLE 3.2, *continued*

Organized Knowledge	Social Relevance-Reconstruction	Self-Actualization	Cognitive Processes	Technology
	1932 PEA—radical social policy	1930s PEA—Eight Year Study		
	1930–'40s Educational Policies Commission stresses social responsibility			
		1945 Life adjustment resolution		
		1947 Stratemeyer's persistent life situations curriculum		
1950–'60s Federal funds for mathematics, science, foreign language studies	1956 Brameld's *Reconstructed Philosophy of Education*		1950–'60s Piaget's work influences American curricula	1958 Skinner reintroduces teaching machines
	1970s Critics call for relevance	1960–'70s Romanticists—humanistic curricula		1970s Boom in CAI
				1970–'90s Mastery learning
1980s National committees call for change in general education	1980–'90s Social-oriented issues added to curriculum	1980–'90s Person-centered curricula	1980–'90s Renewed interest in problem solving	1980–'90s Computer mediated communications systems
	1980–'90s Critics call for change			

this idea several times in the context of the early settlements in the United States, as westward-bound immigrants settled in the great plains, and as modern peoples survive in lands with temperature extremes. When this idea is taught as one that generalizes, students learn to apply this notion to the world's peoples, without studying every continent or every civilization.

A second aspect of scope refers to the decisions about which intellectual processes and affective matters should be included in curricula (Taba, 1962). Not all processes can be worked on simultaneously any more than all affective issues can be involved. Attitudes and sensitivities on many different topics are important in school situations. For example, given the increasing diversity among school children, curriculum developers must decide which types of diversity to emphasize in a particular curriculum. Curriculum scope decisions are among the more important ones that developers make.

CONTINUITY AND SEQUENCE

Continuity and sequence are involved in the vertical organization of curriculum. **Continuity** assures that ideas, themes, and skills are dealt with more than once in school curricula (Goodlad & Su, 1992). Because most students do not grasp an idea in one experience, several iterations must be presented before the notion is clear.

For example, children begin writing paragraphs almost from the outset of their school careers and continue these experiences throughout elementary school, gradually adding to their understanding in succeeding years. Despite the repetition of these experiences, some students reach middle school without a good understanding of "paragraphs." Curricula must be planned to provide multiple experiences involving the same idea in forms suitable for students at different grade levels.

Sequence refers not only to the recurrence and repetition of content, but also to its depth (Goodlad & Su, 1992). Each successive experience with a skill or concept should build on the preceding ones, but the new experience should be broader and deeper than earlier experiences (Tyler, 1949). In the case of paragraphing, for example, young students should be taught that all the sentences in a paragraph pertain to one idea. Soon, the students learn to distinguish between main and supporting ideas. Still later, students should learn that different types of writing call for different types of paragraphs. Using such a sequence shows that the major idea has been presented several times in an increasingly complex way.

Content can be sequenced in several ways, including use of either psychological or logical approaches. Psychological sequencing of content involves arranging the curriculum content in one of the ways that students process information. For years social studies curricula have used a *familiar-to-unfamiliar* sequence by beginning with the students' neighborhood and expanding study gradually to include the community, state, and the wider world, in the belief that this organization makes learning easier for children and youth.

Teachers often find that a *concrete-pictorial-abstract* sequence is helpful in teaching concepts to children. Before attempting to associate a label with a concept, teachers show models or pictures or both, designed to show children the characteristics of concepts as aids to their understanding. Then, when students can associate meanings with ideas, teachers help students attach labels or names, the abstract representations, to the ideas. Chapter 4 points out that learning the meaning of a concept is different from associating the name with the concept.

Other sequences employ logical approaches. The *chronological* approach, which uses calendar time as its organizational focus, is often used in history or literature courses. *Part-to-whole* sequences involve placing the basic elements of content ahead of more complex elements. Pre-algebra, for example, may precede the more rigorous study of algebra, or informal geometry may be offered before formal study of geometry. Typically, the first course in a foreign language contains basic ideas that everyone must learn for continuing study in that language.

Whole-to-part sequences reverse this approach and offer general information ahead of specific information. Survey courses in Western civilization, music appreciation or literature may be taken by high school and college students before they study these disciplines in detail. Taking the survey course first provides background for continued study and learning.

INTEGRATION

Integration of the curriculum brings into close relationship the concepts, skills, and values that constitute a curriculum so that these elements are mutually reinforcing to learners (Goodlad & Su, 1992). Ideally, of course, the integration takes place inside learners.

Because knowledge increases daily, scholars work in ever more specialized areas. For example, whereas once there was "geography," now there is "cultural geography," "physical geography," and "biogeography." The proliferation of subcategories within disciplines and subject areas makes it important for curricula to provide general education in ways that permit its integration within learners.

Chapter 8 contains additional information about organization considerations in the context of preparing a content statement. Then Chapters 10 and 11 provide information about their application in two curriculum projects. However, a sense of what they are should be clear at this point. Check your understandings now, by completing Exercise 3.2.

EXERCISE 3.2

Answer each of these questions related to content organization considerations:

1. Explain how the continued growth of knowledge affects scope considerations for school curricula.
2. Consider a science course (biology, geology, etc.) you took within the past five years. Explain how the content in this course was sequenced.
3. Explain how integration is involved in the production of writing in manuscript-to-cursive-to-word processing sequence.
4. Explain how the instructional practice of asking review questions before a lesson is related to the content organizational consideration of continuity.

CURRICULUM ORGANIZATION

Curriculum organization or design is typically based on one dominant source of curriculum content, including subject matter or the disciplines, needs of society and culture, or needs and interests of learners. Subject matter is the most popular basis for curriculum organization (Beauchamp, 1983). The first three subsections that follow describe curriculum designs that use these sources, comment on the relationships among each group of designs and the content organization considerations, and cite advantages and disadvantages of the designs by groups. Other curriculum designs use content from various single sources or combine content from two or more sources. Descriptions of these designs are found in the final subsection.

SUBJECT MATTER DESIGNS

Designs using subject matter as their organizing foci are popular mostly because learning this content is traditional in the United States. Materials for teaching subject matter are standard fare in schools and both teachers and the public are comfortable with subject matter designs. Such designs typically use one of these approaches: single subject, correlated subjects, fused subjects, or broad-fields subjects, and curriculum is usually developed using the technical approach.

Single subject designs are based on one of the academic disciplines or organized subject matter areas. The obvious advantage is that students studying a single subject learn the content of that subject and the methodologies that authorities in that subject develop and use to organize knowledge. However, with increasing specialization, the subject areas have subdivided and now there are too many to offer each as a single subject in most schools.

Correlated subjects (also known as a multidisciplinary approach) is a plan by which learning experiences in two or more areas are related, but the subject identities are kept. To illustrate, in high schools literature of a given period may be correlated with the history of that era. In elementary school, students sometimes study art in the context of the social studies content or they learn spelling words based on science or social studies content. The intent of correlated studies is to provide students with broader understandings than they would have otherwise by the concurrent treatment of two or more different subjects (Goodlad & Su, 1992).

Fused subjects (also known as an interdisciplinary approach) are similar to correlated subjects except that the individual identities of the courses are lost. The relatively recent use of whole language programs in elementary schools furnishes an example of fused subjects. Reading, writing, speaking, and listening are all taught as language arts, but the distinctions among these subjects are not maintained. Some secondary schools offer Western civilization—a combination of history, geography, music, and literature. Fused subjects are offered infrequently because of the difficulty in obtaining agreements about the theoretical rationales that justify blending content from disciplines commonly viewed as independent of each other.

Broad-fields expands the fused subjects approach by cutting across an entire domain of knowledge to provide an integrated view of subject matter (Goodlad &

Su, 1992). For example, American Studies is a humanities program that blends history and literature with other areas such as art history, social science, and religious studies into a program that has a unique way of looking at the American experience.

The 1918 Commission on the Reorganization of Secondary Education (National Education Association, 1918) called for broad-fields courses, especially in social studies, as a way of helping adolescents develop an understanding of society. Some schools followed these suggestions, but by the late 1960s the social studies returned to being discipline-centered. Though the intent is to bring subject matter together and make it meaningful to students, broad-fields approaches may separate knowledge from real life and fail to reflect the interrelations among the broad fields.

In using any of these subject matter designs, the content to be taught is selected and organized before instruction. Its scope is carefully defined so the content will be as meaningful and integrated as possible for students. Close attention is also given to sequencing content so that learners progress through logical steps (Klein, 1991b).

Generally, using organized subject areas as the basis of curriculum is advantageous because this is a systematic and efficient way to help students learn their cultural heritage. Knowledge of the subject and the intellectual processes involved provide a firm foundation for schooling—and it is the traditional way of designing curricula. Materials and resources are available for content as subject matter, and teachers understand this approach (Klein, 1991b).

Chief among the disadvantages of subject matter designs is the fragmentation of knowledge that students can easily forget. Subject matter designs usually present content out of the context of students' worlds, ignoring their abilities, needs, interests, and past experiences. Also, learning content as subject matter is different from how students learn information naturally. Finally, information keeps being created, so students have more to learn, much of which cannot be learned because it is not presented (Klein, 1991b). The relationships of subject matter designs to curriculum organization considerations are summarized in Table 3.3.

TABLE 3.3
Curriculum Designs Related to Content Organization Considerations

Designs	Organization Considerations		
	Scope	Continuity-sequence	Integration
Subject matter	Well-defined; content pre-planned	Well-defined; preplanned	Weak, except for broad fields; depends on learners
Society-culture	Not well-defined; content varies	Not well-defined	Strong; content relevant to learners
Learners	Not well-defined; content varies	Not well-defined	Strong; content relevant to learners

SOCIETY-CULTURE BASED DESIGNS

Curricula based on the needs of society and culture are rooted in the study of life in society, major activities of social life, or social problems. The emphasis is on problem-solving processes and social-human relations skills rather than on acquiring content. Although these designs do not have a prominent place in regular schools, they may be used as part of the school curriculum, particularly in social studies. Designs based on needs of society and culture exist in some community schools (Klein, 1991b).

Curricula based on needs of society and culture are usually developed through nontechnical approaches. "Although explicit objectives may be used, they do not play as major a role in this design as when subject areas are used as a basis for decision making. There is usually a definite focus for the learning process for all students but definite outcomes are not prescribed in advance" (Klein, 1991b, p. 340).

Social functions and activities designs include three organizational themes: "1) the social living or persistent life situation approaches based on the belief that the curriculum design should follow the persistent functions, areas, or life situations in humanity's existence; 2) approaches that organize the curriculum around aspects of problems of community life; and 3) the social action or reconstruction theories that hold the improvement of society through direct involvement of the schools and their students to be a major goal or even the primary goal of the curriculum" (Saylor, Alexander, & Lewis, 1981, p. 231).

Both persistent life situations and social problems that children and youth need to learn abound in today's society. However, the social reconstruction concept is less fully developed as a curriculum design than it is as an educational philosophy. Society is not ready to support institutions that suggest it needs to be restructured (Saylor, Alexander, & Lewis, 1981).

Advantages of this type of design include the integration of the different subject matters and their relevance to students and society. Students typically see the content as meaningful and are usually motivated to study it. However, the scope and sequence of the curriculum are not well defined and may result in superficial treatment of some topics. Because the content is not well-organized, this design may fail to provide adequate exposure to the cultural heritage.

As a result, students may accept the social situation as it exists and not plan to improve it. Another weakness is that generally teachers are not prepared to teach this curriculum and the usual resources are not readily available (Klein, 1991b). See Table 3.3 for a summary of the relationships between designs based on needs of society and culture and curriculum organization considerations.

LEARNER-BASED DESIGNS

In the 1990s curricula organized around the needs and interests of learners exist in preschools, private schools, and experimental programs in schools and colleges. What makes these curricula unique is that students help select and organize the purposes of learning. The subject areas become the means by which students pursue problems or topics from their interests. Teachers prepare in advance but the idea of "predetermined objectives, either explicitly or implicitly stated is rejected and the purposes of the student or a group of students are used to direct the learning process" (Klein, 1991b, p. 339). These designs typically use nontechnical approaches to curriculum development.

Planned for seven- to 12-year-olds, the *organic curriculum* emphasizes child-centeredness, experience-based learning, integrated content areas, and process-oriented instruction. This approach means that school activities are examined from the child's point of view rather than from the view of adults. Though events may involve traditional content areas, subjects (e.g., mathematics, language, and literacy) are combined in different ways when children are learning (Hunter & Schreier, 1988). Unlike the development of cognitive processes conceptualization that emphasizes intellectual processes, the organic curriculum emphasizes processes in all domains. The intent is to enable children to integrate their learnings.

British educators Blenkin and Kelly (1988) indicate that *developmental* education is curriculum based on children's needs and interests. Developmental education is active learning and genuine, first-hand experiences are the bases of children's knowledge. Children learn *through* subjects rather than learn subjects themselves to build competence. Though developmental education is usually related to early childhood education, no conceptual or empirical reasons limit it to this level of schooling.

Developmental education in the United States is also primarily associated with early childhood education. Curriculum guidelines published in 1991 clarify that early childhood educators believe content should help children achieve goals in all domains. Moreover, curriculum content should reflect and be "generated by the needs and interests of individual children within the group" (National Association for the Education of Young Children, 1991, p. 30). Close reading of the guidelines indicates that educators expect students to meet certain "long-range goals for children in all domains . . . curriculum goals are realistic and attainable" (NAEYC, 1991, p. 29). When goals and objectives are planned, developmental education follows the technical approach similar to the subject designs.

The advantages of designs based on needs and interests of students include the notion that learning is perceived as relevant and meaningful by students. They are actively involved in learning, and typically learn process skills that are beneficial in life. Among the disadvantages: Students do not learn a common body of knowledge. They may not learn the cultural heritage or meet the social goals of education. Learning activities may not be well organized which can lead to serious questions about the scope and sequence of the curriculum. Finally, teachers are not prepared to teach this way and the resources for this curriculum may be hard to acquire (Klein, 1991b). See Table 3.3 for a summary of designs based on needs and interests of learners related to curriculum organization considerations.

OTHER DESIGNS

Several additional curriculum designs defy classification by source of content. The main ones include the following: competency approach, process skills, technology, and core.

The curriculum conception, development of cognitive processes, can use content from any of the sources, although subject matter is the one most frequently chosen. The *competency approach* design uses specific behavioral objectives to define what students need to learn (Klein, 1991b). *Science: A Process Approach,* a federally funded program in the 1970s, is an example of a competency approach (see Figure 3.2 for an excerpt). Although this particular excerpt is from a commentary for teachers, the curriculum for elementary school students followed the same plan of specific objectives and structured learning activities.

Not all process designs are subject specific. *Process skills* designs feature processes that can be transferred to real life (e.g., values clarification, skills for lifelong learning, problem solving skills). In 1968 Berman called for establishing priorities in the curriculum for these processes: perceiving, communicating, loving, decision making, knowing, organizing, creating, and valuing. She showed how to organize the curriculum by blending processes with traditional subject matter and methods.

The *technology* as curriculum design features explicit, behaviorally stated objectives toward which learners are directed through a carefully sequenced set of activities and usually uses subject matter as its source of content. Figure 3.3 shows part of a high school physics program in which the student completes the item and then uncovers the corresponding word or phrase shown at the right. This design focuses on organizing knowledge so it can be learned by students.

The *core* curriculum refers to the experience curriculum, which is organized into a closely integrated and interrelated whole composed of two parts: 1) a core division that seeks to develop common competencies needed by all students, 2) a second division that recognizes differences in interests, aptitudes, and capacities and enables individuals to grow in these areas (Faunce & Bossing, 1958). This design combines subject matter with content based on societal and personal needs.

A core curriculum is necessary in democratic societies where people must exchange views effectively and cooperate in solving common problems (Short, 1986). Problem solving occurs in large blocks of time in which students develop the skills through actual experiences with problems common to youth, jointly planned by teachers and students. In this approach teachers assume some of the functions performed by guidance specialists and counselors and sometimes remain as advisers to a group for two or more years (Faunce & Bossing, 1958).

Exercise 3.3 provides an opportunity for you to reflect on the curriculum designs information. Try this exercise.

EXERCISE 3.3

Provide answers to these questions concerning curriculum designs:

1. From a teacher's point of view, explain why a single subject design might or might not be preferred over other curriculum designs.
2. Identify some social problems that might be used as the basis for a social activities design. Explain your choices.
3. Explain why designs based on needs of society and culture or needs and interests of learners can and do use nontechnical curriculum development.
4. Explain why teachers might like or dislike teaching a core curriculum.

SUMMARY

Five conceptions of curriculum include one each based on subject matter, society and culture, and learners, plus two conceptions that cut across these traditional sources of curriculum: developing cognitive processes and curriculum as technology. Curriculum conceptions imply a purpose of education and content from one or more sources organized to enable learners to reach that purpose. The history of the curriculum conceptions shows that several of these have competed for attention through many years.

Vast amounts of content exist for any curriculum design. To organize that content, planners must consider the scope (breadth), continuity and sequence (vertical articulation), and integration (deepening of the content through the sequence of its use).

Each source of curriculum content provides one or more designs for organizing the content. Subject matter or disciplines designs are the most popular, somewhat because of tradition and the fact that text and resource materials are available for subject matter organization. Subject matter designs typically use a logical organization of content and a technical approach to curriculum development.

Designs based on society and culture are not used as the main approach to curriculum in schools, but are found in less encompassing situations where students study social problems. Designs based on needs and interests of learners are also not popular currently. Such designs require that students be consulted about what they are to learn. Designs based on either of these sources usually use nontechnical curriculum development processes. Competency approaches, process skills, technology, and core curricula offer students unique opportunities to study subject matter.

QUESTIONS FOR DISCUSSION

1. Speculate about the probable reasons why more than one conception of curriculum exists for American schools.
2. Chapter 1 referred to a "societal level of curriculum." Explain how the background information for the curriculum conceptions confirms or refutes the importance of this level of curriculum.
3. In recent years a national curriculum in the United States has been discussed. Identify both pro and con reasons that this idea should be considered.
4. Researchers have found that most curriculum content comes from textbooks. If true, how does this affect the scope of curriculum? Its sequence? Its continuity? Its integration?
5. Which curriculum design appears to dominate in the school where you work? Speculate about why it was selected.
6. Which curriculum designs lend themselves to adaptations by teachers? Which designs require teachers to develop curriculum with students?
7. Would designs based on the needs and interests of students be easier or more difficult for you to implement than designs based on subject matter? Would

the level of the students, whether elementary, middle, or high school, make a difference? Explain.

IMPORTANT IDEAS DISCUSSED INITIALLY IN THIS CHAPTER

conceptions of curriculum
    purposes of education
        cultivate cognitive achievement and
            the intellect
        prepare people for living in an
            unstable, changing world;
            reform society
        develop individuals to their fullest
            potentials
        develop intellectual processes
        make learning systematic and
            efficient

considerations in content organization
    scope
    continuity
    sequence
    integration
curriculum organization
    subject matter designs
    society-culture based designs
    learner-based designs
    other designs

4

STUDIES OF SUBJECT MATTER

OUTLINE

S ubject matter is commonly equated with curriculum content and, in some situations, this equation is accurate. However, society-culture and learners, the topics of Chapters 5 and 6, also contribute to curriculum content. Therefore, curriculum content usually consists of more than subject matter.

This chapter surveys studies of subject matter, including conceptions of knowledge and learning, and their interrelationships. The intent of this chapter is *to encourage you to examine your values and beliefs about subject matter*. Is its acquisition an end in itself? Or is subject matter a means to an end? Because subject matter serves these purposes differently, it is also important to consider questions about the validity and significance of subject matter for helping learners meet alternative purposes. The foundation for these ideas is laid in this chapter, and their application is described in Part 3.

THE INFORMATION EXPLOSION

> During an interview with Isaac Asimov, journalist Bill Moyers referred to a Bell Laboratories report claiming that, "there is more information [data] in a single edition of the *New York Times* than a man or woman in the sixteenth century had to process in the whole of his or her life." (Lenox & Walker, 1994, p. 58)

For at least two decades we have lived in the Information Age. Typically people agree that because of the daily barrage of information, "we risk being overwhelmed by the mass of it" (Lenox & Walker, 1994, p. 57). Where once books, newspapers, magazines, and oral history provided information at our discretion, now most of us are inundated with information, whether or not we seek it, from multiple and far-reaching new sources. Television, radio, electronic information databases, and videotapes are examples.

For purposes of this chapter, it's important to distinguish between the related terms *information* and *knowledge*. Information alone is not knowledge. Data gathered by reading, observation, or hearsay are just information and do not become knowledge until they're "filtered through our experiences and applied to our lives" (Lenox & Walker, 1994, p. 58).

Whereas information is exemplified by sound bites from the nightly news or snippets of printed material, knowledge is orderly and cumulative. Information is passive, but knowledge requires active participation by the knower. A person who is merely informed is at the mercy of the senders of messages because the thinking has been done by others. To be knowledgeable enables a person to become the sender of messages because the knower has done his or her own thinking (Lenox & Walker, 1994). This is the sense in which "knowledge" is used in this chapter.

CONCEPTIONS OF KNOWLEDGE

Only a few of the several ways of thinking about knowledge are discussed in this section. They include traditional disciplines and organized knowledge plus some newer forms. Conceptions of knowledge are important, of course, because they forecast the types of learning in school curricula, discussed in the next major section.

DISCIPLINES AND ORGANIZED KNOWLEDGE

Throughout the history of American education, school curricula have been organized along disciplinary lines. The first secondary school curriculum in 1647 used the classics—Latin and Greek—along with religious principles (Tanner & Tanner, 1990). Gradually the curriculum started to include additional subjects, not necessarily disciplines but organized bodies of knowledge. As early as 1895 the elementary school curriculum proposed by the Committee of Fifteen recommended that children study 16 different subjects! See Figure 4.1.

Until relatively recently curriculum developers held that special methods of thought and inquiry were inherent in the various subjects so that, for example, "history" knowledge differed from "physics" knowledge (Downey, 1960). In a discussion of the unique contributions of school subjects to learning, Taba (1962) indicates that "each subject involves a specific mode of thinking. . . . each science has its own logical language, its own canons of using facts and symbols, its own way of relating facts and principles. . . . each discipline has its own logic" (pp. 181–182). In effect, knowledge was believed to be unique, depending on the subject. The proliferation of subject areas by recombinations, such as biophysics from biology and physics, calls into question these claims.

However, disciplines and organized knowledge continue as the basis of many school curricula. "The principal problem . . . is not how to distinguish *between* disciplines; it is how to *select* which versions of which disciplines to impart at a time when not only the number of disciplines but also the number of *versions* of extant disciplines is constantly expanding" (Schrag, 1992, p. 287). Real disciplinary distinctions may no longer exist.

ALTERNATIVE CONCEPTIONS

Contemporary conceptions of learning acknowledge several knowledge forms. These conceptions include Ryle's declarative-procedural knowledge, Hirsch's extensive-intensive knowledge, and Bereiter-Scardamalia's multiple knowledges. Each conception is sketched briefly here.

Declarative and Procedural Knowledge.   Ryle (1949) conceives of knowledge that distinguishes between "knowing-that" (or "knowing-about") and "knowing-how." *Knowing-that* information encompasses ideas such as "the United States of America comprises 50 states," "white is the color of reflected light containing all the visible rays of the spectrum," and "pi is equivalent to 22/7." People can acquire *knowing-that* information relatively quickly, either through their own thinking processes or by being told the information by other people. Individuals can add to their store of *knowing-that* information, but once acquired, this knowledge is inert and does not improve with time or experiences.

On the other hand, *knowing-how* information involves ideas such as "making correct moves in a chess game," "multiplying numbers accurately," and "arguing

Branches	1st year	2nd year	3rd year	4th year	5th year	6th year	7th year	8th year
Reading	10 lessons a week	5 lessons a week						
Writing	10 lessons a week	5 lessons a week		3 lessons a week				
Spelling lists				4 lessons a week				
English Grammar	Oral, with composition lessons				5 lessons a week with textbook			
Latin								5 lessons
Arithmetic	Oral, 60 minutes a week		5 lessons a week with textbook					
Algebra							5 lessons a week	
Geography	Oral, 60 minutes a week		*5 lessons a week with textbook				3 lessons a week	
Natural Science and Hygiene	60 minutes a week							
U.S. History							5 lessons a week	
U.S. Constitution								*5 lessons
General History	Oral, 60 minutes a week							
Physical Culture	60 minutes a week							
Vocal Music	60 minutes a week divided into 4 lessons							
Drawing	60 minutes a week							
Manual Training or Sewing and Cookery							One-half day each	
Number of Lessons	20 + 7 daily exercise	20 + 7 daily exercise	20 + 5 daily exercise	24 + 5 daily exercise	27 + 5 daily exercise	27 + 5 daily exercise	23 + 6 daily exercise	23 + 6 daily exercise
Total Hours of Recitations	12	12	11	13	16¼	16¼	17½	17½
Length of Recitations	15 minutes	15 minutes	20 minutes	20 minutes	25 minutes	25 minutes	30 minutes	30 minutes

FIGURE 4.1

Curriculum Illustrative of Disciplines and Organized Knowledge

From "The Report of the Sub-committee on the Correlation of Studies in Elementary Education," by Committee of Fifteen, 1895, *Educational Review, 9,* p. 284.

a point in a debate." Understanding is involved in *knowing-how*; a person can understand (or misunderstand) an idea completely or partly. *Knowing-how* information is acquired over time, largely through an individual's own efforts, although these efforts may be facilitated by teaching agents. Such information is dynamic, making it possible for individuals to improve their abilities, and thus their stores of *knowing-how* knowledge. Declarative and procedural information are often referred to as **formal knowledge** and **skills**, respectively, and are the knowledge forms most often taught in schools.

Extensive and Intensive Knowledge.   Hirsch (1985) distinguishes between extensive and intensive knowledge and notes that both types are important and should be taught in schools. But that's where the similarities end. By **extensive knowledge** Hirsch means broad, superficial, and mostly enumerative information akin to specific facts. We all learned our share of extensive information in school as these examples show: "names of the continents and oceans," "Columbus landed in the Americas in 1492," "the chemical name for water is H_2O," and so on.

Intensive knowledge forms relationships among bits of extensive knowledge. To learn about "continents," for example, students study the features of at least one continent. Whether that continent is Africa or North America is unimportant because each has geographic features such as lakes, mountains, and plains that are closely related to its climate conditions. Once the idea is established that a continent is a large land mass with these features, students are able to draw on this information whenever they study ideas such as "continental divide," "continental USA," or "continental shelf."

Hirsch (1985, 1987) proposes that students "gain a store of particular, widely shared background facts" (extensive knowledge) to make sense of what they read. He contends, for example, that newspaper readers must have background information to interpret the news. Unless they know where Croatia and Bosnia are located, readers may have serious difficulty understanding why eastern European countries are concerned about the civil war there in the mid-1990s.

Furthermore, Hirsch believes that "[t]he best time to get this extensive background information is before tenth grade, and the earlier the better" (Hirsch, 1985, p. 13). Hirsch and his colleagues have even gone so far as to construct lists of things that people should know. One of these, titled "What Literate Americans Know," appears in Hirsch's 1987 best seller, *Cultural Literacy.*

Hirsch (1985) says intensive learning should be emphasized in the *later* grades. Some curriculum developers do not agree, however. For example, cognitive psychologists have shown that young children construct their own knowledge, including relationships among ideas and things, at early ages. See Chapter 6 for additional information.

Other curriculum developers do not agree with Hirsch's lists because the knowledge has such strong Anglo-European roots. They believe curricula must reflect the diversity among school populations, many of whom have roots in other locales. Because schools are expected to provide multicultural learning opportunities, these developers believe the scope of Hirsch's lists of the content is too restrictive. (See Chapter 5 for additional information.) Despite these criticisms of

Hirsch's work, the distinction between intensive and extensive knowledge is useful because it reminds developers of the need for both in the curriculum.

Formal, Procedural, Informal, Impressionistic, and Self-Regulatory Knowledge. As a result of their study of expertise, Bereiter and Scardamalia (1993) find that every person has several forms of knowledge in addition to formal (declarative) knowledge and skills (procedural knowledge). Of course, both these forms are well known because people demonstrate their formal knowledge through explanations and their procedural knowledge through performances.

However, people have additional forms of hidden knowledge in varying degrees. One form is **informal knowledge**, best described as intermediate between formal and procedural knowledge (Schrag, 1992). Informal knowledge has been called "educated common sense" because it requires deep understanding not obtained in books (Bereiter & Scardamalia, 1993).

For example, some teachers *know* they should make short assignments at the beginning of class periods that engage students during roll-taking procedures, provide ample table and floor coverings in anticipation of "messy" projects, or have at least one reference in mind for the student who is positive that a report topic isn't available in any school library book. Teachers discover these ideas on their own or "learn" them from veteran teachers. Typically few teachers verbalize these ideas or write them in their lesson plans. Teachers do these things because they make sense.

Impressionistic knowledge involves "feelings" about knowledge that typically operate in the background, but may at times seriously affect the outcomes in some situations (Bereiter & Scardamalia, 1993). For example, would-be curriculum users are usually asked to participate in professional development sessions to help them learn about a revised curriculum. Teachers who have taught for a while are sometimes not enthusiastic about working with a new curriculum because they have impressions of previous curriculum experiences that did not work out well.

For these teachers to look forward to using the revised curriculum, they must form strong positive impressions of the goodness (or beauty or quality) of the revised curriculum. Otherwise, they are unlikely to want formal knowledge about that curriculum because their not-so-positive feelings are in the way.

Although **self-regulatory knowledge** is self-knowledge of one's own intellectual functioning, it may also include informal and impressionistic knowledge. Knowledge of what does and does not work for oneself are prime examples of self-regulatory knowledge (Bereiter & Scardamalia, 1993; Schrag, 1992). Suppose a principal knows she has a low tolerance for teachers who arrive late for work. This principal may figure out that postponing for a few hours any interactions with late-arrivers is beneficial because she will be able to handle the situation professionally instead of personally. This principal is taking advantage of her self-knowledge. Note that one part of self-knowledge is knowing *when* to use it (Bereiter & Scardamalia, 1992). Chapter 6 provides more information about self-regulatory knowledge in the context of learner development.

This section describes several conceptions of knowledge, some of which carry overlapping labels. Exercise 4.1 allows you to check your understanding of these conceptions, which are discussed further in subsequent sections.

Reflect on the conceptions of knowledge as you answer the questions.

1. Mary Germain and Raul Porter are high school biology teachers, but they teach in different school districts. How likely are they to teach the same knowledge forms to sophomores in their respective General Biology classes? Explain.

2. To which conception(s) of knowledge are the following examples related? Explain.
   a. Operating a graphing calculator.
   b. Stating the colors in the rainbow.
   c. "I can't make sense of this situation."
   d. Looking for words in the dictionary.
   e. Choosing a library book because the pictures are "neat."

KNOWLEDGE RELATED TO SCHOOL CURRICULA

For as long as knowledge has been considered as formal knowledge and skills, educators have referred to "content" and "process" designations in discussions of learning outcomes (Taba, 1962). **Content** means the informational aspects of knowledge and **processes** are the skills aspects of creating, using, and communicating knowledge (Bruner, 1960; Parker & Rubin, 1966). However, newer knowledge conceptions elaborate on content and process.

One way of considering knowledge in school curricula is to identify the learning domains represented as cognitive, affective, or psychomotor. **Domains** are areas of learning that share a common characteristic. The cognitive domain is associated with intellectual functions; the affective domain with emotions, attitudes, and values; and the psychomotor domain with physical activities.

Why is consideration of learning domains important? Almost any school-related task includes learning in more than one domain. For instance, shooting basketballs accurately requires not only psychomotor skills, but also a large measure of cognition and affect as well. The shooter must know intellectually the details of the shot, and have the desire to make the basket. Preparing a paper for a curriculum class requires cognitive abilities. Handwriting or keyboarding psychomotor skills, as well as desire or motivation, also must be involved to complete the paper.

Curriculum planners and users must consider the relationships among these domains. Although it is relatively easy to decide the primary domain toward which learning is focused, sometimes learning does not occur as expected because the other domains were not considered. For example, high school English teachers may be excited about teaching students to enjoy literature. Some students will respond positively to class presentations and show suitable cognitive outcomes because they, too, like literature. Others, who may not be so positive, fail to show the expected cognitive outcomes. This difficulty may not be so much in the cognitive area as it is in the affective domain. Perhaps these students would respond differently if literature were tied to a topic having personal value.

TABLE 4.1
Relationships Among
Conceptions of Knowledge,
Learning Domains, and
Classroom Learning Outcomes

Conceptions of Knowledge	Domain of Learning	Classroom Learning Outcomes
Formal Knowing-that Extensive	Cognitive	Verbal information

Skills
Knowing-how
Intensive
	Cognitive	Intellectual skills:
		  Concepts, principles,
		    generalizations
		  Rules

Knowing-how
Informal
Self-regulatory
	Cognitive	Cognitive strategies:
		  Thinking skills
		  Study skills
		  Problem solving skills

Informal Impressionistic Self-regulatory	Affective	Attitudes
Informal Self-regulatory Knowing-that	Psychomotor	Motor skills

The learning domains, along with their respective taxonomies and examples of learning outcomes, are more fully described in the following subsections. A **taxonomy** classifies learning according to levels that are hierarchically related, with each succeeding level encompassing previous ones. Table 4.1 outlines the relationships among conceptions of knowledge, domains, and learning outcomes.

COGNITIVE LEARNING

The **cognitive domain** includes all the intellectual or thinking aspects of learning. Recall or recognition of knowledge, generation of knowledge, and problem solving abilities are among the elements of the cognitive domain (Bloom, 1956). In everyday language, the cognitive domain encompasses the abilities needed in figuring budgets, studying for exams, and the thinking phases of solving personal problems.

Some school-related cognitive learning outcomes are simple, such as the letters in the alphabet, names of the cranial nerves, and words to the Pledge of Allegiance. However, analyzing poetry, reading for main ideas, and carrying out rules for a game require higher-order thinking.

Bloom's Cognitive Taxonomy.   Bloom (1956) and his associates classify cognitive learning outcomes according to one of six levels shown in Figure 4.2. Based on this taxonomy, information cannot be applied in a situation different from the one in which it was learned until a person recalls and understands that information. However, once the first two levels are met, information can be used in appli-

Level	Description
Complex	
Evaluation	Making judgments about the value of information in terms of internal evidence or external criteria
Synthesis	Putting parts of information together to form a whole, in a pattern not clearly present before
Analysis	Breaking information into parts including elements, relationships, or organizational principles
Application	Using information in a slightly different setting from the one in which it was learned
Comprehension	Understanding information at the lowest level; relationships with information on similar topics not intended
Knowledge	Recalling information from memory
Simple	

FIGURE 4.2
Taxonomy of Cognitive Learning Based on the Work of Bloom (1956) and His Associates

cation, analysis, synthesis and evaluation situations. The main organizing principles for this taxonomy are simple-to-complex and concrete-to-abstract sequences (de Landsheere, 1991).

Researchers (Madaus, Woods, & Nuttal, 1973) tested the validity of this hierarchy and found a slightly different structure than the one shown in Figure 4.2. Results show the first three levels are the same, but the hierarchy bifurcates after the application level. One path consists of analysis and the other of synthesis and evaluation, as shown here:

knowledge → comprehension → application → analysis

synthesis → evaluation

For practical purposes this means analysis is not a prerequisite to synthesis, as it appears to be in Figure 4.2.

Curriculum developers who use the taxonomy must be aware of students' backgrounds (de Landsheere, 1991), because a synthesis task for one student might be simply a comprehension task for another student, depending on the students' background knowledge. For example, first-graders typically learn the "addition facts for 6" through instruction with objects. Children can usually show how one item placed with five items totals six items, and can explain this operation. Then they learn the other combinations that make six, as follows:

$4 + 2 = 6, 3 + 3 = 6, 6 + 0 = 6$, etc.

By the end of first grade most children have repeated these experiences so often they can recall these mathematics facts on demand. Despite their ability to recall and explain (comprehend) addition facts, these same first-graders may require additional instruction to apply the facts in solving word problems, *unless* this was the setting in which the information was learned. However, when these students become third-graders, what was an application task in first grade should be simple recall because the students have completed so many repetitions of this information.

It is also difficult to determine the taxonomic level of tasks without knowing what kind of instruction was given. High school students could be asked to elaborate on the effects of World War II on the American economy. On the surface this assignment appears to call for analysis. Suppose, however, that the teacher spends two class periods discussing the economic effects of the war. Under these circumstances student responses to the question would require only comprehension, since the teacher has presented the analyses. If the teacher discusses the war generally and then asks students to analyze the discussion and readings, the task could more properly be termed analytical because the students, rather than the teacher, actually made the analysis.

At least three broad classifications of learning are represented within the cognitive taxonomy. These are verbal information, intellectual skills, and cognitive strategies. Each of these is briefly described here.

Verbal Information.   Declarative or knowing-that knowledge is equivalent to **verbal information**. Examples include "name the musical notes above middle C on the treble clef" or "tell the dates of the Civil War in the United States." Students are able to state or *talk about* what they know as verbal information, which is also related to extensive knowledge.

Students' stores of formal knowledge contain verbal information obtained from reading, listening, viewing videotapes, thinking, or other means. Verbal information, especially if it occurs as organized knowledge, serves students in at least three ways. Verbal information is a prerequisite for further learning (Gagné & Driscoll, 1988). For example, a student who is about to begin study of "equivalent fractions" must know some things about fractions, that numbers can have different names, the significance of an equal sign, and so on. Teachers usually review these pertinent items before beginning on the new topic.

Verbal information provides labels required for communication (Gagné & Driscoll, 1988). The names of locations, days of the week, and addresses are examples of verbal information that people of all ages need and keep in memory. In addition people usually store large quantities of verbal information about their jobs or professions.

Intellectual Skills.   In contrast to verbal information, **intellectual skills** are a form of procedural or knowing-how knowledge. Learners with appropriate intellectual skills can "sing or play the notes of the treble clef" or "identify some battles fought in the Civil War." In other words the knower can *carry out actions* with information, not just talk about it.

Because so much verbal information exists, people learn to deal with it in categories or classes through the use of intellectual skills involving symbols (i.e., letters, numbers, words, or diagrams). Several types of skills exist, but this discussion is limited to concepts, generalizations, principles, and rules.

Concepts are learned as actions on *classes* of objects, object features, and events. Young children, for example, learn what makes something a "book" by pointing out or identifying examples of this concept. They typically learn object features such as color, shape, and size, as well as relational concepts such as "up," "outside," and "near" also by identifying examples. *Naming* these items is declarative or knowing-that knowledge. This should not be confused with *identifying* the example through recognizing its common features with similar items in the class, knowing-how knowledge. Children and young people also learn defined concepts such as "holiday" or "vacation" through words used to describe them and the results of related experiences.

Principles and generalizations take advantage of relationships between concepts. **Principles**, sometimes called *laws*, express relationships between concepts for which there are *no* known exceptions. For example, in the principle "speed is a function of time and distance" the concepts of "speed," "time" and "distance" are mathematically related.

Generalizations are similar to principles, except they express relationships between concepts for which there *are* known exceptions. For example, to say that "people intuitively adapt to their environments" is widely true, but there are exceptions. Of course, to learn principles or generalizations, students must understand the embedded concepts. Concepts, principles, and generalizations are basic learning outcomes in school curricula.

Rules are another form of intellectual skill in which learners *apply* information according to defined procedures. For example, many of us learned the statement "*i* before *e* except after *c*." Contrary to the popular usage of the word "rule," we *know* this rule only when we can apply this statement in spelling words such as "receive" and "achieve." Higher-order rules, made of simpler rules, help us handle more complex situations.

Cognitive Strategies.   Students guide their own learning through the use of **cognitive strategies** such as attending, remembering, thinking, and using language. Learners are able to sing or play the musical notes of the treble clef, for example, because of their *attention* to a request for this activity and their ability to *sort out* treble clef notes from the total set of musical notes. Students who identify Civil War battles do so because they *remember* people, things, and actions associated with those battles. The cognitive strategies mentioned here are just a fraction of the many that students actually use in their demonstrations of learning.

Cognitive strategies develop and can become better and more efficient with instructional experience. On this basis, they qualify as procedural or knowing-how knowledge. By the same reasoning, these strategies are also related to informal and self-regulatory knowledge. Based on their experiences and sometimes on formal instruction, individuals figure out how to deal with situations in ways that work for them. In some school situations, learners' cognitive strategies may go unnoticed, except as the products of their use are displayed. However, in other situations children and youth are actively taught cognitive strategies as part of the curriculum.

Eggen and Kauchak (1994) distinguish among three types of cognitive strategies: study skills, thinking skills, and problem solving skills. **Study skills** are cognitive strategies that enable learners to comprehend and retain the information in written materials and teacher presentations and should be taught in these contexts. Such strategies may be as simple as underlining pertinent information, using efficient note-taking techniques, or preparing summaries. Or the strategies may feature more comprehensive approaches, such as SQ4R—survey, question, read, reflect, recite, and review—that help students learn text material in a series of sequential steps (Eggen & Kauchak, 1994).

Thinking skills, though similar, are broader in scope and cover more learning situations than study skills. Thinking skills include observing, finding patterns and generalizing, forming conclusions based on patterns, and assessing conclusions based on observations. Each of these processes is made of subprocesses such as recalling, hypothesizing, and checking consistency (Eggen & Kauchak, 1994).

In recent years much as been made of higher order thinking or critical thinking. Curriculum developers, particularly in reading and mathematics education, draw on research showing that thinking and learning go beyond the routine (Resnick, 1987). In fact Resnick's working definition of higher order thinking is helpful in several subject areas. For a portion of this information see Figure 4.3.

Thinking skills should be taught with other subject matter because they are part of the acquisition of knowledge (Glaser, 1984; Presseisen, 1988). What's

---

Higher-order thinking:

- Is *nonalgorithmic*. That is, the path of action is not fully specified in advance.
- Tends to be *complex*. The total path is not "visible" (mentally speaking) from any single vantage point.
- Often yields *multiple solutions,* each with costs and benefits, rather than unique solutions.
- Involves *nuanced judgment* and interpretation.
- Involves the application of *multiple criteria*, which sometimes conflict with one another.
- Often involves *uncertainty.* Not everything that bears on the task at hand is known.
- Involves *self-regulation* of the thinking process. We do not recognize higher-order thinking in an individual when someone else "calls the plays" at every step.
- Involves *imposing meaning*, finding structure in apparent disorder.
- Is *effortful*. There is considerable mental work involved in the kinds of elaborations and judgments required.

FIGURE 4.3

Characteristics of Higher Order Thinking

From *Education and Learning to Think* (p. 3), by L. B. Resnick, 1987, Washington, DC: National Academy Press. Reprinted by permission.

more, the learning of thinking skills takes place as certain "dispositions" or contexts permit. If students are expected to learn knowledge exactly as it is presented to them, the thinking skills needed are minimal.

However, if students are "free to make mistakes, try new ventures, see alternative structures that can explain new phenomena" (Presseisen, 1988, p. 8), they need thinking skills to bridge content and context. This topic is reconsidered in Chapter 6 in the context of receptive-generative learning.

Problem solving uses cognitive strategies in situations where a goal is specified but the method of reaching it is not. Dewey (1933) articulates problem solving processes as part of reflective thinking because he believed children should have experiences with content of their choosing. Although it's usually thought about as part of mathematics, problem solving can and should be pursued in other subject matter areas as well.

Polya (1957) offers perhaps the most familiar problem-solving approach. Its four steps include understanding the problem, devising a plan for its solution, implementing the plan, and evaluating the results. Of course, each of these steps involves any number of cognitive strategies that students bring to problem solving situations. Students use their own study or thinking skills in these steps. Problem solving situations can require one correct solution or allow for alternative answers, any of which is equally appropriate (Eggen & Kauchak, 1994).

AFFECTIVE LEARNING

The **affective domain** is concerned with learned emotions or feelings attached to ideas, actions, and objects (Krathwohl, Bloom, & Masia, 1964). Motivation, interests, and appreciations are part of the affective domain. Your feelings about working with students, beliefs about the functions of schools, and concerns about how well you fit in as an educator are all expressions of affective learning. Notice that the examples mentioned do not include action, because feelings, beliefs, and concerns are concealed until individuals express them. Students cannot be expected to acquire feelings, attitudes, or values in the same way they might be required to memorize a sonnet.

Combs (1982) makes a strong case for affective education by stating that unless the affective dimensions of learning are considered, education in the true sense of the word is unlikely. He argues that people are meaning-oriented and that learning is a personal process that cannot be mandated by another. Learners must want to learn. Combs cites four affective factors that critically influence the learning process: self-concept, challenge or threat, values, and the feeling of being cared for or belonging.

Combs says self-concept (i.e., what students believe about themselves) affects every aspect of behavior and learning because learning is mostly a process of discovering personal meaning. How students feel about themselves affects learning and vice versa. Students feel challenged when they face things they believe they can manage. However, if students feel unable to handle things, they feel threatened. Students' values about school subjects and learning affect their abilities to learn in school. Finally, students who believe they belong in the school setting are excited and want to learn. Those who do not have positive feelings about school feel discouragement and apathy. Unless these factors are managed, Combs says, students are not likely to learn cognitive information.

Krathwohl's Affective Taxonomy. Shortly after the cognitive taxonomy was published, Krathwohl, Bloom, and Masia (1964) published a companion affective taxonomy that describes the progressive internalization of affects. At the lowest levels, a person receives and responds to stimuli. At the next level, the learner experiences several ideas or things and sorts them as preferences, thus beginning the valuing of those things or ideas. The remaining levels of the taxonomy involve incorporating the new values within the person's existing values and making them part of that individual's philosophy. Figure 4.4 summarizes the levels of the affective taxonomy and their descriptions.

Close examination of these levels reveals their ordering principle as the degree of internalization or incorporation of the affects into one's personality. The receiving level is the most distant from and external to the person. However "[w]hen the process of internalization is completed, the person feels as if the interests, values, attitudes, etc. were his or her own and lives by them. In Krathwohl's taxonomic terms, the continuum goes from merely being aware that a given phenomenon exists, and giving it a minimum attention, to its becoming one's basic outlook on life" (de Landsheere, 1991, p. 323).

Dispositions, interests, values, and attitudes typify affective learning outcomes. Though these learning outcomes contain formal and procedural knowledge, they also encompass informal, impressionistic, and self-regulatory knowledge. Typically, the latter are not formally addressed in school curricula. Curriculum personnel usually address attitudes as part of curriculum development and classroom use.

Level	Description
Internal to learner	
Characterized by a value or value complex	Making certain values part of one's philosophy of life to direct one's actions
Organization	Thinking about, clarifying, and putting one's values into a system
Valuing	Showing acceptance, preference of one thing over another, becoming committed to that thing
Responding	Showing willingness to respond; participating satisfactorily
Receiving	Showing awareness and willingness to receive or give attention to stimuli
External to learner	

FIGURE 4.4
Taxonomy of Affective Learning Based on the Work of Krathwohl, Bloom, and Masia (1964)

Attitudes.   An **attitude** "is an acquired internal state that influences the choice of personal action toward some class of things, persons, or events" (Gagné & Driscoll, 1988, p. 58). Students' attitudes influence how they conduct themselves in class discussions as well as which books they check out of the school library or the food they select in the cafeteria. Attitudes also affect social interactions, positive preferences for activities, and citizenship. Because schools are social organizations, they are places to help children and youth acquire "tolerance for racial and ethnic differences, kindness to others, helpfulness, [and] thoughtfulness of others' feelings" (Gagné & Driscoll, 1988, p. 57).

In schools students also form preferences for activities, such as working on computers, participating in music or drama productions, reading great literature, or learning for the sake of learning. Most educators also hope that children and youth develop a love for their country, concern for their fellow human beings, and willingness to act as good citizens. Neither these examples of healthy attitudes nor the categories to which they belong are exhaustive.

Attitudes are clearly related to the affective domain because they are rooted in values and what individuals choose to incorporate into their philosophies of life. But attitudes have a cognitive dimension, too. People must have some understanding of situations to form values. Informal, impressionistic, and self-regulatory knowledge are likely sources of this information.

PSYCHOMOTOR LEARNING

The **psychomotor domain** deals with body movement patterns inherent in human beings: running, jumping, climbing, lifting, carrying, hanging, and throwing (Harrow, 1972). What's learned in the psychomotor domain are skillful movements built upon these natural movements.

De Landsheere (1991) makes a case for psychomotor learning as follows: People must be able to move to survive and live independent lives. We need locomotor movement to explore the environment, and sensory motor activities are necessary for the development of intelligence. Activities such as walking and grasping are necessary for physical and mental health. Without body movements artistic and athletic activities would be severely limited.

You make use of psychomotor learning in many ways—getting yourself physically ready to leave home, transporting yourself to school, and forming words with your tongue and lips. Some school subjects are well-suited to psychomotor learning. Elementary school students must learn to handle paintbrushes, writing implements, and other small tools. Physical education, auto mechanics, and art carry expectations for psychomotor learning. However, in a world history class, the psychomotor domain may be limited to map making, model construction, or similar tasks.

Harrow's Psychomotor Taxonomy.   Of several psychomotor taxonomies available, Harrow's (1972) appears to be the most useful. Beginning with reflex and basic-fundamental movements, this taxonomy tracks human voluntary movements through perceptual and physical abilities to skilled movements and nondiscursive communication. Whereas the first two levels are purely motor abilities, the succeeding levels rely on cognition to some extent. People must use cognitive abilities in learning perceptual abilities (e.g., body awareness, body image, body relationship of surrounding objects in space, etc.), physical abilities, skilled movements, and nondiscursive communication. Said another way, while being coached on ways to improve "endurance" or "play games," students must understand the coach's words, expressions, and gestures. Figure 4.5 summarizes the psychomotor levels and their descriptions.

Unlike the cognitive and affective taxonomies, the psychomotor taxonomy does not have an organizing principle. However, individuals handle movements in the general order of the taxonomy. In other words students must exhibit the basic-fundamental movements before the perceptual abilities, which develop ahead of the physical abilities. Within the level of skilled movements, students must also develop *simple* adaptive skills ahead of *compound* adaptive skills and before *complex* adaptive skills (de Landsheere, 1991).

Motor Skills. The development of motor skills is more important at some levels of schooling and subject areas than in others. For example, many young children must learn perceptual abilities in school because they have not learned them elsewhere. Physical education classes at all levels help students learn physical abilities and some skilled movements. However, these abilities are also developed in art classes, science laboratories, music groups, and other classes.

Motor skills represent the major type of learning outcomes in the psychomotor domain. As noted in the discussion of that domain, cognition is required and probably comes from knowing-that, informal, and self-regulatory knowledge.

Level	Description
Complex adaptive skills	
Nondiscursive communication	Involving expressive movement through posture, gestures, facial expressions, and creative movements
Skilled movements	Involving games, sports, dances, and the arts
Physical abilities	Relating to endurance, strength, flexibility, agility, reaction-response time, and dexterity
Perceptual abilities	Relating to kinesthetic, visual, auditory, tactile, and coordination abilities
Fundamental movements	Involving walking, running, jumping, pushing, pulling, and manipulating one's body
Reflex movements	Involving segmental and intersegmental reflexes
Simple adaptive skills	

FIGURE 4.5
Taxonomy of Psychomotor Learning Based on the Work of Harrow (1972)

Exercise 4.2 provides an opportunity to check your understanding of classroom learning outcomes. Because this information is used again, it is a good idea to work through the exercise.

EXERCISE 4.2

For this exercise consider the first two levels in *each* taxonomy as "lower" levels (L) and all succeeding levels as "higher-than-lower" levels (HL). Example: "receiving" and "responding" are L levels in the *affective* taxonomy, but "valuing," "organizing," and "characterized by a value . . . " are HL levels.

For each situation identify both the taxonomy and level—L or HL—most closely related to the students' behaviors, *based on the information given*. Explain your choices.

1. In response to the principal's announcement that visitors from a foreign country would tour their school, several groups of high school students helped clean the campus.
2. Several middle-grade students summarized the main points of their social studies lesson.
3. Third-graders studying electrical circuits found that certain nails, pennies, and dimes were good conductors of electricity but that plastic straws and pencils were not.
4. Ms. S's students were making models of the Earth by applying papier-mâché strips to inflated balloons. Some children were able to do this with greater ease than others because they had better eye-hand coordination.

STUDIES OF SUBJECT MATTER APPLIED IN CURRICULUM PROCESSES

Chapter 1 describes some decisions involved in the curriculum processes. In brief, *development* calls for decisions about a purpose of education as well as the selection and arrangement of content in learning outcomes and learning experiences. *Classroom use* necessitates planning for the scope and complexity of the curriculum change, communication among the people involved, professional development for the users, as well as resource management. *Evaluation* requires decision making about the effects of the curriculum on students and others affected by curriculum change.

This section describes implications of subject matter studies for these curriculum processes. Keep in mind as you read this section that curriculum processes involve change that is almost always incremental and slow. Parts 3 and 4 elaborate on these implications.

DEVELOPMENT

Studies of subject matter have a major influence on the formulation of purposes of education. As pointed out in Chapter 3, the selection of a purpose of education is intimately related to content selection.

Purposes and Content Selection.   Curriculum development is heavily affected by subject matter studies because curriculum IS content in its generic sense. How community members and educators view subject matter is the primary determinant in choosing the purpose of education (see Table 3.1) for a *societal* or *institutional* level curriculum project. Is obtaining and understanding subject matter the ultimate outcome of schooling? If the answer is "yes," then students' acquisition of subject matter is the end in a means-ends relationship.

In many situations the purpose of education is to "cultivate students' cognitive achievement and intellect." The intent of this purpose is to help students acquire as much knowledge as possible, but makes no specific requirements about the form of knowledge. However, curriculum projects typically focus on both formal knowledge and skills offered as subjects (e.g., mathematics, home economics, music).

The purpose of "developing intellectual processes" also usually uses subject matter as its content. However, this purpose focuses on skills or processes, rather than on formal knowledge. In one sense this purpose has a more restricted focus than "cultivating cognitive achievement." Figure 3.2 (Chapter 3) shows an example of a process-oriented science curriculum. Notice that the objectives refer strictly to the skills of science and make no references to the formal knowledge of science subject matter.

Similarly the purpose of "making learning systematic and efficient" also usually uses subject matter as content. In this case, however, subject matter is usually relatively simple formal knowledge organized in a simple-to-complex hierarchy such as the programmed instructional physics curriculum shown in Figure 3.3. Because of restrictions in content scope, this purpose does not call for students to acquire information of the same complexity as "cultivating cognitive achievement." Both "developing intellectual processes" and "making learning systematic and efficient" are process goals without clearly defined ends.

Subject matter may also serve as the means to alternative ends. Subject matter can serve as the *vehicle* by which people "prepare for living in an unstable, changing world or reform society." It can also enable "individuals to develop to their fullest potentials." The first purpose concerns improving living situations for groups of people through study of particular subject matter, and the second purpose centers on helping people better themselves individually. Both these purposes assign subject matter to a supporting role.

To illustrate, the purpose of "reforming society or preparing people for living in an unstable changing world" has as its end improving the society in which students take their places as adult citizens (see Chapter 5). A curriculum with this purpose uses formal knowledge and skills, typically related to societal problems, that enable students to learn problem-posing and problem-solving processes. The purpose of "developing individuals to their fullest potentials" is to help children and youth with their development (see Chapter 6). Therefore, a curriculum with this purpose uses formal knowledge and skills that enable children and youth to meet their needs and interests in unique ways, depending on the learners.

Curricula with either of these purposes also encourage the development of impressionistic and self-regulatory knowledges. Said another way, subject matter is a means to an end in curricula using either of these purposes. Figure 4.6 summarizes these distinctions concerning the role of subject matter in the purposes of education.

For curricula with these purposes, subject matter is the END:
- Cultivating cognitive achievement and the intellect
- Developing intellectual processes*
- Making learning systematic and efficient*

For curricula with these purposes, subject matter is the MEANS to an end:
- Preparing people for living in an unstable, changing world; reforming society
- Developing individuals to their fullest potentials

*Most curricula with these purposes use subject matter as content.

FIGURE 4.6
Role of Subject Matter in Curricula According to Purposes of Education

Once the purpose of education is established, developers of *institutional* and *instructional* curricula choose content that enables students to meet the purpose of education. Developers must be sure that the content is valid and significant, another way of saying that the content is sound and important in helping learners toward the selected purpose of education. Unless this is the case, students studying that content are unlikely to meet the purpose intended by the curriculum. Chapter 8 continues the discussion of this idea.

Developers select particular emphases for learning outcomes by answering questions such as these: Is learning expected in each domain? At which taxonomic levels should learning be targeted? Which learning outcomes are expected—attitudes, concepts, thinking skills, or others? Answers to these questions invariably hinge on developers' beliefs and values toward subject matter. Changes in emphases for learning outcomes are less unusual than are changes in purposes.

Let's see if this discussion about subject matter makes sense. Exercise 4.3 asks you to examine certain curriculum projects in Appendix A to determine how the developers view the use of subject matter.

EXERCISE 4.3

Scan the opening paragraphs in these curriculum projects in Appendix A:

- *Spanish IV Curriculum* (A4)
- *Into Adolescence: Caring for Our Planet and Our Health* (A6)
- *Collaborative Teaching Experiences to Develop Communication Skills in Elementary School Children* (A7)

Answer this question for each project:

Does it appear that students are expected to acquire and understand the subject matter? Or are students using the subject matter as a means to a different end? Explain.

CLASSROOM USE

Curriculum development or revision invariably means changes in classroom use planning considerations, such as the *scope and complexity* of change, of prime concern in classroom use decisions. Chapter 3 points out that most schools use "cultivating cognitive achievement" as their purpose of education. Any change to a different purpose would very likely require massive *professional development* efforts and considerable *communication* among teachers, students, administrators, and community members. These activities would necessitate additional *resources* beyond those normally allocated for these activities.

Decisions to revise the emphases in learning domains or types of learning outcomes, though not as significant as a change in purpose, also mean changes in *scope and complexity* of classroom use decisions. Such decisions are exemplified by changes to include thinking skills or affective concerns in a curriculum that has as its purpose "cultivating cognitive achievement." Most users would need *professional development* to know how to deal with these emphases. A great deal of *communication* must take place among the people concerned so that all understand the "new curriculum," but *resources* needed for changes such as these are probably less than resources required for a change in purpose.

EVALUATION

Curriculum evaluation should be tied to the intended purpose of education, so that studies of subject matter affect curriculum evaluation whenever the purpose of education or the emphases for learning outcomes are altered. For example, evaluation of curricula in which students acquire subject matter typically use instruments (e.g., examinations, demonstrations) that allow students to show subject matter proficiency. Thereafter, evaluation of group outcomes against a predetermined criterion is relatively simple. If the purpose of education is *not* subject matter proficiency, however, evaluation must focus on learners' developmental changes or degrees of societal reform—both of which require different evaluation approaches.

Changes in the emphases for learning outcomes typically require revisions in evaluation processes. Evaluation of thinking skills or problem solving skills, for example, requires changes in methods of data collection and interpretation.

SUMMARY

The Information Age produces such vast quantities of data that no one can possess all of it. Moreover, information becomes knowledge when people think about and process it through their experiences to make it their own. Conceptions of knowledge have changed in the last century so that knowledge has more differentiated forms. From these conceptions of knowledge come changed conceptions of learning.

Domains and taxonomies of learning, known for 40 years to the education community, continue as major classifications of learning outcomes. However, these classifications are further refined as verbal information, intellectual skills, cognitive strategies, attitudes, and motor skills to form the bases for classroom learning outcomes.

The role that curriculum developers assign to subject matter is the key to decisions about purposes of education. Subject matter is considered an end in three purposes: "cultivating cognitive achievement," "developing intellectual processes," and "making learning more systematic." But it is a means in "developing individuals to their fullest potentials" and "preparing people for living in an unstable, changing world/reforming society." Although developers may seldom change the purpose of education, they do change the emphases in learning. Any of these changes require changes in plans for classroom use and evaluation of the curricula.

QUESTIONS FOR DISCUSSION

1. Explain how the information explosion can be considered both an advantage and a disadvantage to curriculum developers.
2. Give at least one original example of declarative/procedural knowledge. Of extensive/intensive knowledge. Of informal/impressionistic/self-regulatory knowledge.
3. To what extent does Combs' case for affective education convince you that curricula should have affective learning outcomes? Explain.
4. Examine the exercises in one textbook used in your school. Do you find references to affective or psychomotor learning? Should either or both be included in the context of the subject matter in the text? Explain.
5. Look at the same textbook exercises again. Do these exercises require lower or higher-than-lower levels of learning? (See Exercise 4.2 for an explanation of these levels.) Explain.
6. Use the same textbook exercises. Determine which type(s) of learning outcomes (e.g., verbal information, attitudes) are emphasized. Explain.
7. Consider the choices curriculum developers have with respect to emphases on certain types of learning. What are the advantages and disadvantages to school-based curriculum decision making (see Chapter 2) in making these choices? Explain.
8. Explain why clarifying one's values about subject matter is necessary for curriculum development.

IMPORTANT IDEAS DISCUSSED
INITIALLY IN THIS CHAPTER

information-knowledge
conceptions of knowledge
   disciplines
   declarative-procedural knowledge
   formal knowledge-skills
   extensive-intensive knowledge
   impressionistic, informal, self-
     regulatory knowledge
knowledge in school curricula
   content-process
   domains   } affective, cognitive,
   taxonomies   and psychomotor

verbal information
intellectual skills
   concepts, generalizations,
     principles, rules
cognitive strategies
   problem solving, study skills,
     thinking skills
attitudes
motor skills

5

STUDIES OF SOCIETY AND CULTURE

OUTLINE

As described in Chapter 3, society usually dictates purposes of education for school curricula. However, the accelerated rate of societal change in the 1990s complicates decisions about purposes of education. For example, change challenges commonly held definitions of literacy as well as the persons/groups traditionally responsible for the literacy of children and youth. Resolution of these challenges, whenever it occurs, is likely to affect school curricula.

Following a description of literacy issues, additional sections briefly survey the literature concerning interrelationships and effects of change in **social institutions**. These institutions are "social arrangements that channel behavior in prescribed ways in the important areas of social life" (Eitzen & Baca Zinn, 1995, p. 42). Changes among and within these institutions result in learners with widely differing backgrounds. The demography of learners, described in a later section of this chapter, provides curriculum developers and users with information about the students for whom curricula are planned.

Specifically, this chapter should help you to *examine your values and beliefs concerning how society and culture relate to curriculum*. For example, to what extent should curricula acknowledge the world outside of school? How do societal-cultural changes affect curriculum processes? How do societal-cultural changes affect choices of learning emphases? Your responses to these questions acknowledge particular social-cultural realities that guide your curriculum content selections. The answers also provide insights into your preferences concerning roles for curriculum users. The foundations for these ideas are discussed in this chapter and applications are provided in Part 3.

LITERACY ISSUES FOR THE 21ST CENTURY

As noted in the previous chapter, we live in the Information Age, in which the amount of available data can be overwhelming. Because of the volume of information, people today cannot *know* as they once did by committing information to memory. Access to information is a major issue. We also use information in sophisticated ways unknown to previous generations. These capabilities are at the heart of functional literacy, the focus of this section.

Educational history in the United States shows that expectations for literacy rise continuously. In 1890 about 7 percent of 14- to 16-year-olds attended high school, but by 1978 the percentage had risen to 94 percent. In this same period "the levels of schooling that contemporary commentators called for as necessary to insure functional literacy rose from three years of schooling to completion of high school" (Applebee, 1994, p. 40).

Whereas "literacy" once referred solely to language abilities, societal changes create additional literacy forms. Families, schools, and community organizations also used to share responsibilities for children's literacy development, but changes in these organizations have shifted accountabilities for this important task. This section elaborates on both issues.

WHAT IS LITERACY?

The term *literacy* is usually associated with the ability to use one's native language and, because children learn language at home, these skills are closely intertwined with culture. Throughout U.S. history the majority of residents have spoken English as their first language and those who did not were expected to learn English to function in society. For practical purposes, this means that literacy is usually defined as *English* language ability. Today, however, this definition is challenged by the diversity of languages spoken in this country.

To complicate matters further, economic changes demand additional forms of literacy (e.g., culture, science, information). Which of these literacies should be accommodated in overcrowded school curricula? Obviously, answers to such complex questions are not easy because they involve people's values and beliefs about what students should learn in school.

Language Literacy.   Standards for **language literacy** have risen since the beginning of formal schooling in the United States. For example, in 1700 people were considered literate if they could produce their signatures. By 1800, in addition to signing their names, literate people were expected to recite a passage from a learned work. According to the first official literacy standard, set by the U.S. Army in 1915, literate people needed to be able to read a short passage and answer a few literal comprehension questions (Butler, 1992).

One measure of recent writing literacy is shown by the tasks required in the 1988 National Assessment of Educational Progress.[1] Students at 4th, 8th, and 12th grades were asked to perform several writing tasks, including informative, persuasive, and narrative writing (Applebee, Langer, Jenkins, Mullis, & Foertsch, 1990). Example tasks from this assessment, shown in Figure 5.1, reveal a substantial increase in literacy standards since 1915.

According to the 1992 National Assessment of Educational Progress, *reading literacy* is defined as "knowing when to read, how to read, and how to reflect on what has been read" (National Assessment Governing Board, 1992, p. 6). Furthermore, this standard prescribes that students should be able to read for the literary experience, to be informed, and to perform tasks. In addition to requiring an initial understanding, reading literacy requires the abilities to interpret, personally reflect and respond, and demonstrate a critical stance (NAGB, 1992).

Despite the need for baseline information, language literacy is difficult to study because its definition is open to interpretation. Both indigenous language minority groups and immigrants who do not speak English make society in the United States multilingual. In some discussions of literacy, "English monolingualism is assumed to have a 'feeding relationship' with literacy; multilingualism is viewed as having a 'bleeding relationship.' In this country, the fact that many people speak languages other than English is assumed to have a negative impact on literacy" (Wiley & Sikula, 1992, p. 75).

---

[1] Writing tasks were identical in the 1984, 1988, and 1990 writing literacy assessments (Mullis, Dossey, Foertsch, Jones, & Gentile, 1991).

> - Summarize a science experiment depicted in a brief series of pictures showing different stages of a plant's growth.* [Grade 4 informative writing]
>
> - Describe an incident or event that you remember well, telling what happened and how you felt at the time. [Grades 8 and 12 narrative writing]
>
> - Take a stand on whether or not funding for the space program should be cut and write a persuasive letter that would convince a legislator of this stand. [Grade 12 persuasive writing]
>
> *The same tasks were used in 1984, 1988, and 1990 NAEP studies.

FIGURE 5.1

Examples of Writing Tasks in the National Assessment of Educational Progress

From *Learning to Write in Our Nation's Schools: Instruction and Achievement in 1988 at Grades 4, 8, and 12* (pp. 61, 71, 85) by A. N. Applebee, J. A. Langer, L. B. Jenkins, I. V. S. Mullis, & M. A. Foertsch, 1990, Washington, DC: Office of Educational Research and Improvement, U.S. Department of Education.

If people do not speak English, should they be considered illiterate or non-English literate? If individuals have limited English proficiency, are they considered illiterate? Do biliterate people have an advantage? These questions, raised by Wiley and Sikula (1992), merit close attention by curriculum developers especially, because cultural background plays such a crucial role in the school adjustment of immigrant, refugee, and other minority children (Delgado-Gaitan & Trueba, 1991; Trueba, 1988, 1989).

Nearly a million immigrants were admitted to the United States in 1992 from countries such as Mexico, Vietnam, India, and China (U.S. Bureau of the Census, 1994). This figure is half the number of immigrants in 1991. Many immigrants choose to live in coastal metropolitan areas, sometimes to be near individuals who speak their language and share their customs. Regardless of where they settle, however, alternative cultural patterns suggest a need for cultural literacy.

Cultural Literacy. People congregate in social groups according to language, ethnic background, religion, or other categories; here their shared beliefs, or *culture,* guide their conduct. Common expectations about how people should act, known as *norms,* develop from social interactions among group members. What is appropriate, correct, moral and important for group members become the criteria or *values* held by the group. Groups also devise expectations, or *social roles,* for members in various positions within the group (Eitzen & Baca Zinn, 1995). People who are NOT members frequently fail to understand the shared beliefs and therefore lack cultural literacy with respect to that group.

Traditionally, school curricula in the United States focused on transmitting the cultural heritage of the Western world and paid little attention to non-European cultures. Advocates of multicultural education believe, however, that schools should impart accurate information about nontraditional cultures. Doing so is expected to reduce prejudice and foster tolerance, improve the academic achievement of minority students, and make the ideals of pluralism and democracy a reality (Willis, 1993). Were these goals realized, students could claim greater cultural literacy than many current situations provide.

Science Literacy.   People from different cultures live and work side by side in a world shaped in large measure by science, mathematics, and technology. **Science literacy** refers to the understandings and ways of thinking, or habits of the mind, needed to function in this environment (American Association for the Advancement of Science, 1990). No longer the province of a privileged few, science literacy is necessary for everyone, not only in the United States, but throughout the world. The problems of survival and living are global; they include unchecked population growth, environmental pollution, and disease, among others (AAAS, 1990).

In devising curriculum standards, the National Council of Teachers of Mathematics (1989) stated that "[t]he educational system of the industrial age does not meet the economic needs of today. New social goals for education include mathematically literate workers, lifelong learning, opportunity for all, and an informed electorate" (p. 3).

Moreover, expectations of scientifically literate workers include these capabilities:

• Knowledge of a variety of techniques for approaching and working on problems.

• Understanding of the underlying scientific-mathematical features of a problem.

• The ability to work with others on problems.

• The ability to cope with open problem situations, because most real world problems do not fit neat formulas.

• Belief in the utility and value of science, mathematics, and technology (AAAS, 1990; NCTM, 1989).

Information Literacy.   In the broad sense, **information literacy** refers to the assembly, analysis, interpretation, integration, and drawing of inferences and conclusions about information from a variety of sources (Adams & Bailey, 1993; Lenox & Walker, 1994). Traditionally, students obtain information from books, which give "random information its pertinence, meaning, and potential" (Breivik & Jones, 1993, p. 28). However, videos, films, and a host of other media offer better information than books on many subjects. For example, "compact disks *are* better for learning about different treatments of a musical arrangement" (Breivik & Jones, 1993, p. 28).

Media provide important fictional and nonfictional information to children and youth on topics including race, ethnicity, gender, religion, intergroup relations, demographic change, government operations, and the environment. Information that is presented represents an interpretation through what is and is not said, the images selected, and the commentary. Media help children and youth organize information and ideas through the repetition of certain themes, interpretations, and word choices. In similar ways media help create, reinforce, and modify students' values and attitudes toward democratic processes, social actions, products, and other activities. Through the repetitive use of certain themes and ideas, media help shape students' expectations and provide models for action. Because of the pervasiveness of media, children and young people need assistance in handling information (Cortes, 1992).

WHO IS RESPONSIBLE FOR LEARNERS' LITERACY?

Since the founding of this country, families, schools, and religious organizations have jointly provided for children's literacy development. However, late in the 20th century, social changes have altered expectations, as well as the actual contributions, of these organizations to literacy development. Currently, schools are expected to provide for learners' literacy development, with minimal assistance from families or other groups.

How well schools can manage these responsibilities, without parental and community assistance, is unclear. However, signs suggest that "economic need and changing social values have combined to make the absentee parent an accepted, if not applauded, social phenomenon. The time the parent spends on career or personal development accords him or her higher status in the current value frame than time spent on children" (Bunting, 1990, pp. 16–17).

This responsibility for literacy issue is an example of the type of problem handled by social institutions. These institutions evolve through the uncoordinated actions of many individuals over time to maintain social stability. Social institutions are conservative by nature, because they use custom and tradition to answer questions of survival. Although social institutions are necessary, they "are often outmoded, inefficient, and unresponsive to the incredibly swift changes brought about by technological advances, population shifts, and increasing worldwide interdependence" (Eitzen & Baca Zinn, 1995, p. 42). Figure 5.2 displays common societal problems and the institutions that handle them.

Societal Problem	Institution
• Sexual regulation; maintenance of stable units that ensure continued births and care of dependent children	Family
• Socialization of the newcomers to the society	Education
• Maintenance of order; the distribution of power	Polity
• Production and distribution of goods and services; ownership of property	Economy
• Understanding the transcendental; the search for meaning of life and death and the place of humankind in the world	Religion

FIGURE 5.2

Common Societal Problems and Their Institutions

From *In Conflict and Order: Understanding Society* (p. 43) by D. S. Eitzen & M. Baca Zinn, 1995, Boston: Allyn and Bacon. Copyright 1995 by Allyn and Bacon. Abridged. Reprinted by permission.

The next two major sections survey the literature related to selected aspects of these social institutions and their struggles with change. The first section describes the economy and polity, and the second section deals with the family, religion, and education. However, before proceeding with study of the social institutions, work on Exercise 5.1. These questions will encourage your continued thinking about literacy issues and how they relate to curriculum.

EXERCISE 5.1

Reconsider the discussion of literacy forms and purposes of education. Then answer these questions:

1. To what extent is the development of each literacy form (language, culture, science, and information) consistent with the purpose of education, "cultivating cognitive achievement and the intellect"? Explain.
2. To what extent does the development of these literacy forms fit with the remaining four purposes of education? (See Table 3.1.)

SOCIAL INSTITUTIONS: ECONOMY AND POLITY

The economy and the polity dominate as social institutions in the United States and greatly influence people's lives. Largely because of the form of the U.S. government, these institutions are inextricably related, with the result that changes in one institution usually predict changes in the other. Of course, some changes are beneficial, but others are not.

This section describes the segmented labor market in the United States and shows how the distribution of power operates to perpetuate the segments. The final subsection describes structural changes in the economy that trigger changes in other social institutions, including education.

THE U.S. LABOR MARKET

The labor market consists of two sectors that provide different livelihoods for people. The *primary* sector consists of "large, bureaucratic organizations with relatively stable production and sales. Jobs within this sector require developed skills, are relatively well paid, occur in good working conditions, and are stable" (Eitzen & Baca Zinn, 1995, p. 374).

Two types of jobs make up this sector. Jobs in the top tier carry high status and are professional or managerial positions. These occupations offer personal autonomy, variety, creativity, initiative, and high pay to the highly educated individuals who have them. Successful workers frequently achieve upward mobility.

Jobs in the bottom tier carry working-class status and are either white-collar clerical or blue-collar skilled and semiskilled positions. Although such jobs are relatively secure because of unionization, these workers can be laid off when the economy is slow. People in these occupations typically find their tasks repetitive and their opportunities for upward mobility limited (Eitzen & Baca Zinn, 1995).

The *secondary* sector contains "marginal firms in which product demand is unstable. Jobs . . . are characterized by poor working conditions, low wages, few opportunities for advancement, and little job security" (Eitzen & Baca Zinn, 1995, p. 384). Most jobs in this sector require little education or skill and individuals have little hope of upward mobility. Workers in this sector usually have poor work histories, attributable in part to the production of marginal products and lack of job security (Edwards, 1975).

The significance of the partitioned labor market is important. First, individuals' positions in these sectors correspond to their socioeconomic status, passed from one generation to the next. Second, the sectors reinforce racial, ethnic, and gender divisions. For example, white males, though found in both sectors, tend to dominate the top tier of the primary sector and white females tend to be clerks in the bottom tier of that sector. White workers appear to be overrepresented in the production lines in the bottom tier of the primary sector, while workers of color are found disproportionately in the secondary sector. Persistent wage differences by race and gender are traceable to workers' placements in the sectors. At least part of this difficulty is traceable to the uneven distribution of power in this country (Eitzen & Baca Zinn, 1995).

DISTRIBUTION OF POWER

As used here, "power is the ability to get what one wants from someone else. This can be achieved by force or by getting that someone to think and believe in accordance with your interests" (Eitzen & Baca Zinn, 1995, p. 415). One popular view of power says that schools, religious organizations, and families work together to influence individuals to accept the status quo. In matters related to the capitalist system of government, obedience to the law, and military solutions for disputes between countries, for example, children and youth are socialized to accept things as they are.

At times almost everyone benefits from the way power is structured in this country. However, power is unequally distributed, and "whenever the interests of the wealthy clash with those of other groups or even of the majority, the interests of the wealthy are served" (Eitzen & Baca Zinn, 1995, p. 417). Consider how energy shortages, inflation, budget cuts, ecological disasters, and corporate fraud are handled. The rich and powerful, and their agents who make up the government, seek to keep their advantageous positions in society. These individuals typically use power to protect their own interests without regard to the damage to the interests of others.

Poor people are generally powerless, in part because they are not organized. As a result the poor absorb the costs of societal changes. For example, when inflation threatens, unemployment increases. When land is needed for different purposes (e.g., gentrification, urban renewal, expressways, parks), poor people may be pushed out of their homes typically in the way of such projects. Even in war, the noncollege-educated are more likely to be killed than the college-educated (Feigelson, 1982; Zeitlin, Lutterman, and Russell, 1977).

During economic downturns some federal funds may reach the poor through unemployment insurance, government jobs, and housing subsidies. However, such help is usually opposed by business people who think federal funds should be used to help businesses instead. Generally, government officials appear to believe that what is good for business is good for the country (Eitzman & Baca Zinn, 1995). The next subsection shows how power operates in the economy.

STRUCTURAL CHANGES IN THE ECONOMY

Within the past two decades several interrelated forces have transformed the U.S. economy. These forces are new technologies based on microelectronics, globalization of the economy, capital flight, and the shift from an economy based on the manufacture of goods to one based on information and services (Eitzen, 1989, 1992; Eitzen & Baca Zinn, 1995).

The Changes.   Advances in the development of microcomputer chips created new industries and changed the operations of existing industries. Information can be stored, manipulated, and retrieved with astonishing speed and accuracy. Information can be sent worldwide virtually instantaneously with the aid of communications satellites. In fact, computers now assist designers and producers of goods and services in almost every industry (Dolbeare, 1989).

As Naisbitt and Aburdene (1990) predicted, the 1990s have seen globalization of the economy. Goods made in the United States are marketed worldwide, but this country imports many more goods than it exports. Stiff competition from other countries has meant sharp decreases in profits by U.S. companies. Acting to protect their interests, businesses merged, contracted work forces, or relocated to locations more favorable to businesses.

Mergers in the 1980s and 1990s lowered business costs as companies reduced their labor forces. Some companies reduced workers' benefits, terminated workers, or encouraged early retirements. In other cases the corporations ceased to operate (e.g., steel companies) or moved to locations where labor costs are less, unions are weaker, or business climates are more receptive. The bottom line is that businesses find they can obtain higher profits by relocating all or part of their operations outside the United States where labor typically costs less and environmental regulations are less stringent (Eitzen & Baca Zinn, 1995).

Economic Effects on the Work Force.   Changes brought about by microelectronics benefit a small number of workers whose skills are needed for the new high-technology jobs. Other workers, primarily women, have low-paying jobs brought about by computer automation in businesses and industries.

However, many workers suffer from economic changes. As companies reduce their work force or close completely, some workers lose their jobs. Although some workers retire early, some individuals take jobs that pay less well to maintain their households. Reduced pay for the family breadwinner often means that both spouses work outside the home just to make ends meet. Workers relocate to other parts of the United States in search of jobs. Still other people give up hope of holding jobs and are counted among the homeless.

By 2005 the work force is expected to include more women and minority group members. Nearly half the labor force (48 percent) is expected to be women. Blacks, Hispanics, Asians and other racial groups are expected to account for about 35 percent of the people entering the labor force. The age distribution is also expected to shift as current workers mature. Whereas in 1992 only about 18 percent of workers between the ages of 45 to 54 were in the labor force, by 2005 that number will increase to 24 percent. Workers 55 years and older are also expected to increase from 12 percent to 14 percent by 2005 (U.S. Department of Labor, 1994).

The industrial profile shows that about 25.1 million new nonfarm wage and salaried jobs are projected between 1992 and 2005 with more than 90 percent of these expected in service-producing industries. Such industries include transportation, communications, and utilities; retail and wholesale trade; services; government; and finance, insurance and real estate (see Figure 5.3). The services division, which includes health, business, and educational services, contains 15 of the 20 fastest growing industries (U.S. Department of Labor, 1994). In the next decade the boom is expected in low-paying jobs.

Literacy in the Workplace. In the past "people with little education or few skills could earn a middle-class living in factories or other blue-collar jobs. That opportunity is dwindling. Manufacturing jobs are dying by the thousands, and the jobs

FIGURE 5.3
Projections of Nonfarm Wage and Salaried Employment

From Tomorrow's Jobs, *Occupational Outlook Handbook: 1994–95.* Bulletin 2450, May 1994 (p. 11). U.S. Department of Labor.

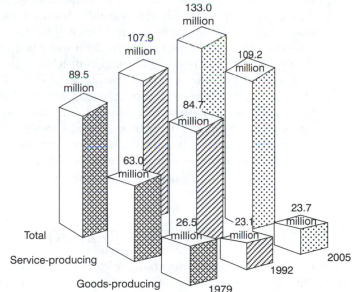

that are left for the unskilled or uneducated are the ones with the smaller pay-checks" (Everett, 1994, p. D1, D8). Almost all jobs that pay well require special training or education. Only a handful of well-paying jobs don't require degrees to begin—and even in those fields, people with better skills usually receive better pay (Everett, 1994).

Demands on workers' literacy are likely to increase significantly. For example:

> In textiles, semiliterate operators used to be able to move into technician jobs because they literally could see how textile machines functioned. Today, many machines have microprocessors and other electronic components that are not observable. To understand, diagnose, and fix the new machines, technicians now have to be able to represent their structures and processes symbolically in their heads by decoding complicated manuals, diagrams, and updates provided by the manufacturers. (Kane, Berryman, Goslin, & Meltzer, 1990, p. 3)

In addition, workers must be able to handle multiple tasks and do them well. Other changes call for workers to work increasingly in teams, both within and across job functions, within supplier-producer-customer networks, and in multi-cultural job settings. These requirements mean that workers need skills in inter-personal communication and conflict resolution (Kane, Berryman, Goslin, & Meltzer, 1990).

A national survey of adult literacy shows a strong relationship between literacy skill and occupation. In this study *literacy* is defined as prose, document, and quantitative knowledges and skills. Examples include finding an item of informa-tion in a newspaper article, using a transportation schedule, and balancing a checkbook (Kirsch, Jungeblut, Jenkins, & Kolstad, 1993).

The survey finds that most adults have jobs requiring literacy skills congruent with the skill levels they are able to demonstrate. Manager-professional-techni-cian, craft-service, and laborer-assembler-fishing-farming groups demonstrate lit-eracy skills at the levels required in their jobs. However, adults in sales-clerical positions vary in their literacy skills, with some people demonstrating more skills than their jobs require (Kirsch, Jungeblut, Jenkins, & Kolstad, 1993).

A separate study finds quantitative literacy skills to be a major factor in raising the likelihood of full-time employment among young adults, both men and women. In particular, this study shows that low quantitative literacy among young black Ameri-cans is a likely explanation for their nonemployment (Rivera-Batiz, 1992).

Structural changes in the economy, in combination with power concerns, also effect changes in other social institutions. The next section continues this discus-sion by highlighting changes in these institutions.

SOCIAL INSTITUTIONS: FAMILY, RELIGION, AND EDUCATION

Family, religion, and education typically handle concerns and problems related to the physical, emotional, and intellectual needs of children and youth. However, these institutions are influenced greatly by changes in the economy and polity. This section surveys the literature on social consequences of economic change and of child care and socialization practices. Implications of both are important to curriculum developers and users.

SOCIAL CONSEQUENCES OF ECONOMIC CHANGE

The structural change in the economy produces negative social changes as well as negative economic effects. Curtailment in upward social mobility and increased awareness of inequalities are two changes highlighted in this section.

Curtailed Upward Social Mobility.   Previous discussion of the segmented labor market showed differentiated possibilities for the upward mobility of workers. Eitzen (1992) cites a common argument related to the economy: "a rising tide lifts all boats." Between 1950 and 1973 this argument generally held as the average standard of living for families steadily increased. However, between 1973 and 1986 the standard of living for most families declined, with weekly wages falling by 14 percent. Wages for white-collar and college-educated workers have declined since 1987 (Eitzen & Baca Zinn, 1995).

The structure of American business, with help from federal tax policies, appears to be heading the United States toward a two-class society. Although a few middle-class people move to a higher social class, many move to a lower social class. For example, in 1959 the top 4 percent of the population, representing 2.1 million individuals and families, earned about the same amount in wages and salaries as the bottom 35 percent, representing 18.3 million individuals and families. However, by 1989 the top 4 percent, representing 3.8 million individuals and families, earned wages and salaries about the same as the bottom 51 percent, representing 49.2 million individuals and families (Bartlett & Steele, 1992). Within a thirty-year period, 16 percent of former middle class individuals and families moved to a lower class. These workers now receive substandard wages, pensions, and fringe benefits and many families are forced to limit their spending to necessities (Eitzen & Baca Zinn, 1995).

The current generation is the first in American history to experience more downward, rather than upward, social mobility. In addition to loss of economic resources, downward mobility has negative effects on self-worth, which is closely tied to occupational status and income. People who suffer downward mobility often feel guilt and embarrassment. Such changes in family circumstances impair the chances that children, both as young people and later as adults, will enjoy economic security and comfortable lifestyles (Eitzen, 1992, p. 587).

Increased Awareness of Inequalities.   Before instant communication, people were less aware of the inequalities in living standards. But the same technology that changed the economy also raised people's consciousness of the inequalities among the social classes. People are inundated with media coverage of events showing discrepancies in Americans' lifestyles. Music, radio, movies, and television, for example, insist that more of almost everything is better. Even locations that were once considered remote are not isolated from these messages. More than 98 percent of all American homes had television service in 1992 (U.S.

Bureau of the Census, 1993). Virtually all Americans, poor and rich alike, are well aware of differences in lifestyles between the "haves" and the "have nots."

In urban areas particularly, news reports provide almost daily coverage of crimes in which perpetrators take valuables that belong to others. Some teenagers steal favored clothing items owned by peers or clothing stores so they can fit with the "in" group. Some individuals turn to drugs for emotional highs and later to crime to support their drug habits. These behaviors suggest that inequalities in American society are widely evident.

CHILD CARE AND SOCIALIZATION PRACTICES

As the original social institution, the family handled problems related to child-rearing and socialization. However, American families have changed, producing consequences that greatly affect how children are raised and schooled (Coleman, 1987; Elkind, 1990; McCarthy, 1992). The following subsection highlights these changes and their effects on learners.

Family-Society Relationships.   When this country was founded, its social and economic organization was founded on the family, where raising children was expected. Children and the aged lived with their families or extended kin groups, as did unmarried adults.[2] Hunger and homelessness were handled by families or extended kin. Income from family members was distributed across households to care for all the members. Fathers and mothers worked at home usually on farms or in nearby shops. As a result, most economic activities were centered in households, with local exchanges providing whatever additional goods were needed (Coleman, 1987).

In the 19th century, however, the Industrial Revolution moved economic activities from households and surrounding neighborhoods to corporate entities not connected with families. Men stopped working at home, mainly in farming, to work in offices or factories owned by corporations. In 1810 about 87 percent of men worked in agriculture, but by 1900 that number had dropped to about 42 percent. In 1980 the number of farmers was only about 3 percent of the male population (Coleman, 1987).

Women also moved out of households to work in businesses, but much more slowly. In 1900 nearly 90 percent of all women worked at home, but by 1980 at least half were in the paid work force (Coleman, 1987). By 2000 more than 60 percent of women are expected to be part of the labor force (U.S. Bureau of the Census, 1993). As the previous section shows, one major reason is need, fueled by structural changes in the economy.

---

[2] In the mid-1990s some blacks and Hispanics continue living in extended family groups. Where ancient African customs prevail, minors and elderly members join existing family units. Hispanic extended families include both relatives and friends who are welcome to stay until they improve their situations (Carrasquillo & London, 1993).

When the economic role of families transferred to private sector businesses, social welfare was taken over by government. Even in colonial days there were a few households without children younger than 18, but the percentage of these households had risen to about 60 percent in 1992 (U.S. Bureau of the Census, 1993). This meant that households with earnings and no children existed alongside households without earnings but with children. Therefore, the federal government taxed the former households and redistributed funds to the latter—sometimes in inefficient ways (Coleman, 1987).

Redistribution occurred chiefly through a federal program, Aid to Dependent Children, created by Congress in 1935, to serve widows until they remarried. Later this program was renamed Aid to Families with Dependent Children (AFDC), but is known colloquially as "welfare" (Jencks, 1992). In Coleman's (1987) view, government has extraordinary difficulty "providing welfare to dependents without creating an incentive for dependency" (p. 34).

Gallman (1994) reports that almost 6 percent of the U.S. population, which includes about 14 million people, is on welfare through AFDC at a cost of about $22 billion a year in 1994. Despite welfare provisions, children younger than 18 were the poorest segment of the population in 1994, accounting for 21.1 percent of the total population below poverty level (U.S. Bureau of the Census, 1994). Although there's much discussion of welfare reform, little real action ensues—largely because support from other sources is not available.

Even when parents work, children can suffer. Conditions at work sometimes affect the relationship between the parents. If this occurs, stress can easily affect children in the family. When the parent/child relationship is seriously disturbed, children at any age level may feel insecure at home and be unable to pay attention in school. "Once they (children) begin to miss out on learning, they feel lost in the classroom, and they begin to seek acceptance elsewhere" (Bronfenbrenner, 1988, p. 121). At this stage children typically seek and find acceptance with peers who have similar histories.

To compound the problem, more and more families are disrupted by divorce. Affected by business cycles and war, divorce rates generally tend to rise (Lauer, 1992). In 1988 more than a million children younger than 18 were involved in divorce (U.S. Bureau of the Census, 1993). Mothers often retain custody of children, but many have to reduce their standard of living because of lowered incomes after divorce. Of course, many adults remarry and reconstitute families with children from previous marriages. But these families pose challenges of their own, and many of these marriages also fail (Lauer, 1992).

Families are also disrupted by violence. Family fights are one of the most frequent reasons for police calls. Spouse and child abuse and even murders among family members are well documented throughout the nation. "Child abuse . . . is more likely when one of the natural parents is missing. Children in a single-parent home, or those with a stepparent, are much more likely to be victims of abuse" (Lauer, 1992, p. 459).

More children younger than 18 live in families headed by grandparents. This was true for about 3.3 million children in 1992, and in more than a quarter of these cases no parent was present (U.S. Bureau of the Census, 1993). According to a study conducted by the American Association of Retired Persons, the major reason given by 44 percent of grandparents for this living arrangement was substance abuse by the children's parent(s). An additional 28 percent of grandparents report that their grandchildren live in their homes because of child abuse, neglect, or abandonment on the part of children's parents (Helser, 1994). Some grandparents find that these living arrangements impose financial difficulties and added stress on the children.

Family-Religion-School Relationships. In the early days of the United States, the social institutions of family, religion, and education were interdependent. As noted in Chapter 3, Latin grammar (secondary) schools taught students the Scriptures at the request of families. Until the 19th century, schooling met "the needs of families rather than broader economic and/or political purposes. Teachers and schools were, in effect, the servants or employees of families" (Elkind, 1990, p. 9).

The American Revolution, however, created the need for a literate electorate and spurred development of universal publicly supported education. "After several decades of trial and error, state systems of education began to emerge between 1830 and 1870" (Elkind, 1990, p. 10). Parents saw a need for schooling because, in this era of the Industrial Revolution, men ceased working in or near home and were no longer able to model adult work for their sons (Coleman, 1987; Grant, 1988). Some young people attended school but others worked in industry; there were no compulsory school attendance laws.

Industrial demand for youth labor diminished as machines became more efficient and waves of immigrants came to work at American factories in the early 1900s. At this point, "social activists were finally able to enact legislation against child labor because industry no longer needed youthful workers" (Sherraden, 1988, p. 139). Families and schools saw themselves as partners, with schools taking over functions that parents once performed. Local, state, and national parent-teacher organizations were started to further this partnership (Elkind, 1990).

Until about the end of World War II, the family, religion, and school complemented each other as social institutions. The Great Depression had ended and the economic boom that accompanied the war carried over into the early 1950s. However, in the late 1950s and 1960s domestic civil unrest and the unpopular Vietnam war changed the social situation. The Civil Rights Act and the War on Poverty helped feed a change in social values among the citizenry that affected social institutions.

This shift in values spawned changes in the relationships among family, education, and religion. Social norms that had guided the behavior of preceding generations relaxed. Each social institution lost ground in its ability to channel behavior in prescribed ways.

In 1966 a landmark study of families and schools showed that schools were more effective for children from strong family backgrounds than for children from weak ones (Coleman et al., 1988). The researchers related this finding to differences between family and school resources devoted to children's education. Although school resources include opportunities, demands, and rewards, these cannot replace what families or households provide—attitudes, effort, and conception of self. Because family resources vary more than school resources, children without the family inputs are at a distinct disadvantage (Coleman, 1987).

Coleman (1987) uses the idea of **social capital** to describe "the norms, the social networks, and the relationships between adults and children that are of value for the child's growing up" (p. 36). Social capital exists within families and also in communities. Family members who display concern for children's school performance manifest social capital. Adults in the community who show interest in children's activities through simple acts such as lending a sympathetic ear to problems not discussable with parents or volunteering as youth group leaders also display social capital.

To check the effects of social capital Coleman, Hoffer, and Kilgore (1982) show that the dropout rate of students from Catholic high schools is substantially less than the rates at public and other private schools (3.4 percent compared with 14.3 percent and 11.9 percent, respectively). The researchers conclude that, rather than greater curricular demands or anything else within the school, the *community* created by the church made the difference. A comparable dropout rate was observed in other religious, but non-Catholic, schools. Coleman and his colleagues conclude that "religious organizations are among the few remaining organizations in society, beyond the family, that cross generations. Thus, they are among the few in which the social capital of an adult community is available to children and youth" (Coleman, 1987, p. 37).

Echoing Coleman's views, Hersh (1994) calls for administrators, faculty, parents, and students to work together to forge a culture of responsibility. Otherwise, he predicts, we will become "a nation of individuals who cannot read or write well, with no sense of major human questions, who cannot think critically or show interest in learning and who are unable to act responsibly in a diverse democratic society" (Hersh, 1994, p. 13). He fears that these individuals would be ill-equipped to compete in any new world order.

In earlier years the labor market helped with social control of young people. However, when youth labor was no longer needed, education assumed most of this social responsibility. For a while, education performed this function effectively, but the responsibility grew as industry required an increasingly literate work force. Students who dropped out of school were and continue to be economically disadvantaged because they aren't equipped to work at skilled jobs (Sherraden, 1988).

As early as 1979 Stannard (quoted in McCarthy, 1992, p. 5) observed that the American family had begun to unburden itself of responsibility to care for and nurture the weak. Adult family members were free to pursue an unprecedented range of self-gratifying endeavors. That observation continues to the present. Parents at all economic levels use much of their elective time for self-pursuits, rather than for childrearing activities. At this point economic need and changing social values make it unlikely that this situation will reverse itself (Bunting, 1990).

These two sections on social institutions present information that bears on schooling and the work of educators. Answer the questions in Exercise 5.2 to help consolidate this information.

1. Reflect on the changes in the economy and polity described here. Describe how these changes affect the school(s) where you are (or were) employed.
2. Repeat the process for the changes in family, religion, and education.
3. To what extent have your professional responsibilities changed over the years? To what extent are these changes related to societal changes? Explain.

DEMOGRAPHIC BACKGROUNDS OF LEARNERS

Previous sections discuss societal-cultural changes in the major social institutions in general. Because these changes should be recognized by curriculum workers, this section summarizes societal and cultural changes as they affect the learners for whom curricula are prepared and delivered.

Much of the information in this section is based on data collected by the U.S. Bureau of the Census and published in the *Statistical Abstract of the United States*. Consequently, groups will be named as they are in the census data. For example, population groups are designated typically by origin as Hispanic or non-Hispanic, with Hispanics representing any of several races. In this discussion whites, blacks, American Indians, Eskimos, Aleuts, Asians, and Pacific Islanders refer to people with non-Hispanic origins, if they are so designated in the census data.

THE POPULATION

The percentage of the total school-age population in the United States is expected to decrease. Whereas about 20 percent of the U.S. population was school-age in 1970, about 14 percent was school-age in 1990. By 2050 the school-age population is expected to decrease further to less than 12 percent (U.S. Bureau of the Census, 1994).

In the 21st century school-age children are expected to reflect increasingly diverse racial backgrounds. Within the population-at-large, the number of school-age children is declining among whites, holding steady among blacks and American Indians-Eskimos-Aleuts, and increasing among Asians-Pacific Islanders and Hispanics. In 1980 white students (ages 5–14) accounted for 74.3 percent of the school-age population, but a decade later this percentage had decreased to 69.4. American Indian-Eskimo-Aleut percentages were 0.8 percent and 1.0 percent for 1980 and 1990, respectively, and the percentages for black students were the same for both years at 14.6 percent. Both Asian-Pacific Islander and Hispanic percentages moved upward, 1.7 to 3.1 percent and 8.6 to 11.9 percent, respectively, between 1980 and 1990 (U.S. Bureau of the Census, 1994).

Table 5.1 shows that the population of 5- to 13-year-olds is projected to increase only about 6 million between 1995 and 2025. The projections also show that the percentage of white students is expected to decline, so that by 2025 about half of school-age students are expected to be white. Percentages of black and American Indian-Eskimo-Aleut students are expected to increase relatively little. However, percentages of Asian-Pacific Islander and Hispanic students are expected to nearly double (U.S. Bureau of the Census, 1994).

Population Mobility.   The United States population is becoming increasingly mobile. For example, in 1990 only 53.3 percent of the population lived in the same house as they did in 1985. During this period another quarter of the population moved from one house to another in the same county, while nearly 10 percent moved to a different county and another 10 percent moved to a different state (U.S. Bureau of the Census, 1993).

The percentage of change in the population by region is uneven. In the Northeast it changed relatively little from 1970 to 1980, accounting for only 0.3 percent of the total change. This percentage increased to 7.5, however, between 1980 and 1990. In the Midwest comparable percentages were 9.8 and 3.6.

However, large population shifts occurred in the South and West. About 54 percent of the changes between 1970 and 1980 and 45.5 percent between 1980 and 1990 took place in the South. The West accounted for slightly more than a third (35.9 percent) of the 1970–80 population change and 43.4 percent in the next decade. Part of the population shift is attributable to business mergers and company relocations from the Northeast to the South and West. Many families and individuals relocated for economic reasons.

Another part of the change in resident population is due to immigration. About 40 percent of the total immigrants to the United States between 1981 and 1990 came from Mexico, islands in the Caribbean, and Central America, but 65 percent of the immigrants came from those areas by 1991 (U.S. Bureau of the Census, 1993). In 1992 this percentage was 37.9 (U.S. Bureau of the Census, 1994). Because they were headed to the United States, many of these individuals settled in the South and West.

TABLE 5.1

Populations of 5- to 13-Year-Olds Projected for 1995–2025, by Percentages

Year	Total Population of 5–13 Year-Olds (in 1,000s)	Non-Hispanic (%)				Hispanic* (%)
		White	Black	American Indian, Eskimo, Aleut	Asian, Pacific Islander	
1995	34,262	67.2	14.7	1.0	3.8	13.3
2000	36,547	64.3	15.1	1.0	4.4	15.2
2005	36,843	61.4	15.4	1.0	5.4	16.8
2010	36,213	58.4	15.8	1.1	6.4	18.4
2025	40,455	52.1	16.6	1.1	7.9	22.3

*Persons of Hispanic origin may be of any race.

Based on U.S. Bureau of the Census, *Current Population Reports,* P25–104 reported in the *Statistical Abstract of the United States 1994,* pp. 24–25.

Plurality of Cultures.   Since 1961–1970 the number of immigrants to the United States more than doubled from about 3 million to more than 7 million in 1981–1990. Immigrants from Europe dropped from 37 percent in the 1961–1970 period to less than 10 percent in 1981–1990, but the percentage of Asian immigrants increased from about 13 percent to 38 percent in the same time period (U.S. Bureau of the Census, 1993).

Although some immigrants share a culture with one extant in the United States, the influx of peoples from other parts of the world is bound to produce additional languages and customs. In some regions,

> most notably in California, the new immigration has created a patchwork of barrios, Koreatowns, Little Taipeis, and Little Saigons. These changes have also created competition and conflict over scarce resources and have led to battles over disputed turf among rival gangs and intense rivalries between members of the white working class and people of color. Moreover, communities, corporations, and schools have had difficulty providing the newcomers with the services they require because of the language and cultural barriers. (Eitzen, 1992, p. 587)

Languages.   According to a survey in April 1990, about 86 percent of the U.S. population speaks English only. However, nearly 14 percent of the population, age 5 years or older, speaks languages other than English. About 7.5 percent of the people surveyed spoke Spanish, the most popular of all languages except English. Fourteen percent of school-age learners speak languages other than English. But the statistic of concern is that, of this group, about 30 percent to 45 percent speak English less than "very well" (U.S. Bureau of the Census, 1994). Learners who are unable to communicate well in classrooms are at a disadvantage and must be a concern to curriculum developers and users.

In summary, the percentage of school-age learners has declined since 1970 and is expected to continue declining into the 21st century. The school-age population early in the next century will have more minority children, representing diverse cultures. Many of these children are likely to speak a native language other than English.

LIVING CONDITIONS

School children grow up under increasingly diverse living conditions. Children younger than 18 in white and Hispanic groups are nearly two times more likely to live with both parents than blacks (78.7 percent, 67 percent, and 38.4 percent, respectively). Less than 4 percent of children in any group live with their fathers only. However, more than half of black children (58.3 percent), more than a quarter of white children (29.1 percent) and 17.8 percent of Hispanic children younger than 18 live with their mothers only (U.S. Bureau of the Census, 1994).

Table 5.2 shows that parental educational attainments vary greatly. More than half of Hispanic parents and a quarter of black parents have less than a high school diploma, but less than 20 percent of white parents lack high school diplomas. White and black parents have significantly better educational attainments than Hispanic parents as measured by high school diplomas and or some college

TABLE 5.2
Parental Educational Attainment by Race, in Percentages, 1993

Educational Attainment	Total Number of Parents All Races (in 1,000s)	Percentage of Parents			
		All Races[1]	White	Black	Hispanic*
Less than 9th grade	3,893	6.0	6.2	3.9	30.5
Grade 9–12, no diploma	7,799	12.0	10.3	21.2	21.4
High school graduate**	22,519	34.6	33.7	42.2	26.6
Some college, no bachelor's	16,307	25.1	25.6	23.6	15.1
Bachelor's degree	9,332	14.3	15.5	6.5	4.4
Graduate, professional degree	5,202	8.0	8.7	2.6	2.0

Based on U.S. Bureau of the Census, unpublished data reported in the *Statistical Abstract of the United States 1994*, p. 67.

[1]Includes other races, not shown separately.

*Persons of Hispanic origins may be of any race.

**Includes high school equivalency.

work. While less than 10 percent of black and Hispanic parents hold bachelor's and or higher degrees, almost a quarter of white parents do.

In 1993 the status of parental employment varied greatly among the races, as shown in Table 5.3. Almost 70 percent of black parents, slightly more Hispanic parents and nearly 90 percent of white parents were members of the civilian labor force. (Children with a parent in the Armed Forces are not counted in these statistics.) The unemployment rates ranged from about 5 percent to 9 percent. However, the numbers of parents *not* in the labor force ranged from 11.6 percent (white) to 21.5 percent (Hispanic) to 31 percent (black). In situations where children live with mothers and fathers, both parents worked among 55 percent of whites and blacks and 40.2 percent of Hispanics.

These employment figures support the fact that a large number of children are reared in poverty, as defined by the federal government's poverty index. Inaugurated in 1964 by the Social Security Administration, the poverty index was revised in 1980 by Federal Interagency Committees. This index uses only money income and does not acknowledge noncash benefits such as food stamps, Medicaid, and public housing. The index, which reflects changes in the Consumer Price Index, takes into account different consumption requirements of families based on their size and composition (U.S. Bureau of the Census, 1994). Table 5.4 displays statistics concerning children under 18 years of age who live in poverty, as defined by this index.

TABLE 5.3
Parental Employment Status by Race, in Percentages, 1993

Employment Status	Total Number of Parents All Races (in 1,000s)	Percentage of Parents			
		All Races[1]	White	Black	Hispanic*
In civilian labor force**	54,345	83.5	87.0	67.0	77.4
Employed	50,603	77.8	81.8	58.5	68.5
Unemployed	3,742	5.8	5.2	8.6	8.9
Not in labor force	9,751	15.0	11.6	31.0	21.5

Based on U.S. Bureau of the Census, unpubliished data reported in the *Statistical Abstract of the United States, 1994.*

[1]Includes other races, not shown separately.

*Persons of Hispanic origins may be of any race.

**Excludes children whose parent is in the armed forces.

Since 1970 the percentage of children in this economic category has grown each year, though the overall percentage appears to be slowing to about a fifth of the total population of children in the United States. However, differences between white and black-Hispanic percentages are dramatic. In 1992 whereas about 21 percent of white children were classified as living in poverty, nearly half of all black children and nearly 40 percent of Hispanic children were in this group.

In summary, if current trends continue, increasing numbers of school children will be reared in homes with only one parent who may be unable to help with school work because his or her educational background is weak. Many school children, especially among minorities, are raised in poverty. Their parent(s) are either unemployed or are not in the labor force. Because of their limited social backgrounds, these children are disadvantaged compared with children from more affluent circumstances.

STUDIES OF SOCIETY AND CULTURE APPLIED IN CURRICULUM PROCESSES

Not only have large scale societal and cultural changes taken place, these changes continue to occur more rapidly than ever in history. As noted in Chapter 3, schools usually follow, rather than lead, societal changes. Therefore, school curricula almost always lag behind the changes. This section describes implications of the studies of society and culture for the curriculum processes of development, classroom use, and evaluation.

TABLE 5.4
Children Younger than 18 Who Live Below Poverty Level by Race, 1970 to 1992

Year	Total Number of Children Below Poverty Level, All Races (in 1,000s)	Percentages of Children Below Poverty Level			
		All Races[1]	White	Black	Hispanic[2]
1970	10,235	14.9	10.5	41.5	(NA)
1975	10,882	16.8	12.5	41.4	33.1
1980	11,114	17.9	13.4	42.1	33.0
1985[3]	12,483	20.1	15.6	43.1	39.6
1990[4]	12,715	19.9	15.1	44.2	39.7
1992	13,876	21.1	16.0	46.3	38.8

Based on U.S. Bureau of the Census, *Current Population Reports,* P–60–185 reported in the *Statistical Abstract of the United States 1994,* p. 475.

NA = Not available.

[1]Includes persons of other races, not shown separately.

[2]Persons of Hispanic origins may be of any race.

[3]Beginning 1983, data based on revised Hispanic population controls and not directly comparable with prior years.

[4]Beginning 1987, data based on revised processing procedures and not directly comparable with prior years.

DEVELOPMENT

Growing demands for literacy at home, in the workplace, and in the community suggest that curriculum revision efforts must acknowledge societal and cultural changes. This subsection elaborates on this statement.

Purposes and Content Selection. Curriculum developers, particularly those concerned about societal-cultural changes, sometimes choose as their purpose "preparing people to live in a rapidly changing world" or "reforming society." The first statement acknowledges that social change affects people in different ways and that students of all ages need help handling change. A curriculum with this purpose assists students *as groups* in coping with change, through study of social problems as the main source of curriculum content. This is the "current" or relevance orientation of the social relevance-reconstruction curriculum conception.

"Reforming society" as a purpose of education, however, means that schools actually shape changes in society. Such proactive curricula are intended to equip students with skills and abilities to solve societal problems through alterations in organizations and institutions. These curricula use societal problems, issues, and concerns as content and set as their goal the betterment of society. Individuals realize their potentials as *group members* in this "futurist" orientation of the social relevance-reconstruction curriculum conception. (See Chapter 3.)

District- and school-based developers with less compelling priorities for dealing with societal and cultural needs than these are also affected by these studies. Planners using the purpose, "cultivating students' cognitive achievement and intellect" acknowledge societal-cultural realities in choosing curriculum content. For example, in recognition of the diversity of cultures and languages, developers frequently select content portraying a multicultural and multilinguistic society. In doing so, these curriculum materials help students understand not only their own culture, but other cultures as well.

What isn't clear is the extent to which developers build into curricula accommodations for learners who:

• Come from cultures other than the dominant one.

• Speak a native language other than English.

• May be "behind" their classmates because they moved with their parents or guardians from one location to another.

• Come from homes where parents are either unable or uninterested in working with school personnel in the education of their children.

• Come from homes where the socioeconomic levels are low, resulting in learners with impoverished outside-of-school learning experiences.

No matter which purpose of education is selected, developers must wrestle with and decide how to handle the literacy questions. Students leaving schools either at graduation or sooner must somehow be equipped for literacy in its different forms.

Projected Roles for Classroom Users of Curricula.   Studies of society and culture suggest that it's increasingly difficult for classroom users/teachers to ignore the world outside of classrooms. The students they face every day bear evidence of the social ills, some of which result from the technological age in which we live.

These studies also suggest that teachers should use interactive methods in the delivery of curriculum. Traditional methods of one-way communication, typically from teacher to students, are NOT very effective in a society that has virtually instant two-way communication globally and into outer space. With a generation of students accustomed to space-age technology, the pace of learning must challenge learners used to video games and other computer technology.

CLASSROOM USE

Studies of society and culture affect classroom use of curriculum to the extent that curriculum content and proposed roles of curriculum users reflect these studies. Choosing either "preparing people for living in an unstable changing world" or "reforming society" as a purpose would require large quantities of *resources* to provide *professional development* for teachers and staff who would need retraining to understand and deliver the revised curriculum. Instructional materials that focus on society don't exist and would have to be developed, requiring even more resources. In addition *communication* among educators, community members, and students with whom this curriculum would be used requires expertise, time, and funds.

Even when curriculum content continues as largely subject matter, studies of society and culture affect classroom use considerations. Increased literacy demands and diversity in student populations are only two of several social changes affecting the *scope* and *complexity* of curriculum use in classrooms. Taking into account either of these factors requires *professional development* for teachers and school staff to help them understand change and to provide coping strategies. Effective *communication* among educators, citizens, and students is a requirement in understanding and managing these social changes. Both people, time, and monetary *resources* are required in order to deal with such social changes.

EVALUATION

Curricular changes that acknowledge societal and cultural studies affect *evaluation* to the extent of their acknowledgement in the curriculum. For example, where the purpose of education is "helping people live in a rapidly changing world or reforming society," evaluation is a *process* of finding the degree to which the curriculum makes it possible for learners collectively to meet this purpose. Methods of evaluation might involve measures of groups' abilities to do problem posing or problem solving.

If the dominant purpose is "cultivating cognitive achievement," evaluation instruments such as tests, scales, or portfolios may be used. However, the subject matter within the evaluation instruments should acknowledge consistency with the social and cultural realities included in the curriculum.

SUMMARY

Recent societal and cultural changes spark issues concerning literacy forms and responsibilities for learners' development of literacy. Both homes and workplaces require additional literacy beyond what they did a few years ago. A major question is who will provide this development.

Social institutions that usually assist in these matters have changed in ways that prevent their functioning as they did in past generations. In particular, technological changes produce structural changes in the economy that greatly modify cities and geographic areas. As a result of economic and other social changes, families, religion, and education have each undergone their own changes.

Census data indicate that the school-age population is declining and becoming poorer. Increased numbers of minority children, some of whom do not speak English, are expected in classrooms. Many school-age children are likely to be reared in homes with only one parent. In some cases that parent may be unable to help his/her child because of a weak educational background.

Studies of society and culture affect all curriculum processes, but are especially important in content selection criteria. Developers' content choices should acknowledge the social realities outside of classrooms because education carries most of the responsibility for producing literate citizens.

QUESTIONS FOR DISCUSSION

1. To what extent would your professional responsibilities change if your school increased its efforts to develop the literacy forms described in this chapter? Explain.
2. In your *residential* community, which social institutions are active in the development of learners' literacy? Describe the contributions made by each institution.
3. The discussion of distribution of power says schools influence students to accept the status quo. Describe indicators from your school that support or refute this idea.
4. Describe the extent to which structural changes in the economy have affected your *residential* community. Your school?
5. Suppose Coleman (1987) is correct about the need for social capital. What recommendations would you make to colleagues working in schools where little social capital exists? Why?
6. Based on information in the section titled Demographic Backgrounds of Learners, describe changes likely within the next five years in the population served by your school. What recommendations for curriculum does this information suggest for school staff, teachers and community leaders in your school?
7. Reflect on the discussion of district- and school-based curriculum development in Chapter 2. Based on the information in this chapter, is there an advantage to one of these approaches over the other? Explain.

IMPORTANT IDEAS DISCUSSED
INITIALLY IN THIS CHAPTER

literacy forms   social institutions
   language   economy-polity
   cultural   family-education-religion
   science   social capital
   information

6

STUDIES OF LEARNERS

OUTLINE

Nurture, nature, or interaction
Behavioral views of development
    Cognitive-intellectual dimensions
    Social-personal-moral dimensions
Cognitive views of development
    Cognitive-intellectual dimensions
    Social-personal-moral dimensions
Humanistic views of development
Physical development
Atypical developmental patterns
    Learning problems
    Physical impairments
Studies of learners applied in curriculum processes
    Development
    Classroom use
    Evaluation

Whereas Chapter 5 discusses learners in broad societal-cultural contexts, this chapter focuses on learners in school situations. The chapter outline mentions the term *development* several times for good reason. As used here, this term applies to the progressive changes that take place over time within children and youth, whether the changes are physical or psychological. Physical changes are also called growth or maturation. Psychological changes frequently carry other labels, too, such as learning or cognitive, intellectual, social, personal, or moral development.

This chapter does not attempt to provide a complete discussion of child and adolescent development because only a fraction of what is known about learners can be addressed. However, this brief survey of the literature *is* expected to show how knowledge of learners' development influences curriculum processes.

More specifically, this chapter is intended to help you *to examine your values and beliefs about learners and learning processes.* For example, what roles do learners play in their own development? Is "learning" construed as behavior? Is "learning" the capacity to demonstrate changes in behavior? Your answers also provide clues to your preferences of roles for curriculum users. They also will provide insights concerning the curriculum content you consider as learnable and necessary for students. The foundation for answering these questions is the topic of this chapter; the ideas are discussed further and applied in Part 3.

NURTURE, NATURE, OR INTERACTION

Fundamental views of the nature and source of human motivation project that learners relate in different ways to their environments. Are learners passive/reactive minds or organisms whose development depends on their being conditioned by outside forces? Are learners active, innately planned personalities that develop as their native instincts, needs, abilities, and talents unfold? Might learners be purposive persons who develop as a result of interactions with their respective psychological environments? (Bigge & Shermis, 1992) These questions elaborate on the section title and provide the foundation for this chapter.

The values and beliefs that curriculum developers hold about learners influence decisions about content, materials, time, and other matters. Teachers and school staff who use or evaluate curricula act on the basis of their views of how students relate to their environments. Therefore, any survey of studies of learners should begin with a discussion of views of the basic nature of children and youth. Differences among these views mean important differences in how individuals work with curricula.

One group of psychologists and educators believes that children develop mainly as a result of **nurture.** In the 18th century John Locke compared children's minds to "tabula rasa" or blank slates. He believed children's experiences were etched into their minds in much the way that one writes on wax tablets (Bruner, 1985; Darling-Hammond & Snyder, 1992).

These ideas evolved further in the early 20th century when "experience" was broadened to include a range of events, both occurring naturally and contrived by people in children's environments. Adherents to the nurture explanation of development believe that events in learners' environments are largely responsible for molding and shaping their intelligences and personalities.

An alternative view of development is held by psychologists and educators who consider that learners shape their own lives and destinies, that they are basically products of **nature** or their heredity. Children are born into the world with the seeds of their personalities locked inside and become who they are as a result of developing their innate talents (Talwar & Lerner, 1991). "The child's original nature is one of positive striving to actualize an inner essence that is good and constructive" (Thomas, 1992, p. 404).

A third perspective of development combines nature and nurture in **interaction** theories. Thomas (1992) explains that where developmental psychologists once argued about the extent to which heredity or environment contributed to development, they now question the manner in which nature and nurture interact. They want to know the width of boundaries set by heredity for various aspects of development (e.g., physical characteristics, cognitive abilities), which environmental forces affect the manifestation of these developmental aspects in children's appearance and behavior, and how the "interaction of inherited potential and environmental forces operates at different stages of the child's growth period" (Thomas, 1992, p. 35).

These perspectives concerning underlying beliefs about development provide the organizing focus for this chapter. Behavioral views of development are based largely on the nurture explanation; cognitive views, on interaction; and humanistic views, largely on nature. Table 6.1 displays key relationships among sources of human motivation, their relationship to learners, types of learning fostered by each source, and views of development. Each of these views is described in a major section that follows. However, cognitive views are more detailed than behavioral or humanistic views because almost all current research on learners uses this perspective.

BEHAVIORAL VIEWS OF DEVELOPMENT

Before 1900 psychologists studied human thought and behavior primarily through introspection. But the first behavioral psychologists strongly rejected this

TABLE 6.1

Comparisons Among Three Views of Development

View of Development	Source of Motivation to Learn	Relationship of Source to Learner	Type of Learning in Which Learners Engage
Behavioral	Nurture	Largely external	Largely receptive
Cognitive	Interaction of nurture with nature	Largely internal	Largely generative
Humanistic	Nature	Internal	Generative

method of study and sought to make psychology a science (Gardner, 1983). To make their study as objective as possible, early behaviorists focused solely on information input and output. However, contemporary social learning researchers also consider the mental processes that occur between input and output.

Two key concepts in behavioral views of development are "conditioning" and "observational learning." Each idea is grounded in the *nurture* orientation, indicating that the learner's environment, including people and their activities, plays a major role in development. In this section cognitive-intellectual development is separated from social-moral development simply for convenience of discussion. Learners' development proceeds in all dimensions simultaneously.

COGNITIVE-INTELLECTUAL DIMENSIONS

In behavioral views, learners' cognitive and intellectual development registers as changes in performance capabilities. **Learning** is "an enduring change in observable behavior that occurs as a result of experience" (Eggen & Kauchak, 1994, p. 255). For changes in behavior to be considered learning, however, they must be long-lasting and result from experiences, rather than maturation or biological processes.

In behavioral views, experiences encompass the activities involved when stimuli such as sights, sounds, and smells become associated with responses or behaviors. For example, the smell of coffee or the reading of words (stimuli) can produce pleasant or unpleasant behaviors (responses), depending on the people involved. Stimuli become associated with responses typically through conditioning or observational learning. As a result, learning is almost exclusively **receptive learning** because it results when learners are subjected to events in their external environments.

Conditioning.   In **operant conditioning** stimuli become associated with responses based on the consequences of learners' actions. For example, suppose that Juan, a first-grader, received a mark of 100 percent on the weekly spelling test. His teacher drew a smiley-face on his paper to express approval of his work. Because he received the smiley-face last week, Juan may study hard for this week's spelling test. The teacher's drawing a smiley-face was the consequence of Juan's achieving a perfect score and was done to increase the probability of the recurrence of Juan's behavior. In the language of behavioral learning, the smiley-face reinforced the response the teacher wants Juan to repeat when he is again faced with a spelling test, the stimulus. Note that in operant conditioning, learners must respond before they can receive reinforcement, a situation that Skinner (1968) refers to as a "contingency" of reinforcement.

Skinner thought people learn complex information with help from discriminative stimuli, or cues, and immediate reinforcement for correct answers, conditions that can be handled by teaching machines (Darling-Hammond & Snyder, 1992). Look again at Figure 3.3, a brief section of a high school physics curriculum. The note accompanying this figure indicates that students use this information in a teaching machine that covers the words in the right column. Sentences with blanks form the stimuli that elicit responses. A skillful reader can figure out responses without much difficulty because of cues in the text. Skinner also believed that by making the correct answers available as *immediate* feedback, students would find them reinforcing and continue to respond to further stimuli. This figure demonstrates operant conditioning as Skinner (1968) envisioned its use in schools.

In operant conditioning, "motivation to learn" is explained as learning, similar to memorizing dates in history or using the proper procedures in driving a car. Skinner (1968) took issue with Dewey's suggestion of allowing children to explore and discover their world. Skinner believed this was more likely to generate idleness than industry. His preference, of course, was for more reliable contingencies, such as programmed learning.

Contingencies or reinforcers include praise, good grades, tokens, and other tangible things and intangible procedures that can be applied by teachers, parents, and others. Unfortunately, reinforcers have different effects on learners and may or may not be reliable. See Stipek (1993) for a discussion of problems with the reinforcement theory of motivation.

Skinner's research contributes to educators' knowledge of sequencing content for learners and the role of feedback and practice in learning. However, his research generally fails to recognize the complexities of classroom life, so it's hard to translate his laboratory-tested procedures into classroom practice. For example, it's difficult to decide *what* is reinforcing *which* behaviors in classroom situations. Also, research shows that learners' abilities to demonstrate specific behaviors, common in behavioral learning, do not mean that students understand the principles underlying those behaviors (Darling-Hammond & Snyder, 1992).

Observational Learning.   In **observational learning,** learners' expectations, beliefs, and goals may influence situations. This view holds that people learn by watching the activities of other individuals who serve as models and by noting consequences (Bandura, 1977, 1989). This statement implies that learners either participate directly with models or observe their behaviors on videotapes or films. For example, young children often learn to "write" their names by copying the marks made by an adult or older sibling. In these cases when children complete writing their names, they usually receive reinforcement in the form of praise or hugs from whoever modeled the behavior.

In other cases learners experience vicarious reinforcement. As an illustration, learners have frequent opportunities to observe how teachers deal with behaviors of their peers. When the foreign language teacher corrects a student's pronunciation, alert learners note the correct pronunciation and use it themselves. Coaches show videotapes of sports contests to aspiring athletes, frequently pointing out strengths and weaknesses of participants. In both situations learners observe the consequences of the models' actions, using this information to make decisions about their own behaviors. Most learners elect to perform only the actions that elicited positive consequences.

Observational learning uses the following mental processes: attention, retention, production, and motivation.

- Attention determines what people observe and the information they take from the situation.

- Retention processes transform and restructure the information so it can be remembered.
- The behavioral production processes translate the remembered information into appropriate actions on the learner's part.
- Finally, motivation processes enable learners to decide which performances they wish to pursue (Bandura, 1977, 1989).

Young children are usually motivated primarily by the sensory and social effects of their actions. As they develop, however, symbolic incentives (e.g., awards, grades) become more important. Children also learn that models provide valuable information for dealing with the environment (Bandura, 1989).

In summary, behavioral views of cognitive-intellectual development stress the importance of learners' responses to events and people in their environments. What is learned is receptive information that has been structured and organized by others. Exercise 6.1 asks you to reflect on these views. Try this exercise as a way of checking your *overall* understanding of these views.

EXERCISE 6.1

Reflect on the behavioral perspectives of *cognitive-intellectual* development. Then read the following situation.

Mr. Xavier, a third-grade teacher, is supposed to help his students learn cursive handwriting—a task that is difficult for some students. He dutifully handwrites assignments for students on overhead transparencies using his best cursive lettering. However, sometimes he's hurried and his lettering is of poor quality. Sure enough, on these occasions he finds that some students who otherwise write legibly, copy his poor quality handwriting.

1. Describe the extent to which the third-graders' learning in this situation is receptive.
2. Based on the information given, which learning domains and types of outcomes are likely in the situation? Explain.

SOCIAL-PERSONAL-MORAL DIMENSIONS

The works of both Skinner and Bandura reflect their interests in aspects of human behavior beyond those normally associated with cognitive-intellectual development. However, these psychologists look on all of development as comprising incremental changes that occur as learners engage in experiences. Because changes are small and gradual, behaviorists generally do not describe developmental stages. Skinner and Bandura approach social, personal, and moral development from different perspectives as the following discussion shows.

Conditioning.   What we know of Skinner's views about development other than intellectual matters must be inferred from his writings. In 1948 Skinner wrote a novel, *Walden Two,* in which he devoted several chapters to child-raising practices in a utopian society. Several chapters on this topic show how social, personal, and moral development are accomplished through conditioning.

Walden Two is a small rural society where children live in age-level groups and are cared for by specially trained caregivers using behavioral engineering principles. For the first five years, *all* the children's important social and personal needs are met so they do not experience anxiety or frustration. Then the children are introduced gradually to the stresses of real life, albeit in a utopia, using carefully controlled learning situations.

For example, in *Walden Two,* the main character Frazier reports that children's ethical training is complete by age 6. He offers an example involving lollipops. Three- and 4-year-old children are helped to overcome their temptation to eat candy in a series of self-control exercises. They are urged to "examine" their behavior while looking at the lollipops. Then the lollipops are concealed, and the children are asked to notice any gain in happiness or any reduction in tension. Next, they are strongly distracted, perhaps in a game. Later the children are reminded of the candy and again encouraged to examine their reaction. After several such instances, children are allowed to wear the lollipops like crucifixes for a few hours, to test their self-control (Skinner, 1948).

Essentially children and youth move through their formative years in carefully crafted experiences that enable them to demonstrate appropriate social and personal behaviors. These experiences, of course, use operant conditioning principles and appropriate reinforcers.

Observational Learning.   Social, personal, and moral development also result from observational learning. In the past socialization occurred primarily in homes and community organizations where models held similar values. However, television has vastly expanded the range of models to which learners are exposed. This expanded social environment increases the likelihood that learners' values, attitudes, and social behaviors are modeled by the media. Through these vicarious experiences, "people acquire attitudes, values, and emotional dispositions toward persons, places, and things" (Bandura, 1989, p. 17).

In sum, in behavioral perspectives learners develop incrementally in social, personal, and moral dimensions. Of course, the same processes bring about these changes as those that foster cognitive-intellectual developmental changes. The impetus for change is in the learners' environments and the results of the changes are behaviors.

COGNITIVE VIEWS OF DEVELOPMENT

Cognitive views developed alongside behavioral views beginning early in the 20th century. Each of several cognitive views discussed here is based on an *interaction* perspective in which learners act on and are influenced by their environments. Whereas "environment" meant only the learner's physical surroundings in behavioral views, cognitivists also recognize psychological environments. Moreover, psychological environments are unique because they encompass each individual's past experiences, present activities, and visions for the future.

COGNITIVE-INTELLECTUAL DIMENSIONS

Under cognitive views *learning* is considered "a change in individuals' mental structures that gives them the capacity to demonstrate changes in behavior" (Eggen & Kauchak, 1994, p. 305). Mental structures are hypothetical constructs by which individuals adapt and organize their environments. These structures are created as the result of mental processes including memory, perception (meanings individuals attach to stimuli), insight, language, and problem solving that occur between information input and output.

Learners create knowledge for themselves as they engage in the mental processes. Therefore, learning is largely **generative learning** because it is unique to the person who creates it.

Three perspectives on cognitive-intellectual development cohere around the theme that learners generate and organize their own learning as a result of their mental processing. Each perspective adopts a different model of the learner and asks related, but slightly different, key questions. Highlights of these perspectives are discussed in this subsection. See Table 6.2 for an overview of major points.

TABLE 6.2
Cognitive-Intellectual Development in Cognitive Perspectives

Perspective	Model of Learner	Key Questions	Thrust of Answers
Developmental	Constructivist	How do cognitive functions develop? How do these functions influence learning?	Learners progress through qualitatively different changes or stages in perception and cognition.
Cognitive structuralist	Hypothesis generator	How is learning influenced by structures used to organize prior learning and current teaching?	Learners develop patterns or configurations to make sense of experiences; language plays large role in learning.
Cognitive science	Novice-to-expert	What do people do when they think? What are the processes that make possible intellectual responses?	Learners build cognitive structures that enable the organization and acquisition of knowledge.

Developmentalism.   Piaget stresses the importance of experiences in which children and youth constantly seek to make sense of their worlds (Darling-Hammond & Snyder, 1992; Gardner, 1983). This desire to understand describes the essence of learners, called constructivists (Bruner, 1985) in this perspective.

Piaget believes that the mind has structures for information processing just as the body has organized systems for its functions. These mental structures adapt and organize learners' psychological environments whenever learners engage in experiences. Adaptation and organization involve actions ranging from sensori-motor activities (e.g., pushing, pulling) to internal intellectual operations (e.g., joining together, sequencing) (Piaget, 1970). Learning, therefore, involves the continual matching of mental structures with experiences.

Piaget's research led him to conjecture that children develop through a series of progressively more powerful mental stages, "each of which represents not just more knowledge but also a different kind of knowledge, born of a new cognitive structure for organizing and using what has been learned" (Darling-Hammond & Snyder, 1992, p. 49). In these stages, qualitative differences evidence themselves in the thinking abilities of learners. Young children at the mercy of their perceptions are unable to reason logically, but slightly older learners can reason if the topic is within their experiences or if they have access to concrete materials as referents for thinking. By adolescence many youths have developed further and are able to reason abstractly; that is, they can deal with hypothetical situations. These learners no longer refer to concrete materials or experiences; they are able to deal with several variables simultaneously and begin to think like many adults (Thomas, 1992).

Part of the reason for differences in thinking is language ability. During early preschool years children demonstrate egocentric speech; that is, they talk to themselves. Researchers have shown that children initially frame their thoughts in words with the result that egocentric speech is really thinking aloud. Over time children internalize their thinking process and develop socialized speech with which they communicate with others (Elkind, 1974).

Piaget's model of development has been called restrictive, because it focuses on logical-mathematical intelligence and does not explain steps toward competence in areas such as art or athletics. Furthermore, "a generation of empirical researchers" have found many details of Piaget's work to be incorrect and that results of the tasks have produced different results when conveyed nonverbally, rather than verbally as Piaget used them (Gardner, 1983).

Despite such criticisms, Piaget's research provides a useful explanation for how children generate knowledge. Some of Piaget's ideas carry over to other cognitive perspectives and his research includes other dimensions of development as well. A discussion of that work follows in the subsection Social-Personal-Moral Dimensions.

Cognitive Structuralism.   This perspective makes use of the developmental notions of active and systematic mental processes. Learners are seen as hypothesis generators, in charge of decisions about which information enters their minds for processing into cognitive maps or structures that guide understanding (Bruner, 1960, 1985). The question raised by cognitive structuralists concerns how learning is influenced by the structures used to organize prior learning and current teaching (Darling-Hammond & Snyder, 1992).

In experiments on perception, Gestalt psychologists observed that individuals interpreted what they "saw" differently and reasoned that differences were based in part on what people already "knew." Thus, their work sought to explain how learners make sense of their worlds or achieve understanding (Rock & Palmer, 1990). One result "emphasized that learning could be more effective if learners were explicitly taught the structure of the content to be learned and the relationships among components" (Darling-Hammond & Snyder, 1992, p. 52).

In the 1960s cognitive researchers tackled this hypothesis in different ways. For example, Ausubel (1963) worked on strategies that promoted meaningful reception learning, while Bruner (1960, 1966) researched discovery learning. Though these approaches seem to be at odds, they share the notion of structuring knowledge to assist learners in its acquisition (Darling-Hammond & Snyder, 1992). Ausubel (1963) developed advance organizers, which provide a framework for processing the information that follows. Bruner's research (1966) focused on mathematical structures, which assist learners in understanding when combined with modes of representing knowledge from Piaget's theory (e.g., enactive, iconic).

Embedded in cognitive structural research are concerns about relationships between language and thought. Vygotsky's (1962) work in this area shows that children's thought and speech begin as separate functions without connections. However, as children develop, these processes become interrelated, but progress is not parallel. The language environment is very important for conceptual thinking. Exposed to only simplistic or "primitive" language, children are likely to think only simplistically or primitively. But exposure to varied and complex concepts leads children to think in varied and complex ways (Thomas, 1992).

Such ideas form the foundation for the whole language approach to literacy. Structuralists believe that language not only provides communication but orders reality as well. Therefore, language literacy skills must be based in the learners' experiences (Goodman, Haussler, & Strickland, 1981). Of course, learners' experiences are culturally based and decisions about knowledge acquisition clearly become value questions.

Cognitive Science.   In recent years cognitive scientists elaborated on the cognitive structuralists' work in several information processing models. In each model, however, the key question is "What do people do when they think?" (Darling-Hammond & Snyder, 1992, p. 55). A good way to find an answer is to compare the abilities of experts with those of novices, hence this becomes the model of the learner for this perspective (Bruner, 1985).

Information processing systems are hypothesized as having structures (e.g., sense organs, or working memory) through which information passes and is managed by cognitive process stored in long-term memory. Information enters as stimuli (e.g., words, pictures, smells) via the sense organs from the external environment into sensory memory. The stimuli are in sensory memory for only a few seconds, and some are lost—but others are encoded or recast into symbols and representations that can be manipulated by the nervous system in the individual's working memory. This is the site at which all "thinking transactions" take place, the person's conscious memory. However, information also stays here only a short while and may be lost unless it is processed into long-term memory through some form of encoding (Thomas, 1992).

Encoding information is facilitated through elaboration, activity or organizational strategies by which learners connect new information with what they have in long-term memory. Teaching agents help students with encoding processes. For example, teachers who ask open-ended questions provide opportunities for learners to connect new information with information already in memory (Eggen & Kauchak, 1994).

Information is stored in long-term memory as mental structures (e.g., schemas, frames, networks) constructed by the learner (Darling-Hammond & Snyder, 1992). The long-term memory is the repository for all knowledge forms and learning outcomes described in Chapter 4. Categories in long-term memory storage include events, goals, relationships, and affects (Thomas, 1992). Theoretically, information that becomes part of long-term memory can be retrieved at any time.

As this discussion shows, the contents of learners' long-term memories are important not only for retrieval and use, but also because what learners already know about a topic affects their construction of meaning on related topics. "The impact of prior knowledge is not a matter of 'readiness,' component skills, or exhaustiveness; it is an issue of depth, interconnectedness, and access. It includes all of the kinds of knowledge . . . and their interrelationships" (Leinhardt, 1992, p. 21). Actual learning outcomes differ among individuals because learning results from the combination of what is already known and how learners make sense of new information.

Differences in learners' information processing strategies result in multiple definitions of *learning styles* as well as research studies to see if accounting for preferred ways of processing information could improve learning. Results of these studies are inconclusive and mixed (Curry, 1990). Cognitive psychologists moved away from study of basic general learning strategies to studies of expert-novice performers (Moran, 1991).

Research shows that experts use sophisticated processing strategies and have highly developed, complex mental structures for organizing and interpreting information. Experts also possess substantial amounts of knowledge about particular topics. In contrast novices seemingly concentrate on specific parts of a problem and fail to use the "big picture" in explanation or interpretation (Darling-Hammond & Snyder, 1992).

Why People Learn.   Unlike reinforcement motivation, no single cognitive view of motivation exists. Instead a number of explanations share the belief that people are motivated to learn to satisfy intrinsic or internal needs such as those for competence, autonomy, or satisfying curiosity. Competence frequently manifests itself as exploration and mastery attempts in a variety of behaviors (White, 1959). Curiosity is motivating because people are predisposed to obtain pleasure from activities and events that provide some amount of surprise or discrepancy from expectations (Berlyne, 1966). Other investigators have shown that people develop in order to control their own lives—to be autonomous (deCharms, 1968, 1984; Deci, 1975).

Cognitive views of motivation suggest that children and youth may respond initially to learning opportunities because of external rewards or reinforcements. In time children accept the values of their social surroundings and, with this acceptance, learners internalize these values as part of self-regulation (Stipek, 1993). Additional information on self-regulation follows in the next subsection.

In summary, each cognitive perspective hypothesizes that language facilitates development and that learners use their individual mental processes in generating their own learning. All forms of learning, including declarative and procedural knowledge, affective learning and motor skills, are learnable under cognitive perspectives. Exercise 6.2 provides an opportunity for you to check your *general* understanding of these perspectives on cognitive-intellectual development.

EXERCISE 6.2

Reflect on the cognitive perspectives of *cognitive-intellectual* development. Then read the following situation.

Ms. Haney, a high school computer science teacher, frequently uses cooperative learning strategies in which mixed-ability learner groups collaborate in efforts to master skills. Sometimes the groups provide instruction for their members. Although the actual procedures vary, students must work together toward a common goal. This goal is reached only when each group member masters the skill.

1. Explain how this situation takes advantage of learners' language abilities.
2. Describe the extent to which students' learning in this situation can be considered generative.
3. Based on the information given, which learning domains and types of outcomes are likely in the situation?
4. Compare and contrast the situations in Exercises 6.1 and 6.2 in terms of teacher and student roles. Describe the extent to which the contrasts may be a function of learners' ages and/or subject matter.

SOCIAL-PERSONAL-MORAL DIMENSIONS

Piaget was also interested in the development of children's affect and moral judgment. This subsection broadens the discussion of developmentalism to include his work in these areas and features contributions from other researchers on social, personal, and moral dimensions of development.

Social-Personal Development.   Piaget's studies show that concurrently with their cognitive-intellectual-language development, children and youth develop through stages in social relations. Young children and young adolescents typically exhibit egocentrism, that is, considering an event from their own point of view. Young children, for example, may suggest taking their mothers to the local fast food restaurant to celebrate Mother's Day, because that's where *they* like to celebrate. However, when children begin socialized speech at about age 6 or 7, they also develop sociocentric social relations that allow them to consider events from someone else's perspective. But, when the growth spurt strikes, teenagers begin to worry unless they look, talk, and feel like their peers. Many youth return to egocentric ways and interpret the social actions of peers and family in terms of themselves (Wadsworth, 1984).

An integral part of social relations is self-regulation or self-discipline. A defining characteristic of all living systems, self-regulation extends Piaget's biologically based principles to affective development. Some areas in which children and youth seek self-regulation include "increasing social independence, integrating social relations in the individual's behavior, internalizing exterior actions into internal and abstract actions, developing a sense of personal control, and controlling one's own development" (Flammer, 1991, p. 1001).

Young children usually depend on adults for direction about activities both at school and at home, provided adults are available. As learners develop, however, they progress to coregulation, a transition stage between dependence and self-regulation in which they share power and authority with adults (Maccoby, 1984). Here adults provide general control, but learners increase the range of activities for which they assume responsibility. By the time children become adolescents, many are self-regulating.

One function of adolescent peer-group activities such as phone calls and journal keeping is "to experience social roles, to try out intellectual and emotional perspectives, to dialogue and to debate" (Flammer, 1991, p. 1002). By engaging in such activities, adolescent learners sometimes learn better organization of their own work through sharing, thinking from different perspectives in debate, or clarifying their own emotions and needs (Flammer, 1991).

Erikson provides useful information on personal-social development from a perspective modeled on Freud's psychoanalytic theory. Erikson conceives of social development as a series of crises in need of resolution. He poses each of these as a challenge in which positive and negative traits exhibit themselves (Erikson, 1963). Ideally, as learners rise to meet these challenges, they develop more positive than negative traits (Eggen & Kauchak, 1994).

By the time children begin kindergarten they are probably moving out of the initiative-versus-guilt crisis. In this stage children increase their cognitive boundaries and are likely to initiate many locomotor and mental activities, some of which may not be appreciated by family or teachers. As with all the stages, the ideal is to maintain some balance between initiative and guilt—too much of either would do children a disservice (Eggen & Kauchak, 1994; Erikson, 1963).

At about age 6, children enter the industry-versus-inferiority stage. Because learners begin to develop their self-concepts during this period, children need to be successful and show accomplishment as a result of their industry. Learners who are thwarted in their quests may develop a sense of inferiority that is difficult to overcome. Teachers and peers have much influence during this stage. Erikson advocates that children "need and enjoy hours of make-believe games and play, but they become dissatisfied with too much of this and want to do something worthwhile. They want to earn recognition by producing something, to gain the satisfaction of completing work by perseverance" (Thomas, 1992, p. 170).

As learners become adolescents, they usually enter the identity-versus-role confusion phase. Given the events of their lives, this stage is named appropriately. Most students change physically, experience new feelings of sexuality, and don't know what to do about them. Concerned about what their peers think, they may experience ambivalent feelings about family members. Above all, students want to know who they are. By early adolescence "self" begins to be understood in more enduring and general terms. By late adolescence some youth systematize the many disparate features of self (Daman, 1991). If they are able to establish their identity during this period, their lives probably proceed more smoothly than if they do not (Eggen & Kauchak, 1994; Erikson, 1963; Thomas, 1992).

Moral Development.   While children develop in other dimensions, they also develop morally. Piaget assumed that cognition and affect developed on parallel tracks and that moral judgment was a naturally developing cognitive process (Reimer, Paolitto, & Hersh, 1983). Piaget (1965) describes moral development as moving from other-oriented to self-oriented moral judgments. Early judgments reflect children's understanding of what parents or authorities conceive as morally acceptable. But at about age 10, as an outgrowth of intellectual development, children's moral structures become more flexible and internally defined (Ward, 1991).

Kohlberg devised a theory of moral development centered on the bases of children's judgments of moral issues. Most young children as well as some older students and a few adults operate at the preconventional level. They follow society's rules of right and wrong, but only in terms of consequences for themselves (Kohlberg, 1967). For example, undesirable consequences typically await people caught with their hands in the cookie jar or those who receive speeding tickets. According to the preconventional level, what's wrong is getting caught (Kaus, Lonky, & Roodin, 1984; Reimer, Paolitto, & Hersh, 1983).

Older children and many adults operate at the conventional level in which they conform to the expectations of others—family, group, or nation. Their actions are guided by the principle "What if everyone did it?" In this level learners recognize that positive relationships among people are based on what they do and how they act toward others. In general, the Golden Rule is the governing idea (Kaus, Lonky, & Roodin, 1984; Reimer, Paolitto, & Hersh, 1983). Highlights of moral reasoning and other social-personal development are displayed in Table 6.3.

To summarize, as learners develop cognitively, they develop in other dimensions as well. Social development is typically egocentric to sociocentric. Following a similar sequence, moral development proceeds from concern for self-consequences to consequences for others.

HUMANISTIC VIEWS OF DEVELOPMENT

Humanistic views of learners are newer than either behavioral or cognitive views, having started about mid-20th century. Whereas behavioral psychologists study

TABLE 6.3

Highlights of Social-Personal-Moral Development of Children and Youth at Three Levels of Schooling

Dimension	Early Childhood and Primary Grades	Elementary School	Middle–Senior High School
Social relations	Egocentrism; play significant	Sociocentrism	Egocentrism gives way to sociocentrism
Social regulation	Largely dependent on adults	Coregulation with adults	Coregulation gives way to self-regulation
Psychosocial development	Initiative versus guilt; beginning industry versus inferiority	Industry versus inferiority	Identity versus role confusion
Moral reasoning	Preconventional	Usually conventional	Usually conventional

performance or behavior, humanistically oriented psychologists study individuals' thoughts and feelings about their personal experiences. Their methods of study are introspection directed toward assisting learners in the **development of self**.

Humanistic theories hold that "the biologically determined inner nature of the human consists of basic needs, emotions, and capacities that are either neutral or positively good" (Thomas, 1992, p. 403). Cruelty and malice are not inborn, but are reactions against frustrations of needs, emotions, and capacities (Maslow, 1968). According to **humanistic views**, development, therefore, fosters the expression of learners' inner natures so they are subject to the least number of unfavorable experiences.

Several psychologists contribute to the literature on humanistic views of development. Among these are Combs and Snygg (1959), Allport (1961), Kelley (1962), and Mahrer (1978). Although these individuals do not agree on details, they adopt the idea that development is largely a function of nature or heredity. Children inherit potentials for growth and self-fulfillment. But the potentials do not materialize unless the circumstances are favorable and foster their development (Thomas, 1992).

As the previous comments suggest, humanistic psychologists have concerned themselves very little with cognitive-intellectual development. Instead, they study individuals' growth and changes of the personal self. Maslow's (1968) work, which embodies the major ideas of humanistic psychology and is known to many educators, forms the basis for the following discussion.

Maslow (1968) proposes that people develop to fulfill certain needs. As Maslow used the term, a *need* exists if its absence breeds illness, its presence prevents illness, or its restoration cures illness. Such needs form a hierarchy of lower to higher-level needs, with lower needs taking precedence over the higher needs. They include the following:

• Physiological needs for air, fulfilling the appetites, rest.

• Safety needs for security and stability, freedom from fear and anxiety.

- Belongingness and love needs for family, friends, affection, rootedness.
- Esteem needs for self-respect and for the esteem of others.

People also have growth needs (Maslow, 1987) toward which they strive once most of their deficiency needs are met. Growth needs are individual and insatiable because they involve the following:

- Knowing and understanding—intellectual achievement.
- Order, truth, and beauty—aesthetic appreciation.
- Self-actualization—doing that for which a person is individually fitted.

People fulfill their needs through psychological development which corresponds generally to two levels of biological change, childhood and adolescence. Children begin life without clear definitions of "self" but gradually attain an understanding of who they are as a result of their exchanges with other people and experiences. In humanistic psychology people grow gradually out of being one kind of individual toward being another.

A person is motivated toward "ongoing actualization of potentials, capacities and talents, as fulfillment of mission . . . as a fuller knowledge of, and acceptance of, the person's own intrinsic nature, as an unceasing trend toward unity, integration . . . within the person" (Maslow, 1968, p. 25). Although time and experience are necessary for the self to emerge, just growing older does not assure self-actualization. Many adolescents and adults do not achieve psychological maturity.

This brief discussion of humanistic views of development completes the presentation on nurture, nature, and interaction theories. Exercise 6.3 is designed to help you clarify your values regarding the nature of learners. This self-knowledge is important for all who work in curriculum.

EXERCISE 6.3

This exercise is intended to help you in clarifying your values and beliefs about learners and learning processes. Specifically, do you view their development primarily as a function of nurture, nature, or interaction of nurture and nature? Figures 2.1 and 2.2 provide basic information about valuing processes. You may find rereading these sections helpful.

1. Reconsider how you relate to learners or those you supervise in your professional position. How many choices or degrees of freedom do these individuals have in their activities? Consider your "usual" ways, rather than any adopted for special occasions. Write two or three sentences expressing your thoughts.
2. Next, reconsider the basic descriptions of behavioral, cognitive, and humanistic views of development. Jot down two or three major ideas representative of each view.
3. With which view of development do your actions best match?
4. How do you feel about the match? Pleased? Concerned? Sad?
5. Do you plan to continue with your usual ways? Why or why not?

PHYSICAL DEVELOPMENT

Physical changes in learners occur simultaneously with development in other dimensions and are discussed here because of their influence in other dimensions. Most noticeable, of course, are overall changes in body size. Children grow rapidly during their first few months, but growth slows in early and middle childhood; learners add about 2 to 3 inches in height and 5 pounds in weight each year. Growth rates again accelerate at puberty and "adolescents add nearly 10 inches in height and about 40 pounds in weight to reach a mature body size" (Berk, 1994, p. 177). Body proportions and composition also change over the school-age span.

In early childhood and primary grades, children of the same chronological age differ in physical size, depending on genetic factors and nutrition, but this is not a problem because the peer group matters little to learners at this age. Children at play make extensive use of their energy in gross motor skills, which means they also require rest periods. In the early grades children's fine motor skills and eye-hand coordination are not well developed. Some have difficulty focusing on small print or objects (Biehler & Snowman, 1993). Because girls generally handle distractions well, they forge ahead of boys in fine motor skill development (Eggen & Kauchak, 1994).

During elementary grades children grow slowly and steadily, but smaller children usually catch up with their peers. However, because learners at this age begin exerting their autonomy, they are sometimes less active and eat less nutritious diets than they did earlier. This can lead to problems with physical fitness (Eggen & Kauchak, 1994). Near the end of elementary school most students begin a growth spurt. Because girls typically begin their spurts a couple of years earlier than boys (Berk, 1994; Tanner, 1991), middle school girls usually tower over boys of the same age. In those two years boys' legs continue growing so that men are usually taller than women (Tanner, 1991).

Delayed growth spurts can worry boys. In early adolescence physical size differences are important because of peer group pressures for conformity. When the growth spurt arrives, students, particularly boys, usually experience awkwardness and clumsiness that can also negatively affect their social and personal development (Berk, 1994).

As a result of their growth spurts, both sexes change physical features, and become physically mature. The biological changes in achieving physical maturity typically affect most students' social and personal development because peer group and friends' reactions are extremely important. For students who do not intend to continue their education, there's concern for life after graduation. Finally, most students feel the need to make personal value decisions about using drugs, premarital sex, and codes of ethics (Biehler & Snowman, 1993). Table 6.4 highlights physical development at different levels of schooling.

ATYPICAL DEVELOPMENTAL PATTERNS

So far this chapter has described normative learner development. However, development does not always follow norms because of genetic, trauma, biological, and/or

TABLE 6.4
Highlights of Normative Physical Development of Children and Youth at Three Levels of Schooling

Early Childhood and Primary Grades	Elementary School	Middle–Senior High School
Gross motor skills refined; fine motor skills develop; wide range in physical sizes among children of same age	Physical growth slow and steady; physical fitness may become an issue	Dramatic differences in growth rates; females mature more rapidly than males

psychological environmental factors. Some children are born with or acquire learning problems or physical impairments that prevent their "normal" development.

Provisions of the Individuals with Disabilities Education Act (Public Law 94-142) made clear that all children, regardless of disability, must have free appropriate public education. This law states that learners with disabilities must be educated in the most normal environment possible (Haring, 1994). Though some learners with disabilities require special placements, many receive most or all their schooling in regular classrooms in inclusion programs.

This section briefly describes atypical patterns of learner development in two major categories, learning problems and physical impairments. The description points out some needs and interests of learners who deviate from the norms.

LEARNING PROBLEMS

For this discussion children/youth with learning problems include those who display giftedness, mental retardation, learning disabilities, or behavioral problems. These individuals exhibit atypical patterns of cognitive-intellectual and or social-personal-moral development.

Giftedness.   Giftedness is associated with advanced cognitive-intellectual development. In the past gifted learners were those with high scores on intelligence tests. However, researchers[1] have broadened the concept of intelligence, so this definition is less meaningful. Although giftedness is now generally considered more than high intelligence, no universally accepted definition exists (Wolf, 1994).

What is agreed is that both the nature of content and the rate of presentation may need modification for gifted students. Creativity, intellectual initiative, critical thinking, social adjustment, responsibility, and leadership should be emphasized. Gifted students are able to grasp and master complex concepts (Wolf, 1994).

---

[1] Gardner (1983) favors seven intelligences: linguistic, logical-mathematical, musical, spatial, body-kinesthetic, interpersonal, and intrapersonal. Sternberg (1985) suggests intelligence as the interaction of the learner's internal and external worlds as demonstrated in experience.

Mental Retardation.   At the opposite extreme on the cognitive-intellectual development continuum is mental retardation, which ranges from mild to profound. Mild retardation is reflected by learners who, before age 18, demonstrate significant subaverage general intellectual functioning (IQ scores of about 70 to 75) and deficits in adaptive behavior (American Association on Mental Retardation, 1992). Adaptive skill limitations are evident in two or more of these areas: communication, self-care, home living, social skills, community use, self-direction, health and safety, functional academics, leisure, and work.

Curriculum options for these individuals must be sensitive to their current and future needs while at the same time challenging them. The content, sequence, and pace of instruction may have to be adjusted. As students age, curricula should increasingly emphasize vocational and life skills (Patton & Polloway, 1994).

Learners with IQ test scores lower than 70 and concomitant scores on measures of adaptive functioning are often characterized as having moderate, severe or profound disabilities. Many individuals in these categories also have other disabilities such as vision, hearing, health and physical impairments that complicate their lives. Because learners in this group are very different from each other, careful evaluation of these individuals' abilities is necessary to plan their curricula. In the main, curricula for these students are organized by life-skill domains and geared to functional, contextually based skills (Wolery & Haring, 1994).

Learning Disabilities.   Children and youth with learning disabilities also display atypical patterns of cognitive-intellectual development. These individuals have an academic problem in one or more areas, that "is not due primarily to emotional disability, mental retardation, visual or auditory impairment, motor disability, or environmental disadvantage" (Mercer, 1994, p. 117). The areas include understanding or using language, reasoning, or mathematical abilities. Said simply, these students are unable to achieve because of learning difficulties.

A heterogeneous group, children with learning disabilities may also have deficits in metacognitive abilities (i.e., thinking about their own thinking), hyperactivity, or problems with language, perception, motor abilities, social-emotional concerns, memory, or attention (Mercer, 1994). Assessing students' learning disabilities is complex and a necessary first step in preparing curricula to meet their needs.

Behavioral Problems.   Learners with behavioral problems have atypical patterns of social-personal-moral development. These are people "who do and say things that interfere substantially with the appropriate functioning of both themselves and others" (Cullinan & Epstein, 1994, p. 169). Sometimes behavior disorders are referred to as emotional disturbances or maladjustments. Learners "may exhibit little or no classroom participation, communication, or other interaction at play or in other contexts; excessive physical aggression, threats, disobedience, destructiveness, or moving around; a lack of basic academic and school readiness skills . . . ; verbal and other extreme fear, sadness, guilt, or self-doubt" (Cullinan & Epstein, 1994, p. 169). Behavioral disorders range from mild to severe. In most cases these learners need training in social skills to promote positive interactions with the adults who work with them.

PHYSICAL IMPAIRMENTS

Children and youth with physical impairments such as visual handicaps, hearing difficulties, or communication disorders may or may not develop according to norms for cognitive, social, and personal change. If physically impaired learners also have cognitive or social difficulties, these must be handled as part of curriculum development and can require specially designed curricula. However, if impairments do NOT involve cognitive or social difficulties, accommodations can usually be made when the curriculum is used in classrooms. Such accommodations include special seating arrangements or equipment (e.g., hearing aids, computers) that permit student access to the curriculum content.

STUDIES OF LEARNERS APPLIED IN CURRICULUM PROCESSES

Studies of learners and their environments contribute to all the curriculum processes. This section highlights these contributions; then, beginning in Chapter 7 these implications are applied in the discussion of initiating curriculum development.

DEVELOPMENT

Nurture, nature, and interaction assumptions about learners usually evoke alternative content selections and projected roles for curriculum users. Although the dominant purpose of education is "cultivating cognitive achievement and the intellect," developers sometimes choose a purpose of education that focuses on learners. This subsection briefly describes both situations.

Purposes and Content Selection.   Developers who place high priority on learners sometimes choose as their purpose of education, "to develop individuals to their fullest potentials." For example, some early childhood curriculum planners use this purpose. These developers, who subscribe to the *nature* perspective of learners, act on this purpose by developing a curriculum that attends to the needs and interests of learners. This action is necessary to enable students to become whomever they are capable of becoming. This purpose does NOT guarantee that students *want* to learn any differently than they do in curricula with other purposes. However, selection of this purpose ensures that the curriculum focuses on people and their needs, rather than subject matter.

Developers who adhere to *nurture* or *interaction* perspectives usually choose an alternative purpose of education. But they may acknowledge the needs and interests of students in curriculum content selections. For example, in a curriculum with the purpose "helping people live in an unstable changing world" the content should include important social issues for young people, such as environmental and health concerns.

By choosing content that interests students, planners with the purpose of "cultivating cognitive achievement and the intellect" expect more and better achievement than if the content disregards students' interests. Developers acknowledge learner *intellectual* interests by letting learners choose subject matter topics or presentation methods (e.g., videos, computer simulations). Developers also acknowledge learners' *social* interests by providing for collaborative as well as individual projects. Planners acknowledge the needs of atypical learners when they arrange scope-continuity-sequence content considerations that accommodate learners' capabilities and particular needs.

By acknowledging learner needs and interests, curriculum developers, depending on their particular views, help foster development in pertinent dimensions. The following illustrations are based on information in this chapter:

1. Learners of any age who are exposed to a variety of models have more opportunities to develop than those in situations with few models. [See behavioral views of cognitive-intellectual or social-personal development.]
2. Curriculum has the potential to help learners through crises in psychosocial development by providing essentially positive experiences that help resolve the challenges at different psychosocial stages. [See cognitive views of social-personal development.]
3. Young children who have multiple language experiences that increase their language abilities may move more rapidly than they would otherwise into the next stage of development. [See cognitive views of cognitive-intellectual development.]

Regardless of which purpose of education the curriculum serves, its content must be learnable by the students. Again, developers' assumptions about learners influence their definitions of this term. Here are examples from both behavioral and cognitive views. Planners who subscribe to *operant conditioning* must sequence information appropriately so that learners can succeed in their performances, that is, receive reinforcement. For the same reason, these developers must also be sure that learners have the prerequisites for any new information presented.

Planners with a cognitive *developmental* orientation tend to ensure that content is appropriate for the intellectual or reasoning capabilities of learners. Developers with a cognitive *structural* perspective arrange the content so that its structure is clear to the learners. In the *cognitive science* orientation planners investigate the extent of students' prior learning (i.e., kinds of knowledge and their interrelationships) related to the new content. This is an indicator of the degree to which learners are likely to encode new content.

Projected Roles for Classroom Users of Curricula. In creating curricula, developers project roles expected in its delivery in classrooms. Sometimes role expectations for teachers and staff are stated directly. Other times, expectations must be inferred by the types of learning expected of students. For example, developers with a nurture orientation typically expect learners to "receive" knowledge. Someone or something within learners' environments prompts their actions because the source of learner activity is external. In these cases instructional delivery is planned substantially as one-way communication (e.g., reading, viewing, or answering questions). Such circumstances assign students to passive or reactive roles where learning is receiving information, or knowledge that someone else generates and/or organizes. This is a time-efficient way of helping students learn.

Students often learn attitudes or other affective behaviors through conditioning or modeling. Also, they can learn declarative or extensive knowledge and motor skills through behavioral approaches because these types of learning call for performance that can be taught through direct instruction or modeling. However, because so many situations exist in which problem solving is necessary, not all of them can be presented by teaching agents using conditioning or modeling. Students who learn the steps in problem solving, including their labels and descriptions, may not know *how* or *when* to *apply* problem solving strategies if the dominant approach is behavioral learning.

On the other hand, developers with interaction or nature orientations typically expect learners to generate their own knowledge because the impetus for learning is, at least partly, within learners. Instructional delivery is projected as discussions, projects, problem solving experiences, and other two-way communication with teachers, peers, and other teaching agents. Such circumstances invite learners to engage in learning, to organize and build their own mental structures. Given the opportunity, learners generate the different types of learning outcomes mentioned in Chapter 4. Although this approach requires time, self-generated knowledge is useful in a variety of situations.

CLASSROOM USE

Knowledge of learners contributes to each planning consideration in classroom use. For example, the *scope and complexity* of curriculum use changes as students, formerly in special education, are mainstreamed into regular classrooms. Regular classroom teachers require *professional development* to understand the developmental backgrounds of these learners, and in many cases, the new demands on teachers precipitate more and newer forms of *communication* among teachers, students, parents/guardians, and administrators.

Additional information about learners' development and the learning processes should be incorporated in curricula as it becomes available. For the information to make a difference, however, curriculum *users* must know and understand it. While professional development can sometimes help, some curriculum users are reluctant to change their views about learners and learning processes because these are inextricably related to their values.

EVALUATION

Curriculum evaluation is affected by studies of learners to the extent that considerations about learners are taken into account in the curriculum. This means, for example, that a curriculum that focuses on learners uses evaluation strategies different from subject matter-based curricula. With the learner-based purpose, there is an obligation to collect and analyze individual learner data with instruments sensitive to personal behaviors (e.g., observations, self-reports) and use these data to describe individual growth and development patterns.

Within subject matter curricula, curriculum evaluation differs depending on the type of learning expected of students. Where students are expected to "receive" information, evaluation procedures use convergent approaches that stress "right" answers. Standardized achievement tests typically require this type of evaluation, by asking students to sort through several responses to multiple choice questions for the correct answer.

On the other hand, where learners generate their own knowledge, evaluation must handle divergent outcomes and processes. Some state and national assessment programs focus on process-oriented evaluation by using questions such as, "How many ways can the outside dimensions of a wastebasket be measured?" or "Write a letter to your state legislator expressing your view on how air pollution should be managed." Scoring such evaluation procedures, of course, requires expertise and time.

SUMMARY

Curriculum development and use require educators to consider their views of the nature of learners in their environments. Those who believe that learners should be nurtured usually adopt a behavioral view of development. This view holds that learners develop in cognitive, social, and personal dimensions in response to events and or people in their environments through conditioning or observational learning. Evidence of development is incremental and shown by learners' behaviors or performances.

In contrast, cognitivists believe learners are products of the interaction of heredity and their environments. Learners develop in cognitive, social, and personal dimensions to satisfy internal needs. Development in one dimension may hinge on development in other dimensions. Cognitive perspectives emphasize learners' mental processes by which they generate their own unique knowledge.

Humanists adopt the notion that learners are born with the seeds of their potentials and that development fosters expression of the self. Learner development, then, is the fulfillment of a hierarchy of needs with the ultimate goal of self-actualization.

Learners' physical development is important to curriculum workers to the extent that physical changes affect development in other dimensions. These changes are most noticeable at adolescence when learners experience physical maturation.

Curriculum workers must also consider that all learners do not develop according to age level norms. This is particularly important because learners with relatively mild learning problems or physical impairments increasingly receive instruction in regular classrooms. Needs and interests of these individuals must be addressed in the curricula.

Studies of learners affect all curriculum processes, but these studies are especially important in content selection criteria. Developers' choices of content are influenced, at least in part, by their views of whether the content meets learners' needs and interests and whether it is learnable. Developers manifest their views also in whether learners are expected to receive or generate knowledge.

QUESTIONS FOR DISCUSSION

1. With which position described in the section titled Nurture, Nature, or Interaction do you feel most comfortable? Does your professional position allow you to act on the basis of your values and beliefs? Explain.

2. This chapter shows that behaviorists, cognitivists, and humanists define "development" differently. Of what importance are these differences in the context of the curriculum processes?

3. Assertive Discipline, a program for classroom management, has been widely used in schools across the United States. The program has three parts: teachers establish specific directions for activities and make sure students know how to behave. When students follow the rules, teachers provide reinforcement. If students do not follow rules, negative consequences are invoked (Canter, 1989). Identify advantages and disadvantages of this program as an aid to learners' development for educators who subscribe to the nurture orientation. To the interaction orientation? To the nature orientation?

4. Identify some advantages and disadvantages of observational learning as an explanation of development.

5. For the particular ages/levels of learners with whom you work (early childhood-primary, elementary, or adolescence), relate the main events in cognitive-intellectual development to those in social-personal-moral development, using the *cognitive developmental* perspective.

6. With which types of development, cognitive-intellectual or social-personal-moral, does physical development share the strongest relationships? Explain.

7. As a teacher or school staff member, to what extent does the curriculum in your school take into account the needs and interests of learners with atypical developmental patterns? Given the opportunity, what modifications would you recommend to curriculum planners? Explain.

8. This chapter mentioned "receptive" and "generative" knowledge several times. Why is this distinction important? Identify at least two original examples of each type of knowledge.

IMPORTANT IDEAS DISCUSSED INITIALLY IN THIS CHAPTER

learner-environment relationships
  nurture
  nature
  interaction of nature and nurture
behavioral views of development
  learning
  receptive learning
  operant conditioning
  observational learning

cognitive views of development
  learning
  generative learning
  developmentalism
  cognitive structuralism
  cognitive science
humanistic views of development
  development of self
  atypical developmental patterns

· ·

PART THREE

CREATION AND VALIDATION OF CONTENT FOR CURRICULUM PROJECTS

Part 3 begins the formal study of institutional curriculum development and depends heavily on information from parts 1 and 2. As the backgrounds of different curriculum conceptions show, educators typically prefer to react to events in society and culture rather than take the lead. As a result, we usually deal with incremental rather than large-scale changes. An opportunity to create a completely new curriculum or to completely revise a curriculum is unusual.

However, whether educators revise a curriculum or develop a new one, curriculum development is "messy," nonlinear, and complicated. Working through the development processes requires knowledge of content, pedagogy, the context, and the curriculum processes. Good human relations skills are also useful in situations where planners have to reconcile differing values and manage several variables at once. Depending on the magnitude of the project, curriculum development can take weeks, months, or longer.

Part 3 contains five chapters designed to help you develop and validate curriculum content using technical and nontechnical approaches. Chapters 7, 8, 10 and 11 each have three or more major sections. Beginning sections in each chapter *describe* the curriculum development processes involved with one of these topics: views of education statements (Chapter 7), content (Chapter 8), learning outcomes and learning experiences in technically developed curricula (Chapter 10), and learning experiences in nontechnically developed curricula (Chapter 11).

The middle sections of each chapter contain *evaluations* of actual curriculum projects, and you are invited to evaluate several projects. Through the study of real world curricula, you can increase your knowledge of the curriculum processes.

Final sections of these chapters offer suggestions on *how to engage* in the curriculum development processes. The results of using these suggestions show in the abbreviated versions of two curricula. Using a technical approach, a health curriculum segment for elementary school students is developed for the purpose, "cultivating cognitive achievement and the intellect." Chapter 7 contains its views statement; Chapter 8, the content statement; and Chapter 10, the learning outcomes and learning experiences. Using a nontechnical approach, an English literature curriculum segment for high school students is developed for the purpose, "developing learners to their fullest potentials." Chapter 7 contains its views statement; Chapter 8, the content statement; and Chapter 11, the learning experiences.

Chapter 9 centers on needs assessment, which is a means of validating content or seeing that it fits its intended context. Three sections *describe* the evaluation processes involved in studying educational contexts. The final section provides suggestions about *how to engage* in needs assessment through planning and specifically refers to needs assessments that might be used in conjunction with the health and English literature curricula developed in Part 3 chapters.

As indicated earlier, most curriculum development efforts call for revisions of existing curricula. Therefore, Chapter 9 has this sequence because the author believes curriculum development groups should consider the purpose of education for their intended project before needs assessment. If the purpose of the intended project is the same as that of the existing curriculum, needs assessment can initiate the curriculum process. However, if the purpose of the intended project differs from the current purpose, curriculum planners must think about that purpose and decide the content necessary for helping students reach the intended purpose, before engaging in needs assessment. For example, changing the purpose from "cultivating cognitive achievement" to "developing learners to their fullest potentials" alters the focus on subject matter. In the first case the focus is squarely on understanding subject matter. In the second case the focus is on developing students' potentials through the use of subject matter.

7

VIEWS OF EDUCATION STATEMENTS FOR CURRICULUM PROJECTS

OUTLINE

How do curriculum developers begin the work of creating or revising curriculum? Some start with a needs assessment if the purpose for the curriculum is unchanged. However, if the purpose is undecided, developers must agree on it before undertaking needs assessment, the topic of Chapter 9.

Clarifying the purpose of education, deciding the roles of teachers and staff in curriculum delivery, and relating the curriculum to the community are tasks in the creation of **views of education statements**. These are important because they guide subsequent curriculum decisions.

This chapter begins with a discussion of planning considerations and change processes, two elements in initiating curriculum projects. Groups who understand and employ these processes advantageously usually develop successful curriculum projects. Curriculum developers work out views of education statements similar to those you are studying here. This chapter also provides the opportunity for you to see how views statements might be formulated for two hypothetical curriculum projects. As a result of studying this chapter, you should be able *to evaluate views of education statements in curriculum documents and to prepare the views of education statement for a curriculum project of your choice.*

INITIATION OF CURRICULUM PROJECTS

Successful educational innovations are characterized by careful attention to the initiation processes (Fullan, 1991). This is not surprising because innovations, especially curriculum revisions, involve many people who may hold different views about schools and purposes of education. As noted previously, community and school personnel typically use social and political processes to work through their differences concerning curriculum decisions.

Planning considerations including the scope and complexity of the curricular change, communication, professional development, and resources are described first as they pertain to the development processes in general. (These same considerations are also involved in planning for classroom use of curricula.) Then the section describes change processes for initiating curriculum projects.

PLANNING CONSIDERATIONS

Curriculum development takes place within district- or school-based groups, usually under the direction of an administrator. The composition of these groups varies depending on the type of governance and curriculum approach. Regardless of who else is involved, however, teachers must be included because they are charged with change processes in classrooms. To the extent that community members can be enticed to work on curriculum committees, they should also be included because they bring outside-of-school perspectives. These individuals may be parents/guardians or citizens interested in school affairs.

Scope and Complexity of the Curricular Change.   Whenever curricula are revised, the development group should be aware of the scope and complexity of the expected changes. *Scope* concerns the breadth of the curriculum to be developed. For example, does the curricular change affect K–12, grades 5–8, a single grade, or a single curriculum area? *Complexity* refers to the magnitude of the change. Adopting a different purpose of education occurs relatively infrequently, but is a complex change with many ramifications. Changing the emphases for learning outcomes (e.g., to higher order thinking skills, to include affective outcomes), though considerably less complex, is also somewhat infrequent.

Regardless of whether they are a district- or school-based team, curriculum developers should know clearly *why* they engage in planning. What problem do they expect to solve at least partially through development of a revised curriculum? What needs of students will be served? How will the community benefit? Without clear answers to questions such as these, curriculum planning may be perceived by those involved as a routine, mechanical activity unworthy of serious consideration. Ideally the intended changes should be large enough to require noticeable, sustained effort, but not so large as to overpower the developers (Crandall, Eiseman, & Louis, 1986).

Curriculum development initiatives usually result from changes in state curriculum guidelines. Such guidelines typically charge school districts with insuring that students have opportunities to learn curriculum content specified in state guidelines. However, the option of pursuing district- or school-level curricula is decided within the district.

Other curriculum development occurs when a community or school raises concerns over a need they believe is not accommodated in the curriculum. For example, concern for information literacy, multicultural education, or increased mathematics achievement can provide the impetus for curriculum development.

Curriculum groups sometimes equate curriculum development with textbook adoptions. Although the processes involved in adopting textbooks can involve curriculum development, those processes alone are not equivalent to curriculum development as envisioned in this text.

Communication.   Leaders of development teams should foster multiple forms of communication both among the participants and any people they represent. To the extent possible, all people affected by the curriculum revision must be aware of the curriculum development activities. School-based development groups may have better communication, because of their cohesiveness, than district groups. Open communication among the participants in curriculum development fosters necessary psychological transitions. As noted in Chapter 1, it's one thing to produce revised curricula on paper and quite another to revise curricula in classrooms.

Professional Development.   Curriculum revision can provide professional development for participants. It is an opportunity for participants to look at concerns through the eyes of fellow participants or outside consultants. Leaders who are sensitive to group needs often go out of their way to locate information sources that invigorate group discussions in curriculum planning sessions. Professional development can assist participants with the psychological transitions involved in curricular change through opportunities to discard outdated ideas (i.e., bring about endings) and to work through neutral zones.

Resources. Curriculum development requires time and energy from all the participants, including the leaders, and may well be the major resources needed. But participants' time sometimes requires extra compensation, and travel expenses-honoraria for outside consultants may also be necessary. Additional resources include instructional materials, supplies, and clerical assistance. Curriculum efforts short on resources are usually less successful than they would be with adequate funding.

CHANGE PROCESSES

Fullan (1991) reports research showing that successful change initiations combine relevance, readiness, and resources. **Relevance** as used here means the interaction of need, the practitioner's understandings of the innovation, and what the innovation offers teachers and students. Relevance issues are addressed, in part, in the scope and complexity of the change, but they also incorporate knowledge of the processes for curriculum development and the benefits of a revised curriculum.

Readiness involves the capacity of individuals and the organization to deal with the innovation (Fullan, 1991). Curriculum developers, both as individuals and as a team, want to know if the curriculum change addresses a perceived need, if the change is reasonable, and if they have time to deal with the processes. Chapter 1 suggests that schools show weak relationships among goals and outcomes and, as a result, are tested by *each* change effort. Therefore, successful curriculum development initiation requires that the number of change efforts occurring simultaneously be minimal; that the change be compatible with the school's culture; and that facilities, equipment, materials, and supplies be available for the change effort. As indicated in the previous section, **resources** are a must for curriculum development.

Exactly what makes a successful combination of relevance, readiness, and resources is unknown because many times these elements cannot be sorted out in advance. In these cases Fullan (1991) suggests initiating the change on a small scale, then using this beginning as leverage for further action. How these change processes operate is exemplified in the section titled Creation of Views of Education Statements.

Deciding on a views of education statement is typically the first task of curriculum development groups, whether district- or school-based. This task is easier when the planning considerations and change processes are thoroughly understood, at least by some group members. As you read the next section, remember that persons on curriculum groups may have very different ideas about the topics involved in a views of education statement. That's why curriculum decision making is considered sociopolitical.

VIEWS OF EDUCATION AS GUIDES FOR CURRICULUM DECISIONS

As used in this text, a **views of education statement** is a vital part of every curriculum document because it contains the essence of the authors' views concerning a purpose for education, roles of teachers and school staffs in using the curriculum with students, and interrelationships of both with the community. The purpose of education is a general statement of the ultimate learning outcome for students. This purpose describes the curriculum developers' notions of how learners are expected to become self-sufficient, self-reliant, productive individuals; socially competent and effective; able to contribute to self and others; and capable of financial independence (Kaufman & Herman, 1991). As discussed previously, the purpose for education also implies the major source of content.

To enable students to meet the stated purpose, developers also project expectations for the relationships among teachers, school staff, students, curriculum content, and the community where the curriculum is used. For example, are teachers expected to make classroom use decisions independently or is decision making shared with students? To what extent are classrooms seen as microcosms of the larger society? Are the challenges of life outside classrooms to be acknowledged or discussed within classrooms? These are a few of the concerns curriculum developers consider as they formulate views of education. Figure 7.1 displays the relationships among the elements in views of education by showing that the purpose of education and the roles of curriculum users must be aligned within the school community.

PURPOSES OF EDUCATION

Developers select a purpose of education largely based on their values toward subject matter. Planners who view the acquisition of subject matter, in any of several forms, as highly important choose a purpose that emphasizes subject matter. Alternatively, planners who emphasize learners or society choose purposes of education in which subject matter serves as a means to these ends. See Figure 4.7.

Alterations in purposes require serious consideration by those affected, including the community and educators. Indeed, should a change be desired, the full range of sociopolitical processes at the local level should be involved. School governing boards establish direction for school systems and employ professional educators to move schools in those directions. Governing boards are responsible for adopting curriculum documents because these represent one major way that schools establish direction (Campbell, Carr, & Harris, 1989).

FIGURE 7.1
Relationships Among the Elements in a Views of Education Statement

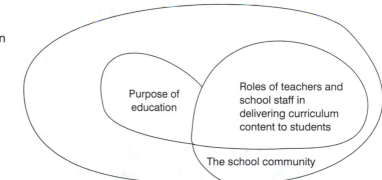

Purpose of education

Roles of teachers and school staff in delivering curriculum content to students

The school community

Chapter 3 discusses five purposes of education:

1. Cultivating cognitive achievement and the intellect.
2. Preparing people for living in an unstable changing world/reforming society.
3. Developing individuals to their fullest potentials.
4. Developing intellectual processes.
5. Making learning systematic and efficient.

These expressions communicate the gist of differences in purposes of education, but the expressions themselves rarely appear in curriculum documents. Rather, curriculum developers typically express their purpose as aims, wording them to clarify one of these expressions. Other developers convey purpose through definitions of *education* that embody their intentions for curriculum.

Broad statements that "give shape and direction to a set of more detailed intentions for the future" (Davies, 1976, p. 12) are called **aims**. By their nature, aims are general, philosophical, and long term. The purposes of education mentioned in the previous paragraph are aims statements. The *Cardinal Principles of Secondary Education* also illustrate aims with their references to health, command of the fundamental processes, worthy home-membership, and others (National Education Association, 1918). Concerned with an ideal that is not measurable, aims seek answers to the question, *why is the curriculum being taught* (Davies, 1976).

Dewey (1916) suggests three criteria for aims: They should 1) grow out of existing conditions, 2) be flexible, and 3) represent a freeing of activities. Dewey indicates clearly that aims should be based on what is already going on within a situation rather than on external activities. Aims imposed by outsiders could limit the planners to choices about means. In indicating that aims should be flexible, Dewey stresses that they must be capable of being altered to meet circumstances, some of which may be unforeseen until the outcomes are tested. Finally, in saying that aims represent a freeing of activities, Dewey expects that aims serve as ends-in-view. "Every means is a temporary end until we have attained it. Every end becomes a means of carrying activity further as soon as it is achieved" (Dewey, 1916, p. 124).

Curriculum developers devise aims to indicate the purpose of education for a district, but they also plan aims for particular programs compatible with those of the school district. Figure 7.2 contains part of the introduction to the curriculum project, *Multicultural Social Studies Curriculum K–12* (1993). The highlighted statement answers the question, "Why is this curriculum being taught?" Aims are revisited in Chapter 10 in the discussion of learning outcomes. (Note: The complete introduction for this curriculum guide is included in Appendix A1.)

Sometimes developers use broadly stated **definitions of education** to represent purposes. Here is an example of a definition from a governing board:

> We believe that education is a process of assisting all students to live and grow in an ever changing, technological society by helping them to acquire skills, attitudes, values and appreciations needed to become independent, creative, productive, sensitive, and self-actualized members of society. (*Computer Education Course of Study*, 1985, p. v)

This definition is elaborated further in a belief statement that calls for a flexible co-curricular program including cognitive and affective content and a strong

> The social studies curriculum is a conceptual catalyst for both teachers and students to gain knowledge, information, and power. The curriculum provides the resources and the opportunities for students to learn. It is assumed that they will *learn and mature into participatory citizens who are self-directed, collaborative workers, complex thinkers, community contributors, and quality producers.* . . .

FIGURE 7.2

Example of Aims Statements (Italics added to highlight aims)

From *Multicultural Social Studies Curriculum K–12,* 1993, p. 3. (Available from Tucson Unified School District No. 1, Tucson, AZ.) Reprinted by permission.

basic skills approach to thinking, reading, writing, speaking, and mathematics. By also considering the belief statement, the purpose emerges as "cultivating the cognitive achievement and intellect," the purpose of education commonly adopted in American schools.

Exercise 7.1 asks you to interpret definitions of education by connecting them to probable purposes of education. See how well you can handle these tasks.

EXERCISE 7.1

Identify the probable purpose of education implied in each of the following definitions of education. Explain.

1. Education is a process for imparting knowledge, skills, and attitudes, and can be undertaken privately or publicly, and in groups or individual situations.
2. Education is providing students with information and helping them to develop abilities and attitudes that will be beneficial to them in their current and future lives.
3. Education is the process of helping another individual become the best person s/he can be.
4. Education is learning about the world in which you live, the people with whom you live, and using this knowledge to make a better place for all.
5. Education is a growing process in which you continually learn about yourself—your hopes and dreams—from year to year throughout your life.

Developers use aims statements or definitions of education as vehicles for stating purposes of education. Through these statements, developers also commit themselves to content from particular sources and to a curriculum design. Recall from Chapters 3 and 4 that strong commitments to subject matter result in subject matter designs. However, commitments to the development of learners culminate in learner-based designs, and commitments to society emerge as social functions and activities designs.

PROJECTED FIT OF CURRICULUM WITH COMMUNITY

Because different people and ideas are represented, curriculum development groups consider their communities, school settings, students, and themselves as they work on a views of education. In most cases the intent of these considerations is to fit the curriculum to the school as it exists within society. Only rarely do curriculum groups attempt changes in the opposite direction.

Studies of society and culture show that the world outside of schools continues to change. As noted in Chapter 5, societal changes have produced major literacy issues. Curriculum developers must wrestle with questions such as, "Which literacy requirements should school curricula handle? Where will learners acquire literacy forms that are NOT part of school curricula?"

In addition, developers find their work complicated by the need to consider other social forces such as increasing cultural and language diversity among students for whom curricula are planned. Projections show that increasing numbers of students will come from seriously disadvantaged social and economic backgrounds. Because of changes in economic situations and social values, schools increasingly serve child-raising functions that were once handled by families. Not only do these require time and expertise from teachers and school staff, they also necessitate additional resources which are usually in short supply.

Several statements in the *Multicultural Social Studies Curriculum K–12* (1993) suggest that this curriculum should fit with the community-at-large. References in the introduction include the following:

> Our lives are affected every day by the challenges of change: political, economic, technological, social, and demographic. The Tucson community is charged with maintaining continuity within these changes. This change and continuity together become the main focus of history, government, and all facets of social studies affecting the lives of our students and the entire TUSD community, which is rich in diverse cultural heritage. (p. 2)
>
> The key challenge is the infusion of various perspectives, references, and content that extend the students' understanding of our complex global society. (p. 2)

These statements address the local context well, generally better than many district level curricula. However, school-based curriculum teams can sharpen the focus on the projected fit of curriculum to community.

Statements about the projected fit of curriculum with the community are necessary to guide the remainder of the curriculum development process. Unless developers consider community needs at the outset, it is doubtful that these will be considered in the remainder of the curriculum document.

PROJECTED ROLES FOR CURRICULUM USERS

The discussion of nurture, nature, and interaction showed that educators hold different views of learners in their environments. These beliefs about the locus of learner motivation affect the choice of learning emphases as well as the projected roles for teachers involved in curriculum delivery.

In school-based curriculum revision, developers are also curriculum users, which makes decisions about both tasks simpler than they are for district-based planners. Some curriculum users may be part of the district development team, but many others are not. Although creating content and projecting user roles is relatively easy, many people affected by these decisions are not involved in making them. Therefore, some individuals may be disinclined to adopt either the content or the projected role.

In the case of *Multicultural Social Studies Curriculum K–12* (1993) projected roles of curriculum implementers are not clearly delineated, but they can be inferred from reading the views of education statements. Several statements imply that teachers should arrange for students to interact with people and ideas within their environments. Here are two examples from the introduction:

> The teacher is a valuable resource, implementing change, and providing the learning environment for the student to understand the various concepts of social studies. (p. 3)
>
> At the elementary grade level through middle school and into high school the student spirals through data and learns to analyze and relate to the material and concepts. These courses of action involve creative problem-solving, thinking, and decision-making skills that empower both students and teachers. (p. 3)

Statements about the projected roles of those who deliver curriculum should be in the views of education for the same reasons that purpose of education and projected relationship with the community statements are there. These are expressions of values about the importance that developers place on certain ideas that will be spelled out as content to be taught in school. Moreover, if these statements are clear, readers do not have difficulty understanding the basis for the remainder of the curriculum document.

VIEWS OF EDUCATION STATEMENTS IN CURRICULUM PROJECTS

With respect to organization, views of education statements are the least standardized section in curriculum documents. Although all projects communicate their purposes, some curricula say little about expectations for teachers, school staff and students or community-society relationships in their views statements. District curriculum projects typically contain little or no information about the context in which the curriculum is to be used.

As illustrated by the curriculum projects in Appendix A, views of education are sometimes recorded in different sections, usually at the beginning of documents. These sections may be labeled philosophy, purpose, mission statement, introduction or have other labels or no name at all. The purpose of education, which is usually described within one of these sections, typically requires extrapolating meaning from one or more paragraphs that describe what the curriculum is supposed to do. Projected roles of curriculum users and the fit of the curriculum with the community are sometimes clearly stated so that developers' intentions are obvious. At other times projections must be inferred from the language of the views statements and are subject to misinterpretations.

Studying views of education statements prepared by other developers can help you think through your own views. How do other developers state their purpose of education? How do they describe the roles of teachers and school staff in delivering the curriculum content? What is the relationship of the curriculum to the school and the community?

To illustrate these points, this section evaluates the views statements in three curriculum documents, *Spanish IV Curriculum* (n.d.), *Into Adolescence: Caring for Our Planet and Our Health* (Hunter, 1991), and *Collaborative Teaching Experiences to Develop Communication Skills* (1992). The reviews discuss purposes of education, content emphases, designs, projected fit of the curriculum with society, and projected roles of curriculum implementers. See Exercise 7.2 for the questions on which these reviews are based. Refer to the questions and the curriculum projects in Appendix A as you read this section.

SPANISH IV CURRICULUM

This curriculum (see A4) for secondary students communicates its predominant purpose as "cultivating cognitive achievement and the intellect" throughout the entire section, Foreign Language Department Philosophy. Notice particularly these references: "It [language learning] enhances the student's ability to think logically, to reason, to memorize, to analyze, to read with inferencing, and to understand his own language." Developers also indicate that students who study foreign language add a new dimension to their personalities and improve understanding of themselves and others.

As noted in the Narrative Description, the content shows a clear emphasis on the subject matter of Spanish, even though language knowledge is applied in social situations. As stated in the philosophy, through this curriculum students are expected to acquire language proficiency, understand themselves and others, and become aware of cultural diversity. This project uses a single subject curriculum design.

The Spanish curriculum philosophy states quite clearly that students need to understand the complexity and cultural pluralism of modern society. Because language reflects culture, students who study this curriculum are expected to adapt better to the multiethnic structure of society than those who do not study foreign language. However, as is true with many district level curricula this one provides no clues to how Spanish could or should be related to students in this particular school district.

By implication, teachers of these students are charged with helping them meet expectations of the curriculum, but their roles are not well-defined. However, students are expected to generate their own knowledge as evidenced by statements such as these: " . . . hypothesize about the past . . . " and "encouraged to use the target language more spontaneously. . . . " Based on such statements, curriculum users are expected to view learners as interactive with their environments.

INTO ADOLESCENCE: CARING FOR OUR PLANET AND OUR HEALTH

This project (see A6) intends to "help people live in a rapidly changing unstable society," a purpose different from the one for *Spanish IV.* The theme of education for change continues throughout the opening sections and the content focuses on social problems in need of solutions. Stated purposes are to provide information about environmental crises, but more importantly to seek individual commitments from students for taking responsibility to do their part in solving the problems. As they develop, students are expected to deal with societal problems. This curriculum uses a social functions and activities design.

Into Adolescence is intimately connected with societal and cultural concerns in and beyond the school. Within the Overview the terms *planet, global issues,* and *rain forests* indicate the breadth of concerns. This curriculum stops short of advocating societal reform, but makes it clear that tomorrow's citizens need to know how to live in a changing world. This curriculum is not related to any particular local context. Users are expected to modify this curriculum to suit local needs.

Curriculum users are expected to arrange activities in which learners interact with their environments, according to implications in the views statements. Throughout this section is a clear call for action on the part of teachers and students to make a difference in the world with regard to pressing environmental concerns. Given the concern of encouraging students' personal commitment, teachers are challenged to work cooperatively with students in problem solving situations.

COLLABORATIVE TEACHING EXPERIENCES TO DEVELOP COMMUNICATION SKILLS

This curriculum (see A7) uses yet a third purpose for education: "to develop individuals to their fullest potentials." Through speech and language skills, this content is seen as serving the developmental needs of prekindergarten through fifth-grade students. The Philosophy statement indicates that teachers of speech-and-language-impaired (TSLI) students should work closely with classroom teachers to encourage the full development of communication skills by all students—at the time those skills develop.

In the appendix of this curriculum excerpt is "The Best Way to Teach: Be Responsive!" which elaborates on the idea around which this project is built, meeting children's needs and interests. Note in particular the references to children's engagement in self-initiated activity and adults working or playing with children at, rather than above, their developmental levels. This curriculum uses a developmental learner-based design.

This curriculum does not specifically refer to community or society, nor is it tied directly to a specific context. However, helping children develop communication skills has high priority and most educators recognize these skills as valued both in school and in the larger society.

Throughout the views statements, and particularly in "The Best Way to Teach," are references to children and teachers, including therapists, interacting in classroom activities. Children are expected to work with materials and generate communication related to their activities.

Exercise 7.2 challenges you to interpret the views of education statements in curriculum projects in Appendix A. See how well you can handle these tasks.

EXERCISE
7.2

Study the views of education statements for these curriculum projects in Appendix A:

- *A Guide for Developing a 1–9 Science Curriculum* (A2)
- *Middle School English Language Arts Curriculum* (A3)
- *Wyoming Arts Education Curriculum* (A5)

Then answer these questions for each project:

1. Identify and discuss the purpose of education and the content emphasis projected for the curriculum. Identify the curriculum design for any guide, course of study, or resource unit.
2. Describe interrelationships between the purpose of education and society-culture, either expressed or inferred in the views statement. Describe the extent to which the local context for the project is taken into account.
3. Describe expressed or inferred roles expected of teachers and school staff in delivering the curriculum to students.

CREATION OF VIEWS OF EDUCATION STATEMENTS

Creation of the views of education takes time because curriculum developers must explore and elaborate their often disparate ideas (e.g., how teachers should handle curriculum delivery). The remainder of the curriculum development processes should proceed smoothly if developers can reach consensus on their purpose, the curriculum's fit with the community, and expectations for curriculum delivery. Because of the need to choose wording carefully, views statements generally develop through several drafts.

As the discussion of views statements in curriculum projects shows, formats for views of education statements vary. Regardless of the format, however, curriculum developers must include the purpose of the curriculum project. In addition, developers who explain their views on subject matter, needs of society and culture, and needs and interests of learners provide helpful information to their readers. In particular curriculum guides and resource units should describe the roles of teachers and school staff in providing curriculum content to students.

The remainder of this section describes the activities of two curriculum development groups in the preparation of views of education statements for hypothetical institutional curricula. One district-level group uses the technical approach in working on the views statement for an elementary school health curriculum. The second group works on a nontechnical school-based English literature curriculum for senior high school students. As you read, note instances of the change processes of relevance and readiness, particularly.

Also, be aware of attempts to take into account the context for the English literature curriculum. The context for the health curriculum will be considered further when this district-based curriculum is translated to a school-based curriculum in Chapter 10. The following are illustrations only, not prescriptions for creating views statements.

HEALTH CURRICULUM

At this point imagine that you are the principal of a relatively small elementary school in a large urban school district. Your school houses three classrooms of students at each grade level 1 through 6 and four sections of kindergarten that meet half days. You have been asked to serve on a development team to develop a district-level health curriculum.

This information is good news to you because you are keenly aware that students in your school should practice better health habits. Students are frequently absent from school because of their own illnesses or because they stay home to care for ailing siblings. Children come from economically deprived backgrounds and their parents or guardians have little practical knowledge about health matters. You anticipate that using the new curriculum could provide at least a partial solution to some of these problems.

The development group has several elementary school teachers of self-contained classrooms as well as physical education teachers, a subject matter specialist from the district office, a consultant from the local university, and two community members. An assistant superintendent initially convenes the group and explains that new guidelines for health recently adopted by the state board of education must be used in the curriculum.

Within five years the district must provide evidence that students have mastered the essential skills for their grade levels. The guidelines, which were crafted by citizens and school representatives from across the state, are expected to upgrade health curricula by integrating several important areas into health curricula (e.g., disease prevention and control, substance abuse prevention) that were formerly scattered in other subject areas or left untaught.

The assistant superintendent explains that district-level curriculum development efforts in other subject areas must remain on hold until the health curriculum is developed. The assistant superintendent also says the district office will communicate with parents and guardians the important points of the new health guidelines and will ask a local radio talk show host to moderate discussions about the state guidelines.

Before the meeting you and other committee members received copies of the guidelines and were asked to review them. At the initial meeting several members point out similarities between the content in the current curriculum and the new guidelines. This assures that the purpose should continue to be "cultivating cognitive achievement and the intellect." The group recognizes that the curriculum must be devised using a technical approach and will have intended learning outcomes because of state requirements. However, your group agrees that a revised health curriculum should relate more closely than the current one to the needs of society and culture.

The next action of the development committee is to request that the district conduct a needs assessment because you want to know how the current curriculum should be revised. Your group agrees to work on a statement of the intended content that could be used in the revised curriculum at your next meeting. (These processes are discussed in Chapter 8, Creation of Content Statements.) Then the content statement will be used by the district evaluation specialists in a needs assessment. (These processes are discussed in Chapter 9, Creation of Needs Assessment Plans.)

After the needs assessment, the curriculum development group resumes its work on a views of education statement. Based on study of recent research on learning, the group agrees to make the revised curriculum one in which teachers and students use more two-way communication than the previous curriculum required. The group believes strongly that hands-on learning experiences by students, including having them participate in the decision-making processes about delivery of the health curriculum, should be included in the revised curriculum. Students are to have increased responsibility for creating their own health knowledge. However, your group is aware that individual school curriculum committees may require information that will convince their members to use this approach when they design the curriculum for students in their schools. (See Chapter 10, Creation of Learning Outcomes and Learning Experiences.)

The group reaches these decisions after long discussion and debate about the relative merits of alternative approaches. In the end, however, group thinking coalesces and you are ready to put the ideas about views on paper. Additional discussion will result because groups invariably find that words have different meanings for people. Nevertheless, you try to word the ideas you agree upon so they communicate well, not only to your group, but to other educators and laypersons who will read the views statement. After several attempts at writing a statement, your group approves the statement shown in abbreviated form in Figure 7.3.

Shift gears!!

The next project is in English literature and concerns school-based curriculum making in a very different locale. You've been promoted—you are now a teacher!

ENGLISH LITERATURE CURRICULUM

Now consider that you are a high school English teacher in a district where "cultivating cognitive achievement and the intellect" is the dominant curriculum purpose. More specifically, you and a colleague teach all the senior level English literature classes. Whenever you and your colleague meet informally in the coffee room, you commiserate about how so many students seem uninterested in literature—including students who read well. Your colleague suggests that students may be used to *seeing* stories unfold on movie screens or television monitors and are *not* used to creating their own images and characterizations. If only there were a way to hook their interests in literature!

Health problems disrupt the lives of millions of Americans of all ages every day. Many of these problems could be prevented if people possessed and acted on the knowledge, skills, and attitudes that this curriculum seeks to provide to elementary school students.

During elementary grades younger students exhibit boundless energy and expand their social horizons as they grow physically. Older elementary school students undergo rapid social-emotional development and many face dilemmas related to their peers. To assist these children and youth in living through these situations, this curriculum seeks *to help students acquire the knowledge, skills, and attitudes that promote sensible, lifelong health habits.* We sincerely expect that students who study this curriculum will improve their own health habits and positively influence those of their parents/guardians and siblings as well.

We believe this aim can be realized through the careful use of up-to-date information from a variety of reputable sources. Teachers and students are expected to engage in meaningful discussions about what it means to be healthy. To this end, we encourage teachers to provide ample opportunities for students to view health issues from several angles and to fully explore the consequences related to the different views. Students should be allowed to choose among options those health issues they wish to study in depth, but every student should take from the health curriculum very clear distinctions between conditions that promote healthy living and those that do not. As students realize the importance of good health, we believe they will be better able to contribute to the society in which they grow and work.

FIGURE 7.3
Illustration of an Abbreviated Views of Education Statement for a District-Based Elementary School Health Curriculum

Alas, you teach in Great Plains Consolidated High School in a small Midwestern town, 125 miles from the nearest city. Some students' parents and grandparents are farmers and ranchers who have lived in the region for generations, while other parents are relative newcomers who own or work in service industries scattered throughout the area. Although parents are generally interested in their children's education, most of them work very hard to earn a living and tend to leave educational matters to the school.

Few of your students have traveled out of state, except by way of television or the movies. Most students expect to graduate and look forward to getting on with their lives either by entering the work force or continuing studies in college. Given this background you and your colleague agree that you must change your approach if you are to succeed in getting the seniors involved in literature study. You jointly agree to think about the students and come up with possibilities for a different approach that you would try during the NEXT school year. Because of past experience you are aware that curriculum development is a lengthy process. This timeline provides the two of you more than eight months to work on the curriculum.

After a lot of thought and discussion with your colleague, you hit upon the idea of recasting the purpose of literature study in the curriculum so that it focuses on the students instead of subject matter. You propose to see if you can "develop students to their fullest potentials." You realize that this represents significant change and that it will take time to develop this approach, but believe that the change is worth the effort. Your colleague agrees to work with you on this project and the two of you discuss your intentions with your department head. This person blesses the project *as an experiment* and asks to be kept apprised of the situation through your written plans. This curriculum will need school board approval.

You and your colleague continue discussions concerning the needs and interests of students that you would like the curriculum to address. You both decide that much teacher-student and student-student communication is necessary and that decision making must be shared among teachers and students. Somewhere in the conversations, your colleague points out that carrying out plans of the type you are discussing might connect school learning with life outside classrooms. You agree this is a worthy intention.

Since the department head wants written information, the two of you tackle writing a views of education statement to guide the remainder of the processes. You, too, must go through the same debates about wording that other curriculum groups have. In the end, you present the abbreviated statement shown in Figure 7.4 to the head.

You also agree to be more observant of the seniors you have *this* year and to note their actions that suggest ways in which students of their age develop. (Note: These activities are described in Chapter 9, Creation of Needs Assessment Plans. The content statement for this curriculum is developed in Chapter 8 and the learning experiences in Chapter 11.)

SUMMARY

Curriculum development projects are likely to be initiated successfully in situations where planning considerations and change processes are understood and handled well. Planning considerations include scope and complexity of the curricular change, communication, professional development, and resources. The change processes combine relevance, readiness, and resources in ways that promote action by curriculum developers.

The processes are used in crafting a views of education statement that sets forth the developers' purpose for education, perspectives on student and teacher/school staff roles in delivering the curriculum, and the interrelationships of these elements with the community. Views of education guide curriculum decisions by pointing direction for the remainder of the curriculum development processes.

Views statements of three curriculum documents show three different purposes of education and content emphases. All three documents call for active student-teacher roles in delivery of the curriculum. All three also connect the curriculum content with needs of society and culture-at-large, but give little indication of the local setting in which they are used.

The world into which high school students graduate is different from what it was when they were freshmen. The new world is characterized by instant communication across vast distances, changing family roles, new information and a multinational global economy, to name only a few changes. Because of such changes, traditional schooling is no longer adequate; it does not measure up to the demands placed on young people entering the workforce or going to college.

This is especially true for the students at Great Plains Consolidated High School where this curriculum is to be used. Most of these youth know little about societal changes, except as portrayed in television and the movies. The population is stable and, because most students have not traveled out of state, few have interacted with people from cultures other than their own.

The students have little experience in exploring the characterizations of people through written materials. To assist these youth in meeting the challenges of young adulthood, this curriculum seeks *to help students expand their consciousness of people portrayed in printed materials, increase language skills and abilities, and improve social relations.*

This purpose can be realized in classrooms where teachers and students engage in the study of literature that portrays people in a variety of settings and time periods. Study of such content is not an end in itself, but is a vehicle by which students come to understand themselves, their peers, and others in the world beyond the classroom.

For this purpose to be achieved, both students and teachers must collaborate in the exchanges of ideas, feelings, and values. Each group must act openly with the other if students are to achieve the purpose for which this curriculum is created.

FIGURE 7.4
Illustration of an Abbreviated Views of Education Statement for a School-Based High School English Literature Curriculum

The final section contains suggestions on creating views of education statements for a district- and a school-based curriculum. Curriculum development is conceived as a group activity in which people work together to consider the purpose of education and projected roles for delivery of the curriculum. Much of the work of developing a views statement involves careful listening and reflective thinking. Afterwards a lot of work is involved in writing the views statements because these must communicate the group's thoughts to people who were not part of the discussions.

QUESTIONS FOR DISCUSSION

1. Recall any experiences in which state guidelines required your involvement in curriculum development. Describe the initiation of these curriculum

processes. Describe any professional development activities that were part of the initiation.

2. From your professional perspective, what suggestions would you offer a curriculum development group about the "readiness" aspect of change?

3. Some developers consider the creation of outcomes and learning experiences more important than the views of education statement. As a result, these curriculum development groups spend little time working on their views statement. Describe possible consequences of this decision.

4. With which purpose of education should this definition of *education* be associated? Explain.

> Education is a lifelong process. At its best, education evolves as a seamless curriculum which, at times, is formal in nature, but much of the time is informal as it occurs in the multitude of experiences outside the formal school setting. Because each child comes to the classroom with a wealth of experience before entering the door, teachers need to account for these experiences as being a natural part of each child's lifelong learning process. In this way the teacher supports education as a seamless curriculum of experiences from birth to old age. (*Personalized Education for Children,* 1982, p. 9)

5. Consider that teachers, school staff, and community members are involved in developing views statements. Should *all* these individuals be concerned about purposes of education? Explain.

6. Describe two reasons that district-based curriculum development groups usually ignore the context for curricula.

7. From your perspective describe the similarities and differences in serving on district- and school-based curriculum development groups in the creation of views of education statements.

8. Explain how the change processes of relevancy, readiness, and resources were addressed (if they were) in the section titled Creation of Views of Education Statements for the health curriculum. For the English literature curriculum?

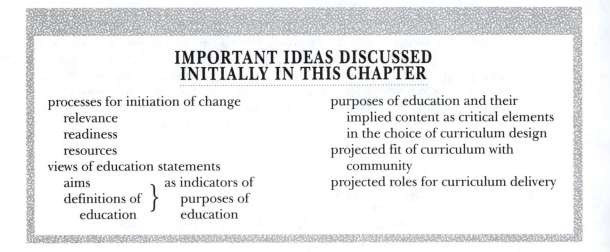

IMPORTANT IDEAS DISCUSSED
INITIALLY IN THIS CHAPTER

processes for initiation of change
   relevance
   readiness
   resources
views of education statements
   aims   as indicators of
   definitions of   }   purposes of
      education   education

purposes of education and their
      implied content as critical elements
      in the choice of curriculum design
projected fit of curriculum with
     community
projected roles for curriculum delivery

8

CONTENT FOR CURRICULUM PROJECTS

OUTLINE

Content statements for curriculum projects
>   Description
>   Rationale

Curriculum content sources
>   Recommendations of professional organizations
>   State guidelines
>   Textbooks and related materials
>   Technology-based materials
>   Professional educators' knowledge bases

Content selection criteria
>   Validity-significance for purpose of education
>   Learnability by learners
>   Appropriateness for needs-interests of learners
>   Consistency with societal-cultural realities

Content in curriculum projects
>   *Spanish IV Curriculum*
>   *Into Adolescence: Caring for Our Planet and Our Health*
>   *Collaborative Teaching Experiences to Develop Communication Skills*

Creation of content statements
>   Health curriculum
>   English literature curriculum

D evelopers decide on purposes of education, which can differ, as part of developing their views of education statements. Because purposes imply content, curriculum content varies from project to project, depending on its purpose. **Curriculum content** is the raw material for student learning in schools. As a result of their interactions with curriculum content and teaching agents, learners are expected to meet the purpose of education established for the curriculum. Because of the dominance of subject matter designs, most projects draw content heavily from subject matter, with lesser amounts from societal problems-issues and needs-interests of learners.

This chapter begins with a discussion of the closely related topics of content statements, curriculum content sources, and selection criteria. Then the selection criteria are applied in analyses of content statements for three curricula serving different purposes of education. The final section offers suggestions for formulating content statements for two hypothetical curricula. After studying this chapter, you should be able to *analyze content statements in curriculum documents and prepare the content statement for a curriculum project of your choice.*

CONTENT STATEMENTS FOR CURRICULUM PROJECTS

Once curriculum developers complete deliberations about their views of education, they are ready to locate and organize content so that learners can satisfy the purpose of education projected for the curriculum. Some developers conceive of content primarily in learning outcomes (i.e., goals and objectives). Others, however, prepare a content statement before developing learning outcomes, a practice recommended in this text. This section describes content statements and their rationale.

DESCRIPTION

As used here, **content statements** are descriptions of the aggregated content for a curriculum. Content statements can use any of several formats including simple outlines, themes, concept maps, and lists. Two-level outlines and themes have the advantage of portraying hierarchical relationships with main ideas and supporting details. Concept maps show how main ideas are connected to related ideas through webbing. However, lists simply display the content without implying relationships. Developers select the format they think best communicates the content.

Figure 8.1 displays the content statement from the *Arizona Social Studies Essential Skills Framework* (1989). Notice that this statement communicates its content as goals and curriculum strands. This is a broad content statement representative of those used in state guidelines. Additional information about this particular content statement follows in the next subsection.

RATIONALE

Many developers find content statements useful because they must "think through" their conceptions of knowledge and learning carefully. For example,

Goals

The goals of the Arizona Social Studies Framework are presented in four broad categories. Each goal is a long-range indication of needed student competency. Each goal is intended to be broad enough so that student learning at all grade levels can contribute to its achievement.

Goal 1. *Knowledge and Cultural Understanding* encompasses learnings from the social science disciplines and the humanities;

Goal 2. *Understanding of Democratic Principles, Values, and Practices* includes the historical derivations and basic principles of American democracy as well as the role and function of the law in our society;

Goal 3. *Individual and Group Participation in Social-Political Affairs* incorporates civic rights and reponsibilities, social-political action, and democratic processes for change; and

Goal 4. *Fundamental Skill Attainment for Effective Citizenship* includes basic study skills, critical-thinking skills, and problem-solving skills in addition to personal, intergroup, and social-participation skills that are necessary for effective living in our democracy.

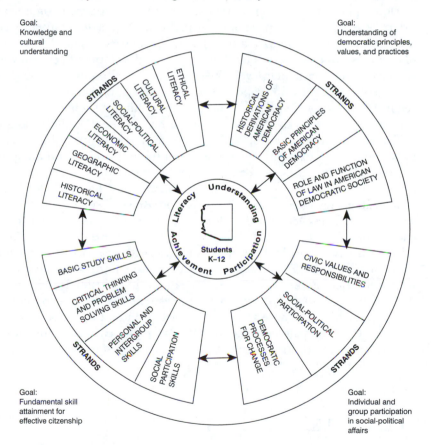

FIGURE 8.1

Example of a Content Statement

From *Arizona Social Studies Essential Skills Framework,* 1989, p. 8. (Available from the Arizona Department of Education, Phoenix, AZ.) Reprinted by permission.

developers who generate statements of "topics" and "skills" signal that both declarative and procedural knowledge are important. Informal, impressionistic, and self-regulatory knowledge do not usually show in content statements because these forms are difficult to pinpoint and rarely taught in school curricula.

Some developers also include "attitudes" in their statements. Although most curricula give highest priority to the cognitive domain, the extent to which affective and psychomotor concerns are included in any particular curriculum is important. Unless references to these domains appear in content statements, outcomes and experiences involving affective and psychomotor learning may remain unplanned.

Content statements help developers clarify the levels of thinking they intend for learners. For example, although "identify" and "recognize" are important in a skills list, "apply" and "evaluate" must also be there. These terms signify lower- and higher-order skills, respectively.

Developers who develop content statements can apply the organizational considerations early in the development process. Organizing content statements by their "scope and sequence," a popular method especially in district-based curricula, carries some benefits. This method allows developers to clarify which content is included at a particular level, as well as whether the range of topics and skills is appropriate (a check on scope). Developers can also examine topics and skills to see if they are repeated (a check on continuity) and if their recurrences and repetitions are progressively deeper (a check on sequence). Finally, by aligning topics, skills, and attitudes developers can determine on a preliminary basis whether these elements are potentially mutually reinforcing (a check on integration).

Figure 8.1 provides the content statement for the *Multicultural Social Studies K–12* (1993), whose views statement is described in Chapter 7. Note that the four broad categories include both cognitive and affective subject matter (e.g., in Goal 1 and Goal 2, respectively). In addition, each goal is explicated as having several curriculum strands, which are also very broad. Because these are state guidelines, school district curriculum developers are expected to focus this content on their particular districts. The results of this focus are shown in the learning outcomes for this curriculum in A1 and their description in Chapter 10.

Finally, the information explosion suggests that creating a content statement is a good idea because there's so much information that could be included in a curriculum. Content statements assist developers in focusing on the most important information. In addition, content statements are useful in needs assessments as described in Chapter 9.

CURRICULUM CONTENT SOURCES

Curriculum content originates in several sources that intermingle in different configurations, depending on local preferences. This discussion describes the following sources: recommendations of professional organizations, state guidelines, textbooks and related materials, alternatives to textbooks, and teachers' knowledge bases.

RECOMMENDATIONS OF PROFESSIONAL ORGANIZATIONS

In recent years several national professional organizations drafted guidelines or standards that have affected curriculum content at state and district levels. Typically organizational leaders work with both members and laypersons to determine the direction and changes needed in existing curricula. Sometimes national recommendations are adopted at state levels, and because states exert much control over district level curriculum matters, the recommendations of national professional groups become influential at district levels.

The National Council of Teachers of Mathematics issued its *Curriculum and Evaluation Standards for School Mathematics* in 1989. These standards call for changes in mathematics curricula by placing high priorities on problem solving, reasoning, communication, mathematical connections, and by playing down mechanistic approaches and computation. In several locations, state curricular requirements are similar to these standards. Illinois' *State Goals for Learning and Sample Learning Objectives* (Illinois State Board of Education, n.d.) are one example.

In 1990 two national organizations jointly adopted guidelines related to appropriate curriculum content for young children. The National Association for the Education of Young Children and the National Association of Early Childhood Specialists in State Departments of Education claim as their purpose to "inform decisions about what constitutes appropriate curriculum content and assessment procedures in programs serving children ages 3 through 8" (NAEYC, 1991, p. 28). These guidelines are used by state agencies and district directors of early childhood programs for planning curricula.

Other professional organizations have followed suit. The National Council of Social Studies released *Expectations of Excellence: Curriculum Standards for Social Studies* in September 1994. The National Research Council issued draft standards for science education in November 1994. In both cases the standards recognize the research on the learning processes and suggest strongly that school curricula focus on the major themes within the disciplines. More importantly both sets of standards promote literacy in several forms.

STATE GUIDELINES

State departments of education issue guidelines that districts within that state are expected to use in designing curricula. For example, developers of the *Middle School English Language Arts Curriculum Guide* (1991) acknowledge the work of the Bureau of Reading and English Education of the New York State Education Department in the introduction to this project. Because the New York state guidelines call for an integrated approach to language arts instruction, that emphasis can be seen in the district-devised curriculum. See Appendix A3 for an excerpt from this curriculum guide. Appendix A also contains an excerpt of state level curriculum guidelines for preparing district-based institutional curricula in the visual arts. See *Wyoming Arts Education Curriculum* (1992) in Appendix A5.

In other states, departments of education issue lists of objectives with various names such as "essential skills" or "minimal competencies." These objectives must be considered by districts whenever curricula are developed, because statewide assessment programs built on these lists are administered to students regularly. (See Figure 8.1.)

TEXTBOOKS AND RELATED MATERIALS

Textbooks and related materials such as workbooks, readings, and teachers' manuals furnish most of the curriculum content taught in schools (Tanner, 1988; Venezky, 1992; Westbury, 1990). In fact Westbury (1990) says " . . . the textbook defines the curriculum" (p. 2).

One study from the Educational Products Information Exchange Institute indicates that "with nearly 95 percent of classroom instruction in grades K–8 and 90 percent of homework time derived from printed materials, textbooks predominate the school day" (Venezky, 1992, p. 444). Secondary school students also confirm that academic work is geared to the textbook available for the class (Sosniak & Perlman, 1990). In addition, teachers themselves acknowledge heavy reliance on textbooks. Seventy-seven percent of the teachers (N=539) said they would not be allowed to teach without their basal workbooks and worksheets (Komoski, 1985).

Although they acknowledge the power of textbooks, Shutes and Petersen (1994) argue strongly against textbooks as definers of the curriculum. Their arguments contend that textbooks do not make their philosophy or goals explicit because the United States has neither a national curriculum nor a consensus about a purpose of education. Because textbooks are commercially prepared, they do not select content, but rather offer wide-ranging content, none in depth. This, of course, is an attempt to appeal to the widest possible audience. Textbooks don't consider instructional pace, and because they are expository, they don't support learning. For example, concepts are sometimes defined, but these are not supported with enough examples or explanatory material to generate complete understanding from reading the text alone (Shutes & Petersen, 1994).

Despite their widespread use as curriculum content, both textbooks and the processes used in their adoption are frequently flawed (Elliott, 1990; Tanner, 1988; Tulley & Farr, 1990; Westbury, 1990). To complicate matters further, the quality of textbooks is intimately related to adoption processes so that both problems must be solved simultaneously if they are solved at all.

The quality problem encompasses related factors such as poor writing, poor content "coverage," and failure to engage students in the skills needed to create the knowledge contained in a particular area of study. Application of readability formulas to text material brings about some difficulties, but prevailing social policy brings others. In the mid-1980s there were charges that textbooks were being "dumbed down" so that anyone could read and understand what was being said (Fiske, 1984; Tanner, 1988 citing Education Secretary Terrel H. Bell under President Reagan). Ironically, examples from some textbooks show that efforts to make them readable actually make them less comprehensible. For an example, read Figure 8.2.

> *This passage from a sixth-grade science text was cited as an example of how, in an effort to simplify the language, authors sometimes make it more difficult to understand:*
>
> > "In the evening, the light fades. Photosynthesis slows down. The amount of carbon dioxide in the air space builds up again. This buildup of carbon dioxide makes the guard cells relax. The openings are closed."
>
> *The center staff (for the Study of Reading at the University of Illinois at Champaign-Urbana) rewrote that passage, restoring the "causal connectives" that had been deleted, as follows:*
>
> > "What happens to these processes in the evening? The fading light of evening causes photosynthesis to slow down. Respiration, however, does not depend on light, and thus continues to produce carbon dioxide. The carbon dioxide in the air spaces builds up again, which makes the guard cells relax. The relaxing of the guard cells closes the leaf opening. Consequently, the leaf openings close in the evening as photosynthesis slows down."

FIGURE 8.2

Example of Textbook Writing

From "A Textbook Sampler," *Principal, 64*(2), p. 46. Copyright 1984 by the National Association of Elementary Principals. Reprinted by permission.

Problems with textbooks are exacerbated by the fact that 22 states use some form of state adoption and most require texts bearing recent copyright dates. Although the other states allow districts to adopt textbooks, the adoption processes in both state- and district-level policies vary widely. Publishers, ever keen on producing texts that sell well, often arrange to release new products to coincide with the adoption dates in populous states such as California and Texas, which use state adoptions. Having a text on either of these state lists usually guarantees the publisher will recoup the expenses incurred in producing the book (Tulley & Farr, 1990).

This also means that people in one or two areas of the country dictate the content marketed in the rest of the United States—a situation that is inherently unfair. The result is that some inferior textbooks are sold across the country and used by many students. In fairness, however, publishers produce textbooks that fit the requirements of the society in which the texts are used. Publishers must provide products that sell or they go out of business!

With all the problems associated with textbooks, it is easy to wonder why they continue to be so popular. Venezky (1992) speculates that elementary teachers, in particular, are trained to use textbooks, rather than develop their own curricula. Maybe this is because elementary teachers in self-contained classrooms teach many different subjects. Also, few teachers at any grade level have time scheduled in their work day to develop curriculum materials. Neither is there sufficient reference or background materials or clerical support to assist with teacher-developed curriculum materials.

What the future holds for textbooks and related materials is hard to predict. Changes in information and its sources are subject to the same barriers to acceptance that other changes in education encounter. Any changes adopted by educators on a large scale endure rigorous trials before they are accepted.

TECHNOLOGY-BASED MATERIALS

Are there alternatives to textbooks? Yes and no. Kerr (1990) recounts a long list of technologies including photographs, films, sound recordings, filmstrips, slides and overhead transparencies, videotapes, television, programmed instruction, and computer-assisted and computer-managed instruction. At the time of its introduction each of these approaches was believed to meet student needs and provide new opportunities for student learning. But there are difficulties—software that is disappointing in quality or novelty, little teacher interest, or little or no gains in student achievement—that prevent these approaches from overtaking textbooks as primary curriculum materials.

Computer-based hardware-software combinations offer teachers and students attractive possibilities not attainable through texts (Adams & Bailey, 1993; Kerr, 1990). Intelligent programs of computer-assisted instruction monitor student work as it is being created. Compact disc–read only memory (CD-ROM) technology allows students access to materials found only in well-equipped libraries at the same time that students engage in controlling their own learning situation. New technology allows students in different physical spaces to collaborate and provides learners with a wider view of their places in the world. Word processing, spread sheets, and data base programs provide opportunities for learning that were not available in the past (Kerr, 1990).

Videodiscs can hold large amounts of information that provide high-quality video and audio presentations. Hypermedia authoring systems allow student authors to create texts with words, graphics, video sound, and special effects. Electronic mail, modems, and fax machines allow learners "to access, retrieve, share, and send information anyplace in the world through high speed telephone networks" (Adams & Bailey, 1993, p. 61). Alternatives to textbooks exist, but so far they are not widely adopted by educators.

PROFESSIONAL EDUCATORS' KNOWLEDGE BASES

Most professional educators have expertise to contribute to curriculum development. Teachers and school staff have varying degrees of knowledge of subject matter, general pedagogical knowledge, educational philosophy, educational contexts, curriculum, learners and their characteristics, and pedagogical content knowledge (Shulman, 1986, 1987). This knowledge must be considered a vital source of curriculum content.

Pedagogical content knowledge is an especially important part of knowledge bases. It is the capacity of teachers to change the content knowledge they have into forms that are understandable by students of different backgrounds and abilities (Shulman, 1987). Although knowing subject matter content is important, teachers need to know how to represent ideas to make them comprehensible to others.

As its name implies, pedagogical content knowledge has two components: content and pedagogy (Grossman, 1989). The content component consists of knowledge that takes into account students, curriculum, and the classroom—the context. Both the teacher's personal values and those embedded in the subject matter contribute to the reorganization of content for teaching. Out of this reorganization, teachers develop orientations to teaching that involve adopting some teaching methods and rejecting others. What this means is that teachers' value orientations to their subject matter influence their content choices, their use of textbooks, teaching strategies, and perceptions of students' instructional needs (Gudmundsdottir, 1990, 1991).

This discussion underscores the critical role that values play in curriculum processes. Because this text is directed to teachers and school staff as curriculum developers, their knowledge bases must be considered as a source of curriculum content.

CONTENT SELECTION CRITERIA

Because so much content exists, developers must choose carefully what they include in projects. Using their views of education as guides, developers select content based on its 1) validity and significance for the intended purpose of education, 2) the learnability of the content by students for whom the curriculum is planned, 3) the appropriateness of the content for the needs and interests of these learners, and 4) the consistency of the content with the realities of society and culture (Taba, 1962).

Most developers can determine validity and significance of content for the purpose of education. However, district- and school-based curriculum planners probably use the remaining criteria differently. School-based developers are likely to be very much aware of the learners and the community where their curriculum is to be used. Therefore, they can probably use the learnability, needs and interests of learners, and consistency with social realities more easily than district-based curriculum developers who have learners with wide-ranging needs. The following subsection describes these criteria.

VALIDITY-SIGNIFICANCE FOR PURPOSE OF EDUCATION

Validity refers to the soundness of content for promoting the purposes of education described in views of education statements. Soundness means the content is logically and firmly grounded in its sources, whether subject matter, needs and interests of learners, or societal problems. In the case of subject matter, principles and generalizations, which are less subject to change than verbal information, should be emphasized. Long-range needs of learners, rather than day-to-day concerns, should be tapped as curriculum content for a purpose that emphasizes learners. Societal problems or issues used as curriculum content should reflect genuine importance for large numbers of people.

Significance refers to the extent to which selected content enables students to perform the intended learning outcomes or engage in learning experiences in meaningful ways. Insignificant content, though not harmful, takes time away from study of more important content that helps students achieve stated goals. Stated simply, unless curriculum content can be related to intended learning, that content should be eliminated from the curriculum.

LEARNABILITY BY LEARNERS

Learnability refers to the fit between learner abilities and curriculum content. Curriculum developers don't consciously select content that is too difficult for students, but this doesn't guarantee that content is always learnable. The author knows an able teacher who sought unsuccessfully for years to teach first-graders the meaning of missing addends (e.g., $2 + ? = 5$, $? + 4 = 7$). Her best efforts failed with all except a few of her really bright students, because the majority of the children were not developmentally prepared for such complex learning. When asked why she pursued attempts to teach this concept, she said simply, because it's in the math book. In this case the content was not learnable by most young students, but the teacher accepted the authority of the textbook rather than use her own good judgment.

Learnability is closely tied to developers' values and beliefs about (1) the nature of learners' development and (2) the abilities of learners for whom content is selected. Presumably, planners discuss their views of development during the preparation of the views of education statement, but their values emerge clearly in content selection.

For example, developers with a *cognitive structural* perspective expect to frame content so that its structure is clear to students. Young children are encouraged to learn that the order in which whole numbers are added does not affect the sum, a mathematics structure known as the commutative property of addition. If children learn this idea in the early grades, they are expected to understand readily in middle school that the order in which algebraic fractions are added does not affect the sum. Similarly, if young children understand the generalization that "people adapt to their environments," these students should have little trouble understanding in high school social studies that for generations people have lived in varied and extreme climates. Consistently helping students understand the fundamentals of subject matter allows learners to add new knowledge to existing knowledge (Bruner, 1960).

Developers with alternative perspectives seek to have those views represented similarly. Subscribers to *observational learning* insist on content with many worthwhile models and *cognitive science* advocates stress the importance of learners' prior knowledge, and so on.

The second element in learnability concerns developers' perceptions of the abilities of learners for whom content is selected. Ideally, developers should know the students for whom they plan curriculum, a situation more difficult for district than school-based groups. However, whenever classroom teachers serve on development teams, they can often provide firsthand answers to questions such as these:

• Do students speak, read, and write standard English well, whether or not it is their native language? Is additional language assistance necessary?

- Are students generally motivated to learn curriculum content? To what extent do students differ in attitudes toward learning?
- To what extent do students vary in their general abilities to learn?
- How should the content be handled for students whose abilities differ significantly from the norm?

Answers to these questions should be considered in the content selection process.

APPROPRIATENESS FOR NEEDS-INTERESTS OF LEARNERS

Curriculum content should meet the long-term needs and interests of students. As noted in Chapter 6, learner development takes place simultaneously in all dimensions—social, personal, moral, cognitive-intellectual, and physical. Therefore, curriculum content should foster learner development in the dimensions implied by the purpose of education.

As is true with learnability, it's helpful if developers know the students who study the content. Developers' views of learner development apply also in decisions about the appropriateness of content for the needs and interests of learners.

Curriculum planners should apply knowledge of developmental patterns of children and youth. That is, they select content for elementary school students that can be tied to concrete reasoning situations. They phase in hypothetical situations for beginning adolescents because students attain formal reasoning capabilities over time. Planners should actively use knowledge of students' social development by suggesting individual and/or group projects according to the ways learners typically interact with peers at different developmental levels. Finally, planners should select content representing all the learning domains pertinent to the purpose of education.

CONSISTENCY WITH SOCIETAL-CULTURAL REALITIES

Content selected for curricula should align with societal and cultural realities. As studies of society and culture show, cultural diversity in American schools is increasing with large numbers of children and youth who speak a native language other than English. Increasing numbers of children do not have homes or are cared for by someone other than family; relatively few children live in homes with two parents or guardians. The content selected must be sensitive to the needs of these learners. Reading materials, mathematics problems, and social issues must not be so separated from the real world that children and youth are unable to grasp their meaning.

Content must also take into account the increasing types and levels of literacy demanded by employers. Jobs without high literacy demands are few and the pay is low. Technology and information services positions are increasing but they require skills that many youth do not possess when they leave school. Curriculum content should provide students with opportunities for learning the skills and abilities needed for work and living in the real world.

Young people must be helped to deal with change because this is and will continue to be part of their lives. Schools are increasingly looked upon as the most important stabilizing force in the lives of some students. Therefore, what students encounter in terms of curriculum content will have much influence on the formation of their values (Smith, 1983). Curriculum workers cannot avoid dealing with these issues as part of the content selection.

This section describes several important selection criteria. Consider that these criteria work like a multiscreen sieve having large holes in the first screen, slightly smaller holes in the second screen, and so on. The screens are validity-significance, learnability, etc. If content fails to pass the initial screen of validity-significance, that content should be eliminated and given no further consideration. Should the content pass the initial test, it must also pass the remaining screens to be included.

Work through Exercise 8.1 to see how well you understand the content selection criteria. This could help your use of the criteria in your own project.

EXERCISE 8.1

For each of these situations, consider that the purpose of education is "cultivating cognitive achievement and the intellect." Reflect on the discussion of content selection criteria. To what extent were these criteria taken into account? Describe recommendations for improvement.

1. Ms. Safire, a fourth-grade teacher, has five students in her class who speak no English. Yet Ms. Safire speaks only English and all the instructional materials available to her are in English.
2. Roundtree Elementary School is in an inner city neighborhood where Mr. Joiner, a brand-new first-grade teacher, has his first paid position. When he arrives, he finds badly outdated and worn preprimers.
3. Mr. Z. has taught English for years at Diablo High School. He looked forward to the new curriculum guide promised by the district office. However, when he read it, he was upset to find that the guide still calls for teaching "sentence diagramming." He believes this topic has lost its reason for existence.

CONTENT IN CURRICULUM PROJECTS

This section presents analyses of the content from *Spanish IV Curriculum* (n.d.), *Into Adolescence: Caring for Our Planet and Our Earth* (Hunter, 1991), and *Collaborative Teaching Experiences to Develop Communication Skills* (1992) located in Appendix A. Because none of these projects has a content statement, the content must be determined by reviewing goals, or other learning outcomes.

Ideally, analyses are based on all the criteria for content selection. However, the analyses here are limited by lack of context information and the author's content background in Spanish. Specifically, without knowledge of the context, "learnability" and "appropriateness for needs and interests of learners" are difficult to assess. Lack of content expertise makes judging the "significance" of Spanish content impossible. Despite these limitations, analysis of the content statements shows important differences among them.

SPANISH IV CURRICULUM

Content for *Spanish IV* (see A4) is recorded under the goals statements in the section titled Goals. Notice the three major categories of content: vocabulary, grammatical structures, and language use with the latter expanded to include dialogue, reading, and listening content information. Additional content is named in the culture goals—geography, culture, customs, and other topics.

This curriculum project uses as its purpose of education, "cultivating cognitive achievement and the intellect." Within the project the purposes are stated as fostering learners' intellectual-personal development, sharing knowledge and culture of the past, and developing skills for participation in society. The project calls for students to apply this information in a number of practical social situations. The content appears to satisfy the validity criterion because it is well-grounded.

The content also appears to satisfy the criterion of consistency with societal and cultural realities largely because of its emphases on using Spanish in social situations, as well as study of the culture and current issues. Students who learn Spanish in these settings are likely to actually use their knowledge in out-of-school situations.

INTO ADOLESCENCE: CARING FOR OUR PLANET AND OUR HEALTH

This project (see A6) lists content for the six lessons both in the overview and the objectives sections. Topics include water usage, garbage reduction, air pollution, rain forests, and protecting the planet. Developers acknowledge that this curriculum is not intended to address all pressing environmental issues.

The purpose of education for this curriculum is to "help people live in a rapidly changing, unstable society." Within this project the purposes are elaborated as providing knowledge about environmental crises and seeking individual commitments from students for taking responsibility to solve problems. The selected content appears to be both valid and significant for the purposes. Developers select as content three problems—water usage, garbage reduction, and air pollution—that are at the very heart of environmental concerns. Helping young people begin to understand the importance of correcting these problems could make a difference in solving these concerns in the future.

This curriculum is not planned for a particular context. However, given the overview of activities, this content appears to be learnable and appropriate for the needs and interests of most students in grades 5–8. It's clear that students are to be active in several types of learning experiences and that engaging in these activities would foster learners' development in several dimensions. Finally, the content is consistent with societal and cultural realities. Newspapers and television news coverage confirm the importance of the need for everyone, young and old, to do his/her part in protecting the environment.

COLLABORATIVE TEACHING EXPERIENCES TO DEVELOP COMMUNICATION SKILLS

The content for this project (see A7) is shown first as a list of communication skills in Evaluating Language Processes and reappears on the Classroom Observation Form. The purpose of education for this curriculum is "developing individuals to their fullest potentials."

The content selected is both valid and significant for this purpose of education because the skills listed represent important abilities needed by people of all ages. Children who learn these skills early are able to move ahead developmentally, but deficiencies in communication can clearly hamper learners' abilities to attain their potentials.

The planned collaboration of speech therapists and classroom teachers provides for *individual* evaluations and assistance with students' needs, both requirements of curricula serving this purpose of education. This collaboration manifests the ideal in learnability; learners are looked upon as individuals. Because these communication skills are universally needed, the content is appropriate for the needs and interests of learners. Societal and cultural realities demand that people be able to communicate with others both at school, in the workplace, and at home.

Now that you've read these analyses, try some of your own, using curriculum documents in Appendix A. Insofar as possible, determine the extent to which the content was selected using criteria described in this chapter. Complete Exercise 8.2.

. . . .

EXERCISE 8.2

Examine the content statements in the following curriculum projects in Appendix A:

- *A Guide for Developing a 1–9 Science Curriculum* (A2)
- *Middle School English Language Arts Curriculum Guide* (A3)
- *Wyoming Arts Education Curriculum* (A5)

To the extent that your expertise allows, determine how well the developers used these content selection criteria:

a. validity-significance for the purpose of education
b. learnability by learners
c. appropriateness for the needs-interests of learners
d. consistency with societal-cultural realities

CREATION OF CONTENT STATEMENTS

Preparing a content statement is a relatively easy task, mostly because it is concrete. The purpose of education suggests major sources of content for the curriculum, but the actual choices of content from those sources should be made using the selection criteria. Once the content has been selected, the development

- State guidelines—list essential or required skills for health education.
- Newsstories—provide timely information on health care from major periodicals.
- Teachers' knowledge bases—provide information about health education, knowledge of the contexts where this curriculum is to be used, and health needs of elementary school students.
- Health textbooks—provide information on a variety of health topics and practices.
- Media catalogs—list motion pictures and videotapes on health topics appropriate for elementary school students.
- Health-care providers—may be school nurses or some other community health-care givers willing to interact with elementary school students about health topics.
- People in the community—may be parents, siblings, guardians, or other people who are willing to donate time for health study activities.

FIGURE 8.3
Examples of Content Sources for an Elementary School Health Curriculum

group is ready to develop the statement in a format of its choice, and make a preliminary recheck of the content against the content organization considerations (e.g., scope, sequence). Final checks occur after the planning of learning experiences and the learning experiences, if these are used.

The remainder of this section describes the work of two different curriculum development groups in the preparation of content statements for hypothetical situations. The health curriculum content statement is prepared by a district-based group using a technical approach. Refer to Figure 7.3 for an abbreviated views of education statement. The English literature curriculum is prepared by a school-based group using a nontechnical approach. See Figure 7.4 for its abbreviated views of education statement.

HEALTH CURRICULUM

Imagine that you are part of a district-based curriculum development group at work on an elementary school health curriculum for students in grades kindergarten through six. You continue as a building principal of an elementary school in the district.

During several meetings you and your colleagues formulate a content statement. As a first step your group lists as many sources as you can imagine that can contribute content to this project. (See Figure 8.3. Note that several sources including news stories, media, health-care providers, or people in the community provide current information.)

Content Selection and Statement Formulation. From these sources your group must select the content that students are expected to learn. This is the point at which the curriculum group actively uses the selection criteria. The group brainstorms topics that belong in health curricula, including "nutrition," "substance abuse," "hygiene," and others. All topics are accepted for the brainstorming list. Then you form subgroups to review the list, split so each subgroup has about the same number of topics.

During this review you consider the validity and then the significance of each topic for helping learners move toward "acquiring the knowledge, skills, and attitudes that promote sensible, lifelong health habits," the aim of your project. You must render a verdict about whether the topic stays in the list. As planners, you are essentially making a preliminary determination about the validity (or soundness), then the significance (or importance) of individual topics. Afterwards, the entire group reconvenes to discuss the preliminary decisions. You attempt to achieve consensus about which topics stay on the list. Once this action is complete, the list is somewhat shorter than it was before the review.

As a whole group, you reexamine your views of education statement and rethink your views about the community and the projected roles of implementors. With these views in mind, you consider the learnability of the topics, their appropriateness for learners' long-term needs and interests, and their consistency with societal-cultural realities. Some topics are discussed at length, while others are barely touched on, largely because of differences in developers' values and their understandings about the learners for whom the curriculum is prepared. Only the topics that survive scrutiny associated with each criterion continue as viable topics for the health curriculum.

Your group decides that a simple two-level content outline is an appropriate way to organize the content statement. A subgroup works out a tentative draft of the content statement and returns it to the whole group for review and comment. After more discussion and compromise, you agree on the content that should form the basis for the health curriculum. Then the group must apply the content organizational considerations.

Preliminary Consideration of Content Organization.   To check this content against organizational considerations, the group reviews the remainder of the district K–12 health curriculum. As a check on *scope*, the K–6 content must be included within the K–12 statement. You also determine whether the K–6 content continues in grades 7–12 as a check on *continuity*. Checks for *sequence* and *integration* will be made in the development of the school-based health curriculum because more information about students and learning experiences is available at that level. The product of all the content deliberations is shown in Figure 8.4. (Note: This statement forms the basis for a needs assessment in Chapter 9 and for learning outcomes and learning experiences in Chapter 10.)

Halt! Refocus—different situation ahead!

ENGLISH LITERATURE CURRICULUM

Suppose you are a high school English teacher working with a colleague on a school-based curriculum project for seniors studying English literature. The two of you agree to change the purpose of the curriculum to the "development of individuals to their fullest potentials" and have the department head's approval to proceed with developing this nontechnical curriculum on a trial basis. You also decide to observe your current students for clues about dimensions in need of development. (Note: These activities are described in a section of Chapter 9 called Creation of Needs Assessment Plans, but their results are incorporated in this section.)

As the two of you begin to consider content, you are aware that pertinent sources are in the needs and interests of students and in subject matter *as seen through their eyes*. Because schooling is definitely a social situation, learners meet many of their developmental needs in schools.

The results of observing your current students show that some need assistance with vocabulary and comprehension exercises and that many could use help with interpretative reading. Even more important are your observations about their

I. Life management skills
   A. Self-concept
   B. Feelings and their effects on thoughts and behaviors
   C. Interpersonal relationships
   D. Stress and management
   E. Decision making and goal setting

II. Environmental health, safety, and injury prevention
   A. Causes, controls, and effects of pollution on health
   B. Prevention, control, and elimination of pollution
   C. Relationship of community health problems and environmental pollution
   D. Types of injuries and their causes
   E. Hazards and their preventions
   F. Emergency care

III. Substance-abuse prevention
   A. Uses of drugs and medicines
   B. Consequences of inappropriate uses of drugs and medicines
   C. Psychological and social forces related to drug abuse

IV. Nutrition
   A. Basic nutritional requirements
   B. Factors that influence food choices
   C. Safe food handling

V. Growth, development, and sexuality
   A. Factors that influence growth and development
   B. Uniqueness of human beings
   C. Factors that influence sexual attitudes and behaviors
   D. Responsibilities to self and others associated with sexuality
   E. Human reproductive processes and related matters

FIGURE 8.4
Content Outline for an Elementary School Health Curriculum

VI. Consumer health
    A. Differences between advertising and educational messages
    B. Advertisements and other influences on selection of health products and services

VII. Community health resources
    A. Community workers and organizations
    B. Community health problems

VIII. Disease prevention and control
    A. Basic causes of illness and disease
    B. Practices that prevent and control diseases
    C. Personal responsibility

IX. Personal health and hygiene
    A. Need for sleep, rest, and exercise
    B. Personal cleanliness
    C. Dental hygiene and care
    D. Fitness
    E. Changes in needs during preadolescence

X. Family health
    A. Different types of family units
    B. Roles, contributions, and responsibilities of family members
    C. Changing roles in families through their life cycles

XI. Physical education
    A. Physical fitness and exercise
    B. Body management skills
    C. Fundamental movement activities
    D. Rhythmic activities
    E. Playground activities
    F. Leisure activities

FIGURE 8.4, *continued*

social needs. Most of the students crave social situations in which they can show themselves to be in control. On several occasions you find students taking opposite sides in a discussion, apparently for the enjoyment of it. In an adolescent psychology text you reread about youth needs for self-regulation and strong peer-group affiliations. These are the concerns that must guide curriculum content selection.

For purposes of this curriculum project, you center attention on a segment of Chaucer's *The Canterbury Tales*. (See Figure 8.5 for additional information.) The challenge is to think about this content in ways that interest and meet the needs of high school seniors. The focus is not on content itself, but on how it helps learners develop socially and linguistically.

For this project you have access to anthologies of English literature as text material, supplemental printed material from the library, and other media presentations. However, the two of you rule out using media presentations, because you want to encourage students to visualize and interpret situations for themselves. Because she took a course there a few years ago, your colleague remembers that the state university has sound recordings of some of *The Canterbury Tales*. You are also aware that communication "experts" such as television personalities or little theater performers could offer assistance in applications of language skills. Grandpa Green, who was an actor on the east coast before he retired to Great Plains, comes to mind as someone who could help. You also consider that several mental health workers in the local area have expertise concerning the needs and interests of students.

Content Selection and Statement Formulation.   From these sources you select content that provides the general area for study. Although you consider the possibility of seeking themes by talking with students, the idea is discarded in favor of preselected themes. This is an experiment that must be reported to the department head and receive school board approval. Both collaborators want to prepare well for the project.

Geoffrey Chaucer (1343?–1400) is considered one of the three greatest English poets, along with William Shakespeare and John Milton. Chaucer's greatest work, *The Canterbury Tales* was written in Middle English and "preserved for all future ages a realistic, detailed, and comprehensive panorama of daily life at the time" (Macmillan Literature Series, 1991, p. 56).

The Canterbury Tales is a long poem consisting of the Prologue, or introduction, and a series of stories told by two dozen-plus people representing a cross-section of medieval English society. The setting for telling the stories is a pilgrimage which took these individuals from London to the cathedral city of Canterbury. Individual stories are of several kinds: "religious stories, legends, fables, fairy tales, sermons, and courtly romances" (Macmillan Literature Series, 1991, p. 57).

Synopsis of The "Prologue": "At the Tabard Inn in Southwark (a London suburb), the narrator joins twenty-nine pilgrims bound for Canterbury to visit Becket's shrine. The pilgrims are from all different walks of medieval life—a Knight, a Squire, a Nun, a Miller, and so on. Each is described with details that make his or her personality clear. As the pilgrims dine at the inn, the Host proposes a contest: Each pilgrim will tell two stories on the trip to Canterbury and two on the homeward journey; the Host will accompany the group and judge the best story; and the winner will receive a free meal at the Tabard on their return. The pilgrims agree to this proposition" (Macmillan Literature Series, *Teacher's Classroom Resources 1*, 1991, p. 41).

Synopsis of "The Wife of Bath's Tale": "A knight in King Arthur's day has been sentenced to die for mistreating a woman, but the queen decides to spare him if he can correctly answer the question 'What is the thing that women most desire?' The knight travels all over and receives many incorrect responses until he finally meets

---

FIGURE 8.5
Chaucer and *The Canterbury Tales*

an old woman who promises to provide the correct answer if he will swear to do her bidding. When he agrees, she tells him the answer, which he then reports to the queen and her court: A woman wants the 'self-same sovereignty' after marriage as she has during courtship. His life is spared, but he now must keep his pledge to the old woman, who demands that he marry her. After the wedding he complains about his wife's age, plainness, poverty, and low birth, but she argues that these are all valued qualities in Christian and ancient teachings. She then asks if he prefers an old and ugly but faithful wife or a young and pretty but faithless one. After some thought, he responds that he must leave such decisions to his wise wife, whereupon—having won the thing that women most desire—she now magically turns into a beautiful young maiden when he kisses her" (Macmillan Literature Series, *Teacher's Classroom Resources 1*, 1991, p. 41).

Synopsis of "The Pardoner's Tale": "While three young men are drinking at a tavern, the funeral of a plague victim passes by. The serving boy speaks of Death's power, but the three men scoff and swear to defeat Death. When they set out to meet Death, they encounter an old man, whom they treat disrespectfully. In answer to their demands, he informs them that Death can be found under a nearby oak tree. The three rush to the tree, where they find a pile of gold coins. Forgetting about Death, they consider how to carry off the gold without being accused of robbery, and they decide to wait until nightfall. While the other two stay behind to guard the treasure, the youngest goes to town for refreshments. During his absence the others plot to kill him to make their shares of the gold larger; however, he has similar ideas, and he poisons the drink he brings back. On his return the other two stab him to death; they then drink the poisoned wine and themselves die" (Macmillan Literature Series, *Teacher's Classroom Resources 1*, 1991, pp. 41–42).

FIGURE 8.5, *continued*

Synopses from *Teacher's Classroom Resources 1*, (pp. 41–42) Macmillan Literature Series. Copyright 1991 by Glencoe/McGraw-Hill Educational Division. Reprinted by permission.

As the two of you consider potential themes, you must consider how they assist learners' development. Students are to be exposed to this content for the express purpose of expanding their consciousness of people in printed materials, increasing language skills and abilities, and improving social relations—as noted in the purpose for this curriculum.

To satisfy the validity criterion, the selected content must promote students' social and language development. This means students must have many opportunities to speak and write in social situations. *The Canterbury Tales* is a good choice for this purpose because its stories are of people living in a different age but engaged in the same social interactions that modern day people encounter. This literary work could allow students to engage in activities where they communicate a great deal, both as themselves, and as characters in the story.

"Everybody has a story. Hear it well if you want to know the storyteller" expresses the major theme for study of this content. Along with related subthemes for each of the *Tales*, these themes could guide the activities in which learners are expected to participate. As a result of participation, learners are expected to grow socially in keeping with the stated purpose. Through the nature of the activities you envision, you anticipate that the content is learnable and will meet the needs and interests of students. You expect to direct the activities so that students understand their intent—this should help make the content significant. Because good communication is vital in school and in the world outside of school, you believe that the content meets the criterion of consistency with societal-cultural realities.

Having sorted through the content using the selection criteria, your two-person group develops a rather simple content statement with a major theme and subthemes to guide the planning of learning experiences. Figure 8.6 shows the major and related themes for this curriculum project. Additional themes will be selected for the remaining parts of the curriculum.

In preparation for your discussion with the department head, you and your colleague reread Rosenblatt (1983) who makes a good case for the significance of studying literature:

> Any insight or clarification the youth derives from the literary work will grow out of its relevance to certain facets of his emotional or intellectual nature. . . . That a literary work may bring into play and be related to profoundly personal needs and preoccupations makes it a powerful potential educational force. For it is out of these basic needs and attitudes that behavior springs. (p. 182)

Preliminary Consideration of Content Organization.   Examining the curriculum for the content organization considerations is probably impossible because the purpose of education for the revised curriculum differs from the purpose of the

FIGURE 8.6
Content Statement for a High School English Literature Curriculum Segment

Themes adapted from *Teacher's Classroom Resources 1,* (p. 41) Macmillan Literature Series. Copyright 1991 by Glencoe/McGraw-Hill Educational Division. Reprinted by permission.

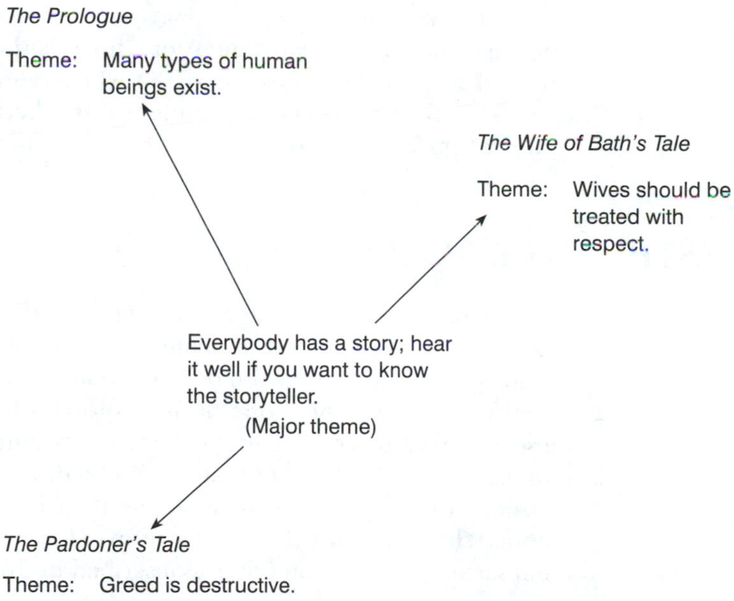

The Prologue

Theme: Many types of human beings exist.

The Wife of Bath's Tale

Theme: Wives should be treated with respect.

Everybody has a story; hear it well if you want to know the storyteller.
(Major theme)

The Pardoner's Tale

Theme: Greed is destructive.

remainder of the English/humanities curriculum at Great Plains High School. You and your colleague can check organization only *within* the English literature curriculum you develop. Typically, content organization is a broader concern than this analysis suggests because it is meant to assure that learners have many opportunities to develop skills and abilities.

Chapter 3 indicates that curricula based on needs and interests of learners have poorly defined *scope, continuity* and *sequence,* but *integration* is expected to be strong because developers use the students' needs and interests. That description describes this case.

SUMMARY

Some curriculum planners translate their purpose of education directly into learning outcomes. But other planners follow a plan advocated in this chapter of devising content statements, before generating outcomes or experiences. These statements encourage planners to consider content carefully from several points of view. Planners draw content from recommendations of professional organizations, state guidelines, textbooks and related materials, technology-based materials, and professional educators' knowledge bases.

Because much more content exists than can be taught, developers use criteria to determine their selections. Proposed content should satisfy the validity-significance and learnability criteria and be appropriate for the needs and interests of students. It also should be consistent with social and cultural realities. Content statements in three curricula, displayed in different formats, showed they are drafted using some of the criteria. Not all criteria could be used, however, because of lack of content expertise in Spanish and because the contexts for the projects are unknown.

The final section offered suggestions for creating content statements for the health and English literature curricula whose views of education appeared in Chapter 7. Both the formats and content differ because the projects are planned for different purposes of education.

QUESTIONS FOR DISCUSSION

1. The rationale for content statements uses information largely from the studies of subject matter in Chapter 4. Explain how information from studies of society and culture in Chapter 5 could also be applied in a rationale for content statements.
2. Identify any professional organizations to which you belong. In what ways do these organizations contribute to curriculum content?
3. Explain why curriculum content should be drawn from multiple sources.
4. Consider the curriculum, or a segment of it, delivered to students in your school. What is its purpose of education? How well does the curriculum or segment satisfy the selection criteria described in this chapter? Explain.

5. Why is it important for teachers to view curriculum content as significant? Is that a prerequisite for making that content interesting to students? What are some ways that teachers make content interesting?
6. Explain why checking the content with the organizational considerations is necessary.
7. Explain how the change processes of relevancy, readiness, and resources were addressed (if they were) in the section Creation of Content Statements for the health curriculum. For the English literature curriculum.

IMPORTANT IDEAS DISCUSSED INITIALLY IN THIS CHAPTER

curriculum content

content statements

curriculum content sources

content selection criteria
    validity-significance for the purpose of
      education

learnability by learners

appropriateness for needs-interests of
    learners

consistency with societal-cultural
    realities

9

NEEDS ASSESSMENTS FOR CURRICULUM PROJECTS

OUTLINE

Needs assessments as context evaluation
      Needs defined
      Standards
Discrepancy needs assessments
      Limitations
      Strategies
Diagnostic needs assessments
Creation of needs assessment plans
      Health curriculum
      English literature curriculum

Soon after curriculum developers initiate planning, they may request a needs assessment to provide information for revising the curriculum. **Needs assessments** are completed to identify strengths and weaknesses of existing curriculum situations and to provide direction for their improvement. The timing of this request depends on whether the developers plan to change the purpose of education. Development may *start* with needs assessment unless the revised curriculum has a purpose different from the one in the current curriculum or the curriculum to be designed is brand-new. In either of these cases developers must decide their purpose and select curriculum content before engaging in needs assessment. A needs assessment in these situations enables developers to put priorities on content.

In technical approaches to curriculum processes, needs assessments can help define a problem within a school or district for which a revised curriculum represents a partial solution. In nontechnical approaches teacher-developers usually use needs assessments to clarify any preliminary information they have about students' needs. Needs assessment enables these teachers to continue improvement of curricula in their classrooms.

This chapter describes needs assessments as context evaluation and outlines two broad approaches that permit evaluators to gather and interpret information for curriculum modification. Needs assessment procedures are illustrated in plans for two hypothetical situations. As a result of studying this chapter, you should be able *to prepare a rudimentary needs assessment plan for a curriculum project of your choice.*

NEEDS ASSESSMENTS AS CONTEXT EVALUATION

Contexts for curriculum development include the people involved in schools and their communities as well as the curriculum content. Ideally context evaluation is an ongoing situation analysis that can provide information to curriculum developers whenever it is needed. However, special needs assessments may be necessary, particularly when curricula are to be revised.

For this discussion, **context evaluation** is used synonymously with needs assessment. The main reasons for undertaking these evaluations are to assess the status of curriculum situations, identify their problems, identify the strengths that could be used to remedy deficiencies or make improvements, and characterize the environment in which the curriculum is used (Stufflebeam & Shinkfield, 1985).

NEEDS DEFINED

As discussed previously, needs are defined in a variety of ways. However, in this discussion of needs assessments the following definitions are used:

Discrepancy view: A need is a discrepancy between desired performance and observed or predicted performance. . . .

Diagnostic view: A need is something whose absence or deficiency proves harmful. (Stufflebeam, McCormick, Brinkerhoff, & Nelson, 1985, pp. 6–7)

Based on such disparate views of needs, evaluators not only approach the assessment tasks differently, but discuss the results in different terms. For example, a discrepancy evaluation reveals whether existing priorities on curricular items serve the group for whom the curriculum is planned. A diagnostic evaluation, however, concentrates on locating and correcting potential difficulties encountered by individuals using the curriculum. This chapter discusses both approaches.

Regardless of which definition curriculum developers adopt, assessments must be handled carefully to protect the people involved. The next section describes standards to be applied in needs assessment.

STANDARDS

Needs assessments inquire into values and preferences of people holding different views of the items under consideration. Therefore, any method of inquiring about those values and preferences must use fair, ethical, and practical methods. Once a decision is made to conduct a needs assessment, those charged with the tasks should prepare and use procedures that satisfy rigorous criteria. The Joint Committee on Standards for Educational Evaluation (1994) provides standards for evaluation of educational programs that are appropriate for needs assessments.

The Joint Committee recommends four types of criteria:

1. *Utility criteria.* For this discussion utility means that needs assessments should provide pertinent information for curriculum developers. Needs assessments should be directed to specified audiences, conducted by competent persons, and obtain information that answers questions pertinent to curriculum needs for the audiences served.
2. *Feasibility criteria.* Feasibility requires that needs assessments be practical, diplomatic, and frugal. The procedures should cause minimal disruptions to school-community situations, solicit cooperation of all pertinent interest groups, and be cost effective.
3. *Propriety criteria.* Needs assessment procedures should serve needs of the targeted participants, be carried out according to formal agreements, respect the rights and welfare of all those involved or affected by the evaluation, be uncompromised by conflicting interests, and be ethical. The evaluators should make sure "that the full set of evaluation findings along with pertinent limitations are made accessible to the persons affected by the evaluation, and any others with expressed legal rights to receive the results" (Joint Committee on Standards for Educational Evaluation, 1994, p. 82).
4. *Accuracy criteria.* Needs assessments should provide accurate and adequate information about the curricular needs in a community, enabling developers to base curriculum modifications on the needs identified. The information-gathering instruments and procedures should be valid and reliable for the purpose of assessing needs, and data should be accurately and appropriately analyzed to support interpretations. Conclusions should be justified by the analyses and reported objectively.

Appendix B contains additional information about these standards, including a brief history, suggested uses, and a summary. Applications of the standards are exemplified in the section titled Creation of Needs Assessment Plans.

DISCREPANCY NEEDS ASSESSMENTS

Technical approaches to curriculum processes frequently use **discrepancy needs assessments** in which evaluators or assessors search for differences between projected "should be" and current "what is" situations. These differences are assessed by school evaluators who obtain information from citizens, parents, students, and school personnel.

Needs assessments typically use deductive or inductive strategies, depending on the questions for which answers are sought. The deductive strategy answers general questions such as "What should the curriculum be?" The inductive strategy seeks answers to questions such as "How can the current curriculum be improved?" These strategies, which are *not* exclusive of each other, can be used jointly (Matczynski & Rogus, 1985).

With either strategy the general procedures are the same. The first step is preparation of statements of desired curricular status for the deductive strategy or statements of current curricular status for the inductive strategy. Next, these statements are transformed into instruments for data collection. The instruments are administered to appropriate groups, evaluators analyze and interpret the data, high priority needs are incorporated into curriculum development planning, and results are reported to the community. See Figure 9.1 for a graphic presentation of these major procedures. An elaboration of these procedures follows in the strategies section after a brief discussion of limitations.

LIMITATIONS

Despite able leadership and well-conceived plans for the selection of participants, needs assessments can sometimes fail to provide accurate information unless assessors are aware of certain limitations. Results of needs assessments are limited by the extent to which any of the following assumptions (Matczynski & Rogus, 1985) about participants and their backgrounds are compromised.

1. *Needs statements have clear meanings both for participants and for people interpreting outcomes.* Simple statements, as free of jargon as possible, should be used in needs assessments. Even simple statements, however, may have different meanings for people because interpretations of written or spoken statements are based on unique backgrounds and experiences. Evaluators must make every effort to use statements that will be understood by the persons who provide information.

2. *Participants know more than one point of view concerning the needs statements.* In needs assessments participants are furnished with lists of curriculum topics, goals, objectives, needs of students, or other information. In order for needs assessments to have meaning, participants must know about alternatives to the items presented by evaluators. In addition, participants must understand what and how the alternatives differ from each other and from the current situation. If participants do not have these understandings, the choices they make are probably meaningless.

FIGURE 9.1

Generalized Procedures for
Discrepancy Needs Assessments

*Note: Use *desired* curricular status
in deductive strategies; *current*
curricular status in inductive
strategies.

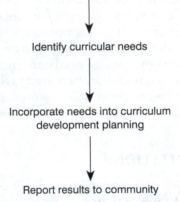

Prepare statements of desired/
current curricular status*

Develop instrumentation for
evaluation of statements

Complete both assessment processes:

- Collect perceived importance data
- Collect perceived achievement data

Identify curricular needs

Incorporate needs into curriculum
development planning

Report results to community

3. *Participants are willing to deliberate seriously about needs statements.* Participants may differ in their philosophical positions about curricular situations, but they must be able and care enough about the assessment to think about/discuss the alternatives with others. While participants must be willing to voice their values and beliefs to others, they should suspend judgments until the different views on needs are presented.

4. *Participants have sufficient knowledge of the school or district to assess its current achievement of needs statements.* As part of needs assessments, participants, including community members, will be called to judge the merit of current curriculum situations. Therefore, they must be aware of what is taking place in the schools. Such awareness may be high in communities with active parent-teacher organizations, with school newsletters that parents read regularly, or where parents volunteer in the school on a regular basis. Plans of a different type must be made in situations where community members are unaware of school affairs. Scheduling a series of forums or town hall meetings can provide community members with opportunities to learn what is happening in schools before asking them to participate in needs assessments. However, some community members will not attend these meetings.

Use Exercise 9.1 to check your understanding of limitations in discrepancy needs assessments.

EXERCISE 9.1

Reflect on the discussion of limitations, then read the following incidents. To what extent were these limitations taken into account in each incident? Describe recommendations for improvement.

1. Mr. and Mrs. Ruiz, parents of elementary school children, have been invited to attend a meeting at their local school concerning a proposal for a literature-based language arts curriculum. Both parents are pleased that they read ably and understand all types of information. They credit having learned to read in elementary schools where a basal reader-phonics approach was used. Based on their own successes, Mr. and Mrs. Ruiz see little reason for the literature-based approach.

2. In Ms. Alexander's school, the needs assessor placed copies of a needs questionnaire in all the teachers' mail boxes with instructions to return the completed questionnaire within 24 hours.

STRATEGIES

Inductive and deductive strategies for discrepancy needs assessments follow the generalized procedures shown in Figure 9.1. However, these approaches differ in the types of questions each seeks to answer.

Questions and Information Needs for Inductive Strategies. The inductive strategy is appropriate in situations where the major questions relate to the *current* situation: Does the current curriculum stress important content?

Answering this question requires an intimate knowledge of the current curriculum, an extremely difficult task in most school districts. Remember the different levels of curriculum in Chapter 1? Deciding which level of curriculum to use in a needs assessment is difficult enough, but deciding content at any of these levels is particularly tough.

To complicate matters further, even if the actual curriculum were known, obtaining objective information about its efficacy is also difficult. Standardized achievement tests provide information about student achievement of general cognitive goals and objectives, but do not necessarily provide information about achievement of the goals and objectives of a particular school or district curriculum. Teacher-made achievement tests provide information about student achievement of instructional objectives, but these results may reflect things other than actual achievement of curricular goals and objectives (e.g., effort, attendance). And how are the goals and objectives in affective and psychomotor domains to be measured? These quandaries make accurate data about curricular achievement difficult to obtain.

As a result, evaluators typically rely on information that yields participants' *perceptions* of the efficacy of the current curriculum as answers to the questions. Information gathered from participants shows their perceptions of priorities concerning the importance of current curriculum goals compared with achievement of current curriculum goals. Discrepancies between these sets of perceptions indicate what should be done to improve the current curriculum.

Questions and Information Needs for Deductive Strategies.   The deductive strategy is used to determine answers to questions about what the situation *should be*. Broadly stated illustrative questions include this: What knowledge or content should be included in the curriculum?

Curriculum developers create a set of tentative statements (e.g., topics, curriculum goals) that answer the question about what *should be*. This approach might well be used in situations where state guidelines suggest goals different from those used currently in the district or school. In this instance information gathered from participants shows their perceptions of priorities to be assigned to the revised goal statements and reveals discrepancies between proposed goals and achievement of current goals.

Data Collection.   Evaluators collect data in several ways, including ranking scales and opinionnaire surveys. Both permit gathering data from several people simultaneously. **Opinionnaire surveys**[1] frequently either ask a question or make a statement to which several answers or responses are possible. Respondents select answers/responses that reflect their judgments about the content of the questions/statements.

When the number of participants warrants, one popular way is to schedule a meeting with participants and ask each one to complete a ranking scale. In using a **ranking scale**, respondents rank statements within a set according to their priorities. A **Q-sort**, also a form of ranking scale, asks respondents to sort cards on which the items are recorded, according to the respondents' priorities.

Consider the following illustrative situation in which a deductive strategy is used. In a meeting to which school-community representatives are invited, each participant is provided with a list of the tentative goals of a revised/new curriculum. Participants are expected to review the goals and revise them, if necessary. Next, participants rank the goals according to their *perceived importance*. Afterwards, they meet in small groups to discuss and reach consensus on their rankings. Evaluators collect the rankings from the small groups and derive an average ranking of goals that is shared with the large group.

Then assessors ask participants to rank only the goals that received high rankings in importance, according to their *perceptions* of how well the goals are being *achieved*. This usually produces a set of rankings different from the rankings by importance. (See Figure 9.2 for an illustration of two sets of rankings for goal statements.)

---

[1] See Appendix C for more information about instruments identified in boldface.

Average Rankings		Program Outcomes
Importance	**Achievement**	
4.1	—	Demonstrate verbal and technological literacy.
6.2	4.9	Demonstrate skills in communication and group interaction.
7.9	4.9	Demonstrate skills in problem solving and decision making.
5.0	—	Demonstrate skills in expressing themselves creatively and responding to creative works of other cultures.
6.9	4.9	Demonstrate civic understanding through the history of American culture and its relationships to concomitant cultures and histories.
5.2	4.3	Demonstrate understanding of past and present cultures.
6.4	2.6	Demonstrate concern, sensitivity, and respect for others.
6.5	3.2	Demonstrate skills in adapting to and creating personal, social, and political change.
4.0	—	Demonstrate capacity for enhancing and sustaining self-esteem through emotional, intellectual, and physical well-being.
6.7	3.5	Demonstrate skills necessary to be self-directed learners.

FIGURE 9.2

Rankings of Program Outcomes for a Social Studies Curriculum

Outcome statements from *Multicultural Social Studies Curriculum K–12,* 1993, p. 18. (Available from Tucson Unified School District, Tucson, AZ.) Reprinted by permission.

Analyses, Interpretations, and Uses. Once information is gathered, assessors study the discrepancies between the importance and achievement rankings using formal analyses procedures. However, the logic of these procedures is straightforward and should be known to teachers and school staff.

In Figure 9.2 assume that high rankings are shown by the largest numbers. Assessors would question the discrepancies in importance-achievement rankings for the following program goals:

• Demonstrate skills in problem solving and decision making.

• Demonstrate concern, sensitivity, and respect for others.

• Demonstrate skills in adapting to and creating personal, social, and political change.

• Demonstrate skills necessary to be self-directed learners.

Note that these program outcomes have average importance rankings that differ considerably from their respective average achievement rankings. These discrepancies suggest outcomes that *should be* achieved are probably not achieved as well as respondents believe they should be. Assessors would try to locate the bases for discrepancies in all four cases. They would also study any situations in which the average achievement rankings were greater than average importance rankings.

Part of the study consists of attempts to diagnose problems that might account for the discrepancies. Evaluators also consider any opportunities in which needs might have been satisfied but were not. They also consider whether any limitations were violated. For example, they could discover that participants resisted listening to other points of view and marked their responses based on their own preconceived ideas. Or evaluators could find that participants had insufficient knowledge of the school to assess current achievement. Should either of these be the case, evaluators would take these limitations into account in their discussions of the outcomes.

Evaluators communicate the needs identified in the assessment to curriculum developers or other authorized school staff. At the appropriate time school staff report the outcomes to community members. Such communication is vital for good school-community relations. Also, curriculum needs identified in assessments may serve as the benchmarks by which the revised curriculum will be evaluated after it is implemented.

Curriculum planners act on as many needs as possible, but give preference to those perceived as having high priority. Where needs are stated as curriculum goals, for example, developers amend existing goals by adding or deleting goals in the original list. The revised goals form the bases for further curriculum development.

As this discussion shows, discrepancy needs assessments are important because they provide the foundation for technical curriculum processes. Use Exercise 9.2 to review the major ideas in such assessments.

EXERCISE
9.2

Reconsider the information about discrepancy needs assessments.

1. Discrepancy needs assessments provide information about group preferences. Explain why this is appropriate in technically developed curriculum situations.
2. Explain why needs assessors collect "importance" data before "achievement" data.

DIAGNOSTIC NEEDS ASSESSMENTS

Diagnostic needs assessments are frequently school- or classroom-based and are conducted primarily by teacher-developers who want more information about their students. Diagnostic needs assessments have at least two limitations. Needs statements must be clearly worded so that students interpret the questions in about the same way as the person who evaluates their responses. Otherwise the results are not dependable. Also, diagnostic needs assessments often measure affective concerns, such as interests and beliefs, that change over time. Interpreters should consider the results as valuable global indicators rather than as prescriptive information.

A diagnostic needs assessment is prompted by the question "What do students need in this curriculum?" Information needs are therefore context-specific in that they answer questions for a specific school or classroom situation. For an adult English as a Second Language (ESL) project, Auerbach (1990) describes the rationale for in-take or start-up activities that "provide 'base-line data' about what students can already do with language and literacy, how they think about it and what they may want to do as a result of instruction" (p. 214). The importance of collecting this information, of course, is that it helps ESL teachers tailor educational experiences to expressed needs of students.

Evaluators collect both quantitative and qualitative data, depending on their purpose and the circumstances in which the data are available. **Observations**[2] can be made of naturally occurring events in classrooms, using both structured and unstructured formats. The curriculum project *Collaborative Teaching Experiences* (see A7) contains a classroom observation form for communication skills that uses a **checklist** format. Either the teacher or therapist notes individual children's communication skills whenever these are demonstrated in classrooms by checking the skills shown by children. This format provides structure for recording observations (see Figure 9.3). Evaluators who are especially interested in the classroom milieu often write notes of their observations in **unstructured observations**. This format provides qualitative data.

Sometimes evaluators gather information in one-on-one interviews with participants. An **interview** involves a person who asks questions and one who answers them. Not only does this allow a personalized approach, it also enables data collectors to probe for reasons behind answers. Interviewers frequently use a set of prepared statements to ensure that data collection is uniform among the respondents.

Auerbach (1990) lists start-up activities for adults that include task-oriented oral language assessment, reading samples, writing samples, goal-setting activities and others. Harste and Short (1988) suggest an activity called Getting to Know You as a way of learning about children's abilities in reading and writing. In this activity children write questions they will ask another child in an interview situation. After the actual interview, the children write their answers. In both these illustrations the behaviors and outcomes that students produce are helpful to teacher-developers for structuring nontechnical curriculum projects. Figure 9.4 provides a sample of interview questions for collecting data from adults in a literacy project.

---

[2] See Appendix C for more information about instruments identified in boldface.

CLASSROOM OBSERVATION FORM FOR COMMUNICATION SKILLS
(√ if skill is observed)

NAME _____ DATE _____

CLASSROOM TEACHER _____ T.S.L.I. _____

_____ Attends to teachers/students and classroom activities

_____ Communicates needs, wants, desires

_____ Gives appropriate responses to questions, commands, or directions

_____ Uses language for a variety of purposes (e.g., naming/requesting, rejection, greeting/answering, possession, location)

_____ Participates in conversational turn-taking activities

_____ Reports, answers, initiates in the presence of small/large groups

_____ Recalls a series of events

_____ Remains on discussion topic

_____ Offers information, states an idea, and generates meaningful communication

_____ Demonstrates appropriate sentence structure

_____ Demonstrates adequate articulation

_____ Demonstrates adequate vocabulary

_____ Demonstrates adequate voice/fluency control

COMMENTS:

FIGURE 9.3
Classroom Observation Form for Communication Skills

From *Collaborative Teaching Experiences to Develop Communication Skills in Elementary School Children, Prekindergarten to Grade 5*, 1992, p. 4. (Available from Speech and Language Department, Jackson County Intermediate School District, Jackson, MI 49201.) Reprinted by permission.

Data from all of these sources require careful analysis and sensitive interpretations. Quantitative data can be tallied so that analysts are able to note trends and draw conclusions. However, qualitative data frequently undergo one or more coding procedures involving **content analyses**, before subsequent processing takes place. During these processes the data collectors also acknowledge any limitations that might have been violated. For example, the data *collector* should acknowledge situations where students asked questions about meanings of needs statements because these students probably do not have a clear understanding of their meaning. Such information is important to interpreters and users of needs assessments.

How about attempting a brief diagnostic assessment on your own? See Exercise 9.3.

Student's background: Where are you from? What was your first language?

Education: Did you go to school in your country? For how long? Are you teaching your children your first language?

Conceptions about literacy: Do most people know how to read and write in your country?

Reading: Do you like to read? Why/why not? Do you read at home? What do you read?

Support systems: What do you do when you have trouble reading/writing something? Does anyone help you? Who?

Needs: What do you need English for? How do you want to use it?

_____ work   _____ talking with friends, neighbors

_____ shopping   _____ housing

FIGURE 9.4

Interview Questions for a Literacy Project

From *Making Meaning, Making Change: A Guide to Participatory Curriculum Development for Adult ESL and Family Literacy* (pp. 216–217), by E. Auerbach, 1990, Boston: University of Massachusetts English Family Literacy Project. Copyright 1990 by Elsa Auerbach. Reprinted by permission.

EXERCISE 9.3

Reconsider the information about diagnostic needs assessments.

1. Describe advantages and disadvantages of checklists compared with interviews.
2. Describe advantages and disadvantages of checklists compared with unstructured observations.
3. Envision some students with whom you work. Select a data collection method and generate at least three appropriate questions or statements that would enable you to obtain diagnostic information about these students.

CREATION OF NEEDS ASSESSMENT PLANS

If school districts have evaluation departments, needs assessments are usually planned and carried out by personnel from that office. In the absence of these departments, school administrators perform the same function or head groups that carry out these projects. Whichever method is used, assessors should be well prepared by training for handling the tasks (at least in part, to satisfy the utility criterion of the standards discussed earlier in this chapter) and should work closely with curriculum developers.

Discrepancy needs assessment strategies require participation by representative groups of community members, students, teachers, and school staff members. The exact numbers of these personnel are decided by the evaluators partly based on the type of needs assessment, the population served, the questions about which information is gathered, the timeline required by the project, the budget, and methods of data collection.

Rarely can the entire community or student body be used in a needs assessment. Therefore, representatives from the school and community should be selected by the evaluators to provide information. For example, if representatives are chosen by one of the systematic methods (e.g., random sampling, stratified random sampling), the results from the smaller representative group should reflect results similar to those that would be obtained from the larger group. The instrument can be made available generally so that community members not chosen as representatives may participate if they wish to do so. However helpful data from volunteer participants may be, it should be analyzed separately from the representatives' data because volunteers' data could bias the results (Stufflebeam & Shinkfield, 1985).

This section illustrates the creation of rudimentary needs assessment plans for the health and the English literature curricula discussed first in Chapter 7. The plan for the health curriculum uses a discrepancy approach and the English literature curriculum uses a diagnostic approach. Keep in mind that these are illustrations only and that other approaches are possible.

HEALTH CURRICULUM

You, as an elementary school principal, serve on the committee that is developing a district level health curriculum. This group determined at its first meeting that the purpose of the revised curriculum would continue to be "cultivating cognitive achievement and the intellect." The next decision was to ask the district governing board to fund a needs assessment and it agreed. Your group completed a content statement showing the topics proposed for the revised health curriculum. At that point, your committee turned the statement over to the district's evaluation specialists.

The evaluation specialists plan a strategy by which information can be gathered from parents/guardians, educators, students, and any other groups interested in health curricula. As the evaluators plan their operations, they consider the Standards. For this project the evaluation specialists decided to collect data in a meeting to which *representatives* of all the context groups (community, school staff, and teachers) would be invited. This meeting is to be scheduled at a time and place that accommodates the schedules of most of the people expected to attend.[3] These processes help satisfy the feasibility criterion.

The meeting itself should be conducted in a manner that respects the rights and welfare of the participants and that provides accurate and adequate information about health curriculum needs, to conform to the propriety and accuracy criteria, respectively. For illustrative purposes only, imagine that the meeting is conducted as follows:

---

[3] Evaluation specialists should also plan some type of follow-up evaluation—mail surveys, for example—in the event that meeting attendance fails to produce a representative group.

An evaluation specialist serves as moderator at the meeting where the participants use a ranking scale based on the content from the development group (see Figure 9.5). As indicated in the directions, participants assign rankings according to their views of the importance of the content. Small group discussions allow participants to talk about their values concerning the different content areas. An attempt will be made to gain consensus on the rankings in each small group.

The moderator of this meeting collects information from the small groups about the IMPORTANCE rankings. Using a nearby word processor and a copy machine, the evaluation specialists take the seven topics that received top rankings and reproduce the statement with new instructions. This time participants are asked to rank the statements according to how well the topics are ACHIEVED currently.

As part of the closing activities, the moderator informs the participants that the results of the meeting will be communicated in the monthly newsletter after the evaluation specialists have had time to analyze and interpret the data.

The rankings of importance are likely to be different from the rankings of achievement, revealing discrepancies between perceptions of what "should be" and "what is." Evaluators must work carefully with analyses and interpretations so that outcomes accurately reflect the preferences of participants. Evaluators are obligated to weigh the evidence collected and interpret it accurately to substantiate their conclusions. Finally, outcomes of the analysis will be reported to your committee and other authorized individuals accurately as a way of conforming to the accuracy criterion. Only when these criteria are satisfied should the information be disseminated to the community.

Your committee will use these data to structure program level learning outcomes. These processes are described in Chapter 10 in the section titled Creation of Plans for Learning Outcomes and Learning Experiences.

ENGLISH LITERATURE CURRICULUM

You and a colleague are the only teachers of senior high school English literature in a small-town high school. The school year is under way and you are teaching literature directed toward the dominant purpose of "cultivating cognitive achievement and the intellect." However, because your students seem to be uninterested, the two of you proposed and received department-head approval to prepare an experimental curriculum to relieve the problem.

You speculate that students are unused to imagining what characters are like because of lack of experiences. You propose to refocus the curriculum on the purpose of "developing individuals to their fullest potentials." You have tentative department-head approval to proceed.

The next step is to find out more about what senior students need in the way of language and social development. What are their interests that could be used in the study of literature? How might their abilities to visualize what they read be improved? In which areas can social relations be improved?

You have already observed that students in this small town do not seem to change a great deal from one year to the next. The two of you agree to gather

Proposed Content for Elementary School Health Curriculum

Listed in **bold print** are 11 major topics proposed for inclusion in the health curriculum for elementary school students in this district. Under each major topic in parentheses are subtopics to help clarify the content in the major topic.

Directions:

1. Study the **major topics** carefully and decide which of these you consider the most IMPORTANT.

2. Write "11" in front of the topic that is the most important, "10" in front of the topic that is second highest in importance, and so on to "1" for the topic with least importance.

In a few minutes you will have an opportunity to discuss your rankings with some of the other people attending this meeting.

_____ **Life management skills**
(self-concept, feelings and their effects on thoughts and behaviors, interpersonal relationships, stress and management, decision making, and goal setting)

_____ **Environmental health, safety and injury prevention**
(causes, controls and effects of pollution on health; prevention, control, and elimination of pollution; relationship of community health problems and environmental pollution; types of injuries and their causes; hazards and their preventions; emergency care)

_____ **Substance abuse prevention**
(uses of drugs and medicines, consequences of inappropriate uses of drugs and medicines, psychological and social forces related to drug abuse)

_____ **Nutrition**
(basic nutritional requirements, factors that influence food choices, safe food handling)

_____ **Growth, development, and sexuality**
(factors that influence growth and development, uniqueness of human beings, factors that influence sexual attitudes and behaviors, responsibilities to self and others associated with sexuality, human reproductive processes and related matters)

_____ **Consumer health**
(differences between advertising and educational messages, advertisements, and other influences on selection of health products and services)

_____ **Community health resources**
(community workers and organizations, community health problems)

_____ **Disease prevention and control**
(basic causes of illness and disease, practices that prevent and control diseases, personal responsibility)

_____ **Personal health and hygiene**
(need for sleep, rest, and exercise; personal cleanliness; dental hygiene and care; fitness; changes in needs in preadolescence)

_____ **Family health**
(different types of family units; roles, contributions, and responsibilities of family members; changing roles in families through their life cycles)

_____ **Physical education**
(physical fitness and exercise, body management skills, fundamental movement activities, rhythmic activities, playground activities, leisure activities)

FIGURE 9.5

Ranking Scale for Use in a Discrepancy Needs Assessment for an Elementary School Health Curriculum

Circumstance: Students were reading silently Swift's *Gulliver's Travels,* in particular "A Voyage to Lilliput."

Observation: Maurice slammed his book closed and glared at me. After a few moments I signaled Maurice to meet me in the back of the room. When I asked why he closed his book so forcefully, he said, "I don't like having to look up so many words just to try to understand the story. I had to look up three words on the first page. It's a crummy story anyway."

I said, "Please, tell me some words you had to look up."

He hesitated and then said haltingly, " 'ligatures' and 'disposed'."

I said, "Do you consider the story crummy just because the vocabulary is difficult or is there something else?"

He grinned and said, "It's just that the words are hard."

I thanked him for the information and he returned to his seat.

Interpretation: If vocabulary difficulties are keeping students from visualizing what they read, we should spend more time in preparation for reading.

FIGURE 9.6

Anecdotal Record from a Diagnostic Needs Assessment for an English Literature Curriculum

data from your current students to help in the curriculum revision. During the next grading period you each use a checklist to keep a record of student performance on selected language skills.

You also agree to keep anecdotal records of two types of instances: 1) those in which students appear to need help with social relations and 2) those in which students show difficulties visualizing what they read. You know that keeping track of learners' social relations[4] is less definitive than working on language skills. If students show difficulties with visualization, you will hold conversations (in private, if the situation merits) with students to try to figure out the elements in the situation that contribute to their responses (e.g., vocabulary, comprehension). See Figure 9.6.

You are aware that the checklists will provide data that can be summarized quickly, but the anecdotal record data may not be as easy to use. You have to read these data several times, then develop and apply a classification system before you are ready to generalize about the results. However, this appears to be a good way of finding out how to help students, so you proceed with these plans, and with your colleague, select a date on which you will compare information.

Before that date, each of you studies the checklist data and summarizes the findings about the status of seniors' language skills. You also review all the anecdotal records and recheck your interpretations to see that they are reasonable

---

[4] For example, one aspect of social relations involves self-regulation—attempts to increase one's social independence or control one's own development (Flammer, 1991). See Chapter 6.

given the circumstances and observations. You sort the anecdotal records according to the primary idea recorded in the interpretation, and summarize this information by categories of things that have proved helpful as well as harmful in discussions of literature.

Next, the two of you meet and discuss your findings. You mull them over and try to see if any alternate interpretations could be made. When you are reasonably confident about the information, you make a joint summary to guide your planning of the content and learning experiences.

SUMMARY

As described in this chapter, needs assessment is a tool that curriculum developers can use in the revision or modification of a curriculum. The procedures selected depend on how needs are defined. Usually, technically developed curricula use discrepancy approaches, and nontechnically developed curricula use diagnostic approaches. Discrepancy approaches yield information about curriculum elements such as goals, topics, and others, while diagnostic approaches provide information about individuals and their needs.

Both types of needs assessments require the application of rigorous criteria to protect the people involved and both have limitations that must be taken into account, especially at the point of interpreting data. Typically evaluation specialists manage discrepancy needs assessments that can involve many people on a districtwide or schoolwide basis. However, teacher-developers arrange for and carry out diagnostic needs assessments because these are context specific and do not usually involve large numbers of people.

The final section illustrates how each of these needs assessments might work in the development of curricula whose views of education statements were presented previously. Both *The Program Evaluation Standards* (1994) criteria and the context were incorporated in these illustrations.

QUESTIONS FOR DISCUSSION

1. Explain why a discrepancy view of needs fits well with a technical approach to curriculum processes. Why does a diagnostic view fit well with a nontechnical approach?
2. Speculate about whether failure with one limitation invalidates the results of a discrepancy needs assessment. Explain.
3. Describe the major difference between inductive and deductive needs assessment strategies.
4. With both inductive and deductive strategies, evaluators study the results for unmet needs and unused opportunities. Explain.
5. Chapter 5 shows that in many cases schools have replaced many child-rearing functions families once had and that children in the future may have parents

with weak educational backgrounds. Given these situations, to what extent should parents/guardians participate with educators in curricular needs assessments? Explain.

6. Explain why evaluators report results of needs assessments to the community.

7. Explain how the standards criteria were applied in the section Creation of Needs Assessment Plans for the health curriculum. For the English literature curriculum?

IMPORTANT IDEAS DISCUSSED INITIALLY IN THIS CHAPTER

needs assessment
context evaluation
discrepancy needs assessments
   ranking scales
   Q sorts
   opinionnaire surveys

diagnostic needs assessments
   observations
   checklists
   unstructured observations
   interviews
   content analyses

10

LEARNING OUTCOMES AND LEARNING EXPERIENCES FOR TECHNICALLY DEVELOPED CURRICULUM PROJECTS

OUTLINE

Intended learning outcomes and planned learning experiences
  Definitions
  Technical approach to development
  Aims, goals, and objectives
  Learning experiences
Learning outcomes and learning experiences in curriculum projects
  Spanish IV Curriculum
  Into Adolescence: Caring for Our Planet and Our Health
Alternative approaches to local curriculum decision making
  revisited
Creation of plans for learning outcomes and learning experiences
  Health curriculum

The preparation of learning outcomes and learning experiences is the culmination of a technically developed curriculum project. In accordance with their views of education, developers prepare learning outcomes and learning experiences using their content statement for the project. Based on expectations in the views of education, learning outcomes and learning experiences also display how the curriculum fits the community and how teachers and school staff are expected to deliver curriculum content to students.

This chapter discusses learning outcomes at several levels of decision making, along with learning experiences that enable students to meet objectives. Next are critiques of the learning outcomes and learning experiences in two curricula. The final section describes the processes of creating learning outcomes and learning experiences, largely through a hypothetical curriculum development situation. The purpose of this chapter is to enable you to *evaluate descriptions of learning outcomes and learning experiences in curriculum documents and to prepare descriptions of both components for a technically developed curriculum project of your choice.*

INTENDED LEARNING OUTCOMES AND PLANNED LEARNING EXPERIENCES

Learning outcomes result from students' experiences with the curriculum content selected by developers and noted in their content statement. To say that outcomes are "intended" acknowledges that teacher-student efforts do not always produce the anticipated results. Curriculum developers plan *intended* learning outcomes, but students achieve *actual* learning outcomes. In a similar vein curriculum developers plan learning experiences, but this does not exclude the possibility that learners learn in unplanned experiences as well.

This section discusses these two components—learning outcomes and learning experiences. The first two subsections describe these curriculum components and the general methods by which they are derived. The remaining subsections provide details and illustrations of learning outcomes and learning experiences.

DEFINITIONS

Intended learning outcomes represent what learners are expected to be able to do with curriculum content as a result of participating in **planned learning experiences** involving one or more teaching agents. Formal knowledge or skills that learners are expected to acquire can be and are stated as intended learning outcomes. But how are learners to develop attitudes, interests, appreciations, thinking skills, and other cognitive strategies? Expectations in these learning domains are not easily framed as intended learning outcomes and must be communicated through plans for learning experiences.

In addition to communicating learning domains, outcomes indicate the developers' emphases on content-process or declarative-procedural knowledge. These knowledge classifications are subdivided as verbal information, intellectual skills, cognitive strategies, attitudes, and motor skills in Chapter 4. Moreover, taken together, outcomes and learning experiences reveal developers' values about curricula delivery, thus revealing their priorities on receptive-generative knowledge.

Planned learning experiences should clarify the means by which learners are to achieve objectives in sufficient detail to allow teachers to plan instruction. Concerns for learners' backgrounds and accommodations for them must be included in planned learning experiences.

Close study of these components shows developers' values and beliefs about societal-cultural needs. Which literacy needs are handled? Which cultural diversity concerns are given attention? What provisions are made for learners from disadvantaged backgrounds? What arrangements are suggested for learners whose development is atypical?

For this discussion learning outcomes involve content conceived broadly to narrowly. In part, degrees of broadness are related to the generality or inclusiveness of the content. For example, because birds are a subgroup of animals, a learning outcome referring to birds has less content generality than a learning outcome about animals. A learning outcome about gymnastics has greater content generality than one focused on tumbling.

Verbs chosen to express actions with/on content are also important measures of broadness-narrowness. Terms such as *understand, think critically,* and *feel* are more ambiguous than *point to, draw,* or *construct.* More ambiguous verbs are used in broad statements of learning outcomes and less ambiguous verbs are used in narrowly stated outcomes. Listed according to the their generality from broad to narrow, learning outcomes include aims, goals, and objectives.

TECHNICAL APPROACH TO DEVELOPMENT

The technical approach to curriculum development suggests a deductive approach by which developers create aims first, then translate them into goals and finally into objectives. Objectives are then transformed into learning experiences. In other words, aims are broad learning outcomes that are systematically made more specific. This approach also implies that aims, representing the broadest statements of educational outcomes, are satisfied by meeting goals. Goals, the next category, represent ends that are satisfied by meeting objectives. Objectives are the ends toward which learning experiences point. (See Figure 10.1.)

This orderly, systematic approach to curriculum decision making works well for some groups of developers. These planners devise intended learning outcomes based on their content statement, then produce the learning experiences that enable students to satisfy those outcomes. "Such a seemingly 'rational' view assumes that you have a very clear idea of the future which you wish to command, for without such a blueprint it is impossible to define in any realistic way the objectives that you wish to reach. Since every step follows from their definition, success is ultimately dependent upon the accuracy of the predictions that are made" (Davies, 1976, p. 6).

Aims and goals SHOULD be devised before objectives and learning experiences. However, some planners create objectives and learning experiences on a

FIGURE 10.1
Relationships Among Learning
Outcomes and Learning
Experiences

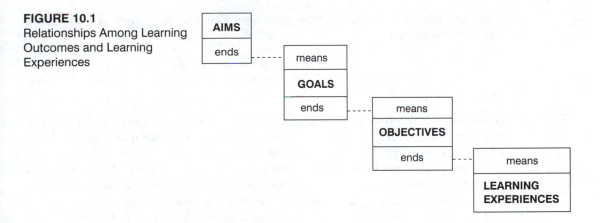

piecemeal basis, which calls for simultaneous development. This back-and-forth process permits several revisions in objectives and learning experiences before these reach final form.

AIMS, GOALS, AND OBJECTIVES

Table 10.1 overviews important information about learning outcomes. As noted in Chapter 7, aims are general, philosophical, and long term and often serve as statements of purpose. They are not measurable and exist to provide shape and direction for a curriculum.

An *aim* can be made operational as a set of **goals** that provide answers to the question, *what destination do you have in mind for learners as far as a particular curriculum or subject is concerned* (Davies, 1976). Because they represent destinations,

TABLE 10.1
Summary Information About Learning Outcomes

Outcome	Question Answered	Function	Measurability	Degree of Generality
Aim	Why is this curriculum being taught?	Gives shape and direction to curriculum	None	Very general
Goal	What destination do you have in mind?	Provides scope for curriculum	Some	General
Objective	What specific destination do you have in mind?	Provides direction for instruction	Much	Less general

goals are less broadly stated than aims and provide indicators of curriculum scope, as shown here:

Aim
- Goal 1
- Goal 2
- etc.

Goals are of different types, depending on content generality and planning requirements at various levels of curriculum decision making (Brandt & Tyler, 1983). Moreover, goals can be measured to the extent of deciding if they are met or if one goal is met better than another (Kaufman & Herman, 1991). Although goals may be considered long term, they are less long term than aims. Depending on their generality, goals may be achievable within a semester.

From goals come **objectives,** which are narrower statements of learning outcomes. Degrees of specificity in objectives vary depending largely on how planners conceive of content and their preferences. In whichever form objectives are cast, however, they provide curriculum developers with opportunities to state operationally what the goal statements mean and provide direction to instructional planners. Objectives also are more time-bound than goals and, due to their specificity, enable evaluation of a curriculum.

Regardless of their learning domain, objectives reveal levels of learning by their wording. Chapter 4 describes these levels as taxonomies in cognitive, affective, and psychomotor domains. For purposes of this discussion, the two-way classification into lower and higher-than-lower taxonomic levels described in Chapter 4 is appropriate. Lower levels (L) include the first two levels and the higher-than-lower levels (HL) refer to succeeding levels of the taxonomy.

L and HL levels indicate developers' values about expectations for learning. Consider these two objectives:

Learners should be able to:

- Identify colors by name from a palette displaying a complete range of colors.
- Create a color scheme appropriate for a living room.

The first objective about the identification of colors calls for lower level learning. However, the second objective requires learning beyond the lower level. Learners must identify colors to create a color scheme, so the L learning is subsumed within the HL learning. Although L learning is necessary, HL learning is important and should be emphasized in curriculum objectives.

Examples of Learning Outcomes.   District curriculum committees frequently prepare intended learning outcomes at two or more levels of decision making. *System* outcomes contain general expectations for all learners, not specifically related to any one subject matter area. For example, citizenship outcomes are considered generally important in all curriculum areas, despite their prominence in social studies curricula.

Program outcomes typically represent expected outcomes in a single subject area, such as mathematics or language arts. In addition to these, *course* or *grade* outcomes and *classroom* outcomes are also developed usually for a single subject area. Sometimes outcomes are clustered for learners across a grade range (e.g., K–3, 5–8).

Figure 10.2 displays learning outcomes at each of these decision making levels from the curriculum project, *Multicultural Social Studies Curriculum K–12* (1993). Heading the list is an aim, which is a system outcome. Three program outcomes follow. Notice that the Program 3 outcome is more focused than the two outcomes that precede it. Although not very precisely, the Program 1 outcome could be measured. Evaluators could determine on a yes-no basis if students were able to perform outcomes such as these and if performances on some outcomes were better than on others (Kaufman & Herman, 1991). For this discussion, statements with the characteristics shown in Program 1 outcome are designated as goals.

The remaining statements for program, grade and classroom are more precise than goals and are called objectives in this discussion. These outcomes describe abilities that students are expected to demonstrate upon completion of learning experiences and their quality and quantity of performance can be evaluated more precisely than that of goals (Kaufman & Herman, 1991). To evaluate objectives,

---

Aims—System

Learn and mature into participatory citizens who are self-directed, collaborative workers, complex thinkers, community contributors, and quality producers.

Goal—Program 1

Know, understand, and be sensitive about culture.

Objective—Program 2

Demonstrate concern, sensitivity, and respect for others.

Objective—Program 3

Practice appropriate social behavior (e.g., respect for personal and public property-environment).

Objective—Grade—second

Recognize the similarities and differences with diverse ethnic and cultural groups.

Objective—Classroom—second

Describe ways in which one group may "borrow" traditions from another group.

Objective—Grades 9-12

Identify examples of the diversity of human cultures through a study of at least four cultural groups in different parts of the world.

Note: The particular linkages between outcomes and levels of curriculum decision making shown here are illustrative; alternative linkages exist.

FIGURE 10.2

Examples of Learning Outcomes in Local Curriculum Decision Making

Learning outcomes excerpted from *Multicultural Social Studies Curriculum, K–12,* 1993, pp. 3, 8, 13, 28, 49. (Available from Tucson Unified School District, Tucson, AZ.) Reprinted by permission.

curriculum implementors usually specify conditions under which students demonstrate their abilities and criteria by which the demonstration is deemed successful.

Exercise 10.1 provides an opportunity to see if you can distinguish among aims, goals, and objectives. Try this exercise.

EXERCISE 10.1

Distinguish between aims, goals, and objectives by labeling aims with A, goals with G, and objectives with O. Explain.

For the *objectives* mark each according to its taxonomic level—L for "lower" and HL for "higher-than-lower." Explain.

1. Apply the rules for forming plural nouns.
2. Execute a perfect forward roll.
3. Understand the economic forces involved in a worldwide trade agreement.
4. Develop universal literacy.
5. Promote fairness in society.
6. Know how to exercise as part of a wellness program.
7. Compare the functions of the three branches of government.
8. Appreciate cultural diversity.
9. Be accountable for own actions.

For the *objectives* mark each according to its level—L for "lower" and HL for "higher-than-lower." Explain.

Unfortunately, labels for learning outcomes are not uniformly and consistently applied. Learning outcomes called goals in one curriculum project are sometimes labeled as objectives in another project. Program outcomes are variously called aims, goals, or objectives depending on the district or school. Course or grade outcomes, while frequently named objectives, are sometimes called goals. Figure 10.3 shows how usage of learning outcome labels overlap.

LEARNING EXPERIENCES

Just as learning outcomes differ, so do planned learning experiences. Planners include *examples* of learning experiences in some curriculum documents to pro-

FIGURE 10.3
Range of Uses for Learning Outcome Labels

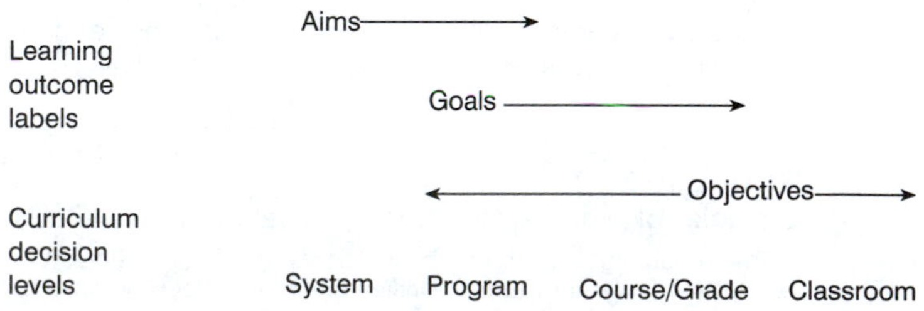

vide implementors with ideas about how learners interact with curriculum content. In these cases implementors are expected to generate their own plans for learning experiences. On the other hand, planners of other documents provide extensive information about expected teacher-learner interactions.

State guidelines typically provide examples of planned learning experiences. On the other hand, district guides generally provide more complete plans for instruction. However, developers are free to select whichever type of planning they wish. The projects in Appendix A attest to this freedom of choice.

So what's included in a planned learning experience? Chapter 2 lists decision making categories including materials and resources, activities and teaching strategies, grouping, time, and space. Decisions in these categories are legitimately involved in the creation of learning experiences.

Regardless of which decisions are included, planned learning experiences must provide information about how learners are expected to connect with curriculum content. What accommodations are suggested for learners with special needs? What types of learning are encouraged? Are students expected to receive or generate their knowledge? Of course, answers to these questions are intimately related to projected teachers' roles in delivering the curriculum. These roles outlined in the planned learning experiences should match those projected in the views of education statement.

Examples of Planned Learning Experiences. Figure 10.4 shows a planned learning experience from the curriculum project, *A Curriculum Guide for Fifth Grade Social Studies* (1990). Although the wording is abridged, all sections are included with some details. As its title indicates, this learning experience is a lesson plan for teachers to follow. It contains information about most of the decision categories.

Recall that Figure 10.1 displays means-ends relationships among learning outcomes and learning experiences from curriculum developers' point of view. Look again at this figure, but read from right to left. This is the sequence in which learners encounter the curriculum. Looked at from this perspective, the figure represents Dewey's (1916) idea that an end is temporary until attained, and then it becomes a means to the next end.

LEARNING OUTCOMES AND LEARNING EXPERIENCES IN CURRICULUM PROJECTS

This section consolidates information about learning outcomes in this chapter with the discussion of aims in Chapter 7 and uses it in the evaluation of curriculum outcomes and learning experiences. Aims are *not* usually labeled, but other outcomes, such as goals and objectives, typically are identified. However, readers must sort learning outcomes according to the level of decision making at which they were made (i.e., program, course/grade). The time to complete this classification is well-spent because it allows readers to see how the purpose of education is put in operational terms.

Lesson: Lydia Darragh—Revolutionary Spy

Forty-eight years old, Irish-born Lydia Darragh was a Quaker housewife in Philadelphia in 1777. The British had taken many homes and buildings, including Independence Hall, as their headquarters. Since the Quaker religion was against fighting, the British believed Lydia to be non-threatening and only used a room in her home. This was an opportunity for Lydia to hear confidential news about the British.

Objectives: Students will be able to:
1. Recognize that women also had contributions to the American Revolutionary War. . . .
3. Understand that some colonists' homes and buildings were taken over by the British for their headquarters. . . .

Time Required: One or two lessons of 40 minutes.

Materials Needed:
- Transparency or copies of Secret Message
- Wall map of the world
- Books (3 listed)

Procedure:
1. Distribute Secret Message handout or use the transparency. Ask students to speculate what it is. . . .
2. Using a wall map of the world, find Ireland to show where Lydia was born. Find Philadelphia to show the setting of the story.
3. Read to the class the story "Lydia Darragh: Revolutionary Spy" found . . . in the paperback book *Secret Missions*. . . .
4. Using *Explorations . . .* , Explain to students that this story is classified as narrative nonfiction. Ask the students to recall the main events of the story in order of occurrence. . . .

Debriefing:

  .

  .

  .

  Name two ways Lydia used for secret communications.
  Why did the British require use of some colonial buildings?

FIGURE 10.4

Example of Planned Learning Experience

From *A Curriculum Guide for Fifth Grade Social Studies,* 1990, pp. 141–142. (Available from Mesa County Valley School District No. 51, Grand Junction, CO.) Abridged and reprinted by permission.

Descriptions of planned learning experiences vary greatly. Some curricula contain only minimal information, which is the case with *Spanish IV Curriculum* (Stoughton Public Schools, n.d.). In other curricula learning experiences are spelled out in detail, in lessons with instructional objectives and detailed procedures, as they are in *Into Adolescence: Caring for Our Planet and Our Health* (Hunter, 1991).

The reviews for both these curriculum projects are organized around the questions in Exercise 10.2. Refer to that exercise and the projects in Appendix A as necessary.

SPANISH IV CURRICULUM

Spanish IV Curriculum (see A4) holds as its purpose "cultivating cognitive achievement and the intellect." Analysis of the learning outcomes by levels of decision making shows that students who satisfy the requirements of the learning outcomes are likely to satisfy this purpose. An explanation follows.

Interrelated learning outcomes appear at four levels of decision making in the project. A *system* level outcome from the first paragraph refers to "sharing with the student the accumulated knowledge and culture of the past. . . . " and dovetails with this *program* outcome: "It (language proficiency) enhances the student's ability to think logically, to reason. . . . " In the Goals section these program outcomes are translated into *course* goals that say simply, "The students will learn language including vocabulary, grammar, dialogue, reading, and listening." Thereafter, the course goals are translated into *objectives,* such as this one: "Students . . . will answer factual and interpretative questions." These curriculum developers have systematically translated their purpose into increasingly more specific outcomes.

Most learning outcomes are cognitive, as well they should be for this purpose of education. Nevertheless, more emphasis on affective outcomes would be beneficial, especially in the case of meeting the program outcome on "becoming a more successful, productive world citizen."

This curriculum uses both lower (L) and higher-than-lower (HL) cognitive objectives. In several instances students are asked for HL thinking, for example, in "make reservations for a hotel room" and "interpret a passage by Quiroga." The learning outcomes appear to emphasize content (e.g., "discuss Latin American currency") and process (e.g., "employ the infinitive after certain prepositions"). This dual emphasis is appropriate for the purpose of education.

In the appendix to this curriculum guide are brief references to reading, conversational, and writing skills, along with a list of basic and supplementary materials. This is the extent to which *learning experiences* are mentioned. Although these items are not tied directly to specific objectives, a skilled teacher of Spanish could use these ideas to good advantage. The roles of teachers and school staff are not defined in the views statements so it is impossible to state whether the planned learning experiences allow these individuals to carry out their roles.

If students engaged in these learning experiences, they would be likely to develop attitudes, interests, and appreciations whether or not affective outcomes were stated. The variety of situations for developing conversational skills alone almost certainly guarantee that students would be involved in the affective concerns. Throw in Hispanic music and movies in Spanish and it becomes clear that there is more than just cognitive learning in this curriculum. Learners' backgrounds do not appear to be taken into account in this project.

INTO ADOLESCENCE: CARING FOR OUR PLANET AND OUR HEALTH

The purpose of education for this project (see A6) was identified in Chapter 7 as "helping people live in a rapidly changing, unstable society." A careful analysis of learning outcomes fails to show that meeting these requirements necessarily leads to satisfying this purpose.

The *program* outcome stated in the second paragraph is intended to help "each individual understand that he or she can make a difference by taking an active role in protecting the planet from further destruction." What could be classified as *course* outcomes appear in the Overview. An example is "to motivate students to take personal responsibility for doing what they can to protect the environment in order to sustain life and to improve human health." Both the program and course outcomes align well with the overall purpose of education, perhaps because all are very broad statements. These outcomes also contain elements of both cognitive and affective learning.

However, the *objectives* are mainly lower level cognitive outcomes that focus on content and appear to be unrelated to course outcomes. Conspicuous by their absence are affective outcomes. For students to meet the course outcomes, they would have to value taking personal actions about some of the issues, which means that affect is involved. Affective objectives that MIGHT have been used include: "students voluntarily make commitments to personally conserve water," or "students, on their own initiative, reduce the amount of their disposable personal garbage."

Usually curricula with the purpose "preparing people for living in an unstable, changing world" develop through nontechnical approaches in which outcomes are not predetermined. The outcomes emerge as students engage in the learning experiences. This project is reevaluated in Chapter 11 from a nontechnical perspective.

The learning experiences clarify the means by which students are to achieve the cognitive objectives in the lesson. Also, teachers and students are able to carry out the participatory roles intended by the views statement. Taking part in the learning experiences probably allows students to develop the affective behaviors commonly associated with this purpose of education, especially if the activities are carried out over a longer period of time than the limited number of class periods suggested in the lessons.

Exercise 10.2 provides an opportunity for you to examine and review intended learning outcomes and planned learning experiences in other curriculum documents in Appendix A. Success in this exercise may help you develop learning outcomes and planned learning experiences for your own curriculum.

EXERCISE 10.2[1]

Locate and study the learning outcomes and learning experiences for these curriculum projects:

- *A Guide for Developing a 1–9 Science Curriculum* (A2)
- *Middle School English Language Arts Curriculum Guide* (A3)
- *Wyoming Arts Education Curriculum* (A5)

Then answer these questions for each project:

1. Study the learning outcomes, which vary with the project. To what extent does meeting the learning outcomes suggest that learners are likely to achieve the purpose of the education? In order to answer this question, consider the following:

   - The learning outcomes by levels of curriculum decision making AND their relationships.
   - The domains of learning represented in the learning outcomes. Note any pertinent domain that is missing.
   - Approximate taxonomy levels, whether lower or higher-than-lower levels.

2. Study the planned learning experiences, which also vary from one project to another. How well do these learning experiences serve their intended functions? To answer this question, consider the extent to which the learning experiences:

   - Clarify means by which students are to achieve objectives.
   - Permit learners to develop a wide range of learning outcomes including attitudes, interests, appreciations, and thinking skills.
   - Take into account learners' backgrounds.
   - Allow teachers to carry out the roles planned for them in the views of education statement.

[1] This exercise assumes that you have completed Exercise 7.2 and are familiar with the views of education statements for these curriculum documents in Appendix A.

ALTERNATIVE APPROACHES TO LOCAL CURRICULUM DECISION MAKING REVISITED

Chapter 2 indicates that district- or school-based groups design local institutional curricula using technical approaches. Where school-based groups exist, they work cooperatively with district groups or independently, depending on the governance structure. (See Table 2.1.)

The advantage of school-based committees is that they typically involve most or all the teachers in a school working together. These groups also have the advantage of considering their particular community's strengths and needs. Their products reflect the collective expertise of the participants.

This section summarizes the tasks involved in developing a curriculum under alternative technical approaches. Figure 10.5 shows how the tasks distribute between district and school committees. Tasks in the left column are typically handled by district groups in the absence of any school-based groups.

However, where school-based groups work with district committees, the tasks diverge at the stage of developing outcomes and learning experiences. The district group prepares program and grade cluster outcomes, lists potential resources, and submits these for governing board approval. Thereafter, the district views statements and learning outcomes may be modified by the school committee for the context where they are implemented. Tasks handled by cooperating school-based groups are summarized in the lower right column of Figure 10.5. This set of tasks is described more fully in the section called Creation of Plans for Learning Outcomes and Learning Experiences.

A third alternative involves school-based groups only, particularly those using site-based management. Independently of district groups, these committees

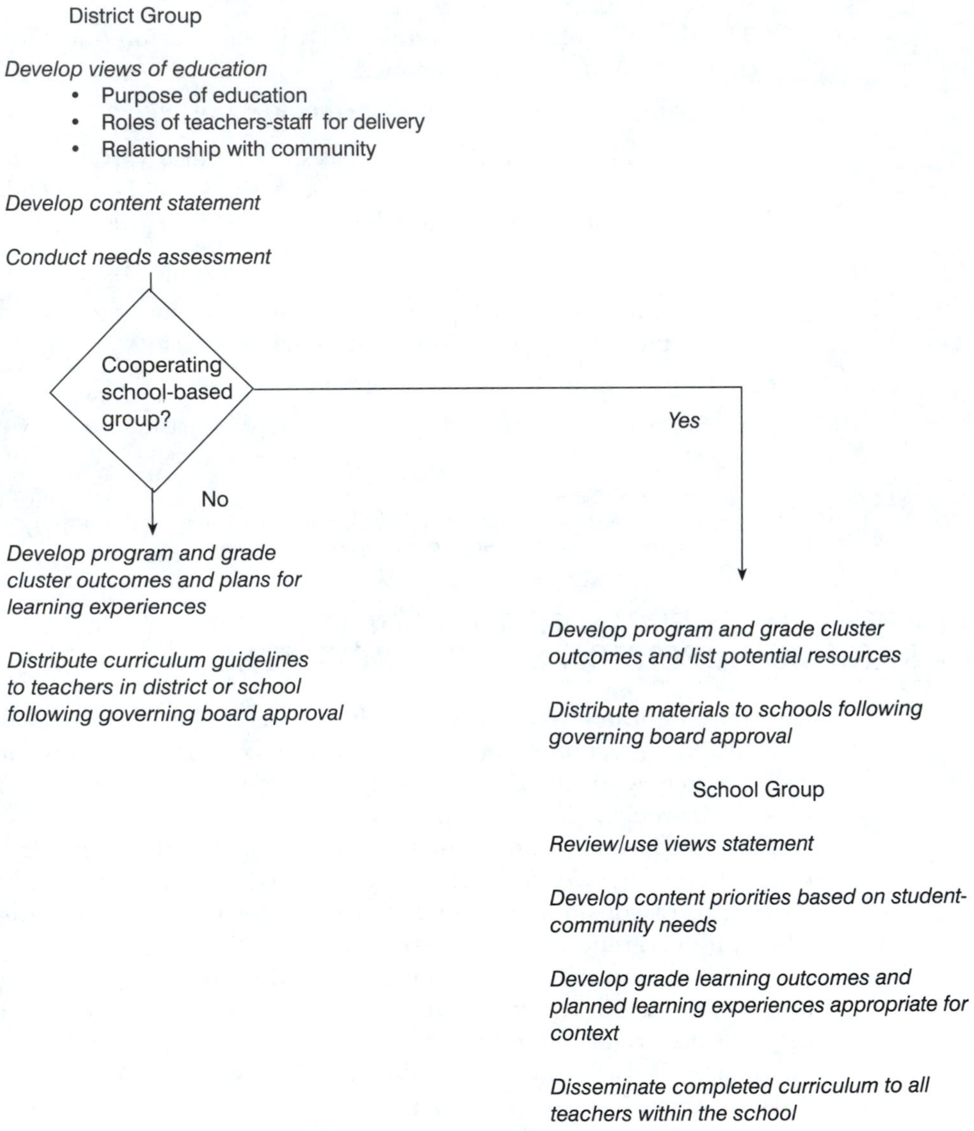

District Group

Develop views of education
- Purpose of education
- Roles of teachers-staff for delivery
- Relationship with community

Develop content statement

Conduct needs assessment

Cooperating school-based group?

Yes

No

Develop program and grade cluster outcomes and plans for learning experiences

Distribute curriculum guidelines to teachers in district or school following governing board approval

Develop program and grade cluster outcomes and list potential resources

Distribute materials to schools following governing board approval

School Group

Review/use views statement

Develop content priorities based on student-community needs

Develop grade learning outcomes and planned learning experiences appropriate for context

Disseminate completed curriculum to all teachers within the school

FIGURE 10.5
Tasks in the Development of Technically Developed Institutional Curricula by District-Based Groups With and Without School-Based Groups

develop their own views of education that take into account their school community. Such groups may also conduct needs assessments, which are then followed by development of grade/classroom learning outcomes and planned learning experiences, especially fitted to the needs of their schools.

CREATION OF PLANS FOR LEARNING OUTCOMES AND LEARNING EXPERIENCES

Creating plans for learning outcomes and learning experiences is usually considered the major thrust of technical curriculum development. As a result, planners spend long hours on these tasks. Well-articulated views of education and content statements provide foundations on which developers build well-chosen learning outcomes and experiences.

This section concludes the development of the health curriculum that began in Chapter 7. A district-based committee formulates *program* and *grade-cluster* learning outcomes. Then the narrative shifts to the work of a *school*-based curriculum committee that modifies the district views of education statement for its community and generates *grade* objectives and planned learning experiences. In the final subsection the school committee reexamines the project against the content organization considerations.

HEALTH CURRICULUM

For the remainder of this section, discussion will focus, for illustrative purposes, on one small piece of the health curriculum. Keep in mind, however, that in a real-world situation both district and school committees work on the complete curriculum.

District Level. Imagine that you, as an elementary school principal, continue service on a district-based curriculum committee charged with planning an elementary school health curriculum. Your group completed its views of education statement and in the process re-adopted the purpose of "cultivating cognitive achievement and the intellect." Actually the aim was stated as helping students "acquire the knowledge, skills, and attitudes that promote sensible, lifelong health habits." (See Figure 7.3.)

The group also drafted a content statement (Figure 8.4) that district evaluators used in a needs assessment. One entry in the content statement that received high priority:

VIII.   Disease prevention and control
      A.   Basic causes of illness and disease
      B.   Practices that prevent and control diseases
      C.   Personal responsibility

For this piece of content and all the other entries with high priority, your district group plans program goals. Although it is easy to see that this content requires a cognitive goal, the aims statement indicates that an affective goal is also needed. So the group proposes the following *elementary school program* goals for this section of the content statement:

Students will:

• Understand the causes, preventive measures, and control of diseases.

• Show interest in measures that prevent illnesses.

The committee also generates health goals by grade clusters K–3 and 4–6. To complete this task, your group extends the outline as follows:

VIII.   Disease prevention and control
      A.   Basic causes of illness and disease
          1.   Differences in wellness and illness
          2.   Communicable and noncommunicable diseases
      B.   Practices that prevent and control diseases
          1.   Knowledge of how illness is spread
          2.   Knowledge of how disease is prevented
      C.   Personal responsibility
          1.   Practice of good health habits
          2.   Application of knowledge of prevention and control

Based on this extended outline, your group prepares learning outcomes for students in two grade clusters, K–3 and 4–6, shown in Figure 10.6. To illustrate, the "basic causes" topic has two outcomes in grades K–3: "understand the differences between wellness and illness (or disease)" and "understand causes of disease." The same topic has one outcome in grades 4–6: "understand causes of

---

Students in grades K–3 should attain these goals:

• understand the differences between wellness and illness (or disease).

• understand causes of disease.

• understand that people can prevent and control disease.

• begin to assume personal responsibility for disease prevention and control.

Students in grades 4–6 should attain these goals:

• understand causes of communicable and noncommunicable diseases.

• understand the role of personal responsibility for disease prevention and control.

• demonstrate personal responsibility for disease prevention and control.

FIGURE 10.6
Examples of Grade-Cluster Learning Outcomes (Goals) for a Health Curriculum

communicable and noncommunicable diseases." Note, too, that the generality of these outcomes is that of goals. They provide scope for the curriculum and can be evaluated generally.

Both sets of outcomes extend and make more specific the aim of this curriculum, but they respect the differences in maturity and general ability levels of children who are to meet them. The learning outcomes for the older students follow logically from those for the younger students. Therefore, these outcomes are clearly within the *scope* of the district health curriculum and they provide *continuity* through elementary school.

Next the district curriculum committee summarizes this information and forwards it to the board of education for discussion and approval. The district committee disbands; its work is completed.

At the next meeting of elementary school principals, your supervisor reports that the board approved the curriculum. The supervisor then discusses the district committee's work on the health curriculum. Of course, this is not news to you because you were there! However, other elementary principals who were not part of the district committee must understand the information because, like you, they will lead the development of school-based curricula in their buildings.

School Level.   Your challenge lies ahead, for you must work with teachers and staff in your school to develop and implement a revised curriculum. Twenty-plus teachers teach at the school where you are principal. Some are just beginning their careers, but others have more years of experience than you. Previous curriculum experiences with these individuals show that some can become involved easily, but others are reluctant. When faced with a new idea, more than one teacher has been known to grumble, "This, too, shall pass," and take cursory notice of a curriculum project. Given this diversity of inclinations toward curriculum development, you know your job won't be particularly easy. What you do know is that children in your school and their parents/guardians need the information in this curriculum.

As the initial step in meeting this challenge, you rethink the change processes for initiating curriculum projects. What combination of relevance, readiness, and resources will make things work in a school-based situation? A few teachers will be ready to start. But others will wonder, "Why do we have to change the curriculum? The one we have is just fine." Which answers are meaningful? This is especially troublesome because you are aware that not every teacher is as concerned as you are about students' absences because of health problems.

Of course, the teachers in your school knew you were working with the district committee. In one sense they knew they would be expected to work on the *school* health curriculum. Your plan is to formally begin this curriculum effort during a regularly scheduled faculty-staff meeting. You talked with the leadership team of the local parent-teacher organization and asked them to recruit community members to work with the faculty and staff on curriculum development.

You hope to engage the assembled group in a discussion that centers on the needs for health education in your school community, the number of students who miss school because of health-related causes, and the highlights and rationale for the new state guidelines for health. From this discussion and informal follow-up conversations, you intend to involve as many people as possible in creating a vision of the revised curriculum.

Before that kick-off meeting, you provide all the faculty, staff, and community members who indicate interest in the curriculum with the district views of education statement, the content outline, program goals, and the grade-cluster goals. Included with the materials is a request that they read them before the meeting. The purpose of the meeting is to begin to clarify what the school curriculum should be—especially how the revised curriculum should differ from what you now have. Some things in the proposed curriculum will remain the same.

At the meeting you moderate a discussion of the views of education statement. Because the purpose of education is unchanged, teachers and community members don't question the aim of the curriculum. However, you ask the assembled group to actively consider how this views statement should be modified to fit your school community. Several teachers and community members contribute ideas centering on the needs of students and their families for practical health information. Others offer suggestions about involving local community health services into curriculum delivery.

The discussion continues about the roles for teachers in delivering the curriculum. Teachers should be asked to explain what their expected role is. (Note: The views statement calls for students to generate their own knowledge. For starters, this implies that health classes must consist of more than reading the textbook and answering questions.) Some teachers will need time to think about the role they are expected to take, so you do not expect acceptance of the views statement at this meeting. You remember that change is individual and that each person must make his/her own way through the meaning-making processes. But, at some point in the deliberations you must see if there is consensus on the projected roles for teachers and school staff.

With the group you examine the program outcomes and the grade-cluster outcomes. Provide the group with whatever explanation is necessary about how these outcomes were derived. But clarify that, within the scope of the grade-cluster outcomes, your school is free to set the next outcomes (grade or classroom) to reflect the needs of your school community. For example, if the need is great to teach substance abuse prevention or environmental health, your school can choose to emphasize those topics and give less attention to topics with less community relevance.

Following this discussion the teachers, staff, and community members should reflect on their school community and students. Based on their perceptions of content needs, they assign high, medium, or low priorities to the grade clusters of outcomes. This discussion must continue until the group is comfortable with the priorities. Community members who wish to continue with curriculum development should be encouraged to do so.

At the appropriate time and with input from the teachers, you devise a multimonth plan for handling the tasks of this project. These include formulating either grade or classroom outcomes, planning learning experiences for these outcomes, developing a timeline for completing the tasks, and a process for communication among the people involved. Ideally, this plan should be approved by the teachers and staff.

Suppose that teachers decide to work in groups on the outcomes and learning experiences. Each group selects one or more "pieces" of content. The media specialist and librarian agree to provide information to the groups as needed. You recommend that representatives from several grades serve on each group to help manage the content organization considerations of *sequence* and *integration*. The repetitions in ideas and activities should deepen students' understandings, but not bore them.

Whether these groups consider creation of more specific learning outcomes first and then learning experiences, or work on them together is immaterial. Sometimes teachers find that thinking about what they want students to *do* in terms of learning activities is helpful in planning learning outcomes. For example, teachers may consider using a videotape about the causes of diseases. Before making a decision, the group must consider what students might learn from viewing the tape. Such back-and-forth thinking about outcomes and experiences is typical of piecemeal planning.

Within their groups teachers will probably have much discussion—some productive and some not—according to group dynamics. As people consider outcomes and learning experiences, they must wrestle with several issues (listed here in no particular order):

- Conceptions and values assigned to knowledge (e.g., content or process, declarative or procedural).
- Beliefs and values about the importance of the content.
- Perceptions of the abilities and interests of students for whom they are planning.
- Beliefs and values about how students should come in contact with content (e.g., be told, read about it, discover it).
- Beliefs and values about the type of learning outcome to be used (e.g., intellectual skills, attitudes).

In the ideal school-based curriculum development project, teachers and school staff reach agreements on these issues. Where this is possible, those who develop the project would "own" the curriculum because their values are represented. In the real world, however, such agreements are rare.

Learning experiences result in cognitive, affective, and/or psychomotor learning for students. Therefore, planners are encouraged to generate outcomes in the appropriate domains and, in the case of cognitive outcomes, to produce measurable objectives. Outcomes and learning experiences vary from one group of planners to another because of differences in views about the issues. For example, consider these grade objectives:

Students should be able to:

1. List diseases that are not contagious.
2. List diseases that are contagious.
3. Distinguish between contagious and noncontagious diseases.
4. Plan appropriate actions for preventing the spread of contagious diseases.
5. Display actions voluntarily on school campuses that prevent the spread of contagious diseases.

Each objective requires cognitive or affective learning about communicable and noncommunicable diseases, based on a grade-cluster goal for 4–6: "Students will understand differences between communicable and noncommunicable diseases." (See Figure 10.6.)

On the surface, outcomes 1 through 4 appear similar, but they require different performances from students and different learning experiences for their achievement. The first two objectives focus on declarative information, but the third and fourth emphasize procedural information. The first two objectives call for learning at lower cognitive taxonomy levels. Objective 3 is also considered a lower level objective even though it requires a slightly higher level of understanding than the first two objectives.

Because Objective 4 requires that students apply their knowledge, it is considered a higher-than-lower cognitive objective. Objective 5 reflects affective learning. Its intent is to enable students to value or become committed to preventing contagious disease. The use of "voluntarily" is important here because an observer would not know if students valued disease prevention unless they took action of their own volition. The learning for Objective 5 should take place alongside cognitive learning.

Prior to these activities introduce learners to the idea that some diseases are contagious from one person to another, but that other diseases are not contagious. Then use the following activities to show how communicable disease may spread.

Activity 1:
Secretly select two students and assign them a communicable disease such as measles, mumps, or chicken pox. Ask each person in the class to walk around the room, shake hands with five different people, and remember who those people were. All students return to their seats.

Ask the two students to identify themselves and tell the diseases they were assigned. Ask for a show of hands of people who came in direct contact with these disease carriers. Invite discussion about how direct contact with a person who has a contagious disease can help spread disease. Follow up with a show of hands of students who shook hands with those who had the direct contact. Continue the discussion about indirect contact and spread of contagious diseases.

Activity 2:
To simulate transmission of communicable diseases by microbes, put a small quantity of cocoa or flour in the hands of several students. Ask them to cough into their hands and note the results. (The action of the cocoa or flour particles is comparable to that of microbes.) Discuss this possible method of spreading diseases.

FIGURE 10.7
Sample Experiences for Learning About Methods for Transmission of Contagious Diseases

Discussions about these matters involve decision making. As developers consider learning outcomes, they must be aware of the implications of their choices. For example, students can increase their *declarative* knowledge for objectives 1 and 2 by adding names of additional contagious and noncontagious diseases. However, students increase their *procedural* knowledge for objectives 3 and 4 through gains in abilities for making "distinctions" and "planning," skills that can be used in a variety of learning situations.

Of what value to students is the information required in objectives 1 and 2? The best answer is probably responding to quiz questions in a health class. But what about the value of the information in Objective 3? For one thing, it is the first step in being able to perform the learning in Objective 4, a learning usually highly valued in society. Must students satisfy Objective 3 before they work on Objective 4? This answer is also a values question. In their roles as curriculum developers, teachers use their knowledge of learners and their characteristics in combination with pedagogical content knowledge to answer these types of questions.

Groups should also consider the developmental levels of students as they deliberate about learning outcomes. More specifically, the group should decide, for example, whether students can be expected to "plan appropriate actions for preventing the spread of contagious diseases" provided they have the prerequisite knowledge. Stated another way, teachers are deciding on the learnability of the content for students in their school.

Some school development groups might decide that students should satisfy all four objectives over a span of three years with objectives 1 and 2 first, followed by Objective 3 and then Objective 4. Other groups might eliminate objectives 1 and 2 altogether, but ask students to meet both objectives 3 and 4. Such decisions would be based on the groups' values involving student abilities and needs and the content to be learned. Most groups would probably want to be sure that students not only satisfied Objective 4 at school, but transferred that behavior to out-of-school situations as well.

Because the objectives call for different types of learning, the planned learning experiences for them differ. For example, students can learn a list of communicable and noncommunicable diseases by reading a book, viewing a motion picture or videotape, or being told what the diseases are by a teacher.

Learning to distinguish between contagious and noncontagious diseases (Objective 3) suggests that students must do something more than read about diseases. For example, students could conduct activities that show how communicable diseases are transmitted. See Figure 10.7 for suggested activities. Note that learners engaged in these activities are expected to generate their own knowledge about how contagious diseases are spread. Discussions within these activities could be used as the basis of learners' plans for actions that prevent the spread of these diseases, required in Objective 4.

Exercise 10.3 extends this discussion of learning outcomes and learning experiences and is intended to prepare you for generating learning outcomes and learning experiences statements for your own curriculum project. Completing this exercise can help prepare you for generating learning outcomes and learning experiences in other situations.

EXERCISE
10.3

Choose a grade-cluster learning outcome other than "understand causes of communicable and noncommunicable diseases" from the display in Figure 10.6.

1. For this outcome generate at least two grade or classroom objectives that require different classroom learning outcomes (e.g., concepts, generalizations, attitudes).
2. Plan a learning experience that would help students meet one of the objectives.
3. Reconsider both the objectives and the learning experience to see that they are complementary. Did you use systematic or piecemeal planning? Explain.

Discuss results with classmates as a check on your planning.

Reconsideration of Content Organization.   Following the development of the classroom outcomes and learning experiences, school curriculum developers should review the project to be sure they adhered to content organization considerations. The grade outcomes, for example, should fall within the *scope* of content established by the grade-cluster outcomes. Presentation or development of the ideas and skills should recur across grades K–6, thus maintaining *continuity*.

Because this is a subject-based curriculum, the developers should also check on *sequence* to see that the repeated ideas and skills require greater depths than those that preceded. Finally, curriculum developers should strive for *integration*, making sure that affective and cognitive learning work together. If any organizational consideration is faulty, the outcomes or learning experiences should be corrected before the curriculum is implemented. When the school committee completes the reconsideration, the curriculum should be distributed to all teachers in the school.

SUMMARY

Chapter 10 describes intended learning outcomes as occupying a continuum of broadness-narrowness from aims to goals to objectives. This continuum conforms to the systematic approach of curriculum development that suggests stating the purpose of education as aims, then making the aims operational as goals, and converting goals to objectives. Each of these learning outcomes serves as both an end and as a means.

Planned learning experiences provide the means to satisfy objectives. Typically, learning experiences indicate with different degrees of specificity how teachers and students are to interact with content. These roles should correspond to those defined in the views of education.

Learning outcomes and learning experiences in two curriculum projects were evaluated to see how well they conformed to these informal specifications. One curriculum fitted the specifications well, but the second curriculum contained learning outcomes not fitted to the purpose of education.

In the final section learning outcomes and learning experiences were created for a hypothetical elementary school health education curriculum. First, a district committee prepared grade-cluster outcomes. Then a school-based group prepared grade objectives and learning experiences. Finally, developers reviewed the project against the content organizational considerations.

QUESTIONS FOR DISCUSSION

1. Explain the advantages that well-prepared views of education and content statements make to the creation of intended learning outcomes and planned learning experiences.

2. This chapter identifies the ambiguity of verbs as one aspect of broadness-narrowness of learning outcomes. Based on this discussion, name additional verbs that could be used in *broad statements*. Other verbs that could be used in *narrow statements?* State reasons for your choices.

3. Labels for learning outcomes at different levels of curriculum decision making are sometimes used interchangeably. Discuss advantages and disadvantages of this practice.

4. Here are two planned learning experiences from *Middle School English Language Arts Curriculum Guide*. (See Appendix A3 for the context in which these experiences are suggested to teachers.) For each experience, decide if learning is intended as receptive or generative. Explain.

   a. "Write a business letter ordering an item that you have seen advertised in a magazine or catalog. Include all necessary information such as a model number, quantity, size, color, price, and method of payment. Be sure to use correct business letter form."

   b. "Take a set of class-generated notes that are disorganized, organize these notes and write a report on a guest speaker, assembly, or a field trip. Decide which notes are main ideas and which are introductory, which are key observations, areas visited and ideas learned. Finally, tell what you and the other students gained from the trip, and how you responded."

5. Explain how the change processes of readiness, relevancy, and resources described in Chapter 7 were addressed (if they were) in the section called Creation of Learning Outcomes and Learning Experiences Statements.

6. Explain advantages and disadvantages of the use of school-based curriculum processes.

7. Explain how teacher expertises were used in the creation of outcomes and learning experiences for the health curriculum.

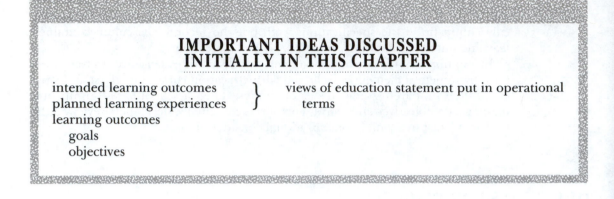

**IMPORTANT IDEAS DISCUSSED
INITIALLY IN THIS CHAPTER**

intended learning outcomes
planned learning experiences   } views of education statement put in operational
learning outcomes   terms
    goals
    objectives

11

LEARNING EXPERIENCES FOR NONTECHNICALLY DEVELOPED CURRICULUM PROJECTS

OUTLINE

The preparation of planned learning experiences is the culmination of a nontechnically developed curriculum project. Based on their views of education, developers prepare learning experiences that point students toward the purpose of education for which that curriculum is intended. Typical purposes for nontechnical curricula include "developing individuals to their fullest potentials" and "preparing people for living in an unstable, changing world." These purposes focus on people as individuals and as groups, respectively. Because outcomes of curricula with these purposes are unpredictable, developers plan learning experiences that foster a variety of learning outcomes and allow them to emerge.

This chapter defines planned learning experiences under the nontechnical approach and details the processes in developing nontechnical curricula including the importance of physical and interpersonal contexts. Next planned learning experiences for two curricula are critiqued. The final section shows how learning experiences are created for a hypothetical nontechnical curriculum. The purpose of this chapter is to enable you *to prepare descriptions of learning experiences for a nontechnically developed curriculum project of your choice.*

PLANNED LEARNING EXPERIENCES

After defining planned learning experiences, this section discusses the development of nontechnically developed curricula. Development includes consideration of the content, the relationships of teacher-planners and learners, interpersonal contexts, and physical contexts. Finally these considerations are illustrated in segments from nontechnical curricula.

DEFINITION

Planned learning experiences in nontechnically developed curricula share some features with those in technically developed curricula. Both provide opportunities for learners to interact with the curriculum content implied by the purpose of education. These opportunities allow for development of a wide range of learning outcomes in all pertinent domains. Planned learning experiences provide for teacher involvement in curriculum delivery in the ways projected in the views of education statement.

But learning experiences in nontechnical curricula have specialized features, too. Their content is typically skills-driven and integrated (e.g., language with mathematics with science). Furthermore, learners have considerable latitude in the choice, timing, and execution of learning experiences, which can complicate resource-space requirements. In general, nontechnical curricula require more resources and space than most technical curricula. Most importantly, these learning experiences feature close relationships between teachers and learners in which each learns from the other (Hunter & Scheirer, 1988; Short & Burke, 1991).

NONTECHNICAL APPROACH TO DEVELOPMENT

Teacher-developers use their purpose of education as a guide in the selection of themes and experiences. These planners use *expedient* planning, in which they determine the learning experiences and allow the outcomes to emerge once experiences are enacted. Several types of learning are possible through this approach, but this is an especially desirable way of helping learners develop values or attitudes (Davies, 1976).

Nature of Content.   Nontechnically developed curriculum documents describe learning experiences built around interdisciplinary themes. Developers sometimes elicit curriculum themes from students, but others use preselected themes, depending on their preferences and degrees of autonomy. For example, adults enrolled in an English as a Second Language literacy project have personal and professional reasons for participation. Some participants want to learn English for assistance with shopping, work, talking with friends and neighbors, or dealing with landlords. Reasons such as these can provide themes addressed in the curriculum (Auerbach, 1990; Nash, Cason, Rhum, McGrail, & Gomez-Sanford, 1989).

On the other hand, the organic curriculum uses preselected themes. Developers choose themes in advance because the curriculum is planned for students over a period of years and preselected themes reduce the possibility of content redundancy. Themes include "growing tomatoes," "a visit to Worsborough Mill," and "the urban farm" (Hunter & Scheirer, 1988). Each theme can easily encompass many cognitive skills related to science, reading, language, and other subjects as well as affective and psychomotor learning.

Relationships of Teacher-Planners and Learners.   Look again at Figure 1.2 and recall the discussion about the relationship between teachers and learners in Chapter 1. It suggests an idea that can be said clearly here. The nontechnical curriculum approach requires that teachers view students as interactive or active on their environments (see Chapter 6). Exchanges between and among learners with learners and with teachers are vital. The focus is on learners learning, rather than on teachers teaching (Hunter & Scheirer, 1988). Teachers and learners together form communities of learners, with each learning from the other (Paris, 1993; Short & Burke, 1991).

This relationship appears to be similar to the one in Kilpatrick's (1918) project method. But the nontechnical curricula described here require teachers with knowledge of curriculum, learners, and subject matter—which were not necessary in the project method. Learners have considerable latitude in their choices of activities, the materials they use, how long they pursue them, and so on. However, teachers coach, encourage and insist that learners engage in activities tied generally to the purpose of education.

For such communities to function properly, strong interpersonal relationships in physical settings must provide freedom among participants. The next two subsections describe these necessities.

Interpersonal Contexts.   The experiences, interactions, and negotiations of meaning among learners and teachers are all part of the **interpersonal context**, which is at the heart of successful nontechnical curriculum projects (Blenkin & Whitehead, 1988). The essence of interpersonal contexts is captured by Short and Burke (1991): "The uniqueness of school is that it is a place where a community of learners can be given opportunities to be reflective about what and how they are learning" (p. 9).

Young children grow in self-knowledge and awareness through play involving materials, people, ideas, and situations. Given the opportunity to freely handle materials, ideas, and language, young children learn a range of feelings as they participate in different roles. In effect, children at play are laying the foundation for using materials in more controlled situations. Here they are able to manifest their feelings and understandings of their world and their place in it (Blenkin & Whitehead, 1988).

Of particular importance are responses to literature, because these permit learners of all ages to deal with their thoughts and fantasies (Blenkin & Whitehead, 1988; Probst, 1987; Rosenblatt, 1983). "It (literature) offers us experience from which we may synthesize knowledge about our values, our beliefs, our relationships with other people and with the world" (Probst, 1987, p. 27). Rosenblatt (1983) suggests that teachers of secondary students be aware that "[t]he areas of intellectual and emotional ferment are the points at which growth is possible in the student's mind and personality. The teacher who learns not to become insecure when lively discussion arises will also learn to sense the right moment to introduce new concepts relevant to these growth points" (p. 247).

Students of all ages also have to learn to deal with "not knowing" or "not doing." Blenkin and Whitehead (1988) report research suggesting that much unacceptable behavior in traditional subject-centered classrooms is caused by young students' feelings of "not knowing" and their inability to handle these feelings appropriately. Observations in classrooms of older children show that situations worsen for some students as they grow older and learning requirements increase. Helping students overcome these difficulties is linked to providing situations in which it is safe and acceptable to "not know." Opportunities for talking, movement, drawing, painting, or other activities are legitimate ways of handling these concerns.

But what about "not doing"? Children usually learn early that school is where you busy yourself producing learning products. However, a key element in self-awareness is reflecting on feelings and experiences, which takes time away from other tasks, literally not doing anything. In classrooms for young children, teachers sometimes create physical spaces where children can daydream and think. Older students have the same needs to reflect, but usually learn to handle their needs in less overt ways.

What all of this means is that students and teachers must act and react to each other with sensitivity to keep the interpersonal context in good working order. In planning nontechnical curricula, developers must allow for individual differences. This discussion also shows the importance of planning the physical situation to support the interpersonal context.

Physical Contexts. Space considerations, learning materials and resources, and time arrangements must be available to stimulate active learning in situations where teachers enact nontechnical curricula. Where social problems furnish content, the physical context includes field trips into the community or laboratory situations in which social experiences can be evaluated. Where learners' developmental needs furnish content, suitably sized physical spaces are necessary for active learners and teachers.

Movable furniture is necessary in both storage and study areas because students work together in groups as well as individually. Storage areas (cupboards, bins, boxes, and others) are required because nontechnically developed curricula typically involve students, depending on their age and grade levels, with multiple materials housed in classrooms.

Classrooms must have age-appropriate and interesting materials and resources. The range of materials is likely to affect the nature of the reaction students have to their experiences with the materials, consequently to expression and development of ideas. Whoever selects materials must judge their potential carefully to bring about the desired involvement of learners. Materials must be important enough that students want to know about and understand them (Blenkin & Whitehead, 1988).

For example, early childhood students should have rooms laid out as workshops with designated areas for arts and crafts, outdoor play and gardens, literacy and literature, mathematics and science, fantasy and role play, and music. Within these areas several types of toys, resources, tools and materials can be arranged so that children use *and return* them to their places. "[T]idying activities such as fitting boxes and bricks back into the correct storage containers or shelves at the end of a day's work can be every bit as demanding, if not more so, on the children's awareness of shape, space and matching as structured tasks such as puzzles which require the child to fit stylized wooden ducks into spaces on a block of wood" (Blenkin & Whitehead, 1988, p. 48).

Older students also need informal classroom arrangements because physical space arrangements draw students into learning activities. Multiple activities require that students be able to move freely about classrooms without disrupting fellow students. Because students work at different rates and for different periods of time, students must have room to work on projects without having to put the materials away early.

The ways teachers display students' work is an important part of organizing space. For example, displays of natural objects and human-made objects can generate language and promote ideas and discussions, especially if students are encouraged to handle the objects. Displaying students' completed work allows for increased positive recognition by teachers and peers. Thus this practice serves an important function, particularly if "developing learners to their fullest potentials" is the purpose.

Time considerations, also part of planning physical contexts, must be considered. Conventional school schedules are usually too restrictive for such learner-based activities. In nontechnical curricula students can choose learning activities that take different amounts of time. Students at all levels, including young children, need time to meditate on what they are learning. To use a nontechnical curriculum, teachers plan large blocks of time in which students initiate, sustain, and extend work. Teachers of self-contained classrooms find time considerations easier to handle than teachers in other situations.

As you read the two subsections that follow, notice how these considerations are managed. Note the content and the roles of teachers and learners, as well as the attention to interpersonal and physical contexts.

Illustration Involving College Undergraduates.   Romey (1988) describes a person-centered approach to world geography for college undergraduates. The goal of this course is to help students reach a broad level of international understanding, based on their own interests and experiences. Students enrolled in the course determine the subject matter and most learning procedures; the teacher facilitates their learning. The class, which is limited to about 20 students, meets as a seminar either once a week for three hours or twice a week for an hour-and-a-half. Class meets in an informal setting with bean-bag chairs, "back-jacks," and other comfortable furniture. Romey indicates that such courses are less successful than usual when they meet in shorter class periods and in regular classrooms. Something about the informality of the meeting place appears to help students take charge of their learning.

Beginning sessions allow students to get acquainted, set up philosophical and operational guidelines for the course, and set a tone for subsequent meetings. Thereafter, students prepare geographic briefings for their classmates using maps and other visual aids on topics they choose. Following their briefings, students lead discussions on their topics.

The instructors' role in such classes is to listen and react to students. They arrange the situation to encourage discussion and help students feel safe expressing their ideas. They help students clarify and sharpen their thinking so that points are understood by fellow students. In addition, they must always be prepared to give their own briefing if students scheduled for briefings miss class. Major reports are used in some semesters. See Figure 11.1 for information about this aspect of this person-centered course.

Illustration Involving Preschool Children.   In a child-centered curriculum Strader and Rinker (1989) use children's (ages 4–6) interests and questions about dinosaurs as the basis for the curriculum. The developers note that several television programs and food products influence children's interest in dinosaurs. Furthermore, a literature search and interviews with teachers confirm that young children are fascinated by dinosaurs. In the 1990s the Public Broadcasting System's *Barney and Friends* is very popular with preschool children and their parents.

The developers recommend materials including books, replicas, models, puzzles, manipulatives, and dramatic play props to be used in the experiences. On the first day children explore large inflated dinosaur models and formulate questions for which they would like answers. These questions furnish the design for two weeks of intensive study. During the first week, children develop terrariums to study dinosaur habitats, discuss dinosaur babies, create dinosaur eggs, read books, sing songs, and create their own books on dinosaurs. In the second week students explore theories of dinosaur extinction, investigate fossils, create dinosaurs, and discuss reptiles.

In some semesters, we have prepared a regular schedule requiring each seminar member to lead a half-hourlong seminar on some topic which they [*sic*] have prepared in depth (commonly the topic of their term papers). When we have done this, the schedule has called for two or three of these per week during the second half of the semester. The presenter is minimally responsible for a 30-minute period of time. At best, these sessions have involved a twenty-minute presentation of major research followed by an active group discussion, much as at a professional meeting. Presenters have the option of making advance reading assignments (on reserve) to the group as a whole, or they may select other students to serve as discussants. They may use slides, videotapes, films, or other audio-visual materials. Maps are required. . . . (A partial) listing of specific topics that emerged in two different semesters (includes):

World distribution of marble
Cuban refugees in Florida
Toxic wastes
Foods of the world
World distribution of sickle-cell anemia
Multi-national corporation and world hunger
World debt

FIGURE 11.1

Description of Learning Experience for a Person-Centered Curriculum Involving Young Adults

From "A Person-Centered Seminar in World Geography" by W. D. Romey, 1988, *Journal of Geography*, *87*(3), p. 91. Copyright 1988 by The National Council for Geographic Education. Reprinted by permission.

The developers report that the most effective learning experiences are those in which children actively participate in answering their own questions. Figure 11.2 illustrates one activity from this curriculum in which dinosaurs are incorporated into various curriculum areas including dramatic play, music, outdoor education, reading, and language arts. However, unlike subject-based curricula, children are not expected to reach the same learning outcomes as their classmates.

Exercise 11.1 concerns potential modifications needed to use nontechnical curricula in most schools. Are nontechnical curricula not used because of the need for these modifications or are there other reasons? Think about these questions.

EXERCISE 11.1

Reflect on the discussion of the requirements for use of nontechnical curricula. Think of a school you know where these curricula are NOT used:

1. Describe any rearrangements in the physical context of classrooms required to use a nontechnical curriculum.
2. Describe any adjustments teachers would have to make in working with students.
3. Describe any adjustments that the school staff would be obligated to make.

In order to answer the children's initial questions: "Where did the dinosaurs live?", "What did the dinosaurs eat/drink?", and "Did dinosaurs live in Hawaii because there are volcanoes there?", the children designed and built their own dinosaur terrariums.

The activity incorporated climatology, geography, and dramatic play. It helped to facilitate group planning, cooperation, and the concepts of extinction. It also provided the children with an opportunity to express their own interpretations of what the dinosaur land might have looked like.

After a discussion on what the land of the dinosaurs was like—through a song and looking through various dinosaur books, the children divided themselves into small groups. Some children were in groups of two, some in groups of three. They were given a flat box (the bottom of a case of soda) and painted or colored the inside of the box. The children were given sand. They placed the sand according to their own ideas on where they felt the land and water should be. Some children created lakes, rivers, oceans, volcanoes, and other geographic settings.

They were then told to go outside and find examples of plants, rocks, "trees," grass, and any other materials that they thought might have been around when the dinosaurs were. They discussed where to put trees, rocks, etc. They placed their "findings" in their terrariums.

Small dinosaur replicas were given to the children to play with in their terrariums. The younger children might enjoy a smaller group or even individual boxes to create their own terrariums.

FIGURE 11.2

Example of Planned Learning Experience for a Child-Centered Curriculum

From "A Child-Centered Approach to Dinosaurs" by W. H. Strader and C. A. Rinker, 1989, *Early Child Development and Care, 43,* p. 69. Copyright 1989 by Gordon and Breach Science Publishers, Inc. Reprinted by permission.

LEARNING EXPERIENCES IN CURRICULUM PROJECTS

This section analyzes the learning experiences in the curriculum projects *Into Adolescence: Caring for Our Planet and Our Health* (Hunter, 1991) and *Collaborative Teaching Experiences to Develop Communication Skills* (1992). These analyses are based on the features of planned learning experiences in nontechnical curriculum discussed in the section titled Definitions.

INTO ADOLESCENCE: CARING FOR OUR PLANET AND OUR HEALTH

Into Adolescence (see A6) has as its purpose the "preparation of people for living in a rapidly changing, unstable society." This project was evaluated previously as a technically developed curriculum because it contains predetermined goals and objectives. That evaluation in Chapter 10 points out the incompatibility between the aim and the objectives.

Reconsidering this document *without* reference to the objectives provides a very different experience. The descriptions of learning experiences show learner involvement in meaningful experiences that support the purpose of education. Much of the learning is cognitive, but some affective and psychomotor possibilities are mentioned. The amount of time suggested for the learning experiences is probably too stringent, but students who engage in these activities over a school year could conceivably develop the values sought by this curriculum. The nature of the learning experiences is such that students explore several sides to environmental issues and choose the side with which they wish to identify.

Reading the learning experiences does not tell whether learners have latitude in their activities, but this could be arranged. Clearly many of the learning experiences involve teachers and students in the active learning intended by the views statement.

COLLABORATIVE TEACHING EXPERIENCES TO DEVELOP COMMUNICATION SKILLS

As indicated in Chapter 7, this project (see A7) has as its purpose the "development of individuals to their fullest potentials." Specifically, this project seeks to expand children's language abilities through the collaboration of regular classroom teachers and teachers of speech-language impaired students. The two sample learning experiences shown in the excerpt support this purpose. The content of the learning experiences is process-oriented and uses the diverse topics of sentence construction and manners. Both experiences allow for cognitive, affective, and psychomotor learning.

The discussion about collaborative classroom activities suggests that learners and teachers have latitude in their use. This curriculum is intended to be individualized. The full extent of how closely teachers and learners work together cannot be judged by reading the descriptions of learning experiences.

However, in these activities teachers and students interact in ways that allow students to take much of the responsibility for their own learning. Even though no dialogue is given, it is easy to imagine teachers using the open-ended questions mentioned in the project to help children think about their actions and develop their communication skills. The activities move students in the direction of the purpose.

ALTERNATIVE APPROACHES TO LOCAL CURRICULUM DECISION MAKING REVISITED

Chapter 2 indicates that school-based curriculum committees sometimes develop institutional curricula using nontechnical approaches, especially at site-based management locations. Developers are principally teachers with strong interests in creating curricula that handle the special needs of students.

As summarized in Figure 11.3, planners prepare a views of education statement, devise content, and sometimes conduct a diagnostic needs assessment. Based on its results, they develop and distribute plans for learning experiences to teachers who use them.

FIGURE 11.3
Tasks in the Development of Nontechnically Developed Institutional Curricula by School-Based Groups

Develop views of education
- *purpose of education*
- *roles of teachers-staff for delivery*
- *relationships with community*

Develop content statement

Conduct needs assessment

Develop plans for learning experiences

Distribute plans for learning experiences to teachers

CREATION OF PLANS FOR LEARNING EXPERIENCES

Creating plans for learning experiences is the major part of developing a non-technical curriculum. However, views of education statements and content statements, usually themes, that are well thought out promote curriculum building to meet the needs of learners and society.

In the section that follows, the two high school teachers, first mentioned in a hypothetical situation in Chapter 7, design learning experiences that help "develop individuals to their fullest potentials." For illustrative purposes the following discussion focuses on *part* of an English literature curriculum. In the real world the developers work on additional curriculum areas and topics. Notice particularly that subject matter is a means of helping individuals develop themselves; its acquisition is not what is important.

ENGLISH LITERATURE CURRICULUM

After gathering information about student needs and interests, you and your colleague select content and develop themes for the curriculum. You are ready to plan learning experiences and expect to forward these plans to your department head because this experimental curriculum requires board approval.

Your intent is to help students expand their consciousness of people portrayed in printed materials, increase language skills and abilities, and improve social relations. This particular curriculum segment uses excerpts from Chaucer's *The Canterbury Tales* as the content. (See Figure 7.4 for information about the views of education statement and Figures 8.5 and 8.6 for information about the content.)

Previous experience tells you that most seniors have studied very little English literature before coming into your course in their last year of high school. This means there's need to establish a setting for *The Canterbury Tales* that permits students to understand what they read. At this point you and your colleague decide to prepare introductory and culminating learning experiences as well as several experiences related to each *Tale* to which you have access—"The Prologue," "The Wife of Bath's Tale," and "The Pardoner's Tale." The intent of the learning experiences is to point learners toward the aims statement.

Introductory Learning Experiences.   The beginning learning experiences concentrate on what life was probably like in the Middle Ages. Among the things that students need to understand are these:

- The purpose of pilgrimages.
- How the church operated during the Middle Ages.
- That the typical person's life span was short because of diseases, such as the Black Death, or wars.
- That the law as we know it had not been written.
- That people spoke Middle English, which is different from English as we know it today.
- That people were assigned to a social status group based on their family background.
- That people living in the Middle Ages were not significantly different in their wants, needs, and desires from people today.

Student editions of literature anthologies provide some background, but teachers' editions provide more information about these understandings as well as suggestions for locating additional information. You plan to relate the most critical ideas at the beginning of this study and add others as the learning experiences are enacted.

Although not all at once nor even in the same week, ask students to read "The Prologue," "The Wife of Bath's Tale," and "The Pardoner's Tale." Point students to the definitions of unusual words that assist their comprehension of the poem and provide assistance with reading as needed by the students. See Figure 11.4 for an illustration of help found in the student text.

Learning Experiences Related to "The Prologue."   The experiences suggested here relate to the theme "Many types of human beings exist." Invite students to read a section of "The Prologue," then allow them to listen to a recording of the section read in Middle English. Discuss similarities and differences between Middle and modern English.

After students have read "The Prologue," the teacher may lead discussion about the Canterbury pilgrims, named in Figure 11.5 according to their societal groupings. However, before the discussion begins, each student should choose a pilgrim to portray for that day. As students interact with the teacher and peers, they try to stay in character. Following this exercise, the students may converse with their neighbors in character. They should try to talk with as many different people as time permits (Wiltsey, 1975). This experience allows students to look at situations through someone else's eyes. In doing so, they may realize, if they have not done so already, that people have individual subjective frames of reference for their actions.

A second learning experience could feature a discussion between pilgrims played by students. For example, ask the Monk and the Prioress to discuss "freedom"; ask the Pardoner and the Miller to discuss "love." These conversations

A Sergeant at the Law[52] who paid his calls,
320 Wary and wise, for clients at Saint Paul's[53]
There also was, of noted excellence.
Discreet he was, a man to reverence,
Or so he seemed, his sayings were so wise.
He often had been Justice of Assize[54]
325 By letters patent,[55] and in full commission.
His fame and learning and his high position
Had won him many a robe and many a fee.
There was no such conveyancer[56] as he;
All was fee-simple[57] to his strong digestion.
330 Not one conveyance could be called in question.
Though there was nowhere one so busy as he,
He was less busy than he seemed to be.
He knew of every judgment, case, and crime
Ever recorded since King William's[58] time.
335 He could dictate defenses or draft deeds;
No one could pinch a comma from his screeds[59]
And he knew every statute off by rote.
He wore a homely particolored coat.
Girt with a silken belt of pin-stripe stuff;
340 Of his appearance I have said enough.

52 **Sergeant at the Law:** lawyer appointed by the king to serve as a judge.
53 **Saint Paul's:** London cathedral outside which lawyers often met clients when the courts were closed.
54 **Assize:** traveling law court.
55 **letters patent:** royal documents commissioning Assize judges.

56 **conveyancer:** The Sergeant specializes in deeds (conveyances) and property disputes.
57 **fee-simple:** property owned outright.

58 **King William's:** referring to William the Conqueror, king from 1066 to 1087.
59 **screeds:** long, tiresome writing.

FIGURE 11.4

An Example of Text from *The Canterbury Tales* Showing Definitions of Uncommon Words

From *English Literature with World Masterpieces,* signature edition, Macmillan Literature Series, p. 66. Copyright 1991 by Glencoe/McGraw-Hill Educational Division. Reprinted by permission.

take place between individual pairs of students whose conversations are viewed and heard by the other students. Observers should note if the participants stay in character during the discussions. Students choose the pilgrim they wish to play and their own discussion topics (Wiltsey, 1975).

A third learning experience uses an inner-outer circle technique. Students, who role-play pilgrims according to their societal class group, discuss their lives. In this technique, one group sitting in an inner circle has a discussion while a second group sitting on the periphery observes the discussion. Each individual in the outer circle observes an individual in the inner circle. The first 10-minute discussion might be among high-class status pilgrims, based on a question such as, "The wars are costing us a great deal of our income. How can we put a stop to them?" After the time expires, the observers and the observed students share perceptions about what transpired in the discussions.

Next, the individuals exchange places and the inner group has a discussion among the middle-class status pilgrims. If time permits, switch a third time and let the discussion center on the lower-class people. The discussion between people role-playing various classes should "help the students to understand the class

The Feudal Group	The Church Group	The City Group
Knight	Nun	Merchant
Squire	Monk	Sergeant at the Law (Judge)
Yeoman	Friar	Five Tradesmen
Franklin	Cleric	Cook
Plowman	Parson	Skipper
Miller	Summoner	Doctor
Reeve	Pardoner	Wife of Bath
		Manciple
		Host (Innkeeper)

FIGURE 11.5

Societal Groupings of the Pilgrims in Chaucer's *The Canterbury Tales*

From *English Literature with World Masterpieces,* signature edition, Macmillan Literature Series, p. 57. Copyright 1991 by Glencoe/McGraw-Hill Educational Division. Reprinted by permission.

society and the differences and similarities between classes. Tying the discussion in with the inner-outer circle gives the students a chance to become closer to each other, practice close observation, and give their fellow students feedback on how they look, talk, and relate to others" (Wiltsey, 1975, p. 260).

During these activities you plan to observe students' social relationships. Are they able to take the perspective of another person? Do these activities help with organizing their own thinking?

Focus a fourth learning activity on a writing experience featuring a modern-day counterpart of *The Canterbury Tales.* Ask students to write a paper in reply to this question: "If Chaucer were writing his tales today, what kinds of people might some of his pilgrims be? Where might their journey take them?" (Macmillan Literature Series, 1991, p. 57). Once the papers have been prepared, ask willing students to share their papers with the class and discuss their ideas. Use these papers as a vehicle to help students sharpen their language skills, according to their needs.

Learning Experiences Related to "The Wife of Bath's Tale."   The theme for these activities is "wives (actually all people) should be treated with respect." Plan to summarize the Prologue to the "Wife of Bath's Tale" for students unless it is part of their reading. Understanding it sets the stage for the tale. In the Prologue the Wife of Bath recounts each of her five marriages and reveals her views on the place of women in society. Said briefly, she is violently opposed to classical stereotypes of women.

After students have read the tale, have them portray various pilgrims and give their reactions to the tale. The Prioress, the Plowman, the Sergeant at the Law, and the Miller, for example, could be expected to express different reactions. In role play the students must consider the characterization of their pilgrim before giving their reactions.

Invite a communications "expert" (Grandpa Green or a mental health expert) to discuss with students how people express themselves differently according to moods and situations. Following this discussion, redo the portrayal of the pilgrims and their reactions. Discuss differences between the first and second characterizations and possible reasons for the differences.

A second learning experience suggests that students, as themselves, discuss perceptions of how the Wife of Bath might be expected to handle different positions—corporation head, clean-up person, instructor, and others—based on her characterization in the tale. How would she solve problems that arise in these job situations? How would her tendency to digress from the task at hand help/hinder the work expected of her in each position?

In "The Prologue" the Host says that each pilgrim is expected to tell two tales on the way to Canterbury and two tales on the way back to London. A third learning experience might challenge students to describe the kind of tale that the Wife of Bath might tell on the return trip. The tale must stay in character, of course.

Learning Experiences Related to "The Pardoner's Tale."   Running throughout these activities is the theme "Greed is destructive." After students have read "The Pardoner's Tale," they might try writing a tale of their own. The tale should begin with a moral such as "Idleness is the devil's workshop" or "Don't cry over spilled milk" or "A bird in the hand is worth two in the bush." They write a brief story that illustrates the point. However, there must be enough detail to make the story as vivid and memorable as "The Pardoner's Tale" (Macmillan Literature Series, 1991).

In another learning experience students discuss the Pardoner's character. After the pilgrimage the Pardoner will no doubt go to confession. What is he going to say? Is he likely to feel any remorse for having told his tale?

In a third learning experience students might discuss whether modern-day counterparts of the Pardoner exist (Wiltsey, 1975). If so, who are they and what do they do that suggests them as his counterparts?

Culminating Learning Experience.   At the conclusion of *The Canterbury Tales* study, students might take a trip together. During the trip they should plan to tell an original tale to one or more classmates that encourages use of their imaginations and language skills. If a real trip is impossible, students could make a hypothetical trip and tell the tale either orally or in writing. In either case ask students to write their tale as a further check on language skills.

Reconsideration of the Project.   You and your colleague reconsider this project before forwarding plans to the department head. You review the learning experiences to see that they do indeed attempt to help students develop their potentials as individuals.

The content themes were selected initially using the content selection criteria—validity and significance, learnability, and others. Now that the learning experiences are planned you must check to see that extraneous content is kept to a minimum to avoid the possibility of violating the validity criterion.

Your preliminary consideration of content organization (see Chapter 8) is unchanged. However, because you formulated the learning experiences based on student needs you anticipate that *integration* is strong. Following the completion of the reconsideration, you send the views statement, content themes, and plans to your department chair. Because of your confidence in the project, you look forward with anticipation to trying this curriculum the next school year.

Exercise 11.2 asks you to reconsider planned learning experiences. This may help with the formulation of your own nontechnical curriculum.

EXERCISE
11.2

Reflect on the planned learning experiences for *The Canterbury Tales*.

1. On which domain(s) of learning is(are) these learning experiences focused? Explain.
2. To what extent are thinking skills likely to be fostered by these learning experiences? Explain.
3. Cite an example from the descriptions in which each type of learning outcome might be developed. Be specific. (Hint: more than one answer exists.)

   a. attitudes
   b. language skills

SUMMARY

Technically developed curricula usually focus on the creation of learning experiences that seek to develop learners as individuals or groups. The outcomes in curricula for either of these purposes cannot be predetermined so the planning focus is the learning experiences, in which interpersonal and physical contexts are critical. Because learners and teachers engage in interactive experiences, informal classroom spaces and carefully selected resources invite learner participation.

The learning experiences for two nontechnical curricula were analyzed to see how well they helped students move toward their intended purposes. In the final section learning experiences were created for a nontechnical English literature curriculum that focused on developing learners' language abilities and consciousness of people.

QUESTIONS FOR DISCUSSION

1. Describe links between nontechnical curricula and student empowerment. Explain.
2. Discuss reasons that critics might argue against the nontechnical learning experiences described in this chapter.

3. Role play is a technique used in several learning experiences for *The Canterbury Tales*. Pretend you are the guide for a school administrator and you visited the classrooms where these activities were in progress. Explain to the administrator whether role play in this curriculum has a purpose different from the one it usually has in subject-centered classrooms.

4. Describe instances in which teachers' expertises were used in the planned learning experiences for *The Canterbury Tales*.

5. Explain how the change processes of relevancy, readiness, and resources described in Chapter 7 were addressed (if indeed they were) in the section Creation of Learning Experiences.

IMPORTANT IDEAS DISCUSSED INITIALLY IN THIS CHAPTER

nontechnical learning experiences requirements for:
    interpersonal context
    physical context

PART FOUR

CLASSROOM USE AND EVALUATION OF CURRICULUM PROJECTS

After the curriculum has been revised by a development group, it is ready to be delivered in the context for which it was designed. Depending on the scope of revision, a technically developed curriculum may be implemented in a few classrooms before it is implemented districtwide.

During trial runs developers and implementors resolve difficulties that might prevent successful implementation of the curriculum in the district. Evaluation of the project is ongoing throughout this period. When the revised curriculum is implemented, evaluation of both the implementation processes as well as curricular outcomes continues. Based on analyses of these data, district personnel decide whether to continue, modify, or discontinue use of the revised curriculum.

Implementation and evaluation of curriculum projects typically involve more individuals than were included as developers. Because these people were not part of development, careful planning of both processes must enable implementors to handle the changes required. These individuals must work out their own meaning of the changes, a lengthy process in many cases.

Nontechnically developed curricula are enacted in contexts where they were developed by teachers. Typically these individuals evolve their own meanings of change during development so that enactment is not a new process. Though formal process evaluation is usually unnecessary, evaluators assess outcomes in terms of the purpose of education because program decisions similar to those for technically developed curricula should also be made about these curricula.

Part 4 contains Chapters 12 and 13 on classroom use and evaluation, respectively. Each has several sections that provide *descriptive* information about the processes for both technical and nontechnical curricula. Final sections in each chapter offer suggestions for *planning the classroom use or evaluation* of curricula.

12

CLASSROOM USE OF CURRICULUM PROJECTS

OUTLINE

The term for introducing a curriculum into the classroom differs according to the developmental approach. Whereas technically developed curricula are *implemented,* nontechnically developed curricula are *enacted* in classrooms. Although enactment is a continuation of development, implementation is typically a separate process.

Implementation represents change whether the curriculum was developed by a district or a school committee. One reason is that some teachers, whether by choice or other reasons, were not part of the development process. These individuals must go through the transitions necessary for considering the revised curriculum (e.g., stop thinking of using the "old" curriculum, wonder about the revised curriculum). Teachers who served as developers are familiar with the curriculum, but they are faced with fitting the revised curriculum to specific contexts. However, because enactment continues the nontechnical development process, the same individuals are involved in both tasks. These educators developed the curriculum for their specific contexts so that using it is not new.

This chapter discusses several considerations involved with planning implementation and enactment as well as change processes associated with implementation. Because of its success in schools, the Concerns-Based Adoption Model is presented as the method of choice for implementing technically developed curricula. Curriculum enactment is classroom use of nontechnically developed curricula.

The final section describes preliminary plans by which the health and English literature curricula developed for hypothetical situations in previous chapters could be used in their respective contexts. After studying this chapter, you should be able *to prepare a rudimentary plan for initiating classroom use of a curriculum project of your choice.*

IMPLEMENTATION/ENACTMENT OF CURRICULUM PROJECTS

Teachers and students are the primary stakeholders in actually using revised curricula in schools, but community members and school staff also hold stakes, particularly in successful ventures. Numerous teachers and students may be involved where a revised curriculum is to be used in all classrooms within a school or district. Their efforts may be helped or hindered by parents/guardians and school staff. These individuals usually support a revised curriculum if they understand its need and rationale. Therefore, involving all the groups from the outset in the curriculum processes (i.e., needs assessment, development) is extremely important.

Each individual must have opportunity to develop personal meaning, if change is to be effective. "One of the failures of understanding about implementation 20 years ago was that we did not accept the reality that a school does not change until each individual teacher within the school successfully implements the innovation" (Hall, 1992, p. 898). The success with which curricula are actually changed in schools is measured one person at a time.

As the term suggests, *change facilitators* intervene to assist teachers and school staff in the change-making processes. Frequently school principals are the ones expected to lead in change facilitation by virtue of their leadership positions. However, other individuals also assist with this function.

In curriculum enactment, the principal's role is crucial because s/he often battles the bureaucracy of the central office. One principal in this situation chose to "interpret the central office administration's curriculum mandates as outlines of goals to be met" (Paris, 1993, p. 54). This interpretation allowed teachers to meet goals in whatever way they believed was best, with the relatively simple requirement of showing that they were following through on them. Because the principal knew the teachers well, she believed they would make good professional decisions. She saw her role in curriculum matters "as catalyst and supporter of teachers' curriculum initiatives" (Paris, 1993, p. 55).

The principal's role is also critical in curriculum implementation. However, a leadership *team* that includes the principal and additional change facilitators has produced good results in school situations (Hall & Hord, 1987). These teams are characterized by differentiated roles, functions, and dynamics. The first change facilitator (CF) should be the principal; the second CF is usually in the school, but not in a classroom (i.e., a curriculum specialist or assistant principal); and an optional third CF may be a teacher or someone from the district office. The principal as first CF has formal authority for curriculum implementation and leads the team. Other facilitators work with the principal using the group's unique dynamics in coaching and helping roles with teachers (Hall & Hord, 1987).

Mendez-Morse (1992) reports that leaders, whether administrators or teachers, who facilitate school change must demonstrate two important abilities: initiating structure (concern for organizational tasks) and consideration (concern for individuals and interpersonal relationships among them). Furthermore, leaders who actually bring about change:

• Possess vision.
• Believe that schools are for learning.
• Value human resources.
• Communicate and listen well.
• Are proactive and risk-taking.

Additional information about the work of change facilitators is provided in this chapter.

Regardless of the label given to the process, the events associated with using revised curricula in classrooms must be planned and managed. The following section describes major planning considerations and change processes in implementation.

PLANNING CONSIDERATIONS

Change facilitators are typically in charge of overseeing a multitude of operations that occur in using revised curricula in classrooms. To obtain a perspective on planning these operations, this section describes four important considerations that include the scope and complexity of the curricular change, communication, professional development, and resources.

Scope and Complexity of the Curricular Change. *Scope* refers to the breadth of the curriculum to be implemented/enacted. Does the change involve a single unit among several that are not changed? Is it a year's work in a subject area? Does the change represent an added responsibility for teachers? A single curriculum unit is probably not a particularly difficult change unless the single unit is an added responsibility. In recent years several units have been added to elementary school curricula (e.g., AIDS education, drug awareness) without taking out any content. Secondary social studies teachers may be asked to include a unit on The Free Enterprise System. Already overwhelmed with content to be taught, some teachers think adding one unit, regardless of size, is a major change.

Complexity refers to the nature of the change. Does the revised curriculum involve a change in the purpose of education? Are teachers expected to think about content in ways that differ significantly from traditional ways? When change is major, as either of these situations would be, the curricular change requires that most teachers undergo significant professional development. Such training is necessary as an initial step toward helping teachers develop their own meaning of change.

To illustrate this point, consider that in the 1970s the "new" mathematics curricula emphasized helping students understand that subject matter. To use these curricula teachers were expected to make significant changes in their own understanding of mathematics. Because many teachers chose not to, or were unable to make the required changes, revised mathematics curricula were implemented in relatively few classrooms in ways corresponding to developers' plans (Elmore & Sykes, 1992).

Communication. As used here, communication refers to all the oral and written ideas concerning curriculum change that flow from one person to another. Though some one-way communication is necessary, most communications should be interactive or two-way. An assumption here is that teachers and change facilitators involved in the nontechnical approach communicate effectively using two-way communication during development activities. Enactment, then, should pose relatively few communication difficulties.

In the technical approach carefully written bulletins may inform teachers and the school community about the revised curriculum and events expected to take place during its implementation. Oral reports at faculty-staff meetings or parent-teacher gatherings serve similar purposes.

Before starting implementation, teachers and change facilitators must exchange information about the activities associated with beginning the revised curriculum. Change facilitators should provide accurate information about the demands of the revised curriculum and teachers must feel free to raise questions, even those that cannot be answered easily. Open communication between these groups is mandatory from start to finish in the implementation processes.

Describing the intricacies of effective communication is beyond the scope of this discussion. The major point is that communication is a major consideration that change facilitators and implementors must address. Regardless of its mode or form, the ideas expressed by senders must be understood by receivers if communications are to achieve desired effects. Sensitivity is required on the part of all people in the curriculum processes.

Professional Development.   In the context of curriculum implementation/enactment "professional development" refers to inservice, training, assistance, or other activities dedicated to helping faculty and staff develop personal meaning for the materials, teaching approaches, and beliefs involved with a revised/modified curriculum. Opportunities for such information and assistance are necessary to help teachers create their own meanings of curriculum change.

However, effective professional development is tailored to specific purposes and audiences. What might be effective in one setting may be ineffective in another. Hall and Hord (1987) describe several tactics and strategies for different types of professional development. For example, "good time workshops" are those in which a specialist makes an entertaining and sometimes provocative presentation in which all participants have a good time. This workshop may provide a change of pace or serve as a morale builder and be appropriate when these purposes are to be served. However, this type workshop is not expected to assist anyone in changing practice or behavior and should not be counted as a way of helping teachers know how to make a change.

Resources.   Time, personnel, and funds are required to use modified curricula in classrooms. All too often these resources are in short supply and the processes of putting curricula into use suffer accordingly. Hall (1992) claims that "implementation *costs* [emphasis in the original] just as much (if not more) as development" (p. 879). Hall pleads a strong case for districts to increase their financial commitments to activities involved in putting revised curricula into classroom use.

Any substantive curriculum change requires a considerable time commitment from change facilitators and teachers. Most principals in their role as change facilitators must devote additional time beyond the usual amount for working with teachers and community members on matters related to the revised curriculum. Teachers must find time in their crowded schedules to learn about the revised curriculum, practice, and reflect on new behaviors. For educators time can be increased only by shifting workload responsibilities or by adding additional personnel. In some situations hiring additional personnel, ranging from clerks to substitute teachers to interim administrators, is a must. In other instances outside consultants may be required to provide professional development for teachers and school staff. Either of these changes requires personnel funds.

Although personnel costs constitute the major part of budgets, funds are also required for operations associated with revised curricula. Instructional materials, supplies, books, and computer hardware and software are examples of items that may be required by revised curricula.

Exercise 12.1 provides a check of your understanding of these planning considerations. Try it now.

EXERCISE 12.1   Reflect on the discussion of planning considerations, then read the incidents. To what extent were these considerations taken into account in each incident? Describe recommendations for improvement.

1. Science teachers at Littlejohn High School each received copies of the revised district curriculum guide with a memo stating that they were to begin using the guides the following semester.
2. During the previous school year teachers at Briarwood Elementary School participated in several activity-based workshops concerned with a literature-based curriculum for language arts. This year five teachers have begun using this approach in their classrooms. On any school day morning at least one of the five can usually be found talking informally with a colleague about using literature in language arts.

CHANGE PROCESSES IN IMPLEMENTATION

Based on analyses of the educational change literature, Fullan (1991) identifies four important issues in change processes in implementation that should be addressed if curricula are used successfully. These issues include **active initiation and participation, pressure and support, changes in behavior and beliefs,** and **ownership.**

Active Initiation and Participation. Some curriculum projects implemented in classrooms require participation by large numbers of people. If change is to be made individually, how the implementation process begins is very important. The literature suggests that projects should start small and let participants learn by doing. Involving a few individuals who are willing to take risks and having them think big is a valuable strategy in initiating successful change (Fullan, 1991).

Sometimes a small group of teachers use a revised curriculum on a trial basis. During this initial use teachers and change facilitators are able to work out some difficulties before implementing the curriculum in multiple classrooms. Also, through the informal communication systems within schools these teachers can sometimes generate enthusiasm for the project that prepares others for using the curriculum.

Pressure and Support. Pressure may serve a positive role in change because many forces within schools strive for maintaining the status quo. In most schools some amount of pressure must be built that results in action. Another reason for a small start may be to help generate pressure for change. Once the change processes begin, interactions among the implementors help integrate pressure and support. "Pressure without support leads to resistance and alienation; support without pressure leads to drift or waste of resources" (Fullan, 1991, p. 91).

Changes in Behavior and Beliefs. Earlier discussion indicated that individuals must develop personal meanings for change. Fullan (1985) states that people do not understand some educational matters until they become involved. Therefore, teachers who start using a curriculum with one set of beliefs may change them as a result of actions with the revised curriculum. "[T]he relationship between behavioral and belief change is reciprocal and ongoing, with change in doing or behavior a necessary experience on the way to breakthroughs in meaning and understanding" (Fullan, 1991, p. 91). For change to be considered complete, however, both behavior and beliefs must change.

Ownership.   Bringing about curricular change is extremely difficult, especially with large numbers of people, because each educator must develop **ownership.** This process requires differing amounts of time, depending on the person's receptivity to change, familiarity with the change, and other factors. However, ownership brings a sense of clarity, skill, and commitment required for the institutionalization of change.

Each of the issues described here must be handled sensitively and skillfully. The job of managing these concerns usually belongs to change facilitators, whose roles are described in the next section.

CONCERNS-BASED ADOPTION MODEL

The **Concerns-Based Adoption Model** (CBAM) provides an effective way of conceptualizing the implementation of technically developed curricula because it handles the planning considerations systematically. Since the early 1970s CBAM researchers have studied the change processes experienced by individual teachers and schools as units as they work with innovations. For this discussion the innovation is considered the implementation of a revised curriculum. CBAM is useful in situations both where district-based curricula are implemented in classrooms throughout a district and where a school-based curriculum is implemented within classrooms in that school.

Three diagnostic dimensions of this model—stages of concern, levels of use, and innovation configurations—provide ways to describe and document the change processes both for individual classrooms and schools as a whole (Hall, 1992). Because it has been successful in many different classroom situations, the CBAM forms the basis for this discussion about implementation.

ASSUMPTIONS

Hord (1987, 1992) describes seven assumptions that have guided research on this model. These assumptions embody and make more specific to CBAM the change processes described previously.

1. *Change is a process, not an event.* Change occurs over time, usually a period of years.
2. *Individuals must change before organizations change.* Change actions must focus on people because their reactions and adjustments are essential. An institution or curriculum is changed only when a sizable number of people associated with it change.
3. *Change is a highly personal experience.* Individuals respond to change in different ways. "Though they (people) are approached individually, they are expected to behave, in effect, collectively. This approach does grave injustice to the staggering diversity and alternately wonderful and maddening unpredictability of human behaviour; it seriously undermines the likelihood of successful implementation" (Hord, 1987, p. 94).
4. *Change entails multilevel developmental growth.* Changing individuals grow in "feelings" and "skills." During the change process, identifiable stages of "feelings" and levels of "skills" emerge.

5. *Change is best understood in operational terms.* Teachers want to know what is expected of them when they implement a modified curriculum. How are their behaviors and those of their students expected to differ from what they were before? How much preparation time is needed? By handling concerns such as these, change facilitators can improve communication and reduce individual resistance to change.

6. *Change facilitation must suit individual needs.* CBAM has built-in diagnostic capabilities that allow change facilitators to help meet the needs of teachers on an individual basis.

7. *Change efforts should focus on individuals, not innovations.* The real meaning of using a revised curriculum is related to people rather than its content. To make this a reality, change facilitators tailor interventions to the needs of teachers and, as appropriate and necessary, alter the curriculum to the needs of the school context.

IMPLEMENTATION PROCESSES

CBAM processes include loosely related strategies subsumed under the headings of **initiation, intervention,** and **institutionalization.** True curriculum implementation evolves through a judicious blending of strategies that encourage participants, mainly teachers, to make personal transitions, develop their own meanings, and reduce their ambiguities about using a modified curriculum.

This section describes three diagnostic tools that CBAM researchers have used over the years in their field-based studies of change. These tools assess participants' feelings about an innovation, their behaviors toward an innovation, and the innovation itself as it is used in specific situations. Following a description of the diagnostic tools is information about ways change facilitators use the results to provide interventions that assist the change processes. Additional information about these tools is provided in the Process Evaluation section of Chapter 13.

Diagnostic Tools. Using the CBAM researchers have found that teachers asked to implement an innovation, such as a revised curriculum, progress through different **stages of concern** ranging from self, to task, and sometimes to impact. Self concerns reveal themselves at awareness, informational, or personal stages. At the next higher levels task concerns relate to management, while impact concerns deal with consequence, collaboration, and refocusing matters. Figure 12.1 displays typical expressions of concern about an innovation. Stated simply, until teachers work their way through the self concerns to the management stage, they are unlikely to begin *using* the revised curriculum.

CBAM researchers have also studied **levels of use** of an innovation and developed behavioral indices for each of eight levels. These levels range from nonuse through mechanical use to integration and renewal. Mechanical use, the lowest user level, is characteristic of teachers who implement the revised curriculum in a poorly coordinated manner and make changes that benefit themselves. At the next higher level labeled "routine," teachers make few or no changes and finally in the refinement level, teachers make changes that benefit their students. Through

	Stages of Concern	Expressions of Concern
I M P A C T	6 Refocusing	I have some ideas about something that would work even better.
	5 Collaboration	I am concerned about relating what I am doing with what other instructors are doing.
	4 Consequence	How is my use affecting students?
T A S K	3 Management	I seem to be spending all my time getting material ready.
S E L F	2 Personal	How will using it affect me?
	1 Informational	I would like to know more about it.
	0 Awareness	I am not concerned about it (the innovation).

FIGURE 12.1

Typical Expressions of Concern About the Innovation

From *Evaluating Educational Innovation* (p. 101), by S. Hord, 1987, London: Croom Helm. Copyright 1987 by Shirley Hord and Croom Helm Ltd. Reprinted by permission.

their actions at each level, individual teachers progressively increase their commitments to curriculum implementation. (See Figure 12.2.) In general these changes in behaviors reflect decreasing self-concerns about the revised curriculum.

On-site classroom visits by CBAM researchers showed that teachers sometimes believed they were using the innovation (i.e., the revised curriculum) even when their actions were quite different from those of colleagues or those described by the developers (Hord, 1987). What emerged from this study was an **innovations configuration** procedure that provides information about what teachers and students should be doing when the curriculum is operational.

Recall that Chapter 1 mentions mutual adaptation as part of the implementation process. For curricula developed at district levels, mutual adaptation can help transform a context-free curriculum into one that fits a school context. Before implementation, district-level developers should meet with teachers to determine how the curriculum looks when put in operation within their classrooms. For example, a revised mathematics curriculum for elementary schools might call for these actions from teachers:

• Use problem solving as the focus of objectives.

• Use manipulative materials as an integral part of instruction.

• Provide daily instruction for a protracted time period.

Developers and teachers might agree that these actions are appropriate in the revised curriculum. However, the groups could differ on what these actions mean.

Levels of Use	Behavioral Indices of Levels
VI Renewal	The user is seeking more effective alternatives to the established use of the innovation.
V Integration	The user is making deliberate efforts to coordinate with others in using the innovation.
IVB Refinement	The user is making changes to increase outcomes.
IVA Routine	The user is making few or no changes and has an established pattern of use.
III Mechanical Use	The user is using the innovation in a poorly coordinated manner and is making user-oriented changes.
II Preparation	The individual is preparing to use the innovation.
I Orientation	The individual is seeking information about the innovation.
0 Nonuse	No action is being taken with respect to the innovation.

FIGURE 12.2

Levels of Use of the Innovation: Typical Behaviors

From "The Local Educational Change Process and Policy Implementation," by G. E. Hall, 1992, *Journal of Research in Science Teaching, 29*(8), p. 893. Copyright 1992 by Journal of Research in Science Teaching. Reprinted by permission of John Wiley & Sons Inc.

For example, some developers might advocate focusing all mathematics instruction on problem solving. Particularly if they are unfamiliar with current emphases, teachers might argue that problem solving is not that important or that students must memorize number facts before they do problem solving.

At this point the developers and teachers should think about each behavior along an acceptable-unacceptable continuum. The developers have in mind what is necessary to achieve the purpose of the curriculum and teachers know their students' abilities and backgrounds and themselves as teachers. The point of these negotiations is to try to fit the curriculum to the context. Both groups must be willing to make adaptations—hence the term, **mutual adaptation**. Their negotiated changes must be approved by the change facilitator.

Figure 12.3 shows sample items for an illustrative innovations configuration for this situation. Note the code that describes behaviors at acceptable and unacceptable levels. Within the acceptable levels are ideals that surpass the acceptable designation. An innovations configuration at a neighboring school using the same revised curriculum might have a slightly different version of the innovations configuration, depending on the changes mutually agreed upon by the developers and teachers. Though these innovations configurations are different, teachers would be expected to use the innovations configuration for their school.

Efforts to achieve mutual adaptation might also be required in situations where a curriculum is school-based, especially in large schools serving very different student populations. Developers of school-based curricula negotiate adapta-

Problem Solving

Each lesson uses problem solving.	At least half the lessons use problem solving.	Problem solving is used as appropriate.
Problem solving deals with items related to student interests.	Problem solving is based on textbook exercises.	No problem solving exercises are done.

Manipulative Materials

Students use materials as teacher assists.	Students watch teacher demonstrations with materials.	Students use pencil-paper only.

Instruction Time

At least 60 minutes are used for instruction daily.	At least 45 minutes are used for instruction daily.	Less than 45 minutes are used for instruction daily.

Key: ————— Variations to the right are unacceptable; variations to the left are acceptable.

- - - - - - - Variations to the left are ideal, as indicated by the developers.

FIGURE 12.3

Sample Items in an Innovations Configuration for an Elementary School Mathematics Curriculum

tions with individual teachers using similar processes to those described here. Changes should be approved by the change facilitator.

Change Facilitators. Change facilitators use the diagnostic tools and provide assistance for teachers implementing a revised curriculum. In CBAM, CFs have training in concerns-based theory. One major tenet of this training helps CFs encourage teachers to change by understanding their needs and easing difficulties with strategies that take these needs into account (Hall & Hord, 1987).

Hord and Hall (1987) document the work of three principals who served as change facilitators for a year-long implementation project. These CFs played important roles "in providing materials, instructional resources, space, personnel, scheduling, and other logistical and organizational arrangements necessary to initiate and sustain school improvement" (Hord & Hall, 1987, p. 83). The principals held frequent one-on-one casual interviews with teachers that led to consultation and coaching activities with teachers. The principals handled these responsibilities well despite the fact that they used different styles. One was a responder; another, an initiator; while the third was a manager.

But change facilitators are human, too, and have concerns about their roles. Sometimes CFs must wrestle with their own concerns at the same time they work with teacher concerns. Supervisors and consultants track change facilitator concerns and provide support for CFs using methods similar to those used with teachers (Hall, Newlove, George, Rutherford, & Hord, 1993).

Initiations.   Activities in which teachers are helped to understand the revised curriculum constitute initiating activities. Many school districts refer to these sessions as professional development or inservice sessions. The main purpose of these activities is to provide information and orientation for teachers seeking to understand their roles as curriculum implementors.

Interventions.   The name given to a variety of activities used by change facilitators as they work with teachers in implementing the curriculum is **interventions**. As mentioned in the initial discussion of personnel, the principal should be the primary change facilitator whose major functions include sanctioning/providing continued support for curriculum implementation and providing resources. Other functions include approving adaptations, monitoring and following up with teachers, reinforcing, pushing, and telling community people about the work. Although the principal bears responsibility for these functions, some of them may be carried out by other CFs. Second and third CFs also handle technical coaching and training responsibilities (Hall & Hord, 1986).

The CBAM diagnostic tools provide change facilitators with information that allows them to personalize the kinds of assistance that teachers need. One CF function is to provide interventions that enable teachers to move through the stages of concern. To illustrate, a CF may provide information to teachers with self-concerns at nonuser levels, either individually for those at the personal level or in group situations for those at the informational level. Other teachers who have begun implementing the curriculum may be stuck at the management level because of concerns about the amounts of time, logistics, or scheduling required by the revised curriculum. In these cases, CFs can provide coaching, reinforcing, or training that enable these individuals to move forward. Change facilitators are well aware that teachers whose concerns are not handled may opt out of actually implementing the curriculum.

CFs also assist teachers when results of the innovation configuration show that they are not performing at acceptable levels. This assistance may be additional instructional materials, training, or opportunity to work with someone who does understand what is necessary to implement the curriculum. Hall and Hord (1987) provide example interventions for each stage of concern.

The goal of the interventions, of course, is to help teachers make the changes required by the new curriculum. CFs provide support, and sometimes pressure, for teachers to change their behaviors. As Fullan (1985) notes, some individuals must change their behaviors before they can begin to change their beliefs. Over time teachers are expected to develop ownership of the revised curriculum.

Despite best efforts of CFs, an "implementation dip" is not unusual. In this indeterminate period "things actually get worse. Student performance may go down; teacher morale and test scores may decline; parent dissatisfaction may increase. This is normal!" (Busick & Inos, 1992, p. 3). Persistence, patience, and time are necessary to sustain implementation. CFs with a clear vision for change are critical in helping move the process out of the implementation dip toward positive growth and change.

In describing a comprehensive management process for transforming organizations, Mink, Esterhuysen, Mink, and Owen (1993) added game plan components to the CBAM. These are clusters of manageable interventions including development of supportive organizational arrangements, training, consultation and reinforcement, monitoring, external communication, and dissemination.

Figure 12.4 displays the systemic nature of relationships among teacher implementors and change facilitators in the CBAM. Change facilitators assess teachers' stages of concern and use of the revised curriculum through the CBAM diagnostic instruments. Based on the results, change facilitators draw upon various resources and intervene in ways that empower teachers to implement the curriculum. As indicated earlier, the relationships portrayed here are intended to balance pressure and support, promote changes in behavior and beliefs, and help implementors own the revised curriculum. None of these actions occurs in isolation; each has spin-offs that affect other actions among teachers.

Institutionalization.   At what point can a curriculum be considered implemented? When is the change process complete? Need for closure, of course, prompts questions such as these. Hord and Hall (1986) provide an operational definition for institutionalization that uses the results of the diagnostic tools. This definition applies to individuals only, rather than the aggregate of implementors, and describes maximum (ideal) or minimum (acceptable) levels. The actual stages of concern, levels of use, and innovation configurations might differ from those in this description, but this discussion provides a notion of how institutionalization works.

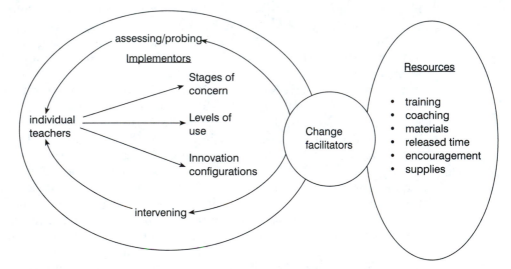

FIGURE 12.4

Relationships Among Implementors, Change Facilitators, and Resources in the Concerns-Based Adoption Model

From *Change in Schools: Facilitating the Process* (p. 12), by G. E. Hall & S. M. Hord, 1987, Albany, NY: State University of New York Press. Copyright 1987 by State University of New York. Reprinted by permission.

Ideal **institutionalization** is reached when individual teachers' initial concerns about using the revised curriculum have decreased to the extent that they use it comfortably. Their concerns focus on the effect of the revised curriculum (see stages 4–6 in Figure 12.1). These teachers have enough experience with the revised curriculum that they can use it at least on a routine basis (maybe at higher levels in some cases—see levels IVA–VI in Figure 12.2). Finally, the teachers perform the expected behaviors at the ideal levels. See the behaviors shown to the left of the dashed (- - -) line in Figure 12.3.

Minimum or acceptable institutionalization can be gauged to have occurred when individual teachers exhibit at least the beginnings of concern for how their use of the revised curriculum affects students in their classrooms (see Figure 12.1 at the consequence stage) coupled with use on a routine basis, at least (see Figure 12.2). Teachers also demonstrate behaviors corresponding to the acceptable variations in the innovations configuration (i.e., behaviors shown to the left of the solid line in Figure 12.3).

How many teachers in a district or building have to meet these criteria? At this point the particular percentage that guarantees institutionalization is not fixed. Obviously, confidence that institutionalization has occurred is greater when many, rather than fewer, teachers meet the criteria. These processes take time, too. Some estimates indicate that implementation may take as long as five years (Hall & Hord, 1987). Given previous discussions concerning change as a "people" process, significant numbers of teachers must demonstrate acceptable stages of concern, levels of use, and innovation configurations to suggest that the change is complete.

Exercise 12.2 provides a brief review of some CBAM concepts. Try this exercise to see how well you understand this information.

**EXERCISE
12.2**

With which stage of concern or level of use should each statement be related? Explain.

1. Teacher to students: "I wonder what would happen if you worked together to . . . "
2. Teacher to principal: "At the next staff meeting, would you please have someone tell us more about the curriculum evaluation procedures?"
3. Change facilitator to teacher: "I spoke a few days ago with Juanita (a colleague), who had a great idea about making this information clearer to students. She . . . (describes the idea). Do you think this might work well in your class?"

CURRICULUM ENACTMENT

Because nontechnical curricula are school- or classroom-based, planning for their use is typically less complicated than the implementation of technically developed curricula. This is true largely because the teachers who generate the curricula handle the planning considerations and enact curricula in a variety of ways.

Because contexts are unique, curriculum enactment does not have a model comparable to CBAM for technical curricula. The following discussion provides general information about the planning considerations in curriculum enactment. This is followed by a brief discussion of one approach to organizing a nontechnical curriculum called The Authoring Cycle.

MANAGEMENT OF PLANNING CONSIDERATIONS

Teachers deal with the *scope and complexity of curricular change* as a regular part of planning. As they find needs for changes in the curriculum, teachers build them into planning. Usually teachers involved in nontechnical curriculum work with their supervisor (who may be a principal or department head), keeping that individual abreast of plans and seeking advice about real or potential problems.

Chapter 11 establishes the idea of interpersonal context as the experience, interaction, and negotiation of meaning between teachers and students. Clearly this means *communication* is a major consideration in planning curriculum enactment. Communication is documented as important when teachers work with colleagues on mutually beneficial arrangements for using classroom spaces (Paris, 1993), negotiate with community members to allow students access to off-campus learning facilities (Hunter & Scheirer, 1988), or solicit content themes from students in a literacy project (Auerbach, 1990). Many situations require that communication be two-way; senders and receivers of messages must understand each other. Interaction and negotiation are usually easier in face-to-face communication.

Professional development is necessary in curriculum enactment just as it is in implementation. Sometimes teachers within a building can provide professional development to their colleagues who have different expertises. However, teachers also need inservice, assistance, or training by others outside their school to help with activities in which they and their students engage. Some professional development opportunities are likely to be unique to those who seek them. For example, not all teachers need the same help with a unit focusing on life management skills. Some teachers have background experiences, not possessed by their colleagues, that permit their leading students in life management learning experiences. In areas where teachers lack background, the supervisor or principal must see that professional development experiences are made available.

Nontechnical curricula involve teachers and students in mutual construction of curricula that require *space, resources,* and *time.* Preparation for curriculum enactment may mean that teachers alter the spaces in which they work with students. Romey (1988) documents the need for less structured physical facilities for situations where students take major responsibilities for their learning. Classroom space and furnishings must promote social discourse because nontechnical curricula require student-student interactions as well as student-teacher interactions.

Curriculum enactment requires planners to locate or produce variety in instructional materials. Although printed materials are important, so are nonprint materials. For example, hands-on materials for students' use must be available in addition to teacher demonstration materials. Because nontechnical curricula encourage student choices of learning activities, learners must be able to manage instructional materials with minimal adult assistance. Also, students within any given classroom may work on different learning activities.

Curriculum enactment requires huge time investments. The open-ended nature of learning activities calls for significant chunks of time that permit student explorations, experiments, and idea formulations. Discussions should be allowed to terminate naturally rather than according to a fixed time schedule. The following discussion of The Authoring Cycle displays how these planning considerations are managed in one nontechnical curriculum approach.

THE AUTHORING CYCLE

This section describes how a nontechnically developed curriculum might work in a classroom. The idea and the framework for this discussion are based on The Authoring Cycle model of curriculum which has been used with elementary, secondary, and college students (Harste & Short, 1988; Short & Burke, 1991). The discussion that follows attempts to capture the spirit of this model rather than provide details. Interested readers should consult the references for additional information.

Figure 12.5 displays the elements of this model in which teachers and students become a community of learners for creating a language literacy curriculum.

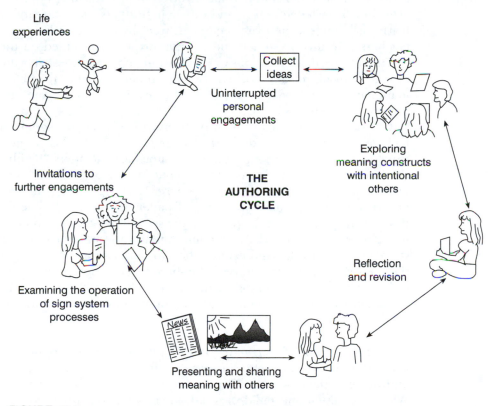

FIGURE 12.5

The Authoring Cycle: An Example of Curriculum Enactment

From Creating Curriculum: Teachers and Students as a Community of Learners (p. 35), by K. G. Short & C. Burke, 1991, Portsmouth NH: Heinemann. Copyright 1991 by Kathy Short and Carolyn Burke. Reprinted by permission.

These elements include life experiences, uninterrupted personal engagements, exploring meaning constructs, reflection and revision, presenting and sharing meaning with others, examining the operation of sign system processes, and invitations to further engagements.

Life Experiences.   What teachers and students know about life comes from their social and cultural experiences. Each person's experiences are invitations to the future and form the springboard for curricular experiences. Strategies for connecting with life experiences provide students with options so they begin with what they know. One strategy, called *Family Stories,* allows students to select and interview family members about their recollections of events. Students may share their interview notes orally with others and later move through the Authoring Cycle. Note that all students, regardless of ability or background, can enter the Authoring Cycle through a strategy such as this one because they choose from their life experiences those they wish to pursue (Short & Burke, 1991).

Uninterrupted Personal Engagements.   Here open classroom structures and activities allow students to become involved in new learning opportunities. However, new knowledge must build on what students know already; they cannot learn new things if these are separated from their world of knowing. The job of teachers is to involve students in learning experiences based on their past that can then be used as invitations to new learning opportunities. Specifically, instead of reading books meant to teach reading, students need to read literature, informational books, billboards, the backs of cereal boxes, maps, and other materials important to learners.

Classroom strategies that provide uninterrupted personal engagements include *Readers Theatre* and *Drawing Conversations.* In the first strategy individual students are assigned character and narrator parts. Readers "highlight the parts that they will read aloud and then, without further preparation, the participants give a reading of the story" (Short & Burke, 1991, pp. 38–39). In *Drawing Conversations* two students share one sheet of paper and a pencil. One person begins drawing and then hands the pencil to the second person who continues the drawing. No talking is allowed. All communication is through the drawing. Both these strategies allow students to explore the process as a way of creating meaning for themselves. Some explorations will be shared and explored with others, and some will remain private. In all cases students need blocks of time, instructional materials that suggest explorations, and the opportunity to use the materials for their own purposes.

Exploring Meaning Constructs.   People who write need opportunities to think about their work from perspectives different from their own. Authors understand and develop their own thinking through trying to explain it to someone else. When they listen and build on what others say about their writing, writers can analyze and think through ideas before trying to produce final draft thinking. *Authors' Circles* is a strategy in which a small group of authors who have work in progress meet together. Each author reads aloud a piece of writing and others in the group ask questions about meaning and indicate particularly effective or confusing parts of the piece. In *Mathematical Circles* students first work through mathematical stories individually, then meet together to compare their strategies for mathematical solutions. In such collaborative situations people learn because they are part of a group involved in thinking together and expanding each other's current ideas and perspectives.

Reflection and Revision.   Following exploration with other people, authors need the opportunity to reflect on the suggestions and comments of the group. Students must have time to think about the relationship between what they intended to do and the actual results. In writing or drawing, they can add, shorten, or change their pieces. In reading students may reinterpret the content of their reading.

Presenting and Sharing Meaning.   Going public with one's meanings requires a real need to do so and additional consideration by an outside person. Authors tend to read their own meanings into what they produce. The outside critic helps the author with social conventions such as mechanics, capitalizations, and others. In some classrooms *Editor's Table* helps with these processes for prospective newspaper or book pieces. The students serving as editors make their own codes fitted to particular documents. After editing, the author types and illustrates the piece and later celebrates with the class. This action encourages students to continue other projects through the Authoring Cycle.

Examining the Operation of Sign System Processes.   Sign systems including language, art, music, and mathematics are the devices by which people create, explore, share, and revise meaning. Using these devices stretches students' limits and creates personal need for new knowledge that can be met through instruction. The teacher or another student plans an experience that attends to that need, then invites learners to participate in the experience that investigates the need. In *Synonym Substitution,* for example, students read a passage with premarked words or phrases that have synonyms. At those marked points the students read anything that makes sense. This strategy obviously requires knowledge of context and stretches vocabularies. In such strategy lessons students consider what they know about language and how they might use new understandings at later times.

Invitations to Further Engagements.   Invitations are the means by which students continue to move through the cycle. As students move through the cycle, they deal with only a part of their intentions, but the processes renew the potential for other learning experiences. *Collaborative Plans* is a regular daily experience when students and teachers list what they will do on a planning sheet and indicate whether they are inviting others to join them. These invitations serve the purpose of making the authoring process an ongoing operation.

These brief descriptions highlight the joint responsibilities that students and teachers have in the creation of the curriculum. They also show that students have choices of learning activities and explain why learning outcomes usually differ among students.

CREATION OF IMPLEMENTATION/ENACTMENT PLANS

After revised curricula receive governing board approval, they are ready to be used in classrooms. Sometimes district-developed curricula are tested in a few classrooms before they are implemented widely throughout the district. The point of these tryouts is to identify changes that might improve the curriculum. This practice is likely to occur in districts where school-based committees do NOT function.

Implementation in even a few classrooms requires preparation. For example, teachers need orientation to the revised curriculum, which may be provided by district personnel. Teachers may participate in professional development activities or training in the use of resources, objectives, evaluation procedures, or other matters required by the revised curriculum. When the teachers deliver the curriculum, a supervisor collects and analyzes information both about how well the curriculum enables students to meet the purpose of education and the implementation processes to determine if changes should be made. After the tryout period evaluators and developers examine their data and adjust the curriculum before it is implemented throughout the district.

Curricula developed by school committees typically do not undergo pilot tests because developers planned the curriculum for their local situation. Change facilitators within the school work with teachers and other staff in using the curriculum. Together they plan the operations involving the scope and complexity of curricular change, communication, professional development, and resources.

The remainder of this section describes incomplete plans for use of the curricula developed in previous chapters for two hypothetical situations. First is a rudimentary plan for implementing the health curriculum devised by a school-based committee. This is followed by a plan for enacting the English literature curriculum.

HEALTH CURRICULUM

Imagine that you are the principal of an elementary school in which a revised health curriculum is to be implemented. You led a group of teachers, staff, and community members in adapting the district curriculum to meet certain needs in your school community. At this point you are especially pleased that you took the training offered by the CBAM Cadre International (Hall & Hord, 1987) because you believe it will help you guide the teachers in your building in using the revised curriculum. That training, for example, helped you deal with your own concerns about change and taught you the importance of good communication with all the people involved.

During curriculum development you communicated with parents and guardians through the school newsletter about the progress of the health curriculum. Several teachers of your twenty-plus group worked on this school curriculum, but several others participated minimally or not at all.

The challenge now is to persuade the reluctant teachers who did not participate in development to use the health curriculum now that is completed. You initially convene teachers of the lower grades separately from teachers in the upper grades to plan implementation of the curriculum. Meeting the teachers in two groups is one strategy to actively involve all of them. You are aware that these two teacher groups may have different concerns about using the revised curriculum. For example, upper-grade teachers must spend more time in health lessons than the current curriculum requires, but lower-grade teachers have about the same time commitment. Also present at these meetings is a lead teacher who serves as a second change facilitator.

Some teacher-developers can help the nondevelopers understand how the new curriculum differs from the previous one—both in content and delivery mode. You expect the discussions to help teachers sort out the scope and complexity of the change. For example, the teachers may decide to implement a few units the first year, then add a few units the next year until all the units are in place.

During these discussions you listen carefully to comments to determine the concerns raised. Whenever possible, you pledge resources for such things as professional development and instructional materials. You also help teachers agree on a projected timeline for implementing the curriculum. You perceive that the developers already feel ownership of the curriculum, and become aware that nondevelopers lack this ownership and want to move more slowly.

Based on the agreed-upon timeline, teachers begin using the revised curriculum. You and the lead teacher work with teachers according to their needs, but insist that the nondevelopers try using the curriculum. After all, unless there is pressure some teachers will not try the revised curriculum. You administer the diagnostic tools for CBAM as needed. (More information about these operations is included in Chapter 13, Creation of Plans for Evaluation.) Depending on the results, you and the lead teacher plan and carry out appropriate interventions that enable teachers to move through the stages of concern and the levels of use hierarchy. As it becomes appropriate, you work with teachers on an innovations configuration for your school. If needed, you work out additional adaptations of the curriculum to suit individual situations.

Your intention is to enable the reluctant teachers to feel successful in using the revised curriculum. You count on the enthusiasm of the developers to help bring some of these individuals along in the implementation processes. Ultimately you hope that all the teachers will sense the value of the revised curriculum as it benefits students and their parents/guardians. You and the lead teacher look ahead to the evaluation of the revised health curriculum described in Chapter 13.

ENGLISH LITERATURE CURRICULUM

The literature curriculum that you and your colleague prepared was approved by your department head and the board. The next step is to plan to use it with students. One of your first concerns is to communicate with next year's seniors, their parents/guardians, and your colleagues about this curriculum. The activities you have planned are a bit different from traditional ones. In the spring newsletter you write a short message that alerts the school community to some impending changes in the English literature classes by briefly describing a few planned activities and calling attention to several that you believe will be of interest to the seniors.

Next you and your colleague must concern yourselves with the physical context in which these classes meet. Normally English literature classes meet in regular size classrooms, but these are too small for the amount and type of discussions that you anticipate. You talk with the department head about another classroom space and find that the auditorium stage area is free a few periods during the school day. There would be plenty of room for discussions and brief dramatic presentations.

Next you request that all English literature classes be scheduled into the open time slots for that space. Your request is granted by the department chair, but you are told that the only available furniture is leftover from drama classes—sofas and odd chairs without arm rests. Although these seating arrangements provide the informality needed for the activities, it would be difficult to do written work there. Eventually you make arrangements for using the computer laboratory on certain dates when students do written assignments. Although this is not the best arrangement, it will serve your purpose for the trial use of this curriculum.

You and your colleague map out as well as you can what the next year's schedule will be—possible dates for the various activities you anticipate. You keep in mind, however, that the schedule must be flexible. Afterward, you divide the responsibilities for making other arrangements. For example, your colleague agrees to schedule the use of the sound recordings for *The Canterbury Tales* from the state university library. You agree to locate Grandpa Green, a retired actor living in your community, to see if he is willing to work with students on language skills. Both of you consider the many arrangements (e.g., permissions, finances, turn-around destination) that must be made to take the seniors on a trip, as you planned in the culminating experience for *The Canterbury Tales*.

Both of you agree that evaluating students using this curriculum is important. But you agree to give yourselves at least half the summer to think about those plans, which are described in Chapter 13, Creation of Evaluation Plans.

SUMMARY

Implementation and enactment are processes by which revised curricula are used in schools. Both sets of processes involve scope and complexity of curricular change, communication, professional development, and resources. Change facilitators, including building principals, manage these processes.

During implementation change facilitators work closely with teachers using the revised curriculum. In the Concerns-Based Adoption Model, CFs assess teachers' stages of concern and levels of use of the revised curriculum and monitor their use of acceptable levels of the innovations configuration for their school. CFs use the results of assessments to provide interventions that assist teachers toward full and appropriate use of the revised curriculum.

The teacher-developers of a nontechnical curriculum are the same ones who put that curriculum into classroom use. They collaborate with other teachers and work under the direction of their building supervisor. Each nontechnical curriculum enactment is unique because teachers use different approaches to organizing the curriculum. The Authoring Cycle is one approach. The final section contained plans for initiating the classroom use of the hypothetical health and English literature curricula developed in previous chapters.

QUESTIONS FOR DISCUSSION

1. Explain what is meant by the statement "Success in curriculum change is measured one person at a time."
2. How are the planning considerations taken into account in the Concerns-Based Adoption Model? Explain.
3. From your perspective as a teacher, principal, or other educational professional describe the type of professional development that either does (or would) benefit you most when you are faced with implementing a revised curriculum. Explain.
4. Describe the correlations between stages of concern and levels of use of a revised curriculum.
5. Speculate about the benefits of institutionalization of a curriculum change insofar as students are concerned.
6. Explain how The Authoring Cycle illustrates the features of the nontechnical approach to curriculum.
7. Explain how the change processes for implementation were addressed in the section Creation of Implementation Plans for the health curriculum.

IMPORTANT IDEAS DISCUSSED INITIALLY IN THIS CHAPTER

processes for implementation of change
    active initiation and participation
    pressure and support
    changes in behavior and belief
    ownership
Concerns-Based Adoption Model
    implementation processes
    initiation

interventions
institutionalization
Concerns-Based Adoption Model
    diagnostic tools
    stages of concern
    levels of use
    innovations configuration
mutual adaptation

13

EVALUATION OF CURRICULUM PROJECTS

OUTLINE

Curriculum evaluation
    Standards
    Limitations
Process evaluation in technically developed projects
    Questions and information needs
    Data collection and analyses
Product evaluation
    Questions and information needs
    Data collection and analyses
Interpretation and uses of analyses
Creation of evaluation plans
    Health curriculum
    English literature curriculum

Evaluation of curriculum projects begins whenever revised curricula are completed and put to use in classrooms. *Curriculum evaluation* refers to the formal determination of the quality, effectiveness, or value of a curriculum (Worthen, Borg, & White, 1993). Major activities include identifying standards for judging quality, gathering relevant data, and applying the standards to determine quality. Ideally curriculum evaluation is part of ongoing school operations that provide information for decisions about school improvement.

For curricula developed through nontechnical and technical approaches, curriculum evaluation answers the question of how well that curriculum enables students to meet the intended purpose of education. For technically developed curricula an additional aspect of evaluation answers questions about the implementation of the curriculum. This chapter focuses on the operations associated with these purposes.

The final section describes preliminary plans by which the health and English literature curricula developed for hypothetical situations in previous chapters could be evaluated in their respective contexts. As a result of studying this chapter, you should be able *to make a rudimentary plan for initiating evaluation of a curriculum project of your choice*.

CURRICULUM EVALUATION

Evaluation of curriculum projects takes place in the same context as needs assessment. In fact outcomes of curriculum evaluation are sometimes compared with outcomes of needs assessment as a check on how well needs were met. As used here, evaluation consists of process and product assessment.

Process evaluation has three purposes: 1) to provide information about the extent to which plans for curriculum implementation are executed and use resources wisely, 2) to provide assistance for changing or clarifying implementation plans, and 3) to assess the degree to which teachers and change facilitators carry out their roles (Stufflebeam & Shinkfield, 1985). Process evaluation is necessary in implementation of technically developed curricula because these are used in multiple classrooms in a school district, usually by teachers who were not developers.

Curriculum enactment, on the other hand, is carried out by the same teachers who developed nontechnical curricula. As noted in Chapter 12 the teacher-developers work with colleagues and their administrators to use the curriculum. Formal process evaluation is unnecessary in these situations.

Product evaluation has as its main purpose gathering, interpreting, and appraising curricular attainments, not only at the end of an implementation or enactment cycle, but as often as necessary. The intent of product evaluation is to determine how well the curriculum meets the needs of the students it is intended to serve (Stufflebeam & Shinkfield, 1985). Process and product evaluation work together to provide a stronger rationale than either one alone to make decisions about technically developed curricula and to explain project outcomes (Stufflebeam, Foley, et al., 1971).

STANDARDS

The same standards apply to evaluation of curriculum processes and products as those used in needs assessments. These standards feature the utility, feasibility, propriety, and accuracy criteria set by the Joint Committee on Standards for Educational Evaluation (1994). Examples of applications of the standards are described in the section titled Creation of Evaluation Plans. Additional information about evaluation standards is included in Appendix B.

LIMITATIONS

Because curriculum evaluation involves people and complex human behaviors, certain limitations are inherent in the processes and must be taken into account in the interpretation of outcomes. Insofar as possible, the limitations should be acknowledged in the evaluation plan so that these can be taken into account when evaluators interpret information. Among the limitations are the degree of *cooperation* among the people involved, the *complexity* of describing or measuring some behaviors or events, *time, access to students* who used the curriculum, and *rationales* (i.e., views of education) for the curriculum (Sanders, 1990).

Curriculum evaluation depends on the *cooperation* of large numbers of people within a school community environment—classroom teachers, principals, curriculum specialists, students, and community members. Unless these individuals cooperate, the evaluation project may not succeed. Allowing others to view their work, identifying issues or problems, participating in data gathering, providing information, and reviewing and correcting draft evaluation reports all require that people work together (Sanders, 1990).

As pointed out in Chapter 1, educators have different views of reality, which makes measuring or describing certain behaviors or events a *complex* undertaking. For example, an "attitude" is composed of affective and cognitive phenomena. Whereas one evaluator might find it easy to determine the extent to which a certain attitude is exhibited, another evaluator might find this task difficult because each is looking for different phenomena.

Consider, also, that classroom activities have different meanings for participants, which may result in students learning different outcomes. Differences may occur between the intended and actual learning outcomes as well as among the actual learning outcomes. These examples point out one complexity of the items about which curriculum evaluation is concerned.

Results of curriculum change may not show up in students immediately. Some changes take years or decades to emerge (Sanders, 1990). Change in students is individual, too, and takes place over *time*. Therefore, assessment may not reveal the changes that developers and implementors seek as quickly as they may look for this information. At whatever point the changes do appear, evaluation may or may not register those changes.

Access to students for curriculum evaluation may pose limitations. Some evaluation procedures, such as observations or interviews, require direct access to students that is not always available to evaluators. Nearly all districts have evaluation plans by which students take various standardized tests, such as achievement and mental ability tests or state-mandated assessment measures. In addition teachers administer tests to evaluate student progress of instructional objectives. These existing evaluation activities require that curriculum evaluation be part of regular school operations because additional time for evaluation cannot be taken in the school calendar.

Curricula may be built on different *rationales* or views of education that involve alternative purposes. Because of these differences, curriculum evaluators choose assessment strategies congruent with particular purposes. Moreover, these choices must not only satisfy the school officials who authorized the evaluation, but the findings must also communicate to all those who use them, including teachers and school staff. Handling these concerns simultaneously is complicated (Sanders, 1990).

For evaluation activities to contribute to school improvement, they must be integrated into regular school operations. Only then can evaluation affect curricular choices, decisions, and practices.

Exercise 13.1 offers an opportunity for you to reflect on these limitations. See how well you understand them at this point.

EXERCISE 13.1

Consider the discussion of limitations on process and product evaluation. Then answer these questions:

1. Suppose an evaluator is unable to obtain information about curriculum effectiveness from community members because of their lack of interest in school affairs. Explain how this affects evaluation efforts.
2. Evaluation of an "attitude" was used as an illustration of a complex behavior in classrooms. Is "achievement" more or less complex than "attitude" for evaluation purposes? Explain.
3. How might making a change in the purpose of education complicate curriculum evaluation?

PROCESS EVALUATION IN TECHNICALLY DEVELOPED PROJECTS

Process evaluation assesses the procedures in implementing revised curricula. These data are especially important in determining the extent to which a revised curriculum is tried with students. Unless curriculum evaluators have process information, they risk evaluating a nonevent, a curriculum that was not actually used (Charters & Jones, 1973; Hall & Loucks, 1974). The following section describes questions and information needs to be answered through collection and analyses of data. It also continues discussion of the Concerns-Based Adoption Model from Chapter 12.

QUESTIONS AND INFORMATION NEEDS

Process evaluation provides answers to the major question about how well a modified curriculum is actually put into operation in schools. Many things can happen when a curriculum begins to be used in classrooms. For example, defects can occur in interpersonal relationships among the teachers, communication, logistics, resource adequacy, physical facilities availability, time schedules or any of many other things that affect smooth operations. Finding defects early is an important way of preventing additional difficulties (Stufflebeam, Foley, et al, 1971).

Implementation frequently requires purchases of instructional materials, professional staff development, changes in the school calendar, or other program decisions. Any of these operations may involve decisions that should be made and acted upon according to a planned schedule. Ordering materials, locating consultants for staff development sessions, and arranging substitutes for teachers on released time are examples of such planned decisions. If these are not handled appropriately, implementation plans can be seriously disrupted. Process evaluation shows how well these decisions are being managed.

Within the major process question are these interrelated subquestions: Were implementation plans carried out? Were these amended when necessary? Were resources used wisely? To what extent was the curriculum implemented? How well did teachers and change facilitators perform their roles?

Information about carrying out plans, resources, extent of implementation, and teacher performance comes from records of teachers' and change facilitators' communications and activities. Data about change facilitators' role performances comes from self-reports or interviews that reveal their personal knowledge of the modified curriculum, its personal value to them, their personal behaviors as a result of the modified curriculum, and knowledge of institutional commitment to the curriculum (Hill, 1986).

DATA COLLECTION AND ANALYSES

When a curriculum is implemented on a trial basis with a few teachers, frequent classroom observations and informal interviews usually provide answers to process evaluation questions. However, when many teachers are involved, change facilitators use systematic data collection techniques such as those provided in the Concerns-Based Adoption Model (CBAM). This subsection describes how stages of concern, levels of use, and innovation configurations are used in the context of process evaluation.

Data Collection From Teachers.   Change facilitators' logs of their exchanges with teachers furnish data for answering process questions. These logs should track teachers' stages of concern, levels of use, and adherence to the innovations configuration required by the revised curriculum as well as the change facilitators' interventions. In addition, written records of teachers' responses to the diagnostic tools are also valuable sources of data. If available, teachers' logs of their experiences in implementing the curriculum are also helpful. Records such as these provide necessary references for the interpretation of analyses and decision making.

Teachers' stages of concern are typically measured in one or more of these ways: **one-legged conferences,**[1] **open-ended statements of concern,** or the **Stages of Concern Questionnaire.** Each measure is appropriate in different settings and for different purposes. One-legged conferences, or unstructured interviews, are informal, brief conversations that change facilitators (CFs) have with teachers, sometimes in classrooms, in hallways, or faculty lounges. Such encounters normally last no more than two minutes. But in that brief time a CF can ask a simple, open-ended question that gets at the teacher's concerns about the revised curriculum and can supply a brief intervention. Two illustrations of open-ended questions are these:

1. "How do you feel about the revised curriculum?"
2. "I am interested in anything you'll share with me about the revised curriculum."

What is important is that the CF listens carefully to the teacher, notes the stage of concern expressed, and replies appropriately.

Change facilitators also ask teachers to describe in writing their concerns about using the revised curriculum. In these open-ended situations teachers receive a page with this statement at the top: "When you think about using the revised curriculum, what are you concerned about?" The remainder of the page is blank and meant to encourage teachers to describe their concerns. Some teachers write only a few lines, but others produce two-page essays. Whatever teachers say, however, is reviewed carefully. Persons trained in content analyses of Stages of Concern responses individually examine and determine the stage at which each teacher is probably functioning (Hall & Hord, 1987).

The Stages of Concern Questionnaire can be used in situations where systematic study of reliable data is particularly important, such as research and evaluation projects (Hall & Hord, 1987). This instrument, which contains 35 items, can be used in all educational settings and requires only 10 to 15 minutes to complete. Because a Likert scale is marked for each item, this questionnaire can be hand- or computer-scored to provide concerns profiles showing the intensity of self, task, and impact concerns. This instrument can be used several times a year to track the progress of teachers' changes from self to impact concerns. (Note: Likert scales are described in the discussion of opinionnaire surveys in Appendix C.)

Whether teachers actually use the revised curriculum is ascertained through classroom observations and interviews. Both data collection techniques are used because change facilitators need information that cannot be collected simply by observing teachers in action in their classrooms. CFs would have to follow teachers through their before- and after-school preparations to determine answers to certain levels of use questions (e.g., the extent to which problem solving is used in mathematics instruction).

Hall and Hord (1987) describe a focused interview that change facilitators employ when multiple teachers implement a curriculum. In this strategy the CF asks teachers a series of carefully structured questions about their *actual* use of the

---

[1] See Appendix C for additional information about the instruments identified in boldface.

curriculum. The interview starts with an open-ended question such as, "Are you using the revised curriculum?" Regardless of the teacher's answer, the interviewer probes with additional questions to determine whether the teacher is or is not *using* the curriculum. Teachers reply with descriptions of the actions they are taking or will be taking. Depending on the responses, change facilitators continue probing to determine the level at which teachers use the revised curriculum.

If, for example, the teacher says he or she IS using the curriculum, the interviewer follows up with the question, "What kinds of changes are you making in your use of the revised curriculum?" The interviewer listens to the answer and sorts it into one of three categories, mechanical use (Level III), routine use (Level IVA), or some form of impact level (Levels IVB, V, VI). If the teacher's answer shows an impact level response, the interviewer continues with other probing questions. Figure 13.1 shows the series of questions in this focused interview. Additional information about assessing levels of use is available in a training manual for this procedure (Loucks, Newlove, & Hall, 1975).

Change facilitators check, too, to see if teachers are using the revised curriculum as it was intended to be used. Chapter 12 briefly describes negotiations between developers and implementors concerning an innovations configuration. The outcome of these negotiations is an instrument containing behavioral statements designated at acceptable or unacceptable levels. Sometimes the acceptable statements are further subdivided into ideal statements (those strongly favored by curriculum developers) and acceptable (those that meet the spirit of the revised curriculum, but not the developers' standards). (See Figure 12.3.) Change facilitators collect data on whether teachers satisfy the appropriate innovations configurations through interviews described previously, but these are supplemented by classroom observations. More information about assessing innovations configurations is available in a training manual for these procedures (Heck, Stiegelbauer, Hall, & Loucks, 1981).

Data Collection From Change Facilitators.   Principals serving as change facilitators are accountable to central administrators for their work in implementing curricula. Therefore, change facilitators must be evaluated on how well they are doing their tasks as part of process evaluation. This evaluation could involve the CFs' preparation of detailed reports of implementation activities that permit the central administration to judge their work. Or evaluation might take the form of interviews by district central administrators.

Interviewers want to know about the change facilitators' knowledge of the curriculum, their values toward the curriculum, their behaviors as a result of the modified curriculum, and their perceptions of support for the curriculum. Figure 13.2 shows some illustrative interview questions related to these major topics. The questions with bullets can be used by interviewers as follow-ups to the main questions. Note also the kinds of comments the interviewers would "listen for" in the responses.

Data Analyses.   Data from CBAM operations are subjected to analyses at least at two levels. Change facilitators perform *ongoing* data analyses to provide personal-

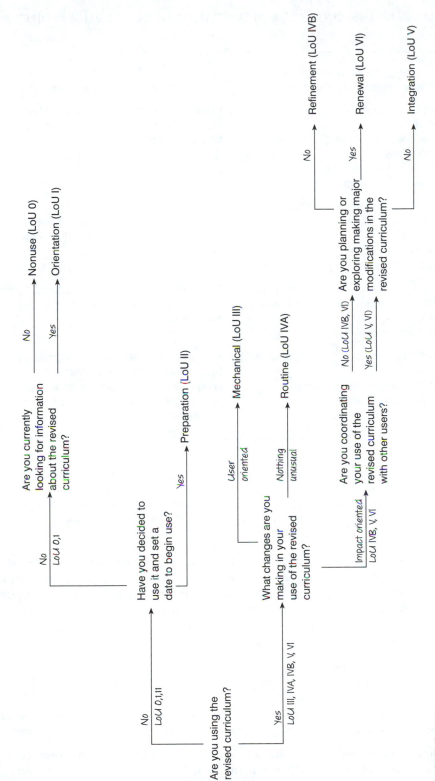

FIGURE 13.1

Interview for Evaluating Levels of Use

Note: Levels of use (LoU) are designated by Roman numerals. See Figure 12.2 for their meanings.

From *Taking Charge of Change* (p. 63) by S. M. Hord, W. L. Rutherford, L. Huling-Austin, and G. E. Hall, 1987, Alexandria, VA: Association for Supervision and Curriculum Development. Copyright 1987 by Southwest Educational Development Laboratory. Adapted by permission.

Suggested Question(s) and *Follow-Up Question(s)	"Listen For" Examples
What is your understanding of this curriculum? * How does it propose that learning takes place? * What are the roles of teachers and students in this curriculum?	Views of learning and roles described are consistent with the views of education statement.
How do you feel about this curriculum? * How would it fit with your own teaching style? * Based on your own views, what are the things you are concerned about?	Positive. CF gives examples of having taught or of wanting to teach this way. Few concerns about the curriculum.
How much support does this curriculum have by the board, the superintendent, the teachers, and the parents/guardians?	Generally perceives support; curriculum reflects community values; teachers support it.
How well are the teachers implementing this curriculum? * Have they run into problems? * How do they feel about it? * Please cite some examples.	Answer mentions concrete examples the CF has seen in classrooms; mentions reactions of teachers, including problems they may have experienced and the solutions applied.

FIGURE 13.2
Illustrative Interview Questions for Use with a Change Facilitator (CF) Concerning Curriculum Implementation

From *Curriculum Evaluation for School Improvement* (pp. 83–85), by J. C. Hill, 1986, Springfield, IL: Charles C. Thomas Publishers. Copyright 1986 by John C. Hill. Adapted by permission.

ized interventions for teachers. CFs analyze results of stages of concern, levels of use, and innovations configuration situations as part of helping teachers implement the curriculum. CFs are aware that they must help teachers pass through the self-concerns to task concerns before teachers actually use the curriculum. For example, teacher comments such as these could emerge from one-legged conferences or open-ended statements:

1. "I need to know more about this new curriculum."
2. "I really don't get through all my plans each day. There is so much to do since I started this new curriculum."
3. "As I use the revised curriculum, I am concerned that my students might not have the opportunity to learn the material before we move to the next topic."

Comments 1–3 represent self, task, and impact level concerns, respectively. Based on the comment, Teacher 1 is not a user at this point and must receive appropriate information before becoming one. On the other hand, teachers 2 and 3 are users, but the content indicates that Teacher 3 is more proficient in using the curriculum than Teacher 2. The second teacher requires an intervention that assists with management, but the third teacher probably needs an intervention that helps him/her keep track of student performance.

Change facilitators analyze data from the CBAM diagnostic tools in this ongoing fashion, making decisions about interventions based on the data from the levels of use or innovations configuration inventories. CFs should also periodically summarize and analyze data for teacher implementors in a formative way. Some time points should be designated when CFs formally evaluate progress of the implementation efforts. Written records of these analyses are helpful to the curriculum evaluators who interpret results.

PRODUCT EVALUATION

Product evaluation assesses planned and unplanned outcomes of using revised curricula in classrooms because both types of information are important in making decisions about school curricula. Results of outcomes evaluations should feed back into the curriculum processes, allowing developers to modify the curriculum in ways that enable students to better meet the intended purpose of education. This section describes questions and information needs concerning product evaluation that are answered through data collection and analyses.

QUESTIONS AND INFORMATION NEEDS

The major purpose of product evaluation is to determine how well a curriculum accomplishes its *intended* purpose. Broad questions involved in product evaluation are these: Is this curriculum bringing about the changes in students that were expected? Are students learning what the curriculum developers intended?

Ideally, for a curriculum with the purpose of "cultivating cognitive achievement," this means that students' intellects are sharpened, that they can and do think with precision, generality, and power in solving problems. If the purpose is "preparing people for living in an unstable, changing world," evaluation should show that students are able to solve societal problems and deal with change. If the purpose is to "develop individuals to their fullest potentials," curriculum evaluation should show that students are personally liberated and developed. These comments, of course, are based on the purposes of education described in Chapter 3.

The term *ideally* suggests the possibility that evaluating curriculum products in the real world does not always proceed as theory says it should. One major reason is that curriculum developers put their purposes, aims, and goals of education into operation in different ways. Even the popular purpose of "cultivating cognitive achievement" carries a variety of meanings among educators and curriculum documents. Aims such as "develop habits of good citizenship" or "learn problem solving" also carry different meanings. Given the variations in interpretations of purposes and aims, direct evaluation of curricular intentions is complex, difficult, and virtually impossible.

As a result of this complexity, evaluators should look broadly at the effects of the curriculum, including the unintended effects and positive and negative outcomes. Product evaluation should gather information from a broad range of people including school and community personnel. In addition, product evaluation should compare the outcomes of the revised curriculum with those of the curriculum it replaced, with the needs assessed in context evaluation, or with alternative programs (Stufflebeam, 1983).

Sometimes *unintended* effects come about because of flaws in the evaluation plan. For example, in recent years developers designed mathematics curricula to help students learn problem-solving or other higher-order thinking skills. In some cases product evaluation shows that students do not achieve this goal. However, this apparent failure may actually be due to inappropriate evaluation methods. Tests that predominantly assess knowledge of facts and execution of algorithms cannot tell evaluators whether students are meeting the higher-order thinking skills (Pandey, 1990). Failure to align the evaluation with the revised curriculum can produce such unintended outcomes.

Unintended effects may also be positive and arise if students learn important things that developers had not planned. To illustrate, in recent years teachers have begun using cooperative learning groups as an instructional strategy. Students who experience learning in such groups may learn not only the content that was intended, but these procedures have been shown to improve race relations, acceptance of academically handicapped students and student self-esteem (Slavin, 1990). Thus, appreciations for the abilities of others, improved human relations skills, and increased self-awareness may be unexpected outcomes that accrue through the instructional delivery approaches for the curriculum.

DATA COLLECTION AND ANALYSES

Evaluators select strategies for collecting information to obtain data from school and community personnel associated with curriculum implementation or enactment. Given the broadness of the questions, several different techniques of gathering information are used to provide a cross-check on the various findings. The strategies selected depend somewhat on the number of people involved, but must take into account the purpose served by the curriculum.

Data Collection From Students. Information about outcomes can and should be collected in a variety of ways from students who use a revised curriculum. These strategies must provide data collection in all the pertinent domains of learning. This discussion can only sample assessment options because a full description is beyond the scope of this book. Education journals periodically devote entire issues to assessment (e.g., *Educational Leadership, Phi Delta Kappan*). Most university libraries have these and other references on this subject.

School districts typically have evaluation plans that designate the instruments to be administered to students according to time-of-year and subject/grade-level schedules. Due to the time and expense required, these plans usually serve dual purposes of providing assessment information about individual students as well as program evaluation. School evaluation plans typically designate teachers as the chief gatherers of student data.

Two popular data collection techniques for cognitive learning include commercial standardized tests (e.g., *Iowa Test of Basic Skills*) and state-mandated assessments (e.g., *California Assessment Program*). **Standardized tests**[2] are assessment instruments "given to a large number of persons under similar conditions, designed to yield comparable scores. The term is most often applied to national norm-referenced tests developed by test publishers" (Hymes, 1991, p. 17). Standardized testing is "perceived to be an efficient, inexpensive, administratively convenient, quantifiable, and objective way of serving the needs of accountability" (Madaus & Kellaghan, 1992, p. 131).

However, standardized tests typically do not measure the curricular goals of particular schools; rather they are based on social criteria of what is regarded as important for all students to learn (Madaus & Kellaghan, 1992). Results from such tests provide one source of data that must be supplemented by information from other sources.

State-mandated assessments were required in 42 states in the early 1990s (Pipho, 1991). In general these instruments measure the outcomes required by state lists of required, basic, or essential skills. In some cases these tests are similar to standardized achievement tests, but in other situations state tests require alternative assessment, sometimes called authentic or performance assessment.

Alternative assessments came into being because most standardized tests do not measure the skills and abilities students need in the real world. Even "low-skill" jobs require technical training and the ability to work with other people in problem solving situations. Multiple-choice, norm-referenced tests put the students taking them "in a passive, reactive role, rather than one that engages their capacities to structure tasks, produce ideas, and solve problems" (Darling-Hammond, 1994, p. 15).

Authentic assessment is "a generic term for alternative assessment methods that test students' ability to solve problems or perform tasks under simulated 'real life' situations" (Hymes, 1991, p. 16). In outlining criteria for authentic assessments, Wiggins (1993) stresses the need for nonroutine and multistage tasks that require a quality product or performance. Tasks should also embody engaging and worthy problems or questions of importance. Eisner (1993) suggests that authentic assessment problems should reveal how students go about solving them and that problems should have more than one acceptable solution. Also, the problems might be solved by students working together. Student assessment that comes nearest to fitting these criteria typically involves performance assessment, systematic observations of students, or portfolios (Hart, 1994).

California's Department of Education is a leader in statewide efforts to reform assessments. In science education, for example, educators from several levels

---

[2] See Appendix C for additional information about the instruments identified in boldface.

worked together to produce a thematic and conceptual outline that set forth science literacy goals for all school children. Subsequently, various groups prepared for the assessment of these goals using "performance tasks, enhanced multiple-choice items, open-ended and justified multiple-choice questions, and portfolios. These assessments provide students with the opportunity to demonstrate conceptual understanding of the big ideas of science; to use scientific tools and processes; and to apply their understanding of these big ideas to solve new problems" (Comfort, 1994, pp. 43–44).

Performance assessments are designed to test the ability of students to use their knowledge and skills in a variety of realistic situations and contexts (Wiggins, 1993). These assessments can be short or extended and use open-ended or enhanced multiple-choice questions. Some performance assessments involve reading and writing, processes, or problem solving and analytical tasks, depending on their purpose.

The mathematics task for upper elementary school students, shown in Figure 13.3, provides an extended situation with several types of questions. This task

---

You and your neighbors are planning a yard sale. You will need to solve several problems to make sure the yard sale is successful. You survey your neighborhood and find out the following information:

People participating	Number of objects to be sold	Space needed
Your family	10	30 sq. ft.
Smiths	15	35 sq. ft.
Andersons	7	10 sq. ft.
Jacksons	13	20 sq. ft.
Saris	12	18 sq. ft.

You call the rental store and find out that they rent tables measuring 6 feet by 2½ feet for $6.00 a day. How many tables will you need for the yard sale? How do you know?

The yard you are planning to use measures 20 feet by 30 feet. Draw a diagram of the placement of the tables in the yard. Be sure to allow about 4 feet of space around the tables for the movement of customers.

You find that the cost of advertising in the local newspaper is $13.50 for the first ten words and $1.00 per word after that. Write an advertisement describing the neighborhood yard sale. Be sure you include the details that the customers would need to know. The items to be sold are all kitchen and garden tools. How much will your ad cost?

FIGURE 13.3

Example of a Performance-Based Task, Featuring an Extended Situation With Several Types of Questions

From "Linking Instruction and Assessment in the Mathematics Classroom" by K. B. Sammons, B. Kobett, J. Heiss, and F. Fennell, 1992, *Arithmetic Teacher, 39*(6), p. 16. Copyright 1992 by the National Council of Teachers of Mathematics. Reprinted by permission.

Listed below are some rights guaranteed to citizens of the United States by the Constitution:

   a. Right to keep and bear arms
   b. Right of assembly and to petition government
   c. Right to a grand jury hearing before being charged with a serious federal crime
   d. Freedom of speech
   e. Right to an attorney
   f. Protection from cruel and unusual punishment
   g. Right to know charges against oneself and to question witnesses in court
   h. Right to due process of the law

Read each of the situations and decide which, if any, rights of citizens (see a–h) were violated. For each situation list the letter or letters of the rights that were violated. Then explain why you answered as you did.

Situation 1:
The leader of a neighborhood gang was arrested on suspicion of blowing up an automobile. For two days he was questioned by police, who did not allow him to call a lawyer. The police said they were not formally charging him with a crime, but were only questioning him.

Situation 2:
At a town hall meeting community members were listening to a speaker describe impending changes in the zoning laws for commercial enterprises. Present at the meeting was a local business owner who believed she would be put out of business if the laws were passed. Each time the speaker began speaking to the community members, the business owner shouted out protests to whatever the speaker said. Finally, one member of the audience called the police and she was arrested.

FIGURE 13.4
Example of a Performance-Based Task, Featuring Enhanced and Justified Multiple-Choice Items

requires an understanding of data analysis, fractions, area, spatial sense, monetary applications, and writing and is intended for individuals or groups of students (Sammons, Kobett, Heiss, & Fennell, 1992). Tasks of this type extend mathematics beyond the classroom to the real world.

Other performance assessment questions involve enhanced or justified multiple-choice questions. An enhanced question involves several questions pertaining to a scenario that provides a context in which students must think about big ideas and show conceptual understanding. Justified multiple-choice items require students to write a brief statement explaining why they chose a particular answer (Comfort, 1994).

The tasks in Figure 13.4 require that high school students apply their understanding of citizens' rights guaranteed by the U.S. Constitution to real-world situations. Students must consider the information provided in the situations, decide which citizens' rights (if any) are violated, and elaborate on their choice of answers.

Systematic **observations** of students can furnish information about the impact of curriculum. "Systematically" means that all students are observed, they are observed often and regularly, the observations are recorded in writing for both typical and atypical behaviors, and the observations are aggregated. Then the observations are studied by a knowledgeable person who interprets them. As an example, over a period of time a knowledgeable teacher who listens to a student read aloud not only notices the words missed, but notes the words the student figures out (Hart, 1994). Observations also furnish one of the better strategies by which affective and psychomotor learning data can be generated.

Portfolios are collections of students' skills, ideas, interests, and accomplishments (Hart, 1994) that span a time period. Portfolios can be appropriately used in almost any subject area. One type of portfolio requires that students select assignments representing their knowledge and effort and prepare personal statements explaining why the particular assignments were important. An algebra teacher who used portfolios of this type changed the curriculum once she became aware of what students put into their portfolios. She chose to use *additional* problem-solving opportunities with written explanations, based on the report that students not only enjoyed them, but remembered and chose these papers for their portfolios (Hart, 1994).

A second type of portfolio is really a process-folio, "or selected works showing the development of students' learning over time" (Zessoules & Gardner, 1991, p. 58). Such portfolios reveal multiple dimensions of students' learning by sampling the depth, breadth, and growth of their thought processes. For example, in an art class students select finished or unfinished works and record notes in journals or on papers attached to the works that explain what they like/don't like, how they judge the piece, and what they learned from it (Zessoules & Gardner, 1991). This portfolio type which involves students in self-assessment provides an additional dimension to curriculum evaluation.

Journals, which may or may not be part of portfolios, have become increasingly popular as a way for teachers and students to interact. Through daily or weekly journal entries, students demonstrate their ideas, interests, and to some extent their skills in a form that is potentially less threatening than other forms of written communication. Journals are particularly appropriate for documenting changes in students' perceptions of themselves or their abilities (Hart, 1994).

Data Collection From School and Community Personnel.   Whereas teachers gather student data, evaluation specialists collect data from teachers, nonteaching school staff, and community members. Teachers often have insights into effects of the curriculum as a result of working with students. Those insights may be revealed in process evaluation, but evaluators who want to know about unintended outcomes should probably also interview teachers about classroom events.

Following the scoring of student measures evaluators may also hold community meetings in which they talk with parents/guardians and/or school staff. The point of these meetings is to obtain additional information that helps explain student performance. Information from these sources may spur additional inquiries among students regarding their perceptions of curriculum effects (Stufflebeam & Shinkfield, 1985).

Data Analyses.   Data from students, teachers, staff, and community members are usually analyzed by curriculum evaluators. These individuals choose, and then use appropriate quantitative and qualitative strategies to treat data. Some analyses are based on the different groups from which data were collected. But evaluators also examine possible outcome effects within subgroups of students or convergences in results when data from all the groups are used. All analyses should be directed toward answering the question about how well the curriculum is meeting the needs of students.

Exercise 13.2 provides a check on strategies for process and product evaluation. Use it to see how well you understand these topics.

EXERCISE 13.2

Consider the different strategies that have been suggested for process and product evaluation.

1. Suppose you are a teacher who is implementing a revised curriculum. From your vantage point are the one-legged conferences, the open-ended statements, and the Stages of Concern Questionnaire equally advantageous for gathering process data? Explain.
2. For each of the following situations, suggest an appropriate strategy for collecting student product data in a curriculum evaluation. Explain each choice.

   a. Abilities in composition
   b. Feelings of self-esteem
   c. Knowledge of history

INTERPRETATION AND USES OF ANALYSES

As stated previously, change facilitators are chiefly responsible for gathering and analyzing process data. Teachers usually gather student outcome data, and district or school level evaluators gather data from other groups such as community personnel or school staff. Evaluators are charged with interpreting the data analyses and selecting the comparisons for the evaluations. Outcomes evaluation can be compared against "a profile of previously assessed needs, pretest performance, selected norms, specified performance standards, or the performance of a comparison group" (Stufflebeam & Shinkfield, 1985, p. 177). In state-mandated assessments, for example, the performance standards are built into the evaluation processes.

Analyses of process data are useful in interpreting the outcomes of product evaluation. For example, if the product evaluation shows that a curriculum is *not* meeting its purpose or is only partially meeting it, analyses of process data may furnish possible reasons. Suppose a modified mathematics curriculum intended that upper elementary-grade students understand certain concepts using decimal notation. Understanding decimals is usually based on knowledge of fractions concepts. In classrooms where students do *not* understand fractions, teachers must take time to establish these prerequisite understandings before moving to work with decimals. This action could disrupt the implementation schedule so that students receive little instruction in decimal notation.

Evaluators should be sensitive to these situations because they can occur in school districts that adopt and begin using a "new" or modified curriculum at *all* grade levels the same year. This practice may jeopardize learning in upper grade levels because students have not had the benefit of using the "new" curriculum at lower grade levels.

In interpreting data analyses the evaluators should take into account the limitations. If, for example, there is any reason to believe that students or teachers were not cooperative in the data-gathering procedures, evaluators would note this lack of cooperation as a potential extenuating circumstance that limits usefulness of the results. Where students' affective learning is concerned, evaluators must interpret outcomes cautiously because of variability in measurement. In either of these examples evaluators would acknowledge these limitations on the generalizability of the results.

When evaluators complete their interpretations, they are able to recommend that the curriculum be continued, continued with modification, or terminated. Their analyses and interpretations, of course, provide the bases for any of these recommendations. Usually recommendations are passed to the governing board for discussion and official action.

CREATION OF EVALUATION PLANS

As was true with needs assessments, personnel from the evaluation office in school districts design and carry out curriculum evaluation plans in conjunction with building administrators and teachers. If this office does not exist, school administrators typically handle these duties as part of their change facilitator roles. Whoever is responsible for evaluation must work closely with teachers and others involved in using curricula in schools.

Because this text takes the position that change is an individual process, all the school people involved in the curriculum change must be involved in evaluation. This makes possible an accounting, however crude, of the extent to which change is taking place. Teachers and school staff develop meaning for the change individually; therefore, each must be part of the assessment procedures. Typically these groups are involved in process evaluation procedures. Students and community members, including parents and guardians, are also involved in product evaluation.

This section provides illustrations of the creation of rudimentary plans for evaluating the health and English literature curricula begun in Chapter 7. Chapter 12 describes plans for implementing the health curriculum and enacting the English literature curriculum in the contexts for which they were developed.

HEALTH CURRICULUM

Imagine that you, as an elementary school principal, are in the process of helping teachers in your building use the revised health curriculum devised by a school committee. This curriculum seeks to help students acquire the knowledge, skills, and attitudes that promote sensible, lifelong health habits. You are also supposed to help insure that the evaluation procedures adhere to the Joint Committee's criteria for utility, feasibility, propriety, and accuracy (Joint Committee on Standards for Educational Evaluation, 1994).

At one of the first meetings with teachers, you administered the Stages of Concern Questionnaire to find out how they felt about the curriculum. As you suspected, responses from several teachers showed self-concerns, but a few others registered task concerns. A few days later in the coffee room you talked with two teachers who appear to be reluctant to start using the curriculum. One said, "I don't understand what's so special about this health curriculum. It looks like what we used before." To help this teacher you asked a few leading questions about her teaching strategies and found that students mostly read their health books and answer questions. Based on this information you suggest different strategies that require students to create their own knowledge, such as hands-on experiences in which students simulate the ways that diseases travel (see Figure 10.7). By prodding gently you help this teacher understand the fundamental differences between "reading the book" and hands-on experiences. You offer to work with her on plans for other learning experiences. The second teacher said he was planning to begin using the curriculum within the next two weeks. You offer him encouragement to start and say that you will check again in two weeks to see how things are going.

Throughout the first cycle of curriculum use, you use one-legged conferences often and the Stages of Concern Questionnaire a couple of times. Based on your analyses of teacher concerns, you and the lead teacher plan and deliver interventions that help teachers progress in using the modified health curriculum.

You also work with the district evaluation office on the product evaluation plans. Because the curriculum content was based on the state guidelines, the state-mandated assessment that measures these skills is one strategy for collecting product data about the intended effects of this curriculum. In addition evaluators suggest the use of checklists or observation schedules that teachers use to keep track of students' behaviors related to the health curriculum. The evaluators offer suggestions for a few items, directions, and a format. You take these suggestions to a faculty-staff meeting where teachers adapt them into checklists and observation schedules for use with their students. All of you agree to use these instruments on a regular basis decided by the teachers.

Evaluators agree to sample community members' perceptions of the effectiveness of the health curriculum near the end of the first cycle. Each of the procedures adopted by the evaluators must also satisfy the criteria of the standards.

ENGLISH LITERATURE CURRICULUM

You are one of two high school teachers who developed an English literature curriculum with the purpose "developing individuals to their fullest potential." The aims of this curriculum are to help students expand their consciousness of other people portrayed in printed materials, increase language skills and abilities, and improve social relations. You and your colleague used a nontechnical approach for curriculum development because you believe students will achieve different learning outcomes.

Before you begin to use the curriculum, however, you know an evaluation plan must be made. For one reason, you are using the curriculum experimentally and must collect some evidence of its efficacy to see if you can be permitted to continue with it. But you also realize that evaluation must find out if you are meeting the intended purpose of education.

You and your colleague talk first with your department head about prospective evaluation strategies. The department head decides to seek assistance from the evaluation office, arranges a meeting with an evaluation specialist, and the three of you develop an initial plan. You all agree that product evaluation of this curriculum should stress collection and analysis of data on how well students are being developed as individuals.

The evaluator suggests a number of possibilities. You could systematically observe students in class activities to document gains in their language skills or improved social relations with peers in English literature. Also, students could keep personal journals that you read periodically to note their changes in language skills and possibilities for expressing thoughts and feelings. You could also offer students opportunities to expand their consciousness of people by asking them to read the beginning parts of certain literature pieces and to act out endings to these pieces as performance assessments. These performances would be evaluated on the basis of how well students performed within the characterizations of the people in the literature pieces. Such strategies would provide information about the intended effects of the curriculum.

As is true of other curricula, however, evaluators should also look for unintended outcomes. The evaluators might search for changes in the students' achievement in other courses. Are there changes, for instance, in student performance in social science classes that could be attributed to the students' growing consciousness of others?

All the procedures described here for process and product evaluation must be prepared carefully to insure their adherence to the standards. For example, only data necessary for product evaluation should be seen by the evaluators (in keeping with the utility criterion). The identities of individual students should be protected out of respect for their rights and welfare (to satisfy the propriety criterion).

SUMMARY

Curriculum evaluation has as its goal the improvement of school programs. Evaluators must acknowledge certain limitations related to cooperation among people, complexity of the behaviors and events, time, access to students, and curriculum rationales. All aspects of evaluation should adhere to the performance criteria of the Joint Committee on Standards for Educational Evaluation.

Process evaluation provides information about the degree to which revised technically developed curricula are implemented. Typically teachers and school administrators are involved in process evaluation and the records of their transactions supply information for process evaluation.

Product evaluation provides information about how well curricula revised in either technical or nontechnical approaches achieve their purposes. Teachers collect information from or about students that provides data for product evaluation. Evaluators collect data from teachers, school staff, and community members to provide additional information on the effectiveness of the curriculum.

Evaluators examine both process and product analyses and interpret them in terms of the limitations. The outcomes of these deliberations result in decisions about continuation, modification, or curtailment of curriculum use. The final section contained plans for initiating evaluation of the hypothetical health and English literature curricula that were developed and put into classroom use in previous chapters.

QUESTIONS FOR DISCUSSION

1. Describe the advantages of ongoing process and product evaluation in school districts.
2. One purpose of process evaluation is to provide assistance for changing or clarifying implementation plans. Explain how this idea is consistent with mutual adaptation in curriculum implementation described in Chapter 12.
3. Assume that curriculum evaluators build into their evaluation plan the appropriate limitations described in this chapter. Explain how acknowledging these limitations increases confidence in the results of evaluation.
4. In most schools teachers are evaluated on their teaching performance. Explain how use of the CBAM helps or hinders these evaluations.
5. Explain why change facilitators should be evaluated on their performance.
6. Describe methods of collecting product evaluation data in your district. How do these methods compare with those suggested in this chapter?
7. Speculate about whether the use of authentic/alternative/performance assessments complicates teachers' workload responsibilities.
8. Explain how the standards criteria were applied in the section titled Creation of Evaluation Plans for the health curriculum. For the English literature curriculum?

IMPORTANT IDEAS DISCUSSED INITIALLY IN THIS CHAPTER

process evaluation

product evaluation

data collection from teacher-
    implementors
  one-legged conferences
  open-ended statements of concern
  Stages of Concern Questionnaire
  interviews

data collection from change facilitators

data collection from students
  standardized tests
  authentic assessments
  observations
  portfolios
  journals
  performance assessments

data collection from school and
    community personnel

Epilogue

. . . .

Pondering the content of Chapters 1–13 confirms the ambiguity of curriculum boundaries mentioned in the Orientation. Additional reflection shows that curriculum change may be difficult to effect, largely because the personnel must undergo psychological changes before they make behavioral changes. Moreover, resistance to change is not unusual when it involves values and beliefs, as is often the case in curriculum.

Remember Figure P.1 in the Preface? For your convenience it is repeated here as Figure E.1. Take a little time now to reflect on the linkages between curriculum foundations and processes suggested by this figure.

A *purpose of education* is the linchpin for the curriculum processes of development, classroom use, and evaluation in ongoing school operations. A purpose of education, projected fit of curriculum with society, and projected role of curriculum users combine in the views of education prepared by curriculum developers as the initial step in development. Here developers express purposes of education as broad philosophical statements that answer "why" questions about their reasons for curriculum development.

Curriculum *content selection,* which follows the creation of views of education statements, depends on the purpose of education. The content chosen must be valid and significant for that particular purpose. In addition content must be consistent with societal and cultural realities, learnable by the learners, and appropriate for their needs and interests. Of course, each of these selection criteria makes use of the developers' values and beliefs about curriculum content.

Frequently, developers solicit planning information from people in the school community, including parents, school faculty and staff, students, and interested citizens through *needs assessments*. Largely because their focus is on subject matter, needs assessments in technical approaches locate discrepancies between what ought to be taught and what is taught. However, needs assessments in nontechnical approaches diagnose strengths and weaknesses of students or societal groups for whom the curriculum is intended. In both cases developers use results in the creation of revised curricula.

Technical curriculum development generally involves deducing *learning outcomes,* called goals and objectives, from the purpose of education. These, in turn,

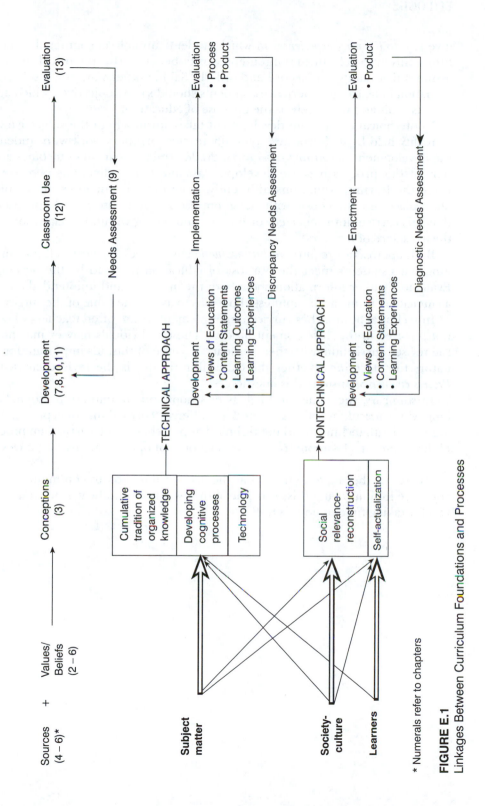

FIGURE E.1
Linkages Between Curriculum Foundations and Processes

* Numerals refer to chapters

277

give rise to *learning experiences* in which students initially encounter the curriculum content. Such an arrangement works because the technical approach assumes that reality is objective and orderly. Said another way, as a result of participation in learning experiences, students should satisfy objectives, which aggregate as goals and ultimately as the purpose of education.

Nontechnical curriculum development takes advantage of the subjective views of reality held by its advocates. Typically teacher-planners work with students in the development of *learning experiences*. Predetermined learning outcomes are *not* part of this process because developers assume that individuals perceive and value the learning situations differently. For practical purposes, development takes place simultaneously with classroom use in the nontechnical approach, so that this curriculum is enacted, or brought into being within the classrooms with the assistance of learners.

Both approaches require *product evaluation* as a check on how well the curriculum helps students meet the purpose of education planned by the developers. Evaluators gather information about both the intended and unintended effects of a curriculum from various interested persons to assess the value of the curriculum.

In technical approaches curriculum implementors are often teachers who were not involved in the development process. These individuals may or may not use the revised curriculum with their students. Because of this, it's important for evaluators to determine whether the curriculum in use is the revised curriculum. *Process evaluation* answers this question.

In summary, the values and beliefs of school and community personnel combine with curriculum sources to produce different curriculum conceptions. These are linked with technical and nontechnical approaches to the curriculum processes of development, classroom use, and evaluation that operate in ongoing cycles.

Please use the suggestion form at the back of the book to communicate ideas you have for improving this text. The author would like to hear from you. Thank you for taking time to do this task.

Answers to Selected Exercises

Exercise 1.1

2. Ms. Chiu's children will probably report to their mother about events experienced during the school day. This is the *experiential* level of curriculum.

Exercise 1.2

Into Adolescence: Caring for Our Planet and Our Health (A6)

1. Two goals for this project are mentioned in the Overview section. The instructional strategies section lists many suggestions for teaching.
2. This project is written primarily for teachers rather than for curriculum developers. The lesson provides instructional level curriculum.

Exercise 2.1

1b. Ms. Blanca's decision to prepare a demonstration on points, lines, and planes for her high school geometry class is primarily an "activities and teaching strategies" decision. Use of a demonstration suggests that this is to be a teacher-directed activity.
2b. Instead of the demonstration Ms. Blanca might have planned a lecture that explained meanings for the topics, conducted an activity involving students in hands-on work with manipulative materials, asked students to study the examples in the textbook, or another experience. These activities are not equivalent because they imply different views of students and learning.

Exercise 3.1

2. The relative positions of curriculum conceptions are related to the social concerns of schooling as shown in the diagram at the top of page 280.

   As indicated in this chapter, the social reconstruction/relevance conception often uses social problems as content, making this conception the one *most* involved with social concerns. The technology conception is the *least* involved with social concerns, primarily because learning in this conception must be predefined and simple, two adjectives that do not apply to social concerns. Self-actualization is nearer social reconstruction on the continuum than are cognitive processes or organized knowl-

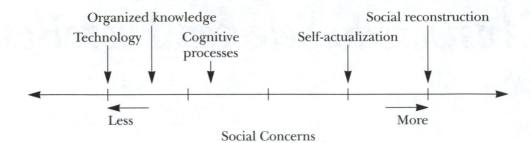

edge because learning centers around learners' growth which includes social concerns. Organized knowledge and cognitive processes tend to lie toward the less social concerns end of the continuum mostly because learning centers on subject matter, rather than social concerns.

Exercise 3.2

1. The continued growth of knowledge means that more information is available for school curricula. Because of this growth, developers must exercise greater discretion than before in their content selections to avoid overloading curricula.

3. A manuscript to cursive to word-processing sequence integrates the concepts, skills, and values associated with the production of writing. Young children typically begin learning to "write" using manuscript letter formations, which may be slow and laborious at first. For example, children learn that the letter "p" is made by a downstroke that hangs below the line connected to a circle placed to the right of the downstroke. Later students learn to join letters in cursive writing—a small stroke connects one letter to another. When children begin to learn keyboarding, they see these letters appear on a screen by simply pressing keys. Usually this occurs at increased speed compared to cursive writing. Throughout the period of learning different ways of writing, students learn that writing grocery lists is similar to writing weekly spelling lists, thereby showing integration.

Exercise 3.3

1. A single subject design is traditional and may be preferred over other designs simply because it is better known by teachers. Also, subject matter designs use readily available teaching materials and can be planned in advance. Other subject designs have some of these features, but none has all of them.

    Some teachers may prefer learner-based or society-culture based designs over subject designs. These designs would allow teachers to focus on learners' needs and interests or the realities of society, rather than subject matter.

3. Designs based on needs of society and needs and interests of learners can and do use nontechnical curriculum development. Outcomes of studying social problems, or needs of society, are usually unpredictable. These outcomes may include changes in values, human relations skills, problem solving abilities, or others. Helping learners gain autonomy or self-reliance or other personal-social growth produces unpredictable outcomes. When a curriculum is set up to use needs and interests of learners, outcomes are likely to vary from one person to another.

Exercise 4.1

2c. "I can't make sense of this situation" is an example of self-regulatory knowledge. The statement reveals knowledge of the person's intellectual functioning.

2e. "Choosing a library book because the pictures are 'neat'" reveals impressionistic knowledge. The statement suggests that the basis for the selection was made with little consideration of words; more attention is given to the pictures.

Exercise 4.2

2. Cognitive taxonomy—lower level (L). Summarizing is essentially a comprehension activity.

4. Psychomotor taxonomy—higher than lower level (HL). The activity described requires largely perceptual and physical abilities.

Exercise 4.3

Collaborative Teaching Experiences . . .

The Philosophy statement suggests that this curriculum is NOT for the purpose of acquiring subject matter. The Philosophy suggests that this curriculum should help children develop better speech and language skills for use with peers and teachers.

Exercise 5.1

1. The purpose of education, "cultivating cognitive achievement and the intellect," provides for the development of language and information literacy because both are primarily cognitive as required by the purpose. Science literacy could also be developed under this purpose. Development of cultural literacy, as described in this chapter, requires a broad interpretation of this purpose for this literacy form to be included. Much of cultural literacy is affective, rather than cognitive.

Exercise 6.1

1. In this situation, learners, who otherwise write legibly, imitate the poor quality handwriting modeled by Mr. Xavier. The students respond to this event or experience in their external environment. This is one of two major ways that students engage in receptive learning.

Exercise 6.2

1. By its nature computer science requires precise language. Language is also very important in cooperative learning strategies where members instruct each other. Language abilities are important to the success of the student groups.

4. In the situation described in Exercise 6.1, Mr. Xavier's handwriting serves as a model for his students, perhaps whether or not he intends this to be the case. The impetus for learning for the students who copy Mr. Xavier's poor handwriting is external. In contrast Ms. Haney coordinates the learning experiences for her students. To a large extent the students in cooperative learning groups generate their own learning because they are in charge of the situation; the impetus for learning comes mainly from within the learners.

Neither the learners' ages nor the subject matter is responsible for the contrasts in the situations. At whatever age children exhibit socialized speech, they can engage successfully in cooperative learning groups. Older learners often imitate behaviors of people they admire. Though it's normal for younger learners to engage in learning to handwrite and older learners to study computer science, the subject matter under consideration is not the deciding factor in how the learning takes place. The important factor in determining whether learning is receptive or generative are classroom climates engineered by teachers.

Exercise 7.1

2. The probable purpose is to "cultivate cognitive achievement and the intellect." This definition primarily emphasizes acquisition of cognitive abilities. "Attitudes" denotes a concern for affective learning, but their development appears secondary.

5. The probable purpose is to "develop individuals to their fullest potentials." This definition emphasizes the development of people.

Exercise 7.2

Wyoming Arts Education Curriculum (A5)

1. This excerpt from the *Wyoming Arts Education Curriculum* contains both a views of education statement for all the arts as well as a brief views statement for the Visual Arts. Subject matter is clearly identified as the content emphasis. The primary purpose of education is "cultivation of cognitive achievement and the intellect" encompassing both content and process.

   The Mission Statement calls for development of a common core of (formal) knowledge as well as a common core of skills. The Introductory Statement to the Visual Arts suggests focus on "production, aesthetics, art history, and criticism."

   As indicated, these are state guidelines rather than a curriculum guide, so that designating a design is inappropriate. These guidelines could be developed by district- or school-based committees into any of several subject designs, including single subject, correlated subjects, or fused subjects.

2. The views statement does not describe a local context because these are state guidelines intended for use by districts in the development of local curricula.

   The views statements emphasize the interrelationships between the purpose of education and society and culture. For example, in the Introduction is this statement: "Arts education is critical to . . . society, and to the future of the global community." These curriculum developers believe that, through the arts, students learn communication skills and analytical thinking skills to help solve societal problems.

3. Neither views statement projects roles for teachers and school staff in delivering the curriculum. However, the sections "Art Equals Basic Skills" and "Art Equals Education" suggest strongly that students are to interact with the curriculum. How else can communication skills and analytical thinking be fostered?

Exercise 8.1

1. Ms. Safire is not well equipped to communicate with non-English speaking students or to provide instructional content in a language students can read. It's difficult to fault the situation insofar as validity and significance are concerned because there's

very little information about the subject matter itself. However, how well the content meets the "learnability" and "needs and interests of learners" criteria is questionable. Without better communication than is suggested by this situation, the teacher and the five non-English speaking students have many obstacles to overcome.

The situation as described seems to have overlooked the criterion of maintaining consistency with societal and cultural realities. The facts show that increasing numbers of students do not speak English.

The situation does not indicate whether the five students speak the same language. Therefore, the obvious recommendation is to provide the five students who do not speak English with assistance from a teacher who can teach them using English as a Second Language. Providing instructional materials in the students' native language would not be helpful unless a teacher or other professional is available to assist students.

Exercise 8.2

Wyoming Arts Education Curriculum

The content for this project is briefly stated in the mission statement including knowledge of aesthetics, criticism, history and production. Each of these is elaborated in three levels of outcomes expected of learners on completion of grades 5, 8, and 12. Students are also expected to develop skills in problem solving, communications, critical thinking and creativity alongside these knowledge outcomes.

Assessments of the extent to which the developers used the content selection criteria require close examination of multiple outcomes and much expertise in the visual arts.

Exercise 9.1

2. According to the statement, Ms. Alexander and other teachers found their needs questionnaires in their mail boxes and were asked to return them shortly. These teachers may know more than one point of view and have knowledge of the school for assessing achievement. However, the needs assessor did not provide teachers with opportunities to clarify meanings of needs statements. The expectation of a 24-hour turnaround does not allow much time to deliberate seriously about the needs statements.

    A better plan might be to distribute the needs assessments, but assemble and allow teachers to talk about the statements. Discussion should clarify terms as well as provide opportunity for debate—before completion of the questionnaires. Of course, questionnaires should be completed anonymously.

Exercise 9.2

1. Discrepancy needs assessments that provide information about group preferences are appropriate in most technically developed curriculum situations. These situations serve large numbers of students so it's important to provide for the greatest number of needs possible. *Diagnostic* needs assessments help with needs of *individuals*.

Exercise 9.3

1. For diagnostic purposes checklists can provide information about the presence or absence of certain skills or behaviors. However, interviews can probe situations to

obtain additional information about learners' skills or behaviors. Skilled interviewers can read interviewees' body language to learn additional information about situations beyond their verbal expressions.

Checklists are unobtrusive, but interviews are not. Checklists are simpler to use and more time-efficient than interviews. Both instruments can be helpful depending on the purpose of data collection.

Exercise 10.1

2. "Execute a perfect forward roll" is a psychomotor objective that names a specific destination and can easily be evaluated. This is HL learning because it calls for abilities clearly beyond the first two levels of the psychomotor taxonomy.

4. "Develop universal literacy" is an outcome that tells why a curriculum is being taught. This statement represents an aim.

6. "Know how to exercise as part of a wellness program" is a psychomotor goal that provides scope for a fitness curriculum. Attaining this goal would likely take several months.

Exercise 10.2

Wyoming Arts Education Curriculum (A5)

1. In Exercise 7.2 the purpose of education is identified as "cultivating cognitive achievement." If students satisfy the learning outcomes in this set of guidelines, they are likely to achieve this purpose for reasons described below.

At least three levels of student learning outcomes appear in the excerpt. The Mission Statement refers to a broad learning outcome equivalent to a *system* statement indicating that "the arts enhance self-esteem, promote understanding of self and encourage lifelong learning." This statement is reiterated in the Visual Arts Introduction Statement with references to provision for "meaningful self-expression" and "creative and divergent thinking."

The major headings (i.e., aesthetics, criticism, history, and production) can be thought of as *Program 1* outcomes for the Visual Arts. Next are *Program 2* outcomes for grades 5, 8, and 12. These learning outcomes represent all three domains and an unusually large number of higher-than-lower taxonomic levels. Consider these Level 2 examples:

Evaluate the works of major artists . . . (higher-than-lower cognitive outcome).

Exhibit increased aesthetic awareness and perception of visual and tactile qualities in works of nature . . . (probably a higher-than-lower affective outcome).

Produce original works in such media as drawing . . . (probably a higher-than-lower psychomotor outcome incorporating cognitive and affective learning as well).

2. These guidelines are intended as a guide by which districts and schools establish arts curricula. Therefore, planning learning experiences is left to the districts and schools.

Exercise 11.2

2. The planned learning experiences for *The Canterbury Tales* foster thinking skills. Throughout these activities students are expected to generate their own knowledge. They have many opportunities to synthesize information from various sources. In many cases students have to listen critically to their peers and distinguish between relevant and irrelevant information. Students also have choices about what they learn.

Exercise 12.1

2. The elementary teachers who participated in literature-based curriculum for language arts and now discuss their experiences provide valuable *professional development* for their colleagues. Their informal discussions may generate interest so that other teachers try some new activities in their own classrooms or take advantage of formal opportunities to participate in inservice meetings on literature-based curriculum whenever these are re-offered.

   The principal should invite each of the five teachers with the training to present brief informational sessions at faculty-staff meetings during the semester. This plan recognizes the work of the five and allows all the teachers access to the information.

Exercise 12.2

2. The teacher who asks for additional information about curriculum evaluation procedures has passed the *self* stages of concern and perhaps the *task* stage as well. This teacher is also a user, possibly at the levels of use stage of *refinement* (IVB). The content of the request suggests that this teacher is looking for ways to make changes to increase outcomes. S/he sees evaluation as the vehicle for these changes.

Exercise 13.1

2. "Achievement" can be as complex as is "attitude," depending on how it is defined. When achievement is considered as the acquisition of declarative knowledge, evaluation is simple and straightforward. However, evaluation of achievement defined as thinking skills or intellectual skills is not simple. To consider achievement as performance in real world situations is quite complex.

Exercise 13.2

2b. Students' feelings of self-esteem can be gathered in self-reports using rating scales. They can also be inferred from students' selections and comments about portfolio entries or from journal entries. Either of these strategies requires careful content analyses of the students' statements.

Appendix A

· ·

Curriculum Projects

This appendix contains excerpts from different types of curriculum documents including guides, guidelines, and resource units. These excerpts illustrate various concepts within the text and serve as sources of content for several exercises.

Documents were selected to provide variety in subject matter areas and grade levels. Excerpts include the following:

Curriculum Guides

Multicultural Social Studies Curriculum, K–12, 1993, Tucson, AZ

A Guide for Developing a 1–9 Science Curriculum, 1991, Wakefield, NE

Middle School English Language Arts Curriculum Guide, 1991, Horseheads, NY

Spanish IV Curriculum, n.d., Stoughton, MA

Curriculum Guidelines

Wyoming Arts Education Curriculum, 1992, Cheyenne, WY

Resource Units

Into Adolescence: Caring for Our Planet and Our Health, Grades 5–8, 1991, Santa Cruz, CA

Collaborative Teaching Experiences to Develop Communication Skills In Elementary School Children: Prekindergarten to Grade Five, 1992, Jackson, MI

Curriculum documents are prepared for different audiences and purposes, which means they differ in content and organization. Guides and resource units are intended for primary use by educators involved in instruction, but curriculum guidelines are used by all educators involved in curriculum development. For example, *Wyoming Arts Education Curriculum* is a document addressed to curriculum workers in a particular state as a source of information for preparing district- and school-level curricula. On the other hand, *A Guide for Developing a 1–9 Science Curriculum* is directed to teachers within a particular educational service unit as a source for planning instruction. A cursory examination of these two documents shows that content in the curriculum *guidelines* is different from that in the curriculum *guide*, reflecting the difference in their purposes. Whereas the guidelines concentrate on learning outcomes, the guides usually contain all the components.

Close examination of the collected curriculum documents shows other differences as well. For example, *Spanish IV Curriculum* contains little information about learning experiences. However, *Into Adolescence: Caring for Our Planet and Our Health, Grades 5–8* is a resource unit that is largely instructional. These differences illustrate the interchangeability of the terms *curriculum* and *instruction* as was mentioned in Chapter 1.

Curriculum documents are also organized differently. About the only generalization possible is that the actual "content of the curriculum" is preceded by "front matter" that describes its intended use. Consequently, for each project in Appendix A, a table of contents shows that document's contents classified according to the labels used in this text: views of education, content statements, outcomes (goals and objectives), experiences (descriptions of learning experiences), and evaluation procedures.

The components of curriculum projects have definite meanings as shown in the following paragraphs:

A **views of education** statement describes the curriculum developers' purpose for education; their perspectives on the roles of students, teachers, and school staffs in implementing the curriculum; and the interrelationships of purpose and participant roles with the school, community and the larger community beyond the school. Purposes of education may emphasize cultivating cognitive achievement and the intellect (also known as transmitting the cultural heritage), developing learners to their fullest potentials, or dealing with societal-cultural issues. Although sections labeled "philosophy" are typically included in many curriculum projects, views of education, as used here, are more inclusive than these. They establish the frameworks that guide the remainder of the curriculum processes.

The **content statement** identifies the major content to be included in the curriculum. In nontechnically developed curricula, the content statement names the major idea or theme that gives rise to related themes, learning experiences, and possible outcomes. In technically developed curricula, the content statement forms the basis for the intended learning outcomes and the descriptions of planned learning experiences.

Intended learning outcomes identify the expected results of learning, also known as aims, goals, and objectives, that learners are expected to acquire. These items form a continuum, with aims as very general statements, goals as general statements, and objectives as more specific statements of the content. Intended learning outcomes are included in technically developed curricula.

Descriptions of learning experiences provide explanations of how learners are expected to have access to curriculum content. These explanations not only provide information about cognitive content, but affective and psychomotor experiences as well, along with their sources and perhaps a time allotment. In technically developed curricula, descriptions clarify which learning outcomes are to be emphasized.

Evaluation procedures suggest methods by which student progress toward program outcomes can be assessed.

You should also be aware of how the material was selected for each project. All pertinent information related to the views of education, content statements, and most goals is included. However, objectives and descriptions of learning experiences were chosen that appear to represent those in the project. Therefore, what is excerpted is the content rather than the front matter.

The author believes these documents reflect the diversity that exists among curriculum projects. Reading them should dispel any notion that curriculum planning follows a recipe.

Multicultural Social Studies Curriculum, K–12

Contents

INTRODUCTION

Our lives are affected every day by the challenges of change: political, economic, technological, social, and demographic. The Tucson community is charged with maintaining continuity within these changes. This change and continuity together become the main focus of history, government, and all facets of social studies affecting the lives of our students and the entire TUSD community, which is rich in diverse cultural heritage.

As educators, parents, and community members, we want our students to perceive the complex nature of all changes in society. Through the inclusive study of democracy, the teacher and the student will gain a deep understanding of individual and social ethics, immersed in a world of change and continuity.

The potential of our community with its ethnic diversity and culturally pluralistic personality serves as impetus for the writers of this curriculum to meet the challenges of change within continuity, and the challenge to respond to the TUSD Creed.

This creed has been formalized in Board Policy 6112, "Diversity Appreciation Education." An excerpt states, "Learning produces an understanding of diverse values. . . . No achievement or contribution is overlooked because of race, color, national origin, language proficiency, sex, religion, disability, or sexual preference. . . . All students have an opportunity to learn their cultural heritage and appreciate its uniqueness as well as that of others. Each student learns to communicate, associate and participate in a diverse community and a pluralistic society. *All staff* is held accountable for implementation of multicultural/non-sexist education. . . ." Adopted in November of 1991, this policy is a mandate for change, transformation of curriculum, and vision.

From *Multicultural Social Studies Curriculum, K–12* (1993), Tucson, AZ. Reprinted by permission.

A1

Together, the global aspects of this curriculum and the goal of education is a lifelong love of learning. The teacher is a valuable resource, implementing change, and providing the learning environment for the students to understand the various concepts of social studies. The key challenge is the infusion of various perspectives, references, and content that extend the students' understanding of our complex, global society.

The emphasis of this curriculum is on a multifaceted culture and society as it has emerged from complex syntheses and transaction of our community's diverse cultural elements. This emphasis will encourage participatory citizenship. Through analyzing values and beliefs, the students and teachers synthesize their knowledge and values to identify alternative courses of action in life situations.

This curriculum is based on a variety of learning, thinking, and multicultural education theories. At the elementary grade level through middle school and into high school the student spirals through data and learns to analyze and relate to the material and concepts. These courses of action involve creative problem solving, thinking, and decision-making skills that empower both students and teachers. The teacher at one grade level provides the means for the student to progress to the next level of understanding.

When viewing the social studies curriculum learner outcomes wheel, one notices the aspect of movement plays a primary role. The arrows indicate not only movement, but also the overlapping relationships inherent in these outcomes. This document provides teachers with suggestions and opportunities along with the responsibility to use professional expertise, skills, and pedagogical practices to provide a more balanced, fuller understanding about our community's history and culture.

The social studies curriculum is a conceptual catalyst for both teachers and students to gain knowledge, information, and power. The curriculum provides the resources and the opportunities for students to learn. It is assumed that they will learn and mature into participatory citizens who are self-directed, collaborative workers, complex thinkers, community contributors, and quality producers. All TUSD students, the culminating products of this curriculum, will value and appreciate the contributions others make to a culturally diverse world and to the Tucson Community.

(Material used in writing this introduction includes that written by Susan Barto, James Banks, Hilda Taba, and Begay and Begay.)

TUSD SOCIAL STUDIES MODEL EXPLANATION

The Social Studies Curriculum Committee wrote the curriculum believing that a comprehensive social studies curriculum must be developed, first of all, from the exit outcomes expected from all TUSD students. From these exit outcomes and the Arizona Social Studies State Essential Skills, the committee focused on general learner outcomes and a framework around which to develop specific grade level curriculum goals.

The explanation that follows delineates each component of the Social Studies Model [Figure A1.1].

Exit Outcomes All Students

The committee reached consensus on Exit Outcomes for all students in the district. These Exit Outcomes verbally describe and define the expectations for all of our students. These Exit Outcomes not only serve as impetus and focus for the Social Studies Curriculum but will serve other curricula to come.

Arizona Social Studies State Essential Skills Framework
Goals and Curriculum Strands

The Arizona Social Studies State Essential Skills Framework is the foundation used to guide the committee in its work. The components of the Essential Skills document are infused throughout the TUSD's Social Studies Curriculum and reflected in the General Learner Outcomes.

TUSD Social Studies K–12 Curriculum General Learner Outcomes

The committee selected ten (10) general learner outcomes and specified the indicators for success for each of the outcomes. These general learner outcomes apply [to] kindergarten through grade twelve.

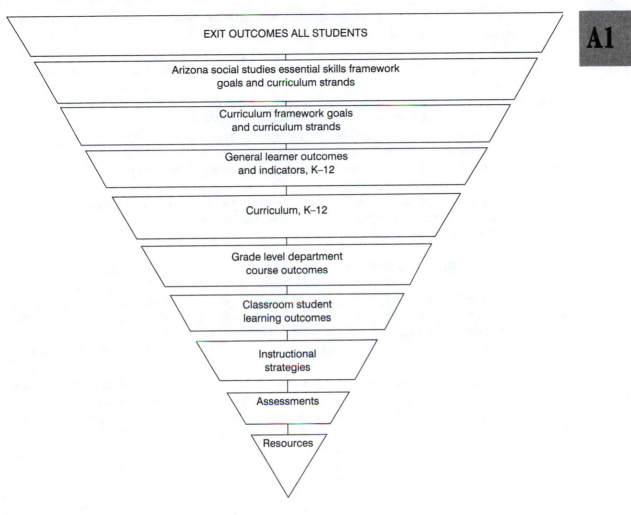

FIGURE A1.1
TUSD Social Studies Model

TUSD Social Studies K–12 Curriculum Framework
Following the goals and strands developed by the Arizona Social Studies State Essential Skills, the Committee developed a visual representation of the desired goals and curricular strands that are the focus of the K–12 curriculum.

Grade Level/Department/Course Outcomes
Each grade level and its departmental unit is expected to apply the curriculum to each grade level.

Classroom/Student Learning Outcomes
Teachers use the Student Learning Outcomes as a guide for developing classroom lessons and experiences for students.

A1

EXIT OUTCOMES ALL STUDENTS

The student will demonstrate that he or she is a . . .

Self-Directed Learner who uses positive values to create a positive vision for the future, sets priorities and achievable goals, creates options, monitors and evaluates progress, and assumes responsibility for his or her actions.

Collaborative Worker who uses effective leadership and group skills to develop and manage interpersonal relationships within culturally and organizationally diverse settings.

Complex Thinker who identifies, accesses, integrates and uses available resources and information to reason, make decisions, and solve complex problems in various contexts.

Community Contributor who contributes time, energy, and talents to improving the welfare of others and the quality of life in diverse communities.

Quality Producer who uses advanced technologies, creates intellectual, artistic, practical and physical products which reflect originality, high standards, and who appreciates and values the contribution of a culturally diverse world and community.

ARIZONA SOCIAL STUDIES ESSENTIAL SKILLS FRAMEWORK
GOALS AND CURRICULUM STRANDS

The goals of the Arizona Social Studies Framework are presented in four broad categories [Figure A1.2]. Each goal is a long-range indicator of needed student competency. Each goal is intended to be broad enough so that learning at all grade levels can contribute to its achievement.

Goal 1. *Knowledge and Cultural Understanding* encompasses learnings from the social science disciplines and the humanities;

Goal 2. *Understanding of Democratic Principles, Values, and Practices* includes the historical derivations and basic principles of American democracy as well as the role and function of the law in our society;

Goal 3. *Individual and Group Participation in Social-Political Affairs* incorporates civic rights and responsibilities, social-political action, and democratic processes for change; and

Goal 4. *Fundamental Skill Attainment for Effective Citizenship* includes basic study skills, critical thinking skills, and problem solving skills in addition to personal, intergroup, and social-participation skills that are necessary for effective living in our democracy.

CURRICULUM FRAMEWORK
GOALS AND CURRICULUM STRANDS, K–12
[The curriculum framework goals are shown in Figure A1.3.]

GENERAL LEARNER OUTCOMES

1. Demonstrate verbal and technological literacy.

2. Demonstrate skills in communication and group interaction.

3. Demonstrate skills in problem solving and decision making.

4. Demonstrate skills in expressing themselves creatively and responding to creative works of other cultures.

5. Demonstrate civic understanding through the study of American culture and history and its relationships to concomitant cultures and histories.

6. Demonstrate understanding of past and present cultures.

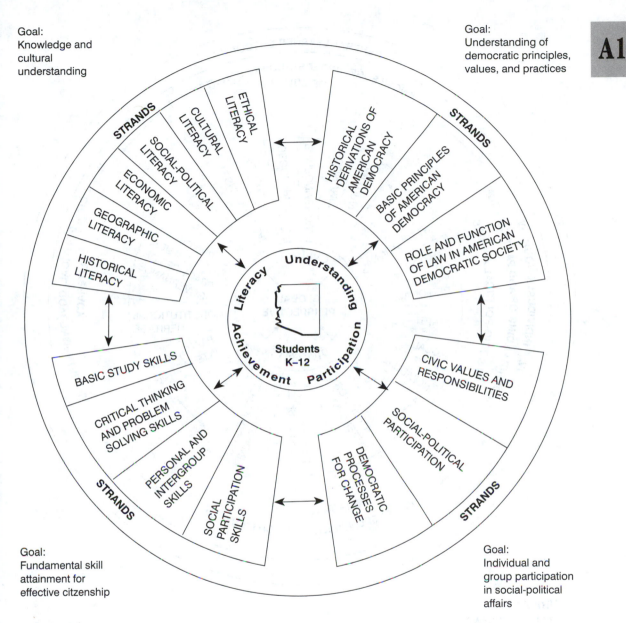

Goal:
Knowledge and cultural understanding

Goal:
Understanding of democratic principles, values, and practices

A1

Goal:
Fundamental skill attainment for effective citzenship

Goal:
Individual and group participation in social-political affairs

FIGURE A1.2
Social Studies Framework Wheel

7. Demonstrate concern, sensitivity and respect for others.

8. Demonstrate skills in adapting to and creating personal, social, and political change.

9. Demonstrate capacity for enhancing and sustaining self-esteem through emotional, intellectual, and physical well-being.

10. Demonstrate skills necessary to be self-directed learners.

A1

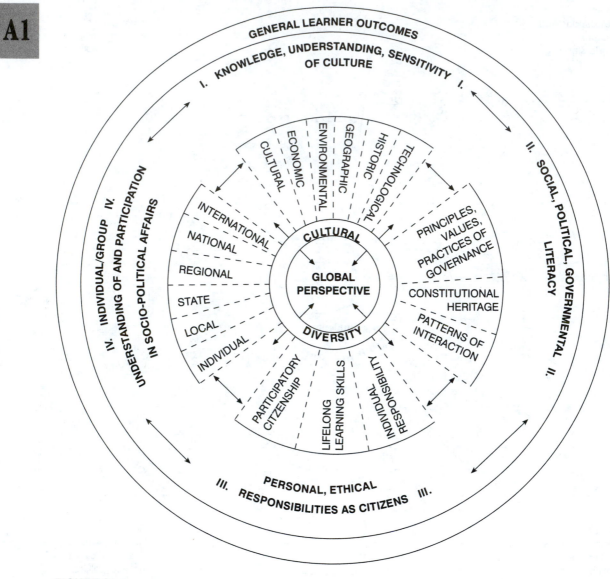

FIGURE A1.3
Curriculum Framework Wheel

GRADE TWO

Focus: Community Diversity

Grade Level Outcome #1
Students will recognize that communities consist of many diverse ethnic and cultural groups.

Student Learning Outcomes
The student will:
1. identify the various ethnic and cultural groups within the community.
2. give examples of contributions made by cultural and ethnic groups to the community (lifestyle, the arts, language, food, and dress).
3. articulate ways in which the community has changed with the migration of each cultural or ethnic group into the area.
4. recognize the way people in the area lived before the migration of diverse ethnic and cultural groups.
5. compare the lifestyle of groups in different environments.
6. recognize that art, music, and literature are a valuable means of passing along the traditions of a cultural group.

Focus: Community Diversity

Grade Level Outcome #2
Students will recognize the similarities and differences in communities with diverse ethnic and cultural groups.

Student Learning Outcomes
The student will:
1. recognize that each neighborhood or community is different from all others in some way.
2. give examples of ways in which groups meet their basic needs.
3. illustrate ways in which cultural groups share music, dance, special celebrations, and sports.
4. describe ways in which one group may "borrow" traditions from another group.
5. develop an awareness of the similarities among diverse cultural and ethnic groups from around the world.

Common Experiences

Outcome: Students will participate in one or more of the following common experiences:
1. Demonstrate an understanding of the importance of an individual within a community by participating in the Kids Voting program.
2. Refer to the TUSD Multicultural Curricular Resources for activities and instructional strategies: African-American, Asian-American, Native-American, and Hispanic-American.
3. Participate in a field trip to a museum, exhibit, or other location that displays ethnic art.
4. Experience community diversity by taking a walking tour of one of the barrios and/or have guest speakers from diverse ethnic groups. Share experiences.
5. Participate in two of the following:
    *   field trip to a police station or other law enforcement agency.
    *   guest speakers from the following list: lawyer, law enforcement officer, geographer, service provider within the community (banker, grocer, fireman, etc.).
    *   field trip to a business (tortilla factory, hospital, or other service provider within the community).

A1

COURSE DESCRIPTION—WORLD CULTURES

Grade Level(s): 9–12   *Prerequisites*: None

Course Outcome:
Students develop culture in the context of the world community, focusing on selected cultures, emphasizing the study of similarities and differences in peoples, families, languages, arts, religions, and values.

Student Learning Outcomes
The student will:
1. explain how the geography of a region affected the development of the region's culture.
2. give examples of cultural transmission of ideas which are passed to and used by different cultural groups.
3. compare the development and structure of two major religions.
4. analyze the impact of land form patterns on society.
5. relate how different climate regions affect human activity.
6. give examples of human migration and mobility.
7. identify examples of the diversity of human cultures through a study of at least four cultural groups in different parts of the world.
8. analyze the dependence and interdependence of different cultural groups.
9. list examples of cross-cultural experiences.
10. compare the forms of basic institutions in different cultures.
11. demonstrate an understanding of the contributions of individual men and women to their respective cultures and to the world.
12. identify the origins of many features of our own cultures.
13. identify cultural diversity in world and regional cultures.
14. locate major cultural units on a map.
15. use information from maps, models, tables, pictures, etc. to locate and show distribution patterns of cultural groups.
16. work effectively in groups by organizing, planning, and making decisions based on information gathered.
17. participate in class discussion.

To Facilitate Student Learning Outcomes—The teacher will
1. present information using lectures, guest speakers, audiovisual aids, field trips, demonstrations, textbooks, appropriate primary and secondary readings.
2. arrange class debates, role-playing activities, mock elections, and mock trials.
3. facilitate small and large group activities which encourage cooperative learning; for example, brainstorming, team learning, and discussion.
4. engage students in process and critical thinking skills by modeling and directing comparison/contrast, data-gathering, analysis, and predicting activities.
5. provide lessons in data gathering and study skills.
6. assign research reports, projects, and case studies.
7. encourage community service activities.
8. evaluate student learning.

A Guide for Developing a 1–9 Science Curriculum

Contents

INTRODUCTION

In the past, science instruction has too often been avoided or limited to instruction from a textbook. This in turn has involved very little use of thought processes on the part of the students and limited opportunities for them to internalize science concepts and scientific methods for everyday use. Therefore it was the desire of this committee to formulate a curriculum guide which would provide school districts direction in planning a science curriculum to maximize students' success in science.

This science curriculum guide—with no claim to completeness—was developed with an attempt to incorporate the latest research, findings, and recommendations of national groups. These sources suggest that the classroom teacher must present learning experiences that will help students develop in four broad areas: 1) a positive attitude for science, 2) a perspective of what science is, 3) process skills to use the scientific method, and 4) powerful concepts for students to better understand the world. These sources also suggest effective science teachers integrate these four strands while providing learning experiences that are tangible and directly accessible to students' senses, so they will develop an ability to understand concepts at the abstract level, manipulate symbols, reason logically, and generalize.

From *A Guide for Developing a 1–9 Science Curriculum: Serving Children Through Their Local Schools* (1991). Available from Educational Service Unit #1, Wakefield, NE. Reprinted by permission.

Students who have been provided with these types of experiences learn to think critically, analyze information, communicate scientific ideas, make logical arguments, work as part of a team, acquire positive attitudes, and develop scientific perspectives that encourage them to use the scientific method over and over in many contexts.

In developing the components of this guide, the committee hopes its philosophy, policies, procedures, and content organization will help school personnel develop an effective science curriculum.

A2

SCIENCE CURRICULUM GOALS

1. Students will apply scientific processes to activities in their daily lives.
2. Students will develop and promote a positive attitude toward science.
3. Students will acquire science facts, concepts, and generalizations.
4. Students will become familiar with the natural world, recognizing both its diversity and its global interdependence.
5. Students will become aware of the interrelationship of science, mathematics, and technology.
6. Students will become aware that science, mathematics, and technology are human enterprises with strengths and limitations.

SCIENCE PHILOSOPHY

We believe . . .

Students:
  • are individuals with unique characteristics and interests.
  • should have an equal opportunity to learn, based on their needs, interests, and abilities.
  • are responsible for learning.
  • are naturally curious.

Learning is enhanced:
  • by using discovery learning.
  • when students actively participate in their learning.
  • when students are able to communicate their experiences.
  • when [students] are developmentally ready.
  • with hands-on material.
  • in an intellectually stimulating environment.
  • when content is relevant to students' lives.
  • when students choose their learning experiences.
  • by using multi-sensory experiences.
  • by working from concrete to abstract.
  • by immediate feedback.

Teachers:
  • primary role is as a facilitator of learning.
  • teach by modeling appropriate behavior.
  • provide a variety of learning experiences to create a positive atmosphere.
  • provide content that is relevant to the students' lives.
  • create learning experiences so that students will succeed and failure is not feared.
  • cooperate with other professionals to benefit students.
  • use a low-profile intervention.
  • continue in professional development.
  • use inquiry instructional strategies.

- provide opportunities for writing experiences.
- assess students' development.
- develop activities which are commensurate with students' abilities.
- continuously evaluate the effectiveness of the program.
- allow students to make decisions.
- develop students' awareness of the roles of women and minorities.

Grouping:
- heterogeneously can provide effective learning.
- is important for students to learn effective social skills.
- promotes cooperation.
- promotes listening to another's opinions without bias.
- develops positive attitudes related to science, scientific perspectives, process skills, and conceptualization of science concepts.

Science Programs:
- provide the best science education possible.
- accommodate students' interests and provide for choices.
- clearly state concepts.
- clearly state its goals, philosophy, policies, and procedures.
- encourage parents to participate in their child's education.
- develop process skills.
- should emphasize quality over quantity.
- should provide experiences to meet the needs of students so all achieve their potential.
- include learning experiences that promotes success.
- foster curiosity and enjoyment of science.
- develop a risk free environment (allowed to make mistakes).
- stimulate open-mindedness and sharing of new ideas.
- encourage/require inquiry.
- develop different perspectives of science.
- use appropriate equipment to measure and analyze data.
- facilitate language development.
- promote cognitive development.
- integrate science across the curriculum.

SCIENCE POLICIES

Students in the community schools will:
- arrive ready to learn.
- cooperate with other students.
- communicate their ideas.
- be tolerant of others' views.
- handle equipment carefully.
- be responsible for their learning.

Teachers in the community schools will:
- insure appropriate amounts of time for science instruction.
- provide a positive risk-free learning environment.
- act as a facilitator of learning.
- model appropriate behavior.
- provide a variety of learning experiences.

A2

A2

- make content meaningful to students.
- communicate with other professionals for the benefit of students.
- create an environment suitable for inquiry learning.
- provide opportunities for writing experiences.
- assess students' development both formally and informally.
- select appropriate materials/equipment provided by the district which are commensurate with the students' abilities.
- care for and handle material/equipment in a safe and responsible manner.
- continuously evaluate the effectiveness of the science program in their classroom.
- provide for decision making.
- allow students to manipulate hands-on materials in the least restrictive environment.
- group students to facilitate effective learning and promote cooperation and good social skills.
- provide an atmosphere which promotes sharing of ideas without bias.
- implement the district's science curriculum.
- communicate with parents in regards to their child's science interests.
- foster curiosity and enjoyment of science.
- use questioning strategies to promote cognitive development.
- integrate science into other curriculum areas as much as possible.

Administrators in the community schools will:
- encourage parental participation in science.
- provide leadership in implementing the science curriculum.
- evaluate science curriculum on a continuing basis.
- supply necessary materials/equipment for the teaching of science.
- insure appropriate amounts of time for science instruction.
- encourage staff members in their development of teaching science.
- evaluate the teacher's implementation of the science curriculum.

CONTENT ORGANIZATIONAL OVERVIEW

The intent of the committee is to have students internalize the necessary content to use science in their everyday lives. When this is achieved, students have meaningful, positive science experiences which they may use to solve everyday problems. This creates an enthusiasm that motivates students to use more science. This increases their process skills and scientific knowledge, which in turn increases understanding of the world.

We believe that to help teachers create learning experiences it is useful to categorize content into four broad categories: 1) scientific attitudes, 2) scientific perspectives, 3) science processes, and 4) scientific knowledge.

While these four content areas are of equal importance and should be totally integrated into a science program they are referenced separately in the following section.

Attitudes

Students are naturally curious, with a variety of interests and abilities. Given the opportunity to actively participate in interesting, hands-on, meaningful science experiences encourages the development of an enthusiastic attitude about science.

The following attributes are desirable when doing scientific investigation and should be encouraged by students and modeled by teachers.

1) Curiosity—a desire to acquire information or knowledge to foster curiosity and channel that curiosity in productive ways.

2) Humility/open-mindedness—respect or tolerance for the ideas and opinions of others and the

importance of carefully considering ideas that at first may seem disquieting or at odds with what one generally believes.

3) Skepticism—instinctively or consistently doubts, questions, or disagrees with generally accepted conclusions.

4) Objectivity—ability to make decisions based on facts.

5) Cooperation—willingness to work together when engaged in group activity.

6) Persistence—reluctance to give up despite obstacles or setbacks.

7) Acceptance of failure as an occasional part of the scientific method.

In addition to these attributes, one must believe that knowledge can be understood in ways that will enable it to be used in solving problems.

Likewise, while there are process skills that are uniquely related to science, there are some skills that are more universal and worth mentioning with respect to science. These skills should be used throughout a science program in a variety of contexts so students will be able to use them in various situations. It is the students' positive attitudes about these skills that will determine if they will initiate them in their everyday life. Because of this, we have included these six skills here for consideration:

- *Computational Skills*—enable a person to judge when computations can be made in one's head or on paper.

- *Calculator Skills*—students easily learn how to figure out steps for solving ordinary numerical problems, which operations to use, and how to check the reasonableness of their answers.

- *Estimation Skills*—are based on a sense of what adequate degree of precision is in a particular situation, which in turn depends on understanding the context of the problem and the purpose of the calculation.

- *Manipulation and Observation Skills*—acquire the ability to handle common materials and tools for dealing with everyday technologies, for making observation, and handling information.

- *Communication Skills*—the ability to communicate ideas and share information with consistency and clarity; and to read and listen with understanding.

- *Critical-Response Skills*—can be applied to one's own observation, arguments, and conclusions; thereby be less limited by their own prejudices and rationalizations.

Finally, an effective teacher, through modeling these attitudes and skills, has an extremely powerful influence on the successful internalization of positive science attitudes and the students' desire to learn and use science both in school and in life beyond school.

Perspectives

All students should leave school with an awareness of how science relates to their culture and their lives. Students should also be aware that science developed historically as a result of culture, time, and the understanding of how things behave.

As teachers need to be aware of the scientific perspectives and integrate them into instruction by targeting particular perspectives at specific grades and appropriately matching instruction to the developmental level of the students. This should not exclude integrating scientific perspectives during instruction for students with needs, during teachable moments, or continuing to expand the scientific perspectives targeted in earlier grades.

Grade 1—Physical and conceptual models are guides to understanding of how systems might work.

Grade 2—Historically significant events in science have a continuing impact on society.

Scientific exploration can lead to everyday world discoveries.

Grade 3—In science, change is predictable, understandable, and controllable.

A2

Technological changes in the world must take into account physical, economic, political, social, ecological, aesthetic, and ethical considerations, and make trade-offs among them.

Systems are designed to display the qualities of stability, equilibrium, conservation, and symmetry.

Grade 4—Science, mathematics, and technology have roots in history and every part of the world.

Knowledge gained from one part of the universe is applicable to other parts.

Scientific views result from a combination of evolutionary changes over a long time and revolutionary changes over a relatively short time.

Grade 5—Science, mathematics, and technology are expressions of both human ingenuity and human limitations.

Scientists challenge ideas to build valid knowledge.

Grade 6—Scientific inquiry requires verifiable evidence, testable hypotheses and logical reasoning in the search for unbiased theories.

Science develops an awareness and understanding of the social and economic aspects of science and technology.

Grade 7–9—In the past scientific progress was based on accumulated practical knowledge, but today it is more often based on scientific understanding of the principles that underlie how things behave.

Natural and social sciences produce verifiable knowledge that is not absolute and beyond change.

Social and economic forces determine which technologies will be undertaken and technology in turn has an enormous impact on the nature of human society.

Process Skills

The following skills are to be integrated into instruction by appropriately matching the development of the students. Certain skills are emphasized as noted in the Grade Level Outline.

Observing

Using the senses to identify properties of objects and events

Seeing: size, shapes, colors, how objects interact
Hearing: loudness, pitch, rhythm
Touching: texture, hot-cold, shapes, size, weight, wet-dry, density
Tasting: bitter, salty, sour, sweet
Smelling: associating objects with odors

Changes in properties and motion of objects

Use scientific instruments to increase observation such as: magnifying glass, ruler, the thermometer, microscope, balance scale, binoculars, telescope, clock . . .

Classifying

Grouping objects according to common properties or differences, and their variations

Arranging objects and events in some order according to some property

These properties could include: color, shape, size, living-nonliving, sequence, behavior, weight, mass, volume, density, taxonomy . . .

Measuring

Making quantitative observations based on a standard unit of measure

Measuring with non-standard units: paper clips, marbles, thimbles, erasers, squares . . .

Measuring with standard units: customary metric

Spatial Relationships

Identifying shapes, relative position, and motion

Shapes include: two and three dimensional geometric, symmetrical . . .

Relative position is locating all objects in space relative to a reference point

Motion refers to any change in position in relation to some reference point; rotation and linear motion are examples

Communication

Using written and spoken word to pass information and ideas to others

Some modes of communication may include: numbers, equations, graphs, drawings, diagrams, tables, exhibits, maps, models

Predicting

Making forecasts of future properties or interactions based on past

Experiences, observations, or organizational schemes (chaos, systems, cycles, models)

Inferring

Interpreting or drawing a conclusion from an observation

Defining Operationally

Making a definition by describing an interaction or observation

Formulating a Hypothesis

Making a prediction based on evidence that may be tested

Interpreting Data

Finding a pattern in collected data that may lead to inferences, predictions, conclusions, hypotheses, or models

Controlling Variables

Identifying variables in a system and holding all variables constant except those that are to be manipulated in the experiments

Experimenting

The ability to use some or all of the process skills in solving problems

KNOWLEDGE CONCEPTS OVERVIEW FOR LIFE SCIENCE (FIRST–JUNIOR HIGH)

Concept

Life Science deals with the structure, functions, and interactions of organisms and their environment. By studying these characteristics we build structures such as systems, cycles, and models which lead to an overall understanding of the importance of organisms.

First Grade

    I.   Living things have properties.

        A. Plants and animals have properties.

        B. People have properties.

   II.   Plants need water to live.

  III.   Animals need food and water to live.

IV.   Plants have different parts with different functions.

Second Grade
I.   All organisms have life cycles.
II.   All organisms grow and change.

Third Grade
I.   Variations in populations affect the propagation of the species for its survival.
II.   Various organisms interact to form a food chain.
   A.   Producers and consumers interact in various ways to affect the food chain.
III.   Various food chains interact to form food webs.
IV.   All vertebrates have an interacting skeletal and muscular system.

Fourth Grade
I.   Organisms are dependent on certain environmental factors to sustain life.
II.   Animals are grouped according to body structures and eating types.
III.   Plants are grouped together according to their structure and the materials they produce.

Fifth Grade
I.   All organisms in an area must have a source of food to survive.
II.   Food webs contain producers, consumers, and decomposers, resulting in a transfer of energy for survival.
   A.   Plants produce energy.
   B.   Animals consume food for energy.
   C.   The process of decomposing makes energy for producers.
III.   Animals have digestive systems to convert food into nutrients.
IV.   Nutrients from food are converted into energy.

Sixth Grade
I.   Food chains and webs form food cycles.
II.   Ecosystems are the result of communities interacting with nonliving materials.
   A.   The ecosystems are dependent upon a carbon dioxide (CO_2) and oxygen (O_2) cycle.
   B.   Animals' respiratory systems utilize oxygen.
   C.   Nature and humans can alter ecosystems.
III.   Pollution can be a product of humans or natural activity and affects organisms.
IV.   Pollution is a major threat to life on Earth.
V.   Evolution is a process that results in change of structure and/or function.

Junior High
I.   Organisms are composed of various protein structures.
   A.   Cells vary in size, function, and types of specialized organelles.
   B.   Groups of cells form tissues, tissues form organs, organs form systems, and systems form organisms.
II.   Different species are classified according to structure and function.

III. Interactions between the living and nonliving result in the continuous cycling of carbon, phosphorus, oxygen, and nitrogen.

IV. Sexual and asexual reproduction are different modes for propagation.

V. Evolution is a product of sexual reproduction or mutation and results in variation.

VI. Organisms are a product of DNA and its intracellular properties and functions.

    A. All organisms get their DNA from parent organisms.

    B. Variations in organisms may occur as a result of natural selection or genetic manipulation.

VII. Humans may alter the environment genetically.

VIII. Medical science can sustain life, but in some cases cannot cure the ailment.

A2

PHYSICAL SCIENCE CONCEPT INSTRUCTIONAL PLAN
GRADE ONE

Concept

I. Matter has unique properties

Supporting Information

1. All things are objects
2. Color, shape, size, feel, and smell are properties of objects
3. Objects are made of materials
4. All matter takes up space
5. Objects have their own sound
6. Matter can be solid, liquid, and gases

Alternate Views

1. Objects only have one property at a time.
2. Objects can only be classified by one variable.

Objective

The student will classify objects by color, size, shape, size, feel, and smell. Activities 1–23 will help achieve this objective.

The students will identify solids, liquids, and gases. Activities 24–28 will help reach these objectives.

Materials

feel boxes	tape	jello	rice	marbles	plastic
smell jars	butter	balloons	flour	socks	letters
paper clips	water	clay	cotton	straws	prism
film cans	coins	fruits	letters	magazines	
Bunsen Burner	seeds	freezer	magazines	scouring pads	

Procedure

Exploration: All the activities need to start with exploration. Allow time for the child's observation.

Invention: Students will return to group and communicate their properties they have observed; share ideas for expansion of ideas.

Expansion: Each activity uses this step-by-step process which allows students to discover more properties and classify by different variables. As they do more of these activities, their ability to observe and describe objects by different properties will increase, as well as the complexity of systems they develop to classify objects.

Evaluation
1. Oral response
2. Checklist
3. Participation
4. Students draw pictures
5. Keep a journal

A2

Activities—Grade One

Matter Has Unique Properties

1. Have the students cut out pictures from magazines showing objects that are each a single color. Tell them to classify the pictures into the six color groups. Divide the class into six groups. Assign a color to each group. Have each group paste their pictures on a large sheet of paper. Put the pages together to make a class book. Title the book "Colors Everywhere."

2. Cut holes big enough for the student to place [his or her] hand in the end of boxes. Place a plastic letter inside the box. Have the student feel the letter and identify the letter.

3. Have the students classify sounds: indoor, outdoor, school, kitchen, home, farm, people, animal, and weather. Make picture book(s) of the students' ideas. Sound words can accompany the pictures the students draw, for example, animal sounds: Sheep—baa; dog—ruff, ruff; chicken—cluck, etc.

4. Gather seeds from a variety of fruits and vegetables. Dry the seeds and mix them up. Have the students classify the seeds by type, size, color, and/or shape. Use the seeds for a creative pattern (i.e., mosaic).

5. Gather sea shells and classify by type, size, color, shape . . .

6. Gather pieces of wood, metal, plastics and classify by type, size, color, shape . . .

7. Gather pieces of fabric and classify by type, size, color, shape . . .

.

.

.

25. Take a stick of butter. Identify that it is a solid. Place the solid in a pan and melt. Now you will have a liquid. Place the pan in a refrigerator and the liquid will return to a solid but a different shape.

26. Use water (liquid), freeze into ice cubes (solid). Take the ice cube and hold it with tongs over a Bunsen burner. Watch the change in form.

27. Blow through straws into water. What causes the bubbles?

28. Push a glass straight down into a larger glass container. Turn the glass over and watch the bubbles. What causes the bubbles?

PERSPECTIVES CONCEPT LESSON PLAN
GRADE SIX

Concept

Physical and conceptual models are guides to understanding of how systems might work. (Concept first introduced in grade one. Sample lesson is an expansion for grade six.)

Supporting Information

    What is a model? (i.e. globe, skeleton)—representation of a real thing
    What is a system? (i.e. solar system)
    What are some examples of models?

Give background and information on these
A model is smaller than what it represents

Alternate Views

Rain comes from clouds
Water or land dries from the heat
Sun is a planet, not a star
Can't rain on sunny days

A2

Objectives

1. Students will construct a terrarium to model a water cycle to determine the interrelationships of water, air, land, sun, and climatic conditions.

2. Globe – World   Students will use models to explain scientific phenomena such as:
   Body Systems   Earth, body systems, solar systems, food chains . . .
   Solar System
   Food Chains

Materials

Soil	Globes	Plants	Solar System Model
Large Container	Model Car	Rocks	"Tommy Torso"
Animals	Skeleton		

Procedure

Exploration
Students will build a terrarium and observe what happens.
Students will collect data on these happenings.

Invention
Become aware that models do represent real life systems.

Expansion
Draw a diagram of what makes up their terrarium.
Different activities—with relationships to models and systems.

Evaluation
Build own model of something that is a model. Example: using an erector set or "tinker toys."

A3

Middle School English Language Arts Curriculum Guide

Contents

INTRODUCTION

It seems that everyone is familiar with the sentiment expressed in Bob Dylan's famous 60's pop song called "The Times They Are a Changin'." More and more, teachers—especially English teachers—realize that what sufficed for instructional approaches even five years ago no longer seems to serve their purposes. It is this awareness, among others, that has prompted secondary English teachers in Horseheads to revise and rearrange the curriculum direction for the 90's. Other factors have served as the impetus for this project as well: The previous curriculum document was dated 1981; it seems reasonable that every five to ten years, a staff should formally re-examine what it is doing. The Bureau of Reading and English Education of the New York State Education Department has developed a forward-looking, integrated approach to language arts instruction which has served to motivate local-level staff to re-think their own curriculum direction. A whole language philosophy and approach to language learning, with its emphasis on real-life, meaningful kinds of language-experiences, is gaining greater acceptance throughout the country. Therefore, to stand still complacently is an unacceptable option.

With this background framework, Middle School and High School language arts revision committees were organized in the fall of 1987 to begin the lengthy step-by-step curriculum revision process, observing the following six-step model to which the District subscribes:

- Stage 1. Overall Review and Needs Assessment

- Stage 2. Development of Philosophy, Goals, and Objectives

- Stage 3. Curriculum Design and Writing
  (Summer Workshops and Released Time)

- Stage 4. Piloting

From *Middle School English Language Arts Curriculum Guide* (1991). Available from Horseheads Central School District, Horseheads, NY. Reprinted by permission.

- Stage 5. Implementation
- Stage 6. Evaluation.

The newly revised District Secondary English Language Arts curriculum guides, one of the most comprehensive curriculum projects ever undertaken in this district, are the product of numerous meetings over the past 3½ years to explore concepts and trends and the viewpoints of department members; develop philosophy, goals, and objectives; and write and refine curriculum strands, using a practical format. Virtually all secondary language arts teachers and principals have been involved in the development, overview, implementation, and/or evaluation of the new guides. Quality and practicality of the new curriculum have been further validated through positive input from State-trained Turnkey Trainers and State Bureau of English and Reading personnel.

Integration of meaningful reading, writing, speaking, and listening experiences is stressed in the new guides, with less emphasis on isolated skill instruction. Staff newcomers, Board of Education members, parents, and students will now have access to [a] specific account of what each language arts course offers.

Our students today face an increasingly competitive and demanding way of life, with ever-increasing literacy requirements at the personal, civic, and career levels. The purpose of this new English language arts curriculum is to address those needs.

A3

PROFILE OF AN EFFECTIVE LANGUAGE ARTS PROGRAM*

A Well-Designed English Language Arts Program ensures that students will learn to use language to

- gain information, discover meaning, understand logical relationships, and make judgments through critical thinking, reading, and viewing.
- speak, write, and solve problems creatively.
- communicate emotions, ideas, opinions, values, experiences, and information.
- discover both the power and beauty of literature as a mirror of human experience, reflecting human motives, conflicts, values, and traditions.

An Integrated Curriculum is one in which

- reading, writing, listening and speaking are taught within a "literate environment" in contexts that are meaningful to students;
- reading, writing, listening and speaking are considered language processes which interact in various ways to allow communication to occur;
- language study happens naturally as part of helping students become clear, precise, effective communicators;
- formal evaluation of subskill mastery is deemphasized in favor of methods that allow for observation of students actively engaged in the communication process.

An Effective Language Arts Program displays these characteristics:

- Management reflects district-wide commitment to a quality English language arts program.
- The program is consistent with current theory and research.
- The curriculum is taught within a language-rich environment.
- The curriculum provides for individual and group needs through a variety of instructional configurations, methods, and materials.
- The curriculum is designed so that language, listening, speaking, composition, reading, and literature support and enhance learning in the content areas.
- The curriculum includes a variety of methods and procedures for evaluating student growth.
- The curriculum establishes methods of program evaluation.

*Produced by The Bureau of English and Reading of the New York State Education Department.

CURRICULUM ESSENTIALS[*]

Meaningfulness	*Active Engagement*	*Integration*
Real book, real writing	Personal investment	Language arts and thinking skills
Attention to skills in context	Writing and talking	Writing as mode of learning
Focus of reading/writing on making meaning	Student ownership of knowledge	Reading to inform writing
Literate environment	Involvement in the process	Literature and content areas
Response-based	Choice and responsibility	Ideas of learners and ideas of "authorities"

A UNIQUE VIEWPOINT OF THE LANGUAGE ARTS TEACHER'S ROLE[**]

A3

The Teacher

Why do I forget question marks.
I am notorious for it.
My students scoff at me.
"How can you teach English when you don't punctuate proper?"

I don't teach you anyway, I think,
just lead you like a scout master
and hope you'll dip your hand
into the brook—cold like no
tap water you've ever felt,
let you marvel, a little frightened,
at a snake, mouth agape,
before it darts between rocks,
an image you'll carry for years,
spur you to anger when I won't
stop to let you rest,
even hope you catch poison ivy,
and, as we race up the hill,
urge you on when you leave me behind,
gasping, a seeming spear
wedged between my ribs.

Of the absent question mark, I say,
"An innocent, harmless error,"
And those of you who aren't smug
point out that I should
extend to you
the same courteous understanding.
I uncap my canteen,
drop to the grass, and,
before I take a long swig,
say, "Why not."

                    by Tom Romano[+]

*Produced by The Bureau of English and Reading of the New York State Education Department.
**Part of presentation by Colleen Talada, State-trained BOCES Turnkey Trainer, at Chemung-Schuyler-Steuben BOCES-sponsored English Language Arts K–12 Awareness Session on November 1, 1989.
+From *Options for Reading and Writing* (Second Edition). Harper and Row, 1989.

The role of the teacher as espoused in *The Teacher* poem:

(1) Adventurer.

(2) Coach.

(3) Decision maker.

(4) Demonstrator of courage.

(5) Encourager.

(6) Evaluator—grades, but also making the grade, encouraging success.

(7) Example of perseverance.

(8) Facilitator of active experiences.

(9) Guide.

(10) Helper of students to go beyond even, perhaps, what the teacher can do.

(11) Indefatigable worker.

(12) Instructor.

(13) Mistake maker.

(14) Model who demonstrates literacy.

(15) Observer who knows students.

(16) One who is more likely to ask about life's new dimensions "Why not?" rather than "Why?"

(17) Participator.

(18) Provider of a learning environment.

(19) Questioner.

(20) Risk taker.

(21) Scholar.

(22) Supporter, not fault finder.

A3

RE-WRITING THE BOOK ON HOW TO TEACH*

School restructuring has been a hot topic for the last decade, and many schools throughout the nation have experimented with their own innovative programs. One such school is Washington state's Cougar Valley Elementary School in Silverdale, Washington, featured in a *USA Today* article. Secondary-level educators could be inspired by this program which stresses regular computer use to supplement textbooks, "doing" rather than just "listening," and written description of student progress instead of report cards.

In contrast to decades-old modus operandi, five new assumptions guide these new approaches:

- Old: The learner is passive. Student is viewed as an empty vessel which can be filled by teachers.

- New: The learner is active. Student brings prior knowledge to the learning task. The learner naturally formulates more sophisticated rules, patterns and generalizations as he or she engages in language activities.

- Old: The student learns what is taught directly.

- New: Children learn much that is not explicitly taught. Personal investment in learning is critical.

- Old: The whole is the sum of the parts. Knowledge is built from smaller parts into a new whole.

- New: The whole is necessary to give meaning to the parts, and then can be broken into parts for further exploration.

- Old: Errors signal a learner's failure to learn or to correctly apply what was taught. Effective teaching can be measured by an absence of errors.

* *USA Today*, Tuesday, November 7, 1989.

- New: Errors indicate developmental levels. They are a demonstration of the learner's current thinking and understanding. Errors are approximations and are necessary in the learning process.
- Old: The product is most important. Skills and acquired knowledge are the main objective in education and should have our primary focus.
- New: The process is more important. "Thinking, reading, speaking, listening and writing are best learned by actually engaging in these activities. When the primary focus is on the process, better products often develop.

PHILOSOPHY, GOALS, AND OBJECTIVES

Philosophy Statement

The Horseheads Middle School Language Arts Program is designed so that the adolescents of our community will acquire the appropriate communication and reasoning skills of viewing, listening, speaking, reading and writing. This program invites the students to master the basic skills in each of the aforementioned areas and to enable them to apply these skills in their daily lives.

The program promotes value-based choices and critical thinking. The various language experiences are intended to create a sense of self-esteem and achievement, which will allow the students to share and to participate more meaningfully in their social, academic, and leisure lives. As a result students will acquire a better understanding of the world around them. Finally, the program recognizes that students are developmentally different, proceeding at varied rates, but nonetheless involved in a life-long learning process.

Goals

Listening and Speaking

- I. Listening and speaking for social interaction.
- II. Listening and speaking for information and understanding.
- III. Listening and speaking for critical analysis and evaluation.
- IV. Listening and speaking for pleasure.
- V. Listening and speaking for personal growth.

Reading and Literature

- I. Reading for pleasure as well as aesthetic and personal response.
- II. Reading for acquisition, interpretation, and application of information.
- III. Reading for critical analysis and evaluation.
- IV. Reading for personal growth.

Writing

- I. To express one's feeling and perspectives.
- II. To narrate a fictional story or an account of a real event.
- III. To explain factual information.
- IV. To describe a person, place, or impression.
- V. To persuade another to change an opinion, or to influence the action of others.

Program Objectives Relating to Goals—Writing Strand

GOALS   OBJECTIVES—The student will:
- I. To express self:
  - A. Journal Entry   (1) Demonstrate introspective thinking.

(2) Develop "voice" in recording feelings, values, attitudes, etc.

(3) Attempt to experiment with language.

(4) Develop a "comfort" level with writing.

B. Friendly Letter

(1) Use informal diction and tone.

(2) Includes topic development.

(3) Use correct form and conventions.

C. Personal Response to Literature

(1) Identify the work or selection and author.

(2) Select one or more element(s) of the work or selection to be discussed.

(3) State reaction(s) to the work or selection.

(4) Provide reasons, examples, or details to support reaction(s).

(5) Draw conclusion about the work or selection.

D. Poem (e.g., haiku, quatrain, ballad, free verse, etc.)

(1) Use the conventions of the form selected.

(2) Use sensory detail and imagery.

(3) Use figurative language, such as metaphor and/or simile.

(4) Demonstrate conciseness in expression.

(5) Use language with awareness of connotation/denotation.

(6) Provides a title, if appropriate.

II. To narrate:

A. Narrative of Actual Experience

(1) Select and limit factual information related to an actual experience.

(2) Begin with an interesting lead.

(3) Develop the narrative chronologically or through some other organizational plan appropriate for the experience (e.g., flashback, cause/effect).

(4) Include details, examples, etc.

(5) Include description and/or other information about other persons involved in the experience.

(6) Include conversation when appropriate, using correct punctuation.

(7) Maintain consistent first- or third-person point of view.

(8) Bring the narrative to a natural closure.

B. Short Story

(1) Sequence events to advance the plot (i.e., rising action, conflict, climax, falling action, resolution).

A3

    (2) Create and describe character(s) and setting.

    (3) Maintain a consistent point of view.

    (4) Include correctly punctuated conversation.

    (5) Use specific, vivid language.

    (6) Suggest a theme.

    (7) Provide a title.

C. Skit

    (1) Select or create a situation, setting, and characters.

    (2) Limit the action to the specific situation.

    (3) Use dialogue to reveal characterization.

    (4) Use dialogue to advance the action.

    (5) Use dialogue format.

    (6) Build to a conclusion.

A3

GRADE 7 CURRICULUM STRANDS

Local Writing

Part 1—Emphasis

Writing for seventh graders should relate to:

- students' needs
- ideas
- purposes
- interests
- feelings
- maturation

as well as subject matter generated through the academic study of literature and other subject matter. The program should offer a balanced approach to personal writing and writing in the content areas. Ideas and strategies should be generated through pre-writing activities which stress inquiry, personal experiences, and critical thinking skills.

    Many of the objectives and activities at the local level will be similar to the regents level; however, characteristics of the learner at the local level necessitate that differences in learning proficiency be considered by the teacher. It is observed that the local level student:

(1)   requires much teacher direction

(2)   is often personally disorganized

(3)   is frequently absent

(4)   is easily distracted

(5)   is more likely to be a discipline problem

(6)   is often chronologically older than students at this grade level

(7)   is often unprepared when homework is assigned

(8)   requires much repetition

(9)   has limited tolerance and attention span.

It is expected that 35% of class time will be devoted to writing-related activities.

Part 2—Goals

(1) To compose sentences.

(2) To combine sentences and vary sentence structure.

(3) To write a well developed paragraph utilizing a variety of approaches and purposes:

    (a) To express one's self:
- journal entry
- personal response to literature
- business and friendly letters.

    (b) To narrate:
- narrative of actual experience
- autobiographical sketch.

    (c) To explain:
- a process essay
- business letter (complaint)
- report based on experience (i.e. guest speaker, field trip).

    (d) To describe:
- a place (real or fictional)
- a favorite person/relative
- a person or place in literature.

    (e) To summarize:
- events of a fictional piece
- a special event
- a news event.

    (f) To persuade:
- book commercial (book review)
- persuasive composition dealing with issues relevant to student needs/student environment (i.e., family, school).

(4) To develop the habit of using the stages in the writing process:
- generating ideas (brainstorming)
- thinking and organizing
- composing
- revising and editing
- sharing
- publishing.

(5) To demonstrate improvement in
- development
- organization
- sense of audience
- purpose.

(6) To demonstrate improvement in the editing and revising stage of writing for correctness in mechanics and usage:
- spelling
- content
- paragraph structure
- sentence variety
- agreement
- correct and varied use of modifiers (specific language-vocabulary).

A3

(7)   To write a pre- and post-sample of writing in order to allow the instructor to determine strengths and weaknesses in planning the writing program for the year, and in measuring each student's progress for the year.

(8)   To keep a folder of writing samples, both those in progress and those completed.

Part 3—Behavioral Objectives

(1)   Given a series of related words (sentence synthesis), the student will demonstrate the ability to compose a meaningful sentence that will indicate an understanding of these words.

(2)   Using connectors (and, but, or, etc.) and using transitional/time words (after, since, because, when, until, whether), the student will demonstrate improvement in combining sentences and varying sentence structure within the context of a narrative piece.

(3)   Given the reading of a short story or novel, the student will write a journal entry as if he were a specific character, indicating an understanding of the character and of the time period.

(4)   Given necessary ordering information, the student will write a business letter demonstrating a knowledge of correct business letter form as well as use of necessary content.

(5)   Given a social situation or experience, the student will write friendly letters (bread and butter letter and thank you), demonstrating a knowledge of correct form including interesting and sincere content.

(6)   Given the planning for a personal narrative or autobiographic sketch, the student will develop a paragraph demonstrating correct sequence.

(7)   Given a simple task (i.e., making a pay telephone call, a banana split, submarine sandwich, making a bed), the student will sequentially describe the steps in completing the process.

(8)   Given a cause for complaint or adjustment, the student will demonstrate a knowledge of correct business letter [form] as well as use in necessary content to address the issue in writing.

(9)   Given a class experience such as a field trip, an assembly or guest speaker, and a set of notes, the student will demonstrate the ability to organize notes, and to write a well developed, multi-paragraph report based on information.

(10)   Given a place or person (real or fictional), the student will write a description using specific language which appeals to the senses and is organized in a specific order such as sequence or order of importance (most to least/least to most).

(11)   Given a special experience, a news event, or a fictional piece, the student will demonstrate the ability to condense information to a summarized form.

(12)   Given a series of writing situations, the student will demonstrate an ability to appropriately write for different audiences (i.e., friend, parent, teacher, principal, older relative).

(13)   Given a writing checklist, the student will demonstrate in pieces of writing an ability to evaluate his/her paper in terms of various areas of mechanics (i.e., spelling, capitalization, punctuation, word usage, etc.), content, and organization.

(14)   Given a topic related to one of the four major methods of discourse, the student will write a pre- and post-test sample indicating improvement from the fall to the spring sampling.

A3

Part 4—Content, Including Suggested Activities

Prewriting Activities

(1) Brainstorming—listing randomly ideas relating to the topic as they come to mind, to be categorized under more general headings and topics later. This can be managed as a teacher-led class discussion, a small-group discussion, or an individual effort.

(2) Branching—determining and listing subtopics for main topics already provided by the teacher or through class discussion.

(3) Mapping—recording brainstorming in a visual format to show details in relation to main ideas.

(4) Nutshelling (think sheet)—focusing on purpose, point of view, audience, introduction, and conclusion statements. (See Milliken Writing Program.)

(5) Interviewing—focusing on classmate, friend, parent, or grandparent to ask questions relating to a given topic as a writing project—to generate responses to a given set of questions.

(6) Notetaking—identifying key ideas from factual passages, field trips, guest speakers, and filmstrips.

(7) Role-playing.

(8) Group discussion.

(9) Conferencing with peers and/or teacher.

(10) Keeping of a journal or diary.

A3

Writing Prompts

(1) Write a letter in which you introduce yourself to the teacher as a person and as a student. Your letter should include age, elementary school, hobbies, talents, things you are proud of, interesting places where you have lived or visited, family, reading interests.

(2) Keep a daily journal using topics assigned by the teacher. Entries should develop the topic sufficiently with interesting details. Sample topics might include these:
   - Describe a perfect day away from school.
   - Tell about your most memorable birthday.
   - An interesting hobby.
   - Discuss your position in your family. Are you the oldest, in the middle, the youngest, or an only child? What are the advantages and problems of your position?

(3) Write a description of a familiar place. Begin with a list of items that appeal to the senses. Expand the list into sentences which emphasize impressions perceived through one or more of the senses. Organize these sentences into an order which might indicate first impressions or greatest impact (i.e., a "greasy spoon" restaurant, florist showroom, cafeteria, bakery).

(4) Write a narrative account of one incident in a book which you have read. Recall the point in the action of the story when the excitement was highest. Explain what happened. Your reader will need to know the time, place, circumstances, and the identity of the persons concerned. Make your reader feel the excitement. Your piece should have a good beginning. Identify the book, the author and the general situation. Make a transition for identification of book and author to narration of specific incident. Orderly arrangement of details and elimination of unnecessary items should be considered, as well as a strong ending.

(5)   Write a thank you letter for a gift. Be sure to specifically name the gift, make some favorable comment about it, and express appreciation. If the gift is money, make some reference to the use which will be made of it.

(6)   Write a letter to the teacher or to the school librarian about a book you have read. Emphasize description of the setting or a favorite character. You may also include a brief summary of the plot. Be sure to use correct letter form.

(7)   Practice writing simple definitions of terms such as these:
   • constitution, amendment, veto
   • harp, trombone, guitar
   • commerce, tariff, embargo
   • cell, organ, system
   • circulatory, skeletal, digestive
   • executive, judicial, legislative
   • area, perimeter, circumference.

A3

The Term to Be Defined	The Class to Which the Object Belongs	The Distinguishing Characteristics
A dinosaur	is a large extinct reptile	which has four limbs and a long tail.

(8)   Write an explanation of a particular process or activity. Before beginning, make a list of the steps involved in this process. Then use transitional words, (first, next, then, meanwhile, after, finally) to organize the list into a logically sequenced paragraph. Topics might include these:
   • make a peanut butter and jelly sandwich
   • tie a necktie
   • bathe a dog
   • buy an item from a pop/candy/snack machine.

(9)   Write a journal entry as if you were a specific character in a given story or book. The entry should identify a specific time in the story and should reflect the feelings of the character in regard to an event which has taken place in that part of the story.

(10)   Write a business letter ordering an item that you have seen advertised in a magazine or catalog. Include all necessary information such as model number, quantity, size, color, price, and method of payment. Be sure to use correct business letter form.

(11)   Write a letter of complaint or adjustment regarding a given situation. Include the specific item or situation involved, the problem, the solution desired, relevant dates, receipts, etc. Use correct business letter form.

(12)   Take a set of class-generated notes which are disorganized, organize these notes and write a report on a guest speaker, assembly, or a field trip. Decide which notes are main ideas and which ones are of an introductory nature, which are key observations, areas visited and ideas learned. Finally, tell what you and the other students gained from the trip, and how you responded.

(13)   Write a personal narrative about an event which has happened to you. Make a list of the steps involved before writing. Sequence these steps. Then write a paragraph or paragraphs using the transitional words to allow the reader to follow the sequence. Conclude with your reaction or feeling about this event.

(14) Write a paragraph in which you tell about a character in a book/story whom you would most like to meet. Describe the person not only physically but with his/her personal characteristics included. Give specific reasons for your choice.

(15) Using a frame with key elements omitted (see framed paragraph ILA Manual), write a summary of a story or book read in class. Be sure to rewrite the entire frame as you add the missing elements.

Part 5—Materials and Resources

(1) Student Textbook:

Basic English Skills (Red Level). New York: McDougal, Littell, and Company, 1985.

(2) For Teacher Reference:

Atwell, Nancie. *In the Middle: Writing, Reading, and Learning with Adolescents*. Portsmouth, New Hampshire: Boynton/Cook Publishers, Inc., 1987.

Calkins, Lucy. *The Art of Teaching Writing*. Portsmouth, New Hampshire: Heineman Educational Books, Inc., 1986.

Composition in the Language Arts Curriculum K-12. Albany: New York State Education Department, Bureau of English and Reading, 1986.

Individualized Language Arts Teacher's Manual. Weehawken, New Jersey: Weehawken Board of Education, 1974.

(3) Computer-Assisted Writing:

Milliken Writing Program by the Milliken Publishing Company, 1986.

PFS Write by Scholastic.

Part 6—Methods of Evaluation

(1) Conferencing with peers and/or the classroom teacher during the pre-writing process.

(2) Conferencing for revision and/or editing.

(3) Analytical scoring of writing using focus areas for corrections.[*]

(4) Holistic scoring.

(5) Primary trait scoring.

(6) Peer evaluation based on a limited number of focused comments on a writing checklist.[+]

(7) Grading the best of several writings.

(8) Pre- and post-quizzes for writing-related lessons on usage and mechanics.

[*]For a detailed analysis of the advantages, disadvantages, and applications of several approaches for writing evaluation, see *A Report of the Writing Evaluation Subcommittee of the Horseheads Central School District Writing Task Force*, June 1985.

[+]For a detailed view of how to use focused comments and writing checklists, as well as methods of organizing an effective writing program for the students, see the November 1985 report on the Rochester Conference of the "Network for Effective Communication" presented by Dr. David Crellin.

A3

A4

. . . .

Spanish IV Curriculum

Contents

FOREIGN LANGUAGE DEPARTMENT PHILOSOPHY

The Foreign Language Department believes that the study of foreign languages is an essential component of the Stoughton High School Philosophy: "To provide an educational program which fosters the widest opportunities for the intellectual strengthening and personal maturation of every student . . . and of sharing with the student the accumulated knowledge and culture of the past, and developing the requisite skills and understanding which enable him/her to participate effectively in society. It is essential that students understand the growing cultural pluralism of today's society, and be made aware of the fragile interdependence of man and his planet."

By acquiring language proficiency, a student is able to communicate with others and become a more successful, productive world citizen. Since language learning involves developing an intellectual skill, it enhances the student's ability to think logically, to reason, to memorize, to analyze, to read with inferencing, and to understand his own language. These skills are valuable throughout life and useful in many careers.

We believe that the study of foreign language adds a new dimension to an individual's personality and a greater understanding of self and others. In the process of language learning, the student develops an awareness of cultural diversity since language reflects culture. The student adapts better to the multiethnic structure of our society and gains insight into the thought pattens and social institutions of other societies. As has been stated: "We begin by saying what we think and end by thinking what we say."

NARRATIVE DESCRIPTION

In Spanish IV, the student will continue using all grammatical structures and vocabulary studied in the previous three years and will move into more advanced vocabulary and complex patterns of grammar. By being habituated to the use of simple grammatical structures, the student is now better equipped to learn those intricate grammatical patterns that facilitate a superior level of expression.

At this level the student will not only enlarge his vocabulary horizontally, by acquiring more words, but will also expand it vertically by gaining a terminology suitable for the communication of the modern man, in a technological society, especially in that pertaining to professions, careers, places of work, job hunting, office equipment and computers.

In terms of grammar, students will be able to hypothesize about the past and about what would happen under certain conditions. Students will be able to describe two simultaneous actions and wishes, feelings, doubts, and intentions in the past. Students will be able to use sentences clarifying purpose, restrictions and sequence of events, as well as what happens or will happen as the result of certain events.

At this point, students will be less constricted by vocabulary items or grammatical structures and will be encouraged to use the target language more spontaneously. The student will be asked to discuss themes such as love, marriage, personality, ethnic foods, health, drugs, sports, exercises, cars, cultures, shopping, travelling, the future, and different pastimes.

The student will understand that we live in a world of competition and interdependence; that one has to be prepared linguistically and technologically to meet the challenges of modern society. No man is an island; no society suffices by itself. It will be through appropriate communication and cultural understanding that man can fulfill the gap of mutual-international interdependence.

GOALS

Perfect communication involves a progressive acquisition of vocabulary, grammatical structures and language use. At this level, students will be taking advanced steps to assure fluent expression.

The students will learn:

A. Language: Linguistic/Communication
   Goals:
   1. Vocabulary
      * words for an advanced level of expression
      * terminology suitable for the communication of the modern man, in a technological society
   2. Grammar
      * describe two simultaneous actions: *al* + infinitive
      * clarify purpose, restrictions, and sequences of events: preposition + infinitive or conjunction + subjunctive
      * clarify what happens or will happen as the result of certain events: *cuando* + indicative or subjunctive
      * describe wishes, feelings, doubts, and intentions in the past: imperfect subjunctive
      * express hypotheses about what would occur under certain conditions: *si*-clauses and sequence of tenses
      * describe the results of an action: *estar* + past participle
      * describe situations in which the subject is acted upon: passive voice or *se* + verb
      * indicate that an agent's action is unintentional: *se* + verb
      * express wishes, doubts, and feelings about previous past actions: pluperfect subjunctive
      * hypothesize about the past: *si* clauses with pluperfect subjunctive and conditional perfect.
      * clarify references: relative pronouns and *cuyo* constructions
   3. Dialogue
      * describe personal experiences

A4

- relate daily activities
- report on events
- react to current issues
- tell a story
- create and act out a dialogue/skit
- interact with teacher and classmates

4. Reading
   - read, understand and interpret passages, novels and culture capsules of the Hispanic world.

5. Listening
   - follow directions
   - comprehend class instruction
   - understand teacher's presentation of different topics
   - do the language laboratory exercises for each unit
   - watch movies

B. Culture Goals
   - students will study the geography, culture, customs, history products, political figures and current issues of the Hispanic world.
   - students will not only accept culture differences, but understand that all nations and cultures have much to benefit from each other.
   - students will regard languages and culture as tools to widen man's horizons, enrich his intellect and complement his aspirations.

SPECIFIC OBJECTIVES

Unidad I

A. Linguistic/Communication

   1. Phonetics: Students will repeat vocabulary words and expressions contained in the lesson and will read aloud the literary passages that precede and follow the unit.

   2. Vocabulary, Structures, Oral/Written Expression
      - Students will be able to make reservations for a hotel room, request hotel services and pay for a hotel bill.
      - memorize vocabulary related to types of lodging reservations, services and personnel.
      - make an oral description of pictures depicting a couple's stay at a hotel, from the moment of checking in to the time of checking out.
      - make a skit related to hotel reservations, discussion of prices, length of stay, type of room and services.
      - role-play this specific situation: You are checking out of your hotel in San Jose, Costa Rica. You would like to pay by credit card, but the hotel takes only cash or travelers' checks. Try to find a solution to the problem.
      - use the construction *al* + infinitive.
      - use *al* + negative infinitive.

- employ the infinitive after certain prepositions.
- differentiate between *para* + infinitive and *por* + infinitive.
- be able to use the subjunctive after the following conjunctions: *para que, a menos que, sin que, con tal (de) que, a condicion de que, antes de que*.
- know whether to use the indicative or the subjunctive after clauses introduced by *cuando, despues (de) que, hasta que, mientras que, luego que, en cuanto, tan pronto como,* and *aunque*.
- answer factual and interpretative questions, based on the reading contained in the unit.

B. Culture

Introduce students to the author Horacio Quiroga

- read and interpret a passage by said author
- discuss the following topics:

    Latin American currency

    Spanish music: guitar and castanets

    Musical comedy: *la Zarzuela*

    Spanish dances: *la yota, el bolero, la sordina*

    Jungles and rain forests in Central and South America

    Missiones region: Iguazu Falls

    Vasco Nunez de Balbao and Fernando do Magallanes

A4

APPENDIX

Reading Skills

Students will read the novel *Don Quixote de la Mancha* by Miguel de Cervantes. This masterpiece will be studied in its historical, social and literary context.

Students will read short stories, versing [sic] the most varied current issues and conducive to discussion.

Conversational Skills

Students will study and discuss the following situations:

El Amor – Love
El Matrimonio – Matrimony
La Personalidad – Personality
La Comida – Food
La Salud – Health
El Alcohol, El tabaco y las Drogas – Alcohol, Tobacco and Drugs
Los Deportes – Sports
Los Ejercicious – Exercises
Los Signos del Zodiaco – The Signs of the Zodiac
Lo Desconociodo – The Unknown
La Moda – Fashion
El Automovil – The Automobile
Artes y Costumbres Hispanicos – The Hispanic Arts and Customs
Intereses y Pasatiempos – Interests and Pastimes
Espana – Spain
Literatur Hispanica – Hispanic Literature

La Immigracion – Immigration
Los Hispanos en los Estados Unidos – The Hispanic in the United States
Compras y Ventas – Shopping and Sales
Como hacerse rico? – How to become rich?
Intereses y Pasatiempos – Interests and Pastimes
Los Viajes y el Terrorismo Internacional – Traveling and International Terrorism
La Evolucion – Evolution
El Futuro – c Adonde Vamos? – The Future – Where are we going to?

Writing Skills

Students will write several compositions on some of the topics previously listed under Conversational Skills, or any other topic assigned by the teacher.

METHODS OF EVALUATION

A. Oral Quizzes

 1. Sight translation
 2. Answering factual or interpretative questions, in Spanish, based on assigned readings
 3. Directed dialogues
 4. Construction of dialogues
 5. Situational skits
 6. Description of pictures, drawings, situations or events

B. Written Quizzes

 1. Grammatical structures
 2. Vocabulary
 3. Answering factual or interpretative questions, in Spanish, based on assigned readings
 4. Description of pictures, drawings, situations or events

C. Major Exams

 Consisting of the four components: listening, reading, speaking and writing

D. Composition Work

 1. Paragraph writing, involving complex grammatical structures
 2. Compositions
 3. Construction of dialogues and skits
 4. Letter writing
 5. Description of people, things, situations and events

E. Homework

 Assignments using one or more of the four language learning components (listening, speaking, reading and writing) are given and corrected every day.

F. Class Participation

 1. Following directions
 2. Oral comprehension
 3. Answering/asking questions

4. Substitution drills of complex grammatical structures.

5. Spontaneous class participation, intervention or comments.

BASIC AND SUPPLEMENTARY MATERIALS

1. Textbook: *Spanish for Mastery, Level III*, Valette-Valette, 1988

2. Workbook

3. Tape Program: Language Laboratory and Classroom Use

4. Hispanic Music

5. Video tapes of Hispanic Culture

6. Movies in Spanish

7. *De Aqui y de Alla*, D. C. Heath and Company

8. *Temas y Dialogos*, Holt, Rinehart, and Winston, Inc.

9. *Don Quixote de la Mancha*, Grafisk Institute A/S, Copenhagne

10. Teacher-prepared materials

A4

A5

Wyoming Arts Education Curriculum

A5

Contents

MISSION STATEMENT

The arts enhance self-esteem, promote understanding of self and encourage lifelong learning.

The Wyoming Arts Education Plan is intended to provide a road map for quality sequential arts education for all students. The plan aids in the development of a common core of knowledge in aesthetics, criticism, history and production. The plan provides for a common core of skills in problem solving, communications, critical thinking and creativity.

INTRODUCTION

The Need for Arts Curriculum

In response to several state and national initiatives, a number of educators in the state of Wyoming, in conjunction with the Wyoming Arts Council, the Wyoming Department of Education and the Wyoming Alliance for Arts Education, determined that guidelines were needed in the visual, performing and literary arts to assist colleagues with the task of developing performance-based outcome objectives.

In 1990, the State Board of Education mandated that each Wyoming school district develop student performance standards or outcomes around a common core of skills and a common core of knowledge. The Fine Arts and Performing Arts are identified as an integral part of the common core of knowledge skills, and creativity and life skills are among the six common core of skills areas in these standards. Section 10 reads:

From *Wyoming Arts Education Curriculum,* 1992. Available from Wyoming State Department of Education, Cheyenne, WY. Reprinted by permission.

a)   Each school shall adopt district student performance standards and site-specific student performance standards.

Additionally, the state legislature, in Enrolled Act 50, Section 5 (ii) requires:

"Establishment of a core curriculum developing basic learning and thinking skills and maintenance of a curriculum available to all students which encourages students to pursue traditional, technical or vocational post-secondary educational opportunities and trains them for employment in a highly technical and global economy."

Art Equals Basic Skills

Art has always had a place in our schools, but now research has shown that arts education is critical to learning, to society, and to the future of the global community.

Our world has become increasingly complicated. Communications are now instantaneous and universal, more intricate than ever before. Science, government, industry, community, and school leaders are finding that old formulas no longer solve today's problems. How can we come up with fresh approaches and inventive solutions? We need a generation that can attack problems creatively—with imagination and initiative. We must ensure that students can deal with this new complexity.

Communication Skills:
A primary mission of arts education is to teach effective communication. And because art is communication, arts education provides more tools for exchanging information than any other field of study.

Discipline:
The study of art fosters self-discipline, essential to educational success, satisfactory employment, and personal growth. A student who can understand a demanding concept in art is bound to be a life-long learner able to vigorously address challenge.

Analytical Thinking:
Creativity and critical thinking are fundamental to arts education. Students who receive quality arts instruction will master skills to solve today's difficult problems.

Quality of Life:
The arts have a profound influence on an individual's ability to live richly and fully, giving us a vehicle for self-expression, inspiring our imaginations and renewing our enthusiasm.

Future:
Nearly everything we know of earth's earliest civilizations has come to us through the arts. The quality of our modern civilization will be measured by the quality of contemporary artistic expression—the cultural heritage we leave. How will we be viewed?

A5

Art Equals Education

What are forward-looking schools doing? Now that we know arts are at the core of learning itself, public schools throughout the country are making profound changes in the way it's taught.

Integrated Approaches
Confronting arts problems develops critical thinking skills. Teachers have discovered that students learn more, and retain it more effectively, when art is integrated with other academic subjects, reflecting math and science concepts, the course of history and the development of our society, and themes in literature.

Sequential Curriculum
Arts education is becoming a basic component of the standard curriculum for students in grades K–12. States are designing sequential and comprehensive arts programs to include a careful balance among

history, aesthetics, skills, and production experiences. These programs provide not only a sense of civilization's progress but, additionally, foster communication skills.

Teacher Training

Most elementary school teachers have had little training in the arts, and many students have little exposure to arts specialists. When there are specialists in a school, their background is often limited to music or visual arts. There's a growing awareness that more teachers need more expanded arts training.

Expanded Arts Experiences

Study of the arts is no longer confined to the traditional classroom. Artists are regarded as important resources, and are frequently invited to perform for students, to work with individuals and classes, and to participate in extended residencies. Class site visits to museums, theatres and other arts environments also occur.

Arts Requirements

School systems concerned about educating the whole child with a well-rounded curriculum include standards in the arts, requiring that art be taught in elementary schools, and that art credits in fine and performing arts be required for high school graduation. They're establishing a core of subject content, scopes of skills, and systems for defining course objectives, performance-based outcomes and means of evaluating mastery.

Funding and Involvement

Many school districts are increasing the funds available for arts instruction. Parents, artists, arts organizations, businesses, and state and local agencies—all of whom increasingly recognize the value of the artistic process—have become advocates for increasing services and funding.

A5

The Purpose of These Guidelines

These guidelines have been created to assist schools and communities as they work together to develop student performance standards or outcomes. Five separate task forces devoted long hours to developing outcomes-based objectives and resource lists in the areas of dance, drama, music, visual and literacy arts. This publication, which resulted from their work, is intended to serve as a guideline for educators throughout the state as they work to accomplish these goals and ultimately improve the quality of instruction of Wyoming educators and the achievement of Wyoming students.

Each task force has designed a document that is appropriate for Wyoming schools. In some cases, the task forces borrowed from other states which have already undergone this planning process. In others, new information has been provided. In all instances, this is information to review and adapt as districts and communities see best. We have included many resources for those who feel they need more information.

Differences of style are apparent in the actual presentation of the information. This accommodates the various styles of the five task forces and their respective disciplines. Each group determined how it wanted to present respective outcomes and resources, just as individual schools will do.

If you have questions on any of this material, feel free to call the State Department of Education or the Wyoming Arts Council. If we can't answer your questions, we'll find someone who can!

Future Directions

The Wyoming Arts Council and the Wyoming Alliance for Arts Education will provide inservice opportunities for schools that would like to participate in hands-on sessions with task force members. Teachers will have an opportunity to work their way through a "mini-planning" process similar to the one task force members undertook. It's an opportunity for educators to work specifically with arts education goals and out-comes, with added perspective and input directly from the task force. If your district would like to schedule one of these sessions or attend one that is occurring nearby let us know. For more information on these inservice opportunities contact the Arts in Education Program Manager, Wyoming Arts Council, (307)777-7742.

VISUAL ARTS

Introductory Statement

The Visual Arts Task Force believes that schools must implement a qualitative and sequential (K–12) visual arts curriculum that provides for meaningful self-expression of all students. The ideal curriculum integrates production, aesthetics, art history and criticism in a wholistic way that accommodates individual learning styles. This approach must also provide for creative and divergent thinking.

Important goals should include involving parents and the community in planning and implementation, sharing and integrating with other subject areas, creating awareness of career opportunities and acquiring administrative support.

We encourage local school districts to use this curriculum document as a guide when they begin developing their own arts education curriculum. We present what we consider an ideal. Each district must take into consideration its own school and community needs and desires.

Level One Outcomes

Aesthetics

By completion of grade five, students will:

- Recognize that certain human drives (religious fervor, the quest for beauty or prestige) continually motivate artistic expression, that common objects used in daily life, such as furniture and clothing, have been designed by artists, and that everyone makes visual decisions in daily life.

- Demonstrate knowledge of the persuasive function of visual art as it is used to promote beliefs or influence behavior, such as through advertisements or design of certain publications.

- Understand the impact that architectural forms, such as churches, shopping malls, restaurants and government buildings have on people's behavior.

- Indicate familiarity with art career opportunities represented by painters, sculptors, graphic artists, designers, craftsmen, photographers, architects, teachers, etc.

- Relate sensory elements and structural principles of the visual arts to other art forms, such as dance, music, drama, poetry and literature.

- Identify the effects of the elements in natural and man-made form (line, shape, color, hue, texture, perspective).

- Demonstrate an understanding of structural principles of natural and man-made form and be able to:
  - experiment with arrangements that illustrate various forms of rhythm and movement
  - experiment with arrangements that illustrate kinds of balance in two-dimensional and three-dimensional works, (e.g., symmetrical, asymmetrical)
  - employ a variety of sensory elements and structural principles in producing visual images

- Demonstrate knowledge of relationships in visual form and an open-mindedness which allows the student to:
  - value and assess the roles of visual art and artists in our society
  - demonstrate an appreciation of design and craftsmanship in man-made objects
  - seek out new art experiences and methods

- Exhibit appreciation of the visual arts through participation in:
  - school exhibits and contests
  - leisure time artistic endeavors
  - seeking new knowledge about art in books, magazines and newspapers
  - community art exhibitions, including museum offerings and the work of local artisans.

A5

Criticism: Making critical judgments

By completion of grade five, students will:
• Perceive and respond to visual qualities in both natural and man-made objects
• Focus attention on visual stimuli; the student will see rather than merely look
• Discriminate between original art and reproductions of art
• Develop a vocabulary of art terms
• Describe the sensory elements and structural principles in works of art
• Interpret visual imagery in works of art by:
    • identifying the feeling or mood derived from the work of art
    • discussing the meaning of subject matter and theme in works of art
    • describing how sensory elements and structural principles contribute to the expressive quality of a work of art
• Justify aesthetic judgments about individual work, that of peers and that of professionals, demonstrated in daily life.

History

By completion of grade five, students will:
• Be familiar with art of cultures throughout the world and be able to
    • identify major artists and their work
    • identify and describe major styles in the history of art
    • demonstrate an understanding that art reflects the relationship between artists and their culture
    • recognize the effect of technology on art
    • demonstrate familiarity with the arts and crafts of local, state and regional artisans and the development of their crafts

A5

Production

By completion of grade five, students will:
• Make choices of subjects and themes, independent of the views of others
• Produce imaginative and expressive visual images:
    • in response to specific subject matter
    • with a specified composition
    • with a particular function
    • which express particular feelings, moods or beliefs
• Use sensory elements in producing visual images which explore:
    • the qualities of line

Level Two Outcomes

Aesthetics

By completion of grade eight, students will:
• Exhibit increased aesthetic awareness and perception of visual and tactile qualities in works of nature, art, events and objects within the total environment
• Indicate ability to identify images and symbols in works of art, natural events, and objects within the total environment
• Demonstrate appreciation for images and symbols in works of art, natural events, and objects within the total environment
• Demonstrate an awareness and sensitivity to natural and human-made environments

- Evidence familiarity with applicable uses of design in the environment and society as a whole
- Show proficiency in categorizing various art forms exhibited in public forums
- Demonstrate an appreciation of their own art work, that of their peers and the art of recognized artists from past and present
- Discuss verbally and in written form concepts of art periods, schools of art, and definitions of art, applying:
  - informed judgment rather than personal opinion
  - skills involved in philosophical inquiry
  - aesthetic appreciation of sensory perception and response to art and the environment
  - critical thinking to a definition of what art is philosophically
- Evidence familiarity with various philosophers' ideas of how art may be an imitation or expression of feelings (expressionistic) or formed order (formalist) or usefulness (functionalist)

Criticism

By completion of grade eight, students will:
- Evaluate works of major artists, students and selves
- Analyze, compare and show relationships as a means of making informed judgments on works of art
- Interpret a work of art by referring to the subject matter, sensory elements, formal qualities and technical features in artwork
- Demonstrate the knowledge that interpretation is effected by understanding the artist, culture, and time period of the work
- Provide supporting reasons for interpretation of work including sensory, formal, technical, cultural, and historical reference
- Indicate a knowledge of some standards that have been used by critics to judge art, including expressiveness, originality, formal order, utility, content and craftsmanship
- Defend how a work of art can be judged by more than one standard
- Create and defend a judgment of a work of art

A5

History

By completion of grade eight, students will:
- Indicate a knowledge of historical and cultural developments which occur as a result of varying needs and aesthetic points of view, including:
  - a variety of artworks and accomplishments of contemporary, historic, and prehistoric cultures
  - the aesthetic values of a particular culture
  - contemporary and historical art as an integral part of all art experiences
  - an awareness of the nature and usefulness of art careers in society
- Evidence familiarity with the historical impact on contemporary artists in the local community and on public displays of art

Production

By completion of grade eight, students will:
- Demonstrate understanding of the importance of personal experiences and originality in their own visual expressions and in the art work of others by developing:
  - manipulative and organizational skills to use visual arts media effectively
  - inventive and imaginative skills to organize and depict ideas, feelings and moods
  - the ability to design items used in everyday living incorporating design elements and principles

- • the ability to make choices of subjects and themes independent of the views of others
- • Produce original works in such media as drawing and painting, constructing, printmaking, crafts, graphics, film animation, environmental and architectural design

Level Three Outcomes

Aesthetics

By completion of grade twelve, students will:
- • Identify specific characteristics in hue, line, shape, color, texture, dark and light (art elements) in increasingly sophisticated works of art
- • Analyze works of art to illustrate how the artist organizes and unifies the work so that all parts of the composition work together to express ideas and feelings
- • Identify an artistic medium (oil, paint, watercolor, colored pastels, charcoal, paper), artists' tools and equipment (brushes, drawing pencils, pens, printing press); and ways of working to produce the work (sketching, carving, painting, printing)
- • Respond to the expressive character of the work, that is, the feeling of the work

Criticism

By completion of grade twelve, students will:
- • Demonstrate increased ability to evaluate art from a variety of perspectives, forming opinions about personal artistic expression, that of peers and the work of past and present recognized artists
- • Demonstrate the ability to understand the difference between liking and judging works of art
- • Show proficiency in understanding the interpretation of artworks by recognized art critics and historians

- • Develop a vocabulary of art terms for describing art work and other visual compositions including the subject matter, theme, style and historical content in works of art
- • Analyze the relationship between expressive content in works of art and the cultural context of the work
- • Identify the relationships among design elements that give the work of art a particular emphasis, sense of unity and expressiveness

History

By completion of grade twelve, students will:
- • Evidence familiarity with a variety of world, national, regional and local art cultures by recognizing and describing:
  - • major styles in the history of art, (i.e., Impressionism, Cubism, and Pop)
  - • the diversity of art forms produced in cultures throughout the world
  - • similarities as well as differences in the art of various cultures, (e.g., similarities in form, material, function and style)
  - • the effect of technology on contemporary art, (i.e., the generation of electronic images, the emergence of new materials and methods)
- • Identify artists and artist periods along the historical timeline

Production

By completion of grade twelve, students will:
- • Create works of art that are imaginative and original, incorporating:
  - • choices of subjects and themes independent of the views of others
  - • design elements and principles in creating art in several media
  - • creative thought processes

- control of techniques that add craftsmanship to the personal statement (working from observation and imagination) in a variety of media
- Produce expressive visual images in response to specified subject matter which:
  - express particular feelings and moods
  - use exaggeration, abstraction and simplification
  - demonstrate developed skills and increased expressive ability gained through use of material tools and processes

EVALUATING THE ARTS

Evaluation for the student's total experience requires consideration of the individual's attitudes, aesthetic growth, understanding of art culture and heritage, and development of skill and work habits, as well as the quality of creative work.

Evaluation is more than the grading of a finished product. For example, it includes appraisal of the students' growth in self-evaluation. This ability develops as students become aware of their increased skill in the use of materials and continue to appreciate their unique modes of expression. Students should be able to use established criteria as well as to determine standards for evaluating or judging their own work. Using both methods of evaluation, they can see and understand their individual progress and growth.

In both objective and expressive evaluation, educators use a variety of formal and informal means: observation, demonstration, tests, discussion, self evaluation, check lists, portfolios, sketch books, exhibitions and group critiques.

Teacher Observation—Teachers make objective and subjective judgments based on their observations of student behavior, including attitudes, interests, enthusiasm, originality and independence.

Student Performance—Recording the results of students' demonstrated competence reveals their values, ability to perform a certain task, personal expression and ability to organize and express ideas and feelings. Performance tests can be written or completed through making an end product (e.g., painting, drawing).

Individual Inventories—Students' responses to an individual inventory reveal their preferences of attitudes toward learning activities.

Skill Tests—The results of skill tests make possible an assessment of student abilities to use specific skills, including both technical and physical skills and abilities to make aesthetic decisions based on these skills.

Objective Tests—Students' responses to oral or written questions demonstrate acquired knowledge.

Subjective Tests—Essay assignments encourage students to demonstrate their ability to think through problems, applying their total experience to the solution rather than merely repeating what they have been told.

Discussion—These discussions allow students to express orally their opinions, knowledge, and judgments.

Self-Evaluation—This process involves students in the assessment of their own progress and deserves special attention. Students need help in learning to assess accurately their own growth.

Checklist—These lists are used by the instructor to evaluate students' ability to perform outcomes.

Portfolios—Used to assess students' artistic performance of individual/or exit outcomes.

Sketchbook—This process demonstrates the students' daily responses to conceptualize and to express creativity.

Exhibitions—Students' responses demonstrate visually a command of material, organizational skills, and expressive abilities.

Group Critiques—This process involves student response to their and others' work in a sharing environment.

A5

A6

. . . .

Into Adolescence: Caring for Our Planet and Our Health, Grades 5–8

Contents

INTRODUCTION

Environmental issues hit the news almost every day—endangered species, oil spills, toxic waste, the hole in the ozone layer, destruction of the rain forests. Concern for the environment is often focused on our families, neighborhoods and regions, but the issues are played out globally.

A major goal for our time is that each individual understand that he or she can make a difference by taking an active role in protecting the planet from further destruction.

Thinking at a global level is a useful and exciting intellectual activity, but no substitute for the work needed to solve practical problems at home. If we really want to contribute to the welfare of humankind and of our planet, the best place to start is in our own community, and its fields, rivers, marshes, coastlines, roads, and streets, as well as with its social problems (Rene Dubos, 1981, in Samuels, M. and Bennett, H.Z., *Well Body, Well Earth* [San Francisco: Sierra Club Books, 1983], 199).

Encouraging young adolescents to accept this individual responsibility is the purpose of this curriculum. Young people must respect the natural environment in which they live and understand that their well-being and that of the planet are intertwined. Youth who develop environmentally sound habits will become adults who create policies and practices that nurture the earth rather than exploiting its resources.

Through the collective efforts of individuals, it is possible to reverse this trend of natural destruction, which had already begun in 1855, as described in this letter from Chief Sealth of the Lakota Sioux Duwamish Tribe of Washington state to President Franklin Pierce in 1855.

Every part of the earth is sacred to my people. Every shining pine needle, every sandy shore, every mist in the dark woods, every clearing and humming insect is holy in the memory and experience of my people. The white man . . . is a stranger who comes in the night and takes from the land whatever he needs. The earth is not his brother but his enemy and when he has conquered it, he moves on. . . . All things share the same breath—the beasts, the trees, the man. . . . What is man without the beasts? If all the beasts were gone, men would die from great loneliness of spirit, for whatever befalls the earth befalls the sons of earth. . . . The whites too shall pass—perhaps sooner than other tribes. Continue to contaminate your bed, and you will one night suffocate in your own waste. When the buffalo are slaughtered, the wild horses all tamed, the secret corners of the forest heavy with the scent of many men, and the view of the ripe hills blotted by talking wires, where is the thicket? Gone. Where is the eagle? Gone. And what is it to say good-bye to the swift pony and the hunt, the end of living and the beginning of survival (Ehrlich, A. H. and Ehrlich, P. R., *Earth* [New York: Franklin Watts, 1987], 161).

Into Adolescence: Caring for Our Planet and Our Health is oriented toward informing students about the global environmental crisis we face, their implications for human health and what each of us can do to protect our planet.

Overview

Into Adolescence: Caring for Our Planet and Our Health is written for middle school students, grades 5-8, with two goals. The first is to enable students to study environmental issues in relation to their own health and well-being. The second is to motivate students to take personal responsibility for doing what they can to protect the environment in order to sustain life and to improve human health.

This module is not intended to be comprehensive. It does not cover all the pressing environmental issues we face in all their complexity. The module is deliberately focused on a few issues that will interest young adolescents. They are issues where students can make a difference, as well as issues that lend themselves to enjoyable activities. Our hope is that students will begin to be aware of environmental issues and initiate lifelong habits of protecting the earth.

The link between environmental issues and personal health is often obvious, as in the case of air pollution leading to respiratory diseases or polluted drinking water leading to cancer. But sometimes the link will be less obvious to students.

For example, wasting water does not make one immediately ill, but the effect of ultimately running out of water would kill us all. Likewise, creating more garbage than can be disposed of doesn't seem, on the face of it, to be related to health. What is in garbage—and how it's disposed of—are the health issues.

The second goal, that of feeling personal responsibility for the environment, must be tied to a sense of efficacy—that one's individual action will make a difference. Each lesson stresses the exponential growth of individual action and encourages students to examine what they can do on both individual and group levels.

The lessons include opportunities to assess current situations at school or at home (how much garbage is created in one day, how much water is used, etc.). After investigation, students decide what individual action they can take to change the situation. Students also have options to take on class projects, for example, to reduce indoor air pollution at school.

The first lesson introduces the goals of the curriculum and the importance of individual action in caring for our planet and our health. Students study newspaper articles about current environmental issues and are encouraged to share what they know about the environment.

In Lesson 2, students monitor their water use for a day and figure the total gallons of water used by the class in one day. This figure is expanded to indicate water use in the larger community, so students can understand the importance of water conservation. The activities in this lesson encourage a personal commitment to actions that conserve water.

Lesson 3 continues the theme of personal responsibility for the environment with a student assignment to collect all personal garbage for a day. Class activities urge students to examine the links between their personal garbage, the environment and health. Students make a commitment to personal action to reduce the amount of garbage they generate.

The next lesson deals with air pollution. Students survey sources of air pollution at home or at school and commit to an action to help reduce air pollution.

A6

Lesson 5 broadens the focus from local aspects of environmental issues to global issues. Students are introduced to the important environmental resource of rain forests. Once again, students commit to personal actions they can take that can help save rain forests.

For the final lesson, students are encouraged to review the commitments they've made during the module and assess their progress toward an environmental ethic. Students then create their own pictures of a healthy planet.

Encourage Personal Commitment

Throughout the lessons, students should be told to save the commitments they make to environmental actions. The worksheets with these commitments are titled **My Part in** . . . You may want to encourage students to keep a special notebook or a special section in their binders for these worksheets.

At the completion of the module, these worksheets will provide students a record of their goals for environmental action. Encourage students to keep the worksheets as a reference even after the module is completed. These commitments can remind students of the importance of individual action in caring for our planet and our health.

If you have a science background, or can team-teach with someone who does, *Caring for Our Planet and Our Health* could be expanded to cover the issues of acid rain, ozone depletion and the greenhouse effect in more detail. Be sure to emphasize students' ability to have an effect on these seemingly overwhelming problems.

Objectives

Lesson 1	*Caring for Planet Earth*	Students will be able to define important environmental terms.
Lesson 2	*The Water We Need*	Students will be able to list three ways in which water is important to the life of human beings and to the earth.
		Students will be able to describe ways they can personally conserve water.
Lesson 3	*Too Much Garbage*	Students will be able to list three ways to manage garbage.
		Students will be able to describe ways in which they can reduce the amount of garbage at school or at home.
Lesson 4	*Clean Air, Please*	Students will be able to describe sources of indoor and outdoor air pollution.
		Students will be able to describe some health consequences of air pollution.
		Students will be able to identify action steps to reduce or prevent indoor air pollution at home or at school.
Lesson 5	*Save the Rain Forests*	Students will be able to explain why rain forests are important to human beings around the world.
		Students will be able to identify consequences of the destruction of rain forests.
		Students will be able to identify personal actions to help save the rain forests.
Lesson 6	*Protecting Our Planet*	Students will be able to identify ways they can help care for the environment.

Time

The time indicated for each lesson is an approximate measure, based on a 45–50 minute class period. The actual time required to complete all activities in a given lesson will vary, depending on student interest and ability. Lessons that will probably require more than [one period] to complete are indicated.

A6

Instructional Strategies

Throughout this module, students explore environmental issues in their own lives, and pledge through self-contracts to take action to create change. Students should be encouraged to collect these pledges and review their efforts periodically.

The module incorporates a variety of instructional strategies to develop and maintain student motivation and interest at peak levels. Some of the strategies are traditional, while others are more interactive, encouraging students to help each other learn. The specific strategies used in each lesson are clearly identified. An alphabetical list of instructional strategies and their descriptions follow:

Brainstorming   Overhead Transparencies
Class Discussion   Teacher Lecture
Cooperative Learning Groups   Worksheets
Creative Expression

Brainstorming

Brainstorming is used to stimulate discussion of an issue or topic. Students are asked to give their ideas and opinions without comment or judgment from the teacher or other students. Ideas can be listed on the chalkboard, on butcher paper or newsprint, or on a transparency. Brainstorming should continue until all ideas have been exhausted or a predetermined time limit has been reached.

Class Discussion

A class discussion led by the teacher is one of the most valuable strategies used in education. It can be used to initiate, amplify or summarize a lesson. Most of the lessons in this module include some form of class discussion.

Cooperative Learning Groups

Cooperative learning is one of the most common and effective strategies used in this module. Students work in small groups to disseminate and share information, analyze ideas or solve problems. The size of the group depends on the nature of the lesson and the make-up of the class. Groups work best with two to six members.

Group structure will affect the success of the lessons. Groups can be formed by student choice, random selection or a more formal, teacher-influenced process. Groups seem to function best when they represent the variety and balance found in the classroom. Groups also work better when each student has a responsibility within the group (reader, recorder, timer, reporter, etc.).

While groups are working on their tasks, the teacher should move from group to group, answering questions and dealing with any problems that arise. At the conclusion of the group process, some closure should take place.

Creative Expression

Asking students to write short stories or poems or make drawings or collages about topics they are studying integrates language arts, fine arts and personal experience into a lesson. This technique can be used as a follow-up to most lessons.

Overhead Transparencies

Overhead transparencies are an effective visual aid to use in presenting information and graphic examples. Most of the lessons in this module provide teacher resources that can be used as transparencies.

Teacher Lecture

A traditional teacher lecture disseminates information directly from the teacher to students. In some lessons, this approach is the best way to provide information. Generally, this method is combined with other methods to assure high-level motivation and learning.

A6

Worksheets

Most lessons in this module include worksheets. Students may be asked to complete the worksheets individually or in cooperative learning groups. Some worksheets include an activity to be completed outside of class. Completed worksheets should generally be reviewed with the whole class to provide relevant and timely feedback.

Make It Real

The natural environment is a critical and dynamic part of our social and political world. There are individuals at all levels within your community who are concerned about environmental issues. You can make this unit more real to students by inviting guest speakers to visit your class and share their experiences and concerns. Again, such local visitors can help make global issues more relevant by explaining the link to the local situation.

LESSON 2—THE WATER WE NEED

Objectives

Students will be able to list three ways in which water is important to the life of human beings and to the earth.

Students will be able to describe ways they can personally conserve water.

Time   Two class periods

Overview

When students understand the impact of human beings' use of water, they are better able to see the importance of conservation. To begin this lesson, students monitor their water use for a full day. They then figure the total number of gallons of water they have used. Total water use for the class is calculated from these figures.

The impact of our water use becomes obvious when the class's total water use is expanded to the school and the community. Students also discuss the importance of water to health. Students make a commitment to conserve water and suggest ways to encourage others to conserve also.

Instructional Strategies

Brainstorming, class discussion, worksheets.

Teacher Materials and Preparation

HAVE:
- √ Overhead projector.
- √ Transparency marker.

COPY:
- √ **One Day of Water Use** worksheet, one for each student.
- √ **Tips for Saving Water** worksheet, one for each student.
- √ **My Part in Water Conservation** worksheet, one for each student.
- √ **Wasting Water** experiments, copies of each of four experiments to distribute to student volunteers or to as many students as you choose (optional).

MAKE:
- √ Transparency of **One Day of Water Use Example.**
- √ Transparency of **One Day of Water Use** worksheet (blank).

REVIEW:
- √ The Water We Need *Teacher Background Information.*

A6

Procedure

Begin a class discussion of the importance of water to living things—human beings, animals, plants. Use Teacher Background Information as a guide for this discussion.

Distribute the One Day of Water Use worksheet. Tell students they will be keeping track of all the water they use for a 24-hour period—at school, home or anywhere else, tallying each type of use. *Note:* Handle this assignment with sensitivity, as some students could be embarrassed about certain items on the worksheet. Assure students that information about personal habits will be kept confidential. Tell students **not** to write their names on the worksheets.

Show students the One Day of Water Use Example transparency, and explain the assignment. Each time they use water, students should make a tally mark in the *Times* column of the worksheet next to that type of water use.

When students have charted their water use for 24 hours, they should calculate their total water use for each activity. Tell students to multiply the number of tallies they marked for each use by the number of gallons in the middle column. The result will indicate the total number of gallons of water they used in each category.

Students should then add the number of gallons they used in each category to find their total water use for the 24 hours. Ask if there are any questions about the worksheet. Tell students to bring the completed worksheet to the next class. Stress that the worksheets are *anonymous*; students should *not* write their names on them.

When students have completed the **One Day of Water Use** assignment, have them turn in the completed, unsigned worksheet. Ask one or two students to quickly tally all the worksheets to obtain classroom totals for each type of water use. Have these students fill in a blank transparency of the **One Day of Water Use** worksheet with the class totals for each type of use.

Show the class the filled-in transparency, and add up the total gallons used by the class. Mark this number on the transparency.

Multiply that number by the number of students in the school, then by the number of people in your town or city, etc. Ask students, "Is it possible for human beings to use up all the water there is on Planet Earth?"

Discuss the importance of water conservation, using the following questions to guide the discussion:

Imagine a day without water. What would that be like?

How much of the water you used in a day was wasted water, like letting water run while you brushed your teeth?

What is water conservation, and why is it important?

What is the relationship between water conservation and your health?

Distribute the **Tips for Saving Water** worksheet. Have students read the suggestions, then brainstorm more ideas to add to the list of tips.

Ask students to brainstorm some ways to change the water-use habits of their friends and families. How could they convince other people to conserve?

Optional: Suggest that students do some research on how much water is wasted in homes. Review the four **Wasting Water** experiments with students, and ask for volunteers to conduct each experiment. Ask students to report their findings to the class at a later session.

(These experiments were adapted from *50 Simple Things Kids Can Do to Save the Earth,* published by the EarthWorks Press, Berkeley, CA. Copyright 1990.)

Distribute the **My Part in Water Conservation** worksheet. Have students complete it in class or as homework.

Evaluation

Ask students to list (in class or as homework) three reasons water is important to us and one way in which conserving water relates to our health.

A6

Assess students' responses on the **My Part in Water Conservation** worksheet for their knowledge of water conservation techniques.

The Water We Need
Teacher Background Information

Why is water important to us?

About two-thirds of our bodies is water. Water covers three-quarters of the earth's surface. Water is essential to maintaining life; it is the basic source of all hydrogen and oxygen, the chemical foundation of all energy and life.

Not only is water necessary to us to live. We also use it to bathe and swim in, and to cook, clean dishes and wash clothing. Water is used for energy and transportation. Many, many creatures live in water. Without their watery habitats, these creatures would die.

What is water conservation and why is it important?

Water conservation means *careful* use of the water we need for our survival, whether it be water for drinking or water in rivers, oceans and lakes that sustains other life forms. Every time we turn on the faucet, fresh water flows out from reserves in the ground and from rivers and streams.

In the Middle Ages, most people probably used about 3 to 5 gallons of water a day. In the 1800s, that amount jumped to about 95 gallons a day in the West. Today, in the United States, water use for recreation, cooling, food production and industrial supply equals about 1,500 gallons a day per person. However, each of us *could* live on a gallon or so of water a day for drinking, cooking and washing—although we seldom do.

Conserving water saves energy and preserves fresh-water habitats. So much water is already diverted from rivers and lakes to meet the demands of farming, industry and personal water use. This diversion is particularly necessary in areas of the country where there is an insufficient water supply, such as the Southwest.

Water diversion often leads to the destruction of wildlife. When rivers shrink, fish can no longer follow their normal paths of migration to spawn and may fail to reproduce. Diminishing water also destroys animal habitats in wetlands.

When ground water is the source of our water supply and is used faster than it is replenished, it can cause land to sink, a process called subsidence. Once subsidence occurs, the underground aquifers where water is stored cannot be reformed. According to the U.S. Geological Survey, 35 states are pumping ground water faster than it is being replenished.

How can we conserve water?

Individuals can make a difference in solving the problems of water waste. By conserving water in the home, the average household can save more than 30,000 gallons of water per year.

One Day of Water Use
Example

Directions: Keep a record of how much water you use in one day. From the time you get up in the morning until you go to bed at night, put a tally mark next to each type of water use every time you do it.

Then count the tallies for each type of water use. Multiply the number of times for each use by the number of gallons indicated in the center column. Write the total gallons for each use in the right-hand column. Then add this column to find the total number of gallons of water you used in one day.

Bring the completed worksheet to class to turn in. No name, please. The information is all that is needed.

A6

Type of water use	Times	Gallons each time	Total gals.
1. Take a shower	/	30 gal.	30
2. Take a bath		36 gal.	
3. Brush teeth, tap running	//	5 gal.	10
4. Flush toilet	//// ////	6 gal.	48
5. Wash hands, tap running	///// /////	2 gal.	20
6. Use dishwasher	/	16 gal.	16
7. Use washing machine		60 gal.	
8. Wash car		10 gal. per min.	
9. Water yard or garden		12 gal. per min.	
10. Get a drink of water, tap running	///// /	1 gal. (includes washing glass)	6
11. Prepare and cook food	/	2 gal.	2
Total gallons used in one day			132

Tips for Saving Water

Don't let the water run while you're brushing your teeth or washing your face or hands. Wet your tooth-brush, washcloth or hands. Then turn off the water while you scrub. Turn the water back on to rinse.

Convince your family or the school administration to put something in the toilet tank to save water when the toilet is flushed. You can buy a water displacement device or use a plastic bottle filled with water. Don't flush the toilet each time you use it.

Take a shower instead of a bath. A shower can use about one-third as much water as a bath if you have a low-flow shower head and keep the shower short. Cut down the amount of time you spend in the shower, and don't turn on the water full-blast.

Ask about installing a low-flow shower head in your shower.

Check faucets, toilets and pipes for leaks. One small leak can waste 20 gallons of water a day. A leaky toilet can waste as much as 100 gallons of water a day!

Don't let the water run to cool the water when you're thirsty. Keep a bottle of water in the refrigerator for a cool, refreshing drink.

If you have a yard, ask your family to water the garden or grass only when it needs it. Water in the early evening, so the hot sun doesn't evaporate the water.

If you wash a car, turn the water off when you're not using it. You can put a turn-off nozzle [on] the hose.

Don't run a washing machine or a dishwasher unless there is a full load. Use the energy-saving or short cycle switch on the machines if they have it.

Save the water that runs while you wait for hot water to start, and water plants with it.

Use a bowl filled with water to wash vegetables rather than running the water; then water plants with it.

Can you think of other ways to save water?

Wasting Water

Experiment 1—Meter Reader

Directions: One way to check for water leaks in toilets, sinks and pipes in a building or house is to check the water meter. Get someone to show you where the water meter is and how to read it.

Pick a time when no one will be using any water in the building. This should be a time when every-one is gone and no water is being used to run dishwashers or washing machines or water the yard.

Read the water meter before you leave, and write the number on the first line. Read the meter again when you return. Write that number on the second line. Compare the two numbers. If the numbers have changed, that means there's probably a leak somewhere in the building.

A6

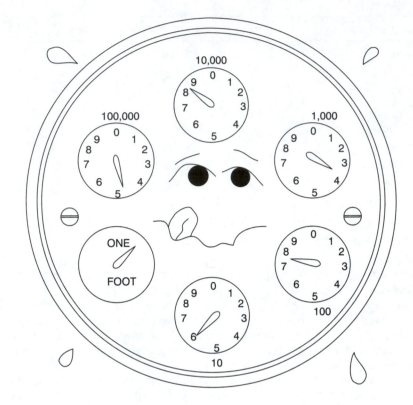

1. _____

   First reading

A6

2. _____

   Second reading

3. Do the numbers indicate that there is a leak?

Collaborative Teaching Experiences to Develop Communication Skills in Elementary School Children: Prekindergarten to Grade Five

Contents

PHILOSOPHY

Whole language, cooperative learning, peer tutoring and developmentally appropriate practices are promoting more verbally interactive classrooms. These educational practices help all children in the elementary school to develop better speech and language skills. While this is better for all students, emphasis on verbal interaction may place increased expectations on speech and language impaired children. Therefore, it is essential that the T.S.L.I.* become more involved in the classroom in order to expand language while it is occurring. This allows the therapist to facilitate the language impaired students and encourage communication skills for all students in the most realistic educational setting, the classroom. This document includes sample lesson plans for collaborative teaching. They are designed for use as large and small group activities in the classroom setting. These activities provide the opportunity for the speech and language impaired child to model from their normally developing peers.

From *Collaborative Teaching Experiences to Develop Communication Skills in Elementary School Children: Prekindergarten to Grade 5* (1992). Available from Speech and Language Department, Jackson County Intermediate School District, Jackson, MI 49201. Reprinted by permission.

*Teacher of speech-language impaired (therapist)

CHANGING ROLES

The T.S.L.I.'s role in public schools is changing to include more consultation with regular and special education teachers.

The most successful model for consultation is that of being a collaborator and joint problem solver. The basic principles for collaborative teaching/consultation are:

1. The classroom teacher is the individual who has the opportunity to implement and reinforce new language and communication skills for children.

2. The T.S.L.I. can help to implement language skills by providing expertise to the classroom teacher and assisting children in attaining the necessary language skills for school success.

COLLABORATIVE TEACHING MODEL

A collaborative teaching model can vary greatly and depends upon individual teaching and interactional styles. There are times when the classroom teacher may take the lead with support from the therapist. At other times, the therapist may lead a lesson while the classroom teacher takes part of the group or supports the lesson being taught.

Consultation/collaboration is successful when both the T.S.L.I. and teacher are committed to the process. Joint teaching also requires careful planning and a flexible approach.

The classroom teacher and the T.S.L.I. should:

1. establish a joint foundation upon which to work. The teacher will want to share classroom instructional goals and the T.S.L.I. will want to share individual/group communication goals for the students.

2. determine a scheduled time for planning and reviewing lessons.

3. discuss basic rules of the classroom and the individual teacher's classroom management style.

EVALUATING LANGUAGE PROCESSES IN THE CLASSROOM SETTING

The most valuable tool for evaluating student's progress in the classroom is observation. The general focus of the observation is the child's overall functioning in the classroom. The teacher and therapist are specifically interested in seeing the students utilize the following communication skills:

1. making requests
2. following and giving directions
3. asking and answering questions
4. carrying on a conversation
5. speaking alone in the presence of a group
6. offering information
7. remaining on a discussion topic

The therapist's checklist on the next page helps to provide a framework for evaluating communication skills in the classroom.

The T.S.L.I. may observe the child's language functioning in a variety of settings including the therapy room, classroom, home, playground, etc. Standardized testing supports observational findings and adds to the total educational evaluation.

Recording Progress

The clinician's log form is used to document the child's ongoing progress and the number of therapy sessions held during the year.

A7

CLASSROOM OBSERVATION FORM FOR COMMUNICATION SKILLS
(√ if skill is observed)

NAME _____   DATE_____

CLASSROOM TEACHER_____   T.S.L.I._____

_____   attends to teachers/students and classroom activities

_____   communicates needs, wants, desires

_____   gives appropriate responses to questions, commands or directions

_____   uses language for a variety of purposes (e.g., naming/requesting, rejection, greeting/answering, possession, location)

_____   participates in conversational turn-taking activities

_____   reports, answers, initiates in the presence of small/large groups

_____   recalls a series of events

_____   remains on discussion topic

_____   offers information, states an idea and generates meaningful communication

_____   demonstrates appropriate sentence structure

_____   demonstrates adequate articulation

_____   demonstrates adequate vocabulary

_____   demonstrates adequate voice/fluency control

COMMENTS:

WORKING IN THE CLASSROOM

There are two important components for teaching shared language lessons in the classroom. The first component of a good language lesson is the T.S.L.I.'s ability to adapt to the philosophy, style and personality of the individual classroom teachers. The second component is use of good communication strategies.

Programs currently utilizing these components are the:

High Scope Foundation
Transactional Intervention Program
K-T.A.L.K.—Kindergarten Teacher Language Administered Kit
T.A.L.K.—Teaching Activities for Language Knowledge

The following section on Communication Strategies uses concepts from the above programs as well as new ideas implemented by the T.S.L.I.s in Jackson County.

COMMUNICATION STRATEGIES

The T.S.L.I. and the classroom teacher maintain a heightened awareness of the students' total functioning and their communication skills.

The collaborative teaching team uses observation to understand the children's discussions and interactions while they are involved in the activities. Throughout these activities, the students spontaneously demonstrate their level of language functioning.

Awareness
The definition of silence, observation, understanding and listening used by the High Scope Foundation are:

silence—as a first step be silent and follow the child's lead

A7

observation—observe with a focus

understanding—be sensitive to what you have seen and develop a plan of action based on your observations

listening—listen carefully and wait for the child to finish whatever he/she is saying

Interaction

The process of interaction begins after the teaching team is aware of the children, their developmental levels and their interactive style. The teacher/T.S.L.I. may discuss what they are doing (self-talk), describe what the children are doing (labeling) and repeat what the children have said (clarification).

The teacher or T.S.L.I. listens to the students, taking turns in conversation while expanding upon and extending the elements of the discussion. Adults often add new ideas and thoughts into the conversation responding as evocateurs as opposed to provocateurs. In other words, adults are ready to change their styles of interaction according to the student's language needs and personality.

The transactional objectives listed below describe the basic steps of interaction:

Observe the child

Match their developmental level

Match the child's interests

Take turns with the child

Match the child's behavioral style

Expand and extend the child's use of language

Increase the length of turn-taking episodes in conversation

Open-ended Questions

The team uses questions in group activities that are open-ended or divergent whenever possible. Open-ended questions stimulate more language and creative thinking and encourage a variety of solutions. Some examples of open-ended questions include:

1. What do you think of. . . . . ?
2. Where could the child be. . . . . ?
3. How do you think that might work. . . . . ?
4. Why. . . . .?

A complete list of open-ended questions is listed in Appendix A. These communication techniques help the adults to become better listeners and become more involved in children's play or work. The adults communicate with the child at his/her developmental level. Within the framework of the activity the interests of the child are primary. This style of interaction facilitates language and conceptual growth.

A7

COLLABORATIVE CLASSROOM ACTIVITIES

The following are sample activities that can be used for collaborative teaching. The success of these activities is dependent on the joint planning that takes place. Some questions to consider in joint planning are:

1) Whose responsibility is it to gather the necessary materials?

2) Who will introduce the activity? (How will the lesson be supported?)

3) Who will divide the students into groups and determine the number of groups and the size of each group? A class of 24 students may have:

a) 2 groups of 12 students

b) 4 groups of 6 students

c) 6 groups of 4 students

4) How much time will be needed for the activity?

5) How is this integrated into the total curriculum?

ACTIVITY #3

TITLE: Cooperative Quotes

DESCRIPTION: Each group will have to decide how parts of a sentence fit together.

POSSIBLE OUTCOME:

Students will be working cooperatively as well as reading and constructing a sentence.

MATERIALS:

1) Variety of construction paper shapes with written words on each shape to form a sentence.

| The | Cat | Is | Black |

2) You may use cut out bears, stars, hearts, anything you want.

3) Cooperation sentences that may be used:

    a) Cooperation means we are all in this together.
    b) Cooperation means we like to share.
    c) Cooperation means we care about each other.

INTERACTION STYLE:

Small group - Whole group

INTRODUCTION:

1) Break the children up into cooperative groups.

2) Hand the groups their shapes and tell them their job is to decide how the parts of the sentence will fit together.

3) When each group is finished with a sentence, someone from their group may write the sentence on the chalkboard.

Each group will be responsible for working together in their group to decide how the parts of the sentence will go together.

DISCUSSION:

Each group will read their sentences aloud to the rest of the class. Each group will discuss how they worked together to figure out the sentences.

EXTENSION:

This same idea can be used with reading or spelling words. Match opposites, compound words or word definitions. This activity can also be used for sequencing steps in a recipe or parts of a story.

ACTIVITY #10

TITLE: Thingamajigs

DESCRIPTION: Learn about good and bad manners.

POSSIBLE OUTCOME:

Development of nouns, verbs, adjectives, concepts, rhymes and proper social manners.

MATERIALS:

Suggested reading is "The Thingamajigs Book of Manners" by Irene Keller.

| socks | feathers |
| buttons | netting |

A7

lace	scraps of materials
curly ribbon	yarn
ribbons	ric rac
hot glue guns	ice cream
toppings	

INTERACTIVE STYLE:
Whole group/small group/centers

INTRODUCTION:
Discuss with whole group "What are good manners/bad manners?"
Read and discuss "The Thingamajig Book of Manners" by Irene Keller. Show a finished "thingamajig" puppet. Talk about breaking into centers to make a "thingamajig" sock puppet. Encourage creativity.

PROCEDURE: Break into centers to make sock puppets:
1) Eyes, nose, mouth center

2) Hair center

3) Extra trimmings for elaboration

4) Hot glue center

DISCUSSION:
Share finished puppets with whole group.

EXTENSION:
1) Each child uses his/her puppet to share a good manner with the teacher. The teacher writes it down and creates a classroom book of good manners.

2) Invite another class in and have an ice cream social to provide opportunities for proper etiquette techniques.

THE BEST WAY TO TEACH: BE RESPONSIVE!*

In most classrooms, adult/child interaction styles and strategies are inconsistent with a developmental approach and our understanding of how to optimize engagement and developmental growth for young children.

An alternative to the directive approach is the Responsive model of interaction. This responsive approach is a nondidactic, child-oriented style in which the adult follows the child's interests and activities.

Research studies indicate that when adults are responsive to and supportive of children's interests, they learn that their behavior is accepted and valued. This results in feelings of confidence and high self-esteem. The child is also likely to feel a sense of control over his surroundings, and this sense of control is likely to lead the child to confidently explore familiar and novel aspects of his environment.

This approach may also work because adults are playing with children at rather than above their developmental level. It is believed that only activities and interactions that are within the range of the child's developmental functioning will contribute to the developmental growth. Further research supporting the responsive approach includes:

• Children perform best on measures of social, cognitive and language development when in child-care environments in which caregivers are characterized as warm, responsive, and where children are allowed to engage in self-initiated activity.

*Wolock, Ellen. (1990). *The Relationship of Teacher Interactive Style to the Engagement of Developmentally Delayed Preschoolers*. Doctoral Dissertation, University of Michigan, 1990.

A7

- Children also perform higher on measures of persistence and initiative when teachers are responsive and nonintrusive, and incorporate activities that are at the children's developmental level.

- This level of child involvement is extremely important as the extent to which children persist on tasks during play and teaching situations is correlated with developmental test scores. The most critical influence in facilitating children's involvement and engagement is a responsive adult/child relationship.

- Children of parents/teachers who enjoy their children and are oriented toward following and supporting their interests/behavior have been found to achieve higher scores on the Bayley Scales of Mental Development, than children of parents/teachers who were high controlling.

ACTIVE LEARNING CHECKLIST

This checklist assesses the degree to which an activity engages children in active learning. For each check mark, record specific examples to support your assessment.

1. Materials. Each child uses one or more of the following types of materials:

    _____ Real, functional, everyday objects
    _____ Found and natural materials
    _____ Tools
    _____ Messy, sticky, gooey, drippy, squishy materials
    _____ Heavy, large materials
    _____ Easy-to-handle materials
    _____ Own body

2. Manipulations. Children use materials in one or more of the following ways:

    _____ Exploring with all senses
    _____ Discovering relations through direct experience
    _____ Transforming and combining of materials
    _____ Acquiring skills with tools and equipment
    _____ Using the large muscles

3. Choices. Children make the following choices:

    _____ Which materials to use
    _____ What to do with materials
    _____ How to take care of their own needs

4. Language from children. Children talk about the following:

    _____ What they are doing
    _____ What is important to them
    _____ Their observations, thinking and reasoning

5. Support from adults. Adults do the following:

    Environment support

    _____ Provide a variety of materials to choose and use
    _____ Provide enough materials for each child
    _____ Provide enough space for children to use materials

    Nonverbal support

    _____ Watch what children do with materials
    _____ Imitate children's actions
    _____ Use materials themselves

A7

_____ Photograph children's actions
_____ Listen to what children say
_____ Put themselves on children's physical level
_____ Use their bodies to express interest
_____ Wait while children solve problems, care for needs
_____ Remain calm in the face of children's "mistakes"

Verbal support

_____ Acknowledge children's actions, choices
_____ Repeat children's language
_____ Converse with children about what children are doing
_____ Refer children to each other
_____ Encourage children to answer their own questions
_____ Ask children questions that relate to their play
_____ Accept children's answers and explanations
_____ Converse with nonverbal children

A7

Appendix B

· ·

The Program Evaluation Standards

The Program Evaluation Standards (Joint Committee on Standards for Educational Evaluation, 1994) are the focus of this appendix. First is a brief history of the *Standards,* followed by information on their possible uses in curriculum situations, and then a summary of the four standards.

Background of the Standards

Based on his work in the 1930s, Ralph Tyler advocated that educators should define objectives and gather data to see if these had been achieved, an approach that has remained important since its beginning (Joint Committee on Standards for Educational Evaluation, 1981). By the 1950s, standardized testing had become so important that the professional organizations concerned with assessment began to regulate the actions of their members. In 1954 the American Psychological Association (APA) prepared the first set of recommendations on psychological tests and diagnostic techniques. The next year the APA joined with the American Educational Research Association and the National Council on Measurements Used in Education to develop standards for educational and psychological tests. Updated versions of these standards, published in 1966, 1974, and 1985, were widely used in professional settings as well as the courts to evaluate tests and the uses of test scores (Stufflebeam, 1991).

The *Standards for Evaluations of Educational Programs, Projects, and Materials,* published in 1981, were the result of several years of work by a broad-based joint committee of persons representing 12 organizations. By 1989, however, the Joint Committee began the processes of revising the standards to make them applicable in broader contexts.

The Joint Committee that authored *The Program Evaluation Standards* is composed of members from the following groups who sponsor the standards:

American Association of School Administrators

American Educational Research Association

American Evaluation Association

American Federation of Teachers

American Psychological Association

Association for Assessment in Counseling

Association for Supervision and Curriculum Development

Canadian Society for the Study of Education

Council of Chief State School Officers

Council on Postsecondary Accreditation

National Association of Elementary School Principals

National Association of Secondary School Principals

National Council on Measurement in Education

National Education Association

National School Boards Association

Uses of the Standards

The *Standards* are applicable both in curricular needs assessments (see Chapter 9) and in evaluations of curriculum processes and products (see Chapter 13). Although the *Standards* are useful in many different situations, they are particularly pertinent in these situations:

- *Deciding whether to evaluate.* Should a special needs assessment be conducted? Is there sufficient value in doing an evaluation to spend the time, energy, and resources needed? Has the modified curriculum been in use long enough to merit an evaluation?

- *Defining the evaluation problem.* What are the questions that require answers in this particular curriculum situation?

- *Designing an evaluation.* Who should be involved in the evaluation? How should information be collected? How should collected information be analyzed to provide answers to the evaluation question?

- *Producing and communicating evaluation reports.* Who is involved in producing and communicating evaluation results? Who can make good use of evaluation information?

Summary of the Standards

The Joint Committee identified four important attributes of an evaluation: utility, feasibility, propriety, and accuracy. Using these attributes as a foundation, standards were developed that helped define each of these characteristics. Utility standards, for example, are concerned with whether an evaluation serves the practical information needs of a particular audience. The feasibility standards require that evaluations be "realistic, prudent, diplomatic, and frugal" (Joint Committee on Standards for Educational Evaluation, 1994, p. 63). The propriety standards require that evaluations be "conducted legally, ethically, and with due regard for the welfare of those involved in the evaluation, as well as those affected by the results" (Joint Committee on Standards for Educational Evaluation, 1994, p. 81). The accuracy standards are designed to ensure that an evaluation will reveal information for judging accurately the merit or worth of a program.

Figure B.1 contains a summary of the *Standards*. Readers who desire additional information should read the complete document, available in most university libraries.

Utility Standards

The utility standards are intended to ensure that an evaluation will serve the information needs of intended users.

U1   Stakeholder Identification Persons involved in or affected by the evaluation should be identified, so that their needs can be addressed.

U2   Evaluator Credibility The persons conducting the evaluation should be both trustworthy and competent to perform the evaluation, so that the evaluation findings achieve maximum credibility and acceptance.

U3   Information Scope and Selection Information collected should be broadly selected to address pertinent questions about the program and be responsive to the needs and interests of clients and other specified stakeholders.

U4   Values Identification The perspectives, procedures, and rationale used to interpret the findings should be carefully described, so that the bases for value judgments are clear.

U5   Report Clarity Evaluation reports should clearly describe the program being evaluated, including its context, and the purposes, procedures, and findings of the evaluation, so that essential information is provided and easily understood.

U6   Report Timeliness and Dissemination Significant interim findings and evaluation reports should be disseminated to intended users, so that they can be used in a timely fashion.

U7   Evaluation Impact Evaluations should be planned, conducted, and reported in ways that encourage follow-through by stakeholders, so that the likelihood that the evaluation will be used is increased.

Feasibility Standards

The feasibility standards are intended to ensure that an evaluation will be realistic, prudent, diplomatic, and frugal.

F1   Practical Procedures The evaluation procedures should be practical, to keep disruption to a minimum while needed information is obtained.

F2   Political Viability The evaluation should be planned and conducted with anticipation of the different positions of various interest groups, so that their cooperation may be obtained, and so that possible attempts by any of these groups to curtail evaluation operations or to bias or misapply the results can be averted or counteracted.

F3   Cost Effectiveness The evaluation should be efficient and produce information of sufficient value, so that the resources expended can be justified.

Propriety Standards

The propriety standards are intended to ensure that an evaluation will be conducted legally, ethically, and with due regard for the welfare of those involved in the evaluation, as well as those affected by its results.

P1   Service Orientation Evaluations should be designed to assist organizations to address and effectively serve the needs of the full range of targeted participants.

P2   Formal Agreements Obligations of the formal parties to an evaluation (what is to be done, how, by whom, when) should be agreed to in writing, so that these parties are obligated to adhere to all conditions of the agreement or formally to renegotiate it.

P3   Rights of Human Subjects Evaluations should be designed and conducted to respect and protect the rights and welfare of human subjects.

FIGURE B.1
Summary of the Program Evaluation Standards

P4   Human Interactions Evaluators should respect human dignity and worth in their interactions with other persons associated with an evaluation, so that participants are not threatened or harmed.

P5   Complete and Fair Assessment The evaluation should be complete and fair in its examination and recording of strengths and weaknesses of the program being evaluated, so that strengths can be built upon and problem areas addressed.

P6   Disclosure of Findings The formal parties to an evaluation should ensure that the full set of evaluation findings along with pertinent limitations are made accessible to the persons affected by the evaluation, and any others with expressed legal rights to receive the results.

P7   Conflict of Interest Conflict of interest should be dealt with openly and honestly, so that it does not compromise the evaluation processes and results.

P8   Fiscal Responsibility The evaluator's allocation and expenditure of resources should reflect sound accountability procedures and otherwise be prudent and ethically responsible, so that expenditures are accounted for and appropriate.

Accuracy Standards

The accuracy standards are intended to ensure that an evaluation will reveal and convey technically adequate information about the features that determine worth or merit of the program being evaluated.

A1   Program Documentation The program being evaluated should be described and documented clearly and accurately, so that the program is clearly identified.

A2   Context Analysis The context in which the program exists should be examined in enough detail, so that its likely influences on the program can be identified.

A3   Described Purposes and Procedures The purposes and procedures of the evaluation should be monitored and described in enough detail, so that they can be identified and assessed.

A4   Defensible Information Sources The sources of information used in a program evaluation should be described in enough detail, so that the adequacy of the information can be assessed.

A5   Valid Information The information gathering procedures should be chosen or developed and then implemented so that they will assure that the interpretation arrived at is valid for the intended use.

A6   Reliable Information The information gathering procedures should be chosen or developed and then implemented so that they will assure that the information obtained is sufficiently reliable for the intended use.

A7   Systematic Information The information collected, processed, and reported in an evaluation should be systematically reviewed and any errors found should be corrected.

A8   Analysis of Quantitative Information Quantitative information in an evaluation should be appropriately and systematically analyzed so that evaluation questions are effectively answered.

A9   Analysis of Qualitative Information Qualitative information in an evaluation should be appropriately and systematically analyzed so that evaluation questions are effectively answered.

A10   Justified Conclusions The conclusions reached in an evaluation should be explicitly justified, so that stakeholders can assess them.

A11   Impartial Reporting Reporting procedures should guard against distortion caused by personal feelings and biases of any party to the evaluation, so that evaluation reports fairly reflect the evaluation findings.

A12   Metaevaluation The evaluation itself should be formatively and summatively evaluated against these and other pertinent standards, so that its conduct is appropriately guided and, on completion, stakeholders can closely examine its strengths and weaknesses.

FIGURE B.1, *continued*

From *The Program Evaluation Standards: How to Assess Evaluations of Educational Programs,* 2nd ed. (pp. 23–24, 65–66, 81–82, 125–126) by the Joint Committee on Standards for Educational Evaluation, James R. Sanders, Chair, 1994. Thousand Oaks, CA: Sage. Reprinted by permission.

Appendix C

. . . .

Instrumentation for Curriculum Evaluation

This appendix extends information about instruments for data collection mentioned in Chapters 9 and 13. It also provides general information about the instruments' uses and construction. Even here, however, the information is not exhaustive. Readers interested in additional information should consult the references.

No matter which data collection strategy evaluators select, the processes involved in using the instrument and the data generated must satisfy the utility, feasibility, propriety, and accuracy criteria of the Joint Committee on Educational Evaluation (1994). These criteria are intended to insure that the evaluation will serve the information needs of the users; be realistic, prudent, diplomatic, and frugal; be conducted legally and ethically; and reveal and convey technically adequate information about the program being evaluated.

Data collection strategies can be classified in different ways depending on the purpose of classification. This discussion groups instruments according to degrees of intrusiveness or the amount of contact data collectors have with those from whom data are collected. Instruments are grouped in three categories ranging from most to least intrusive: interviews, observations, and tests/work products. Interviews usually involve one-to-one contact between the data collector who asks questions and the person who answers them. In observations data collectors place themselves in positions to witness actions taken by one or more persons from whom data are needed, but no contact is involved. In tests and work products respondents reveal their thoughts and feelings in forms (e.g., written, oral, visual) that are transmitted impersonally to data collectors.

Instrumentation categories have elastic boundaries because specific data collection techniques can be and are classified more than one way. For example, some performance tests result in work products, but others use observations requiring an audience and raters who score an actual performance (e.g., speeches, concerts). Some surveys are made in an interview format, but others result from group meetings as work products. Checklists can be used in tabulating observations or in self-reports of work. The three major classifications suggested here are just ways of organizing this discussion.

Interviews

Interviews are typically one-on-one situations where an individual asks questions to which a second individual responds. Interviewers may work from a script in which the questions are carefully worded and organized in sequence, or they ask questions spontaneously. The former situation is referred to as a focused or structured interview and the latter is unstructured (Rosenthal & Rosnow, 1991).

Focused (Structured) Interviews

The Levels of Use interview shown in Figure 13.1 furnishes sample focused-interview questions. So do the annual Phi Delta Kappa/Gallup polls mentioned in Chapter 2. Figure C.1 contains a sample question from the PDK/Gallup poll. In both cases the interviewer asks questions of the interviewee in a prescribed form to assure consistency in response opportunities for all individuals who are interviewed.

Questions in the PDK/Gallup poll are nonbranching, which is to say every respondent is asked the same question in the same order. In this poll the questions contain answer prompts for the interviewees. Some examples: "Do you favor or oppose such a program?" and "Which one of the following three approaches do you think is the best way . . . ?"

On the other hand, the Levels of Use interview uses branching questions in a given order. The interviewee's answer to one question determines the question to be asked next. The questions are also more open-ended than the Gallup poll questions, allowing the interviewer to probe responses that need elaboration.

Unstructured Interviews

In unstructured situations interviewers do not follow scripts. Although this format may allow for greater flexibility than the structured approach, keeping track of responses is more difficult. Especially where interviews are unstructured, interviewers usually record responses. Otherwise, they make extensive notes of the interviewee's comments. Even so, the results of unstructured interviews may be less reliable than those from structured question-and-answer sessions because the questions asked of one respondent can vary from those asked of others.

Unstructured interviews allow data collectors to gather a variety of information. In particular interviewers may ask questions about the interviewee's knowledge, beliefs, or feelings toward a particular curriculum situation. If the interviewer is inclined, s/he may use follow-up questions to which the interviewee supplies clarifying information.

The one-legged conferences that change facilitators have with teachers are classified as unstructured interviews. Chapter 13 suggests that these interviews begin with open-ended

---

Monoculturalism or Multiculturalism?

First question:

In your opinion, which should the public schools in your community promote—one common, predominant cultural tradition only, or both a common cultural tradition and the diverse cultural traditions of the different populations in America?

Second question asked of respondents who said that schools should promote both one common tradition and diverse traditions of different peoples:

Which one do you think should receive more emphasis—one common cultural tradition, diverse cultural traditions, or should both receive the same emphasis?

FIGURE C.1

Illustration of Structured Interview Questions

From S. M. Elam, L. C. Rose, & A. M. Gallup (1994). The 26th annual Phi Delta Kappa/Gallup poll of the public's attitudes toward the public schools. *Phi Delta Kappan, 76*(53). Copyright 1994 by Phi Delta Kappa. Reprinted by permission.

questions, such as, "How are things going with the revised curriculum?" Questions like these allow teachers to give positive or negative answers. They also permit interviewers to follow up with other questions that reveal more of how teachers feel about the curriculum and whether or not they are using it (Hall & Hord, 1987).

In constructing interviews evaluators should be aware of several guidelines. Evaluators should ensure that each question is relevant for its intended purpose; otherwise the question should be discarded. The sequence of questions is also important. Because respondents sometimes give similar answers to related questions, evaluators should avoid asking related questions in sequence. Questions should be worded so that their meanings are readily understood by all the respondents (Rosenthal & Rosnow, 1991).

No matter which interview approach is taken, data must usually be translated into a different form for analysis. Where possible and appropriate, evaluators code qualitative data into quantitative categories that permit aggregating responses from individuals. These tasks must be done carefully not only to preserve accuracy, but also to maintain the sense of the data. Uncodable data must be studied carefully to determine trends and appropriate generalizations.

Observations

Observations occur when data collectors are able to see or hear the people from whom data are needed, but no interactions take place among these individuals. Data collectors sometimes record responses to predetermined questions or place information in planned categories, making these structured observations. They may also record information spontaneously as unstructured observations.

Structured Observations

The first aspect of structure relates to categories of behaviors about which the data collector wants information. These categories may include demonstrations of abilities, skills, interests, values, or others. Each behavior is assumed to have at least two values. That is, the behavior is either shown or not shown. In these cases a **checklist** is an appropriate way of collecting data. Two different checklists are part of the curriculum project *Collaborative Teaching Experiences to Develop Communication Skills in Elementary School Children* (see A7).

In one case a Classroom Observation Form for Communication Skills is maintained for each student. The classroom teacher or therapist who observes a student demonstrating any of the communication behaviors checks the behavior shown. The second checklist focuses on active learning. Collectors are to mark any behavior demonstrated that corresponds to an example behavior on the list. By implication, then, evaluators assume that categories left unmarked mean that data collectors did not observe students demonstrating those behaviors.

Other structured observations make use of **rating scales** that provide indication of the degree to which a behavior is shown. Sometimes the different degrees of behavior are described in words, but in other scales degrees are noted with numbers or letters to which values are assigned. For example, the teachers who designed the English literature curriculum in Part 3 chapters might use a rating scale, a segment of which is shown in Figure C.2, to record performance of students' language skills. The extreme positions of this rating scale are behaviorally described, but raters can also mark students' performance at intermediate points. Gitomer (1993) says that scales discipline evaluation in form and function by structuring it within a common framework and reporting it on a common scale. Scales also reduce a complex performance to one or a limited set of numbers allowing evaluators to aggregate data for comparison purposes.

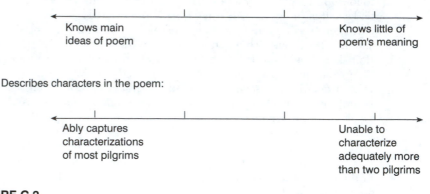

Tells what the poem is about:

Knows main
ideas of poem

Knows little of
poem's meaning

Describes characters in the poem:

Ably captures
characterizations
of most pilgrims

Unable to
characterize
adequately more
than two pilgrims

FIGURE C.2
Segment of a Rating Scale for Measuring Student Performance in the Nontechnical
Curriculum Project Using *The Canterbury Tales.*

Structured observations serve a variety of purposes in curriculum evaluation. They are particularly helpful in tracking student progress in skills acquisition. Checklists and rating scales are frequently used in assessments where the performance must be viewed while it is in progress such as in speeches, oral reading, auto repair demonstrations, and the like. Either form of recording observations usually also has a comments section for recording items that do not fit into categories.

Unstructured Observations

Anecdotal records provide a way of recording unstructured observations. Some data collectors simply make notes about what they see and hear. In either strategy the behaviors demonstrated are separated from interpretations of those behaviors. This distinction is important because observations should include what anyone viewing or hearing the situation would observe; interpretations bring the interpreter's values into the situation.

Unstructured observations can be beneficial in recording data in small-scale curriculum situations. However, these require a sizable investment in time, both for recording and interpretation. Therefore, using these methods in large-scale projects is improbable. Once data are gathered, these records must be organized to determine trends. Actual interpretation may involve content analyses which are described in the final subsection of this appendix.

Tests and Work Products

This category includes situations in which respondents provide responses indirectly to persons seeking data. Tests include both actual pencil-paper instruments as well as information recorded onto computer-scorable sheets or onto data files processed by computers. Work products encompass collections of student work, sets of rankings, survey results, and others.

A variety of behaviors can be evaluated with tests and work products including achievement, aptitude, preferences, and so on. Obviously tests are advantageous because data can be collected from many people at once. This means they are also relatively inexpensive to use. Tests measuring lower-level abilities are typically easy to score, but scoring those that measure higher-level abilities requires time and expertise. Work products usually require careful examination and sometimes expert judgments are necessary.

Tests

In the context of this discussion, tests provide product evaluators with data about student performance for determining the extent to which the curriculum is serving its intended purpose. As long as tests relate to purpose, they can be teacher-made or commercially published standardized tests, norm-referenced or criterion-referenced, and so on. Tests provide data for evaluating cognitive outcomes in any of several categories including verbal information, concept acquisition, and problem solving. Both lower- and higher-level thinking skills can be evaluated using tests. What tests have in common is the requirement that students respond to questions that produce data about their achievement of learning outcomes.

Usual test procedures assess student ability to answer "well-structured, unconditional, knowledge-lean tasks" (Gitomer, 1993, p. 245). "Well-structured" means that the question is clearly framed, information for its answer is recognizable, and procedures for moving from question to answer are clear. "Unconditional" means the problem interpretation is not subject to dependent considerations. "Knowledge-lean" indicates that limited external world knowledge is needed to solve the problem (Gitomer, 1993). Examples of questions fitting these conditions include the following:

- Name the states that share borders with Nebraska.
- Sodium hydroxide added to hydrochloric acid produces _?_ and _?_ . Or, stated as a chemical equation:

  $NaOH + HCl = $ _?_ $+$ _?_

Tests fitting this well-structured, unconditional, and knowledge-lean description often use a multiple choice format in which only one of the responses is the *correct* choice. This is the predominant format for standardized achievement tests. Such tests are excellent for measuring *lower* cognitive tasks.

Less structure and fewer prompts in test questions require students to use *higher* level cognitive abilities. For example, the Assessment of Performance Unit (APU) is a British national assessment effort that evaluates student performance in science using lifelike situations (Hein, 1991).

Figure C.3 shows a question that measures the abilities of older students to apply chemistry concepts in a real world situation. Note the open-endedness of the question and the dearth of answer prompts. To frame answers students must handle dependent considerations (e.g., environmental toxicity, wind conditions) and external world knowledge. They also must puzzle through their knowledge of the chemical composition of marble and the atmosphere to decide reasons. This question reflects many of the criteria for performance tests suggested by Wiggins (1993) and Eisner (1993).

Enhanced or justified multiple-choice test questions described in Chapter 13 provide information to curriculum evaluators about students' knowledge of relationships among events, reasoning, and other *higher order* thinking. Students actively generate their own knowledge in answering these questions.

Scoring tests that tap students' higher levels of thinking requires analytical skills by evaluators. In state assessment programs raters often use scoring rubrics that specify characteristics of the answers to be demonstrated at several levels of proficiency. Readers assign ratings to papers based on the degree to which they show characteristics of one of these levels. For example, Figure C.4 contains a rubric for scoring student responses to a state

FIGURE C.3

Example of an Open-Ended Performance Test Question

From "Active Assessment for Active Science" by G. E. Hein, (1991), In V. Perrone (Ed.), *Expanding Student Assessment* (p. 121). Alexandria, VA: Association for Supervision and Curriculum Development. Copyright 1991 by ASCD. Reprinted by permission.

Category 4: Applying Chemistry Concepts (Age 13)
A smooth marble fountain was built in the middle of the city.

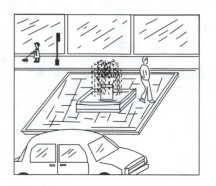

After several years, the surface was worn and covered with small holes.

Think of three reasons, other than damage by people, that could have caused the small holes to form.

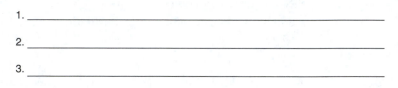

1. _____

2. _____

3. _____

assessment in mathematics. This instance describes four categories, but rubrics can have more or fewer classifications depending on the test designers.

Ranking Procedures

Ranking procedures include simple pencil-paper procedures used in group settings where individuals are expected to reach consensus on a set of rankings through discussion of the merits of the various items. Rankings typically display respondents' values toward the items in question. Figure 9.4 exemplifies this type of ranking procedure for program goals in a health curriculum.

Another procedure, called a **Q sort**, uses cards containing individual items and requires respondents to order these cards into a defined number of categories, ranging from most to least valued. The number of categories is decided in advance by the evaluator and depends on the number of items. With items on separate cards, respondents can freely experiment with rankings. After respondents complete their rankings, however, a collector must examine the particular card sort in order to record the data (Hill, 1986). Because of the time involved and the necessity for an evaluator to record individual results, Q sorts are valuable in situations where the number of respondents is relatively small.

Ranking procedures are typically used in needs assessments to collect perceptions of the importance or achievement of existing or intended goals and/or objectives according to the respondents' priorities. In successful procedures the number of items to be ranked is probably no more than seven or eight. Cognitive psychologists indicate that is about the maximum number of items that can be held in memory at any one time (Eggen &

Kauchak, 1994). Whether the items for ranking are goals, needs, or interests, here are principles for constructing the procedure:

- Use only one idea per item.
- State each idea in the simplest terms possible.
- Write items as free of values as possible.
- Give clear directions for answering (Hill, 1986).

Surveys

On other occasions data collectors use surveys to collect information from students, school staff, teachers, and community personnel. Surveys require responses on topics as diverse as the desirability of certain goals or needs/interests as bases for curriculum revisions, attitudes toward particular subject areas, or context factors in curriculum development. Surveys are methods of collecting information about the "same variables or characteristics from at least two (normally far more) cases and end up with a data matrix" (de Vaus, 1991,

---

4-Point Rubric:

A **4** response represents an effective solution. It shows complete understanding of the problem, thoroughly addresses all points relevant to the solution, shows logical reasoning and valid conclusions, communicates effectively and clearly through writing and/or diagrams, and includes adequate and correct computations and/or set up.

A **3** response contains minor flaws. Although it shows an understanding of the problem, communicates adequately through writing and/or diagrams, and generally reaches reasonable conclusions, it shows minor flaws in reasoning and/or computation or neglects to address some aspect of the problem.

A **2** response shows gaps in understanding and/or execution. It shows one or some combination of the following flaws: an incomplete understanding of the problem, failure to address all aspects of the problem, faulty reasoning, weak conclusions, unclear communication in writing and/or diagrams, or a poor understanding of relevant mathematical procedures or concepts.

A **1** response shows some effort beyond restating the problem or copying given data. It shows some combination of the following flaws: little understanding of the problem, failure to address most aspects of the problem, major flaws in reasoning that lead to invalid conclusions, or a lack of understanding of relevant mathematical procedures or concepts.

Assign a **0** if the response shows no understanding of the problem or if the student fails to respond to the item.

Assign **N/S** (Not Scorable) if the response is illegible or written in a language other than English.

FIGURE C.4

Sample Rubric for Scoring Mathematics Examinations

From *Arizona Student Assessment Program Mathematics Scoring Guide.* 1993, p. 2. Copyright 1993 by The Riverside Publishing Company. Reprinted by permission.

p. 3). A data matrix is a simple table with cases (responses from different people) listed on the horizontal and variables (different survey questions) listed on the vertical dimension. The data or responses gathered from the people are recorded within this table.

As an example, a survey could assist a school board in gathering information from parents about the numbers and descriptions of children and youth for whom curricula must be planned. Households representing the cases and questions related to numbers of children and youth and their descriptions (e.g., grade levels, primary language) would be listed on the horizontal and vertical dimensions of the matrix. Information actually gathered from the community would be placed in the body of the table. With such information data analysts could tabulate the number of students by grade levels, by primary language spoken or other characteristics. With such information curriculum developers could realistically plan appropriate programs.

Surveys may be conducted in interview situations, but more frequently they are administered as **opinionnaires** to large groups in meetings or mailed to participants. Theoretically, surveys can contain any number of questions or statements; however, people are generally inclined to answer surveys that have fewer rather than more questions. Responses may use a Likert-type scale where individuals mark degrees of agreement with statements, such as "I enjoy doing word problems in mathematics" or "Writing poems is my least favorite activity in language arts." Usually these degrees correspond to five scale points: "strongly agree," "agree," "neutral," "disagree," and "strongly disagree." When students are too young to understand these terms, the scale may contain a series of pictures such as those shown in Figure C.5. Each scale point or picture has a numerical value of 1–5, determined by the evaluator. For example, either 1 or 5 could be assigned to the "strongly agree" scale point. This scoring plan allows evaluators to aggregate and analyze results using quantitative methods.

Portfolios

Portfolios are purposeful collections of students' work that exhibit effort, progress, and achievements. "The collection must include student participation in selecting contents, the criteria for selection, the criteria for judging merit, and evidence of student self-reflection" (Paulson, Paulson, & Meyer, 1991, p. 60). Collections of students' work can and do provide data for answering process and product questions. Because they provide indices of students' progress, portfolios can be examined at several points for information about students' skill development, their attainments, or their interests. Typically teachers evaluate

Directions given orally by the evaluator:

"Mark the picture that best shows how you feel about the sentences I say to you:

    I like to read about dinosaurs."

FIGURE C.5
Example of Likert-Type Scale for Use with Young Children

portfolios, but students also do self-evaluation to provide data for curriculum evaluators. Kieffer and Morrison (1994) explain in detail how using portfolios enables teachers to perform authentic assessments in classrooms.

Camp (1993) points out three desirable features of portfolios for evaluation of writing abilities. Portfolios contain writing samples representative of a variety of performances for different audiences and purposes. Within portfolios students can include evidence of the processes used in creating the writing samples with items such as brainstorming ideas, rough drafts, and notes. Students can also provide evidence of their awareness of the processes and strategies used in writing. Similar arguments for portfolios could be made in other curriculum areas such as science through elaborations of the processes involved in laboratory sessions, in mathematics with explanations of how problem solutions were derived, or music where students provide tapes and self-reflections on practice sessions and performances.

Students may develop ownership of their work if they are actively involved in creating and evaluating their activities. Paulson, Paulson, and Meyer (1991) offer a set of guidelines for use of portfolios that take into account students' roles. Ideally portfolios contain information showing students' self-reflections, offer students concrete ways to learn to value their own work through self-reflection, and show growth on the part of students (Paulson, Paulson, & Meyer, 1991).

Portfolio assessments can be very helpful. For example, the assessment shown in Figure C.6 combines features of a rating scale with those of rubrics. Three major components of writers' abilities are highlighted in the sections on accomplishment, use of processes and resources, and development as a writer. Within each section are several criteria that evaluators apply to the writing samples. Then, based on the degree to which those criteria are demonstrated, an evaluator marks one of the ratings. The final open-ended statements provide a summary of the evaluator's assessment.

Content Analyses

Some written products are responses to open-ended questions (e.g., Stages of Concerns, performance test responses) whose content must be judged by persons with training in making valid inferences from text (Weber, 1990). Applied in curriculum evaluation situations, content analyses are used to code open-ended questions in surveys, determine the psychological state of individuals or groups (as in Stages of Concern), audit communication content against objectives (as in evaluating responses to open-ended questions), and others.

Essentially content analysis requires the creation and interpretation of classifications of content. These procedures involve defining categories and deciding whether they are mutually exclusive and how broad or narrow they are (Weber, 1990). Consider again the open-ended question asked of teachers who implement a revised curriculum: "When you think about using the revised curriculum, what are you concerned about?" Content analysts devise and define a set of categories by which to classify their responses, examples of which might be the Stages of Concerns such as "awareness," "management," or "consequence." Using these categories and their definitions, analysts code and interpret teachers' written responses. Evaluators make informed judgments about teachers' probable stages of concern depending on the category in which their comments aggregate. As this explanation shows, content analysis requires judges trained in its methodologies.

Summary

This appendix describes instruments for gathering curriculum evaluation data in three classifications of interviews, observations, and tests/work products. No instrument or classi-

The contents of the student's portfolio demonstrate:
(Please check where appropriate)

	Significant Evidence Present	Satisfactory Evidence Present	Some Evidence Present	Little Evidence Present
Accomplishment in writing	_____	_____	_____	_____

- setting and meeting worthwhile challenges
- establishing and maintaining purpose
- use of the techniques and choices of the genre
- organization, development, use of detail
- control of conventions, vocabulary, sentence structure
- awareness of the needs of the audience
- use of language, sound, images, tone, voice
- humor, metaphor, playfulness

	Significant Evidence Present	Satisfactory Evidence Present	Some Evidence Present	Little Evidence Present
Use of processes and resources for writing	_____	_____	_____	_____

- awareness of strategies and processes for writing
- use of processes: prewriting, drafting, revision
- awareness of features important to writing
- ability to see strengths and opportunities in own and others' writing
- ability to describe what one sees and knows about writing
- use of classroom social context for writing
- use of available experience and resources (one's own, the school's, the community's)

	Significant Evidence Present	Satisfactory Evidence Present	Some Evidence Present	Little Evidence Present
Development as a writer	_____	_____	_____	_____

- progress from early to late pieces, growth, development
- increased understanding of features and options important to writing
- engagement with writing, investment, pursuit
- use of writing for different purposes, genres, and audiences
- sense of self as a writer, achievements and purposes as a writer
- personal criteria and standards for writing

This student's strengths in writing include:

This student's developmental needs as a writer include:

FIGURE C.6

Example of a Portfolio Exit Assessment

From "Assessment as an Episode of Learning" by D. P. Wolf, 1993. In R. E. Bennett & W. C. Ward (Eds.), *Construction Versus Choice in Cognitive Achievement* (p. 230). Copyright 1993 by Erlbaum Associates. Reprinted by permission.

fication of instruments is necessarily better than any other. Evaluators choose among instruments based on the purpose and context to be served.

When data are needed from large numbers of respondents, tests and surveys are efficient collection methods. Interviews, observations, and content analyses take time to administer and interpret. These instruments are used typically when there are relatively few people involved. Teachers often administer and score tests, portfolios, and checklists. However, content analyses, Q sorts, and rating scales are usually administered and scored by curriculum evaluators.

Glossary

· ·

Active initiation and participation. Initial change processes in implementation of curriculum; usually involve a few individuals willing to take risks at learning by doing.

Affective domain. Area of learning concerned with affect, including values, interests, dispositions, and attitudes.

Aim. Learning outcome stated generally and philosophically, and as long-term intentions; not measurable.

Appropriateness for need-interests of learners. Content selection criterion used to insure that curriculum content meets the long-term needs and interests of learners for whom the curriculum is planned.

Attitudes. Class of classroom learning outcomes that reflects learner's choices of personal actions toward things, people or events.

Atypical developmental pattern. Learner development that does not follow norms because of genetic, trauma, biological, or psychological environmental factors.

Authentic assessment. Data collection technique in which students demonstrate skills and abilities in lifelike tasks and situations.

Authoring Cycle. A nontechnical curriculum for literacy learning.

Behavioral view of development. Approach to study of human development based on nurture; focuses mainly on input and output of information.

Belief. Idea accepted as true, but more susceptible to change than a value.

Broad fields. Curriculum design based on an entire domain of knowledge.

Change facilitator. Person responsible for helping teachers use modified or revised curricula in classrooms.

Changes in behavior and beliefs. Change processes in curriculum implementation; both must occur for change to be complete.

Checklist. Data collection technique in which the collector gathers data regarding the presence or absence of behaviors according to a predefined list.

Classroom-based curriculum decision making. Level of decision making at which teachers, and sometimes students, make judgments about curriculum concerns.

Classroom learning outcomes. Broad name for all the types of learning that result from learner interactions with curriculum content and teaching agents.

Classroom use. Arrangements for using revised curricula in classrooms. Called implementation in technical approach, enactment in nontechnical approach.

Cognitive domain. Area of learning concerned with intellectual matters, including verbal information, intellectual skills, and cognitive strategies.

Cognitive science. Cognitive explanation for learning based on cognitive structures that enable the organization and application of knowledge.

Cognitive strategies. Class of classroom learning outcomes that guides learners' learning processes of attending, remembering, thinking, and others.

Cognitive structuralism. Cognitive explanation for learning based on patterns or configurations by which learners make sense of their experiences.

Cognitive view of development. Approach to study of human development based on interaction of nature and nurture; focuses on development of learner's unique mental structures.

Competency approach. Curriculum design based on the use of specific behavioral objectives that define what students need to learn.

Concept. Classroom learning outcome that reflects learner's ability to distinguish between objects, object features, and events as classes; an intellectual skill.

Conception of curriculum. An idea concerning curriculum that implies a particular purpose of education, content, and organization.

Conception of knowledge. An idea concerning ways of thinking about what people do in order to own information; involves filtering it through experience and applying it in daily living.

Concerns-Based Adoption Model (CBAM). Model for implementing curricula that recognizes and systematically accounts for change processes on the part of participants.

Concerns-Based Adoption Model diagnostic tool. Used by change facilitators in curriculum implementation; includes measures of stages of concern, levels of use, and innovation configurations.

Concerns-Based Adoption Model implementation process. Includes the activities associated with initiation, implementation, and institutionalization of curricula in school settings.

Considerations in content organization. Concerns related to management of curriculum content; include scope, sequence, continuity, and integration.

Consistency with societal-cultural realities. Content selection criterion used to insure that curriculum content aligns with the real world outside of schools.

Content. Class of classroom learning outcomes that reflect the informational aspects of knowledge.

Content analysis. Evaluation procedure in which responses are subjected to coding and classification to make informed judgments about them.

Content selection criterion. Standard by which content can be included in or excluded from curricula.

Content statement. Contains the major information, processes, values, and/or attitudes to be included in the curriculum.

Context evaluation. Means of identifying strengths and weaknesses in curriculum situations; needs assessment.

Continuity. Content organization consideration that assures the repetition of ideas, themes, and skills within a curriculum.

Core. Curriculum design that develops common competencies needed by all learners but recognizes differences in learners' interests, aptitudes, and capacities.

Correlated subjects. Curriculum design in which learning experiences in two or more areas are related, but the identities of the subject areas are kept.

Course of study. Curriculum product containing specified content, learning outcomes, and time allocations. Also known as a **Syllabus.**

Cultivate cognitive achievement and the intellect. Purpose of education in the cumulative tradition of organized knowledge/academic rationalism curriculum conception; uses the academic disciplines or subject matter as primary source of content.

Cultural literacy. Understandings and ways of thinking needed to function in social groups according to language, ethnic background, religion, and so on.

Curriculum. What is taught to students; both intended and unintended information, skills, and attitudes.

Curriculum content. The raw material for student learning in schools.

Curriculum content sources. Refers to recommendations of professional organizations, state guidelines, textbooks and related materials, technology-based materials, and professional educators' knowledge bases.

Curriculum development. Creation of new or revised programs of study for the purpose of school improvement.

Curriculum evaluation. The delineation, obtainment, and provision of descriptive and judgmental information about the merit of a curriculum for the purpose of school improvement; includes needs assessment, process, and product evaluation.

Curriculum guidelines. Curriculum product containing learning outcomes.

Curriculum guides. Curriculum product containing details about topics to be taught, predetermined learning outcomes, and suggestions for instructional strategies.

Curriculum processes. Includes all the considerations with which curriculum workers deal as they develop, use, and evaluate curricula.

Curriculum products. Result from curriculum development; include guides, courses of study, syllabi, resource units, and others.

Curriculum projects. Same as **Curriculum products.**

Declarative knowledge. Conception of knowledge associated with "knowing-that" information.

Definition of education. Statement containing developers' purpose of education.

Develop individuals to their fullest potentials. Purpose of education in the self-actualization curriculum conception; uses content that helps learners develop in all domains—cognitive, affective, and psychomotor.

Develop intellectual processes. Purpose of education in the development of cognitive processes curriculum conception; may use content from any source, but typically uses subject matter.

Development of self. Major focus of humanistic views of development; concerns that learners' inner natures be subjected to the least number of unfavorable experiences.

Developmental education. Curriculum design based on needs and interests of learners; emphasizes firsthand experiences as the bases of learners' knowledge.

Developmentalism. Cognitive explanation for learning based on qualitatively different stages in perception and cognition through which learners pass with age and experiences.

Diagnostic needs assessment. Method of context evaluation that reveals needs of individual students; associated with nontechnical approach.

Discipline. Conception of knowledge; one of the branches of knowledge.

Discrepancy needs assessment. Method of context evaluation that looks for differences between projected and current curriculum situations; associated with technical approach.

District-based curriculum decision making. Level of decision making at which district administrators, other school personnel, and citizens make judgments about curriculum concerns.

Domain. Area of learning that shares common characteristics; includes cognitive, affective, and psychomotor areas.

Economy. Social institution responsible for handling social problems related to the production and distribution of goods and services and ownership of property; in recent years responsible for large-scale societal changes.

Education. Social institution responsible for handling socialization of newcomers into society.

Enactment. Arrangements for using a nontechnically developed curriculum in classrooms.

Extensive knowledge. Part of a conception of knowledge, the other of which is **Intensive knowledge;** refers to broad, superficial, and mostly enumerative information.

Family. Social institution responsible for handling problems related to sexual regulation and maintenance of stable units that ensure continued births and care of dependent children.

Formal knowledge. Part of a conception of knowledge, the other of which is skills; refers to declarative or "knowing-that" knowledge.

Fused subjects. Curriculum design in which learning experiences in two or more areas are related, and the identities of the subject areas are lost.

Generalization. Classroom learning outcome that reflects learner's ability to express relationships between concepts, for which there are known exceptions.

Generative learning. Involves self-organized information, occurs in response to internal needs; associated with cognitive views of development.

Goal. Learning outcome at an intermediate level of generality between aim and objective; can be measured to the extent of deciding if it is met or if one goal is met better than another.

Humanistic view of development. Approach to study of human development based on nature; focuses mainly on the development of learner's inner self.

Implementation. Arrangements for using a technically developed curriculum in classrooms.

Impressionistic knowledge. A form of knowledge involving "feelings" about situations and issues; usually operates in the background of one's consciousness.

Informal knowledge. A form of knowledge intermediate between formal and procedural; often called "educated common sense."

Information. Data from all sources such as printed materials, television, laboratory experiments, and others; has not been filtered through the receiver's experiences nor applied.

Information literacy. Understandings and ways of thinking needed to handle data from media, printed materials, television, or technology-based sources external to the learner.

Information processing systems. Hypothesized structures and processes by which learning occurs in the cognitive science explanation of development.

Initiation (CBAM). Refers to processes used at the outset of implementing a curriculum under the Concerns-Based Adoption Model.

Innovations configuration. Diagnostic tool used in CBAM to see if teachers are using revised curriculum at levels acceptable for the particular school situation.

Institutionalization (CBAM). Refers to processes to determine the degree to which a revised curriculum is fully implemented.

Instruction. Delivery of the curriculum to students by teaching agents.

Integration. Content organization consideration that describes the close relationships among concepts, skills, and values in a curriculum so they are mutually reinforcing to learners.

Intellectual skill. Class of classroom learning outcomes generally related to processing information; includes discriminations, concepts, rules, and higher-order rules.

Intended learning outcomes. Statements representative of what learners are expected to be able

to do with curriculum content following their interactions with teaching agents.

Intensive knowledge. Part of a conception of knowledge, the other of which is **Extensive knowledge;** refers to relationships between bits of extensive knowledge.

Interaction of nature and nurture. Explanation of the relationship between learners and their environments; recognizes reciprocal actions between nature and nurture.

Interpersonal context. Experience, interaction, and negotiation of meaning between learners and teachers; especially important in nontechnical curricula.

Interventions. Activities that help teachers use revised curricula in classrooms; usually directed by change facilitators.

Interview. Data collection technique in which a data collector asks questions of respondents in one-to-one format, usually face-to-face; questions may be predetermined in a focused interview or extemporaneous in an unstructured interview.

Journal. Data collection technique in which respondents reveal ideas, interests, and skills in narrative form.

Knowledge. Information that has been filtered through the receiver's experience and applied in personal situations.

Language literacy. Abilities to understand and use one's native tongue to express ideas.

Learnability. Content selection criterion used to insure that curriculum content can be learned by those for whom the curriculum is planned.

Learner-environment relationships. Views of development; encompass nature, nurture, and interaction of nature with nurture.

Learning. Knowledges, techniques, and values that students take from classrooms.

Learning (behavioral views). Enduring change in observable behavior as a result of experience.

Learning (cognitive views). Change in one's mental structures that allows for the expression of changes in behavior.

Learning outcomes. What learners are able to do with curriculum content.

Levels of curriculum. Degrees to which curricula are related to the students for whom they are intended; include societal, institutional, instructional, and experiential.

Levels of use. Diagnostic tool used in CBAM to check the degree to which teachers are actually using a revised curriculum.

Literacy forms. Language, cultural, science, and information literacy.

Make learning systematic and efficient. Purpose of education in the technology curriculum conception; may use content from any source, but typically uses subject matter.

Motor skills. Class of classroom learning outcomes generally related to psychomotor learning.

Mutual adaptation. Refers to processes for implementing curriculum in a particular situation; these processes are negotiated between change facilitators and teachers using the curriculum.

Nature. Explanation of the relationships between learners and their environment; maintains that learners are born with the seeds of their potential and environmental conditions help or hinder their development.

Needs assessment. Means of identifying strengths and weaknesses of curriculum situations; context evaluation.

Nontechnical approach. Method of developing curricula in which learning outcomes evolve as students and teachers enact the curriculum in classrooms; does not include predetermined learning outcomes for students.

Nurture. Explanation of the relationships between learners and their environment; maintains that learners' development is influenced largely by people or events in their environments.

Objective. Learning outcome stated specifically; can be measured to the extent of deciding how much better one objective is met than another.

Observation. Data collection technique in which the collector is in a position to witness the actions and gather information about persons from whom data are needed.

Observational learning. Behavioral explanation for learning based on formulating expectations, beliefs, and goals by watching the actions of other people.

One-legged conference. Data collection technique in which the change facilitator schedules an informal, brief conference with a teacher concerning curriculum implementation.

Open-ended statement of concern. Data collection technique in which teachers express their thoughts and feelings concerning curriculum implementation.

Operant conditioning. Behavioral explanation for learning based on reinforcement for a learner's response increases the probability of that response in similar situations.

Opinionnaire survey. Data collection technique in which large numbers of respondents provide information on perceived needs, concerns, attitudes, values, and beliefs.

Organic curriculum. Curriculum design based on needs and interests of learners; emphasizes child-centeredness, experience-based learning, integrated content areas, and process-oriented instruction.

Ownership. Change processes in curriculum implementation; signify that teachers have made the psychological changes required to use the curriculum.

Pedagogical content knowledge. Teachers' special knowledge of content that takes into account students, curriculum, the classroom, and their own values.

Performance assessment. Data collection technique in which persons providing data must demonstrate abilities and skills to the data collector; sometimes used interchangeably with **authentic assessment.**

Physical context. Spatial-temporal situation in which a curriculum is used, especially important for nontechnical curricula.

Planned learning experiences. Situations that allow students to come in contact with curriculum content appropriate for the intended purpose of education.

Polity. Social institution responsible for handling problems related to maintenance of order and the distribution of power.

Portfolio. Data collection technique in which students' skills, ideas, interests, and accomplishments are revealed in a series of their works.

Prepare people for living in an unstable, changing world; reform society. Purpose of education in the social relevance-reconstruction curriculum conception; uses content based on societal needs, interests, and problems.

Pressure and support. Change processes in curriculum implementation; usually external and necessary to bring about action within school.

Principle. Classroom learning outcome that reflects learner's ability to express relationships between concepts, for which there are no known exceptions.

Problem solving. Classroom learning outcome that reflects learner's ability to use cognitive strategies in situations where a goal is specified but the method of reaching it is not.

Procedural knowledge. Conception of knowledge associated with "knowing-how" information.

Process. Class of classroom learning outcomes that reflect the skills aspects of knowledge.

Process evaluation. Provides descriptive and judgmental information about the implementation of a modified curriculum.

Process skills. Curriculum design featuring processes such as problem solving, decision making, critical reading, and others that are transferrable to real life.

Processes for implementation of change. Strategies for effecting changes necessary for actually revising curriculum situations; involves active initiation and participation, pressure and support, changes in behavior and belief, and ownership.

Processes for initiation of change. Strategies for beginning the effecting of changes necessary for developing new curricula; involves relevance, readiness, and resources.

Product evaluation. Provides descriptive and judgmental information about the impact of a curriculum on students.

Psychomotor domain. Area of learning concerned with development of motor skills.

Q sort. Data collection technique that reveals respondents' priorities of curriculum statements; involves card sort technique.

Ranking scale. Data collection technique that reveals respondents' priorities toward curriculum statements.

Rating scale. Data collection method that reveals degrees of respondents' behaviors toward curriculum statements.

Readiness. Change process in curriculum development; involves the capacity of individuals and school to deal with curriculum revision.

Receptive learning. Involves learning information organized by others; occurs in response to events in learner's environment; associated with behavioral views of development.

Relevance. Change process in curriculum development; involves interaction of need, understandings of curriculum development, and what the revised curriculum offers.

Religion. Social institution responsible for handling problems related to understanding the transcendental or the search for meaning of life and death and the place of humankind in the world.

Resource unit. Curriculum product containing learning outcomes, suggestions for teaching, sources of information, and prepared instructional units.

Resources. Change process in curriculum development; refers to facilities, equipment, materials, and supplies.

Rule. Classroom learning outcome that reflects learner's ability to apply information according to defined procedures; an intellectual skill.

School-based curriculum decision making. Level of decision making at which school administrators and teachers within that school make judgments about curriculum concerns pertinent to their school context.

Science literacy. Understandings and ways of thinking that enable people to live and work in a world shaped largely by science, mathematics, and technology.

Scope. Content organization consideration that describes the breadth of curriculum at a particular time; the horizontal organization of content.

Sequence. Content organization consideration that describes the deepening of recurring and repetitious curricular experiences.

Self-regulatory knowledge. A form of self-knowledge about one's own intellectual functioning.

Skills. Part of a conception of knowledge, the other of which is **formal knowledge;** refers to procedural or "knowing-how" knowledge.

Significance for purpose of education. Content selection criterion used to insure that curriculum content helps learners perform the intended learning outcomes or engage in the learning experiences in ways meaningful to the purpose of education.

Single subject. Curriculum design based on one academic discipline or organized subject matter area.

Social capital. Refers to the norms, social networks, and the relationships between adults and children that are valuable for children growing up.

Social functions and activities. Curriculum design based on needs of society and culture.

Social institution. Uncoordinated actions of many people that furnish solutions to societal problems largely by custom or tradition.

Stages of concern. Diagnostic tool used in CBAM to show the degree of feelings that teachers have about using a revised curriculum.

Stages of concern questionnaire. Data collection technique by which change facilitators formally collect information on teachers' feelings about using a revised curriculum.

Standardized test. Data collection procedures by which teachers collect information from students using instruments that have been used with large numbers of other students and designed to give comparable information; usually measures cognitive learning.

Study skill. Classroom learning outcomes that reflect learner's abilities to use cognitive strategies in comprehending and retaining subject matter.

Syllabus. Same as **Course of study.**

Taxonomy. Measures of complexity within learning domains.

Technical approach. Method of developing curricula that uses systematic decision making; includes predetermined learning outcomes for students.

Technology. Curriculum design that features explicit, behaviorally stated objectives.

Thinking skill. Classroom learning outcome that reflects learner's abilities to use cognitive strategies in processing information.

Unstructured observation. Data collection technique in which the collector records or makes notes of information but does not use a predetermined set of questions or categories in gathering data on the actions of persons from whom data are needed.

Validity for purpose of education. Content selection criterion used to insure that curriculum content supports the purpose of education for which it is intended.

Value. Idea chosen from alternatives, based on considerations of consequences, cherished enough to be made public, and acted on in some way.

Verbal information. Class of classroom learning outcomes related to declarative knowledge.

Views of education statement. Contains the developers' purpose for education; perspectives on roles of students, teachers and school staffs in implementing curricula; and the interrelationships of these elements with the community beyond the school.

References

· ·

A curriculum guide for fifth grade social studies. (1990, July). (Available from Mesa County Valley School District No. 51, Department of Curriculum Services, 2115 Grand Ave., Grand Junction, CO 81501-8063)

A guide for developing a 1–9 science curriculum. (1991). (Available from Educational Service Unit #1, P.O. Box 216, Wakefield, NE 68784)

A textbook sampler. *Principal, 64*(2), 46.

Adams, S., & Bailey, G. D. (1993). Education for the Information Age: Is it time to trade vehicles? *NASSP Bulletin, 77*(553), 57–63.

Allport, G. W. (1961). *Pattern and growth in personality.* New York: Holt, Rinehart & Winston.

Ambrosie, F., & Haley, P. W. (1991). The role of the curriculum specialist in site-based management, *National Association of Secondary School Principals' Bulletin, 75*(537), 73–81.

American Association for the Advancement of Science. (1990). *Science for all Americans,* Project 2061. New York: Oxford University Press.

American Association on Mental Retardation. (1992). *Mental retardation: Definition, classification, and systems of supports* (9th ed.). Washington, DC: Author.

Applebee, A. N. (1994). English language arts assessment: Lessons from the past, *English Journal, 83*(4), 40–46.

Applebee, A. N., Langer, J. A., Jenkins, L. B., Mullis, I. V. S., & Foertsch, M. A. (1990). *Learning to write in our nation's schools: Instruction and achievement in 1988 at grades 4, 8, and 12.*

Princeton, NJ: National Assessment of Educational Progress, Educational Testing Service.

Arizona Student Assessment Program. (1993). *Sample rubric for scoring mathematics examinations.* Chicago: Riverside.

Auerbach, E. (1990). *Making meaning, making change: A guide to participatory curriculum development for adult ESL and family literacy.* Boston: University of Massachusetts English Family Literacy Project.

Ausubel, D. P. (1963). *The psychology of meaningful verbal learning: An introduction to school learning.* New York: Grune & Stratton.

Bandura, A. (1977). *Social learning theory.* Englewood Cliffs, NJ: Prentice Hall.

Bandura, A. (1989). Social cognitive theory. *Annals of child development: Six theories of child development: Revised formulations and current issues, 6,* 1–60.

Bartlett, D. L., & Steele, J. B. (1992). *America: What went wrong?* Kansas City, MO: Andrews and McMeel.

Beauchamp, G. A. (1983). Curriculum design. In F. W. English (Ed.), *Fundamental curriculum decisions* (pp. 90–98). Alexandria, VA: The Association of Supervision and Curriculum Development.

Ben-Peretz, M. (1990). *The teacher-curriculum encounter: Freeing teachers from the tyranny of texts.* Albany, NY: State University of New York Press.

Bereiter, C., & Scardamalia, M. (1992). Cognition and curriculum. In P. W. Jackson (Ed.), *Handbook of research on curriculum* (pp. 517–542). New York: Macmillan.

373

Bereiter, C., & Scardamalia, M. (1993). *Surpassing ourselves: An inquiry into the nature and implications of expertise.* Chicago: Open Court.

Berk, L. E. (1994). *Child development,* 3rd ed. Boston: Allyn and Bacon.

Berlyne, D. (1966). Curiosity and exploration. *Science, 153,* 21–33.

Berman, L. (1968). *New priorities in the curriculum.* Englewood Cliffs, NJ: Prentice Hall.

Biehler, R. F., & Snowman, J. (1993). *Psychology applied to teaching* (7th ed.). Boston: Houghton Mifflin.

Bigge, M. L., & Shermis, S. S. (1992). *Learning theories for teachers* (5th ed.). New York: HarperCollins.

Blenkin, G. M., & Kelly, A. V. (1988). Education as development. In G. M. Blenkin & A. V. Kelly (Eds.), *Early childhood education: A developmental curriculum* (pp. 1–31). London: Paul Chapman.

Blenkin, G. M., & Whitehead, M. (1988). Creating a context for development. In G. M. Blenkin & A. V. Kelly (Eds.), *Early childhood education: A developmental curriculum* (pp. 32–60). London: Paul Chapman.

Bloom, B. S. (Ed.). (1956). *Taxonomy of educational objectives: Handbook I: Cognitive domain.* New York: McKay.

Boyer, E. L. (1983). *High school: A report on secondary education in America.* New York: Harper & Row.

Brameld, T. (1956). *Toward a reconstructed philosophy of education.* New York: Dryden.

Brandt, R. S. (1988). Conclusion: Conceptions of content. In R. S. Brandt (Ed.), *Content of curriculum* (pp. 187–197). Alexandria, VA: Association for Supervision and Curriculum Development.

Brandt, R. S., & Tyler, R. W. (1983). Goals and objectives. In F. W. English (Ed.), *Fundamental curriculum decisions* (pp. 40–52). Alexandria, VA: Association for Supervision and Curriculum Development.

Breivik, P. S., & Jones, D. L. (1993). Information literacy: Liberal education for the information age. *Liberal Education, 79*(1), 24–29.

Bridges, W. (1991). *Managing transitions: Making the most of change.* Reading, MA: Addison Wesley.

Bronfenbrenner, U. (1988). Alienation and the four worlds of childhood. In K. Ryan & J. M.

Cooper (Eds.), *Kaleidoscope: Readings in education* (5th ed.). (pp. 119–126). Boston: Houghton Mifflin.

Bruner, J. S. (1960). *The process of education.* New York: Viking.

Bruner, J. S. (1966). *Toward a theory of instruction.* New York: Norton.

Bruner, J. (1985). Models of the learner, *Educational Researcher, 14*(6), 5–8.

Bunting, C. (1990). Schools and families: The tie that bonds. *School Administrator, 6*(8), 16–18.

Busick, K. U., & Inos, R. H. (1992). *Synthesis of the research on educational change.* Honolulu, HI: Pacific Region Educational Laboratory. (ERIC Document Reproduction Service No. ED 349 705)

Butler, A. (Speaker). (1992). *Defining literacy in the 21st century* [Exploring Reading #1 Videotape]. Crystal Lake, IL: Rigby Education.

Butts, R. F. (1975–1976). The search for purpose in American education, *The College Board Review, 98,* 3–19.

Camp, R. (1993). The place of portfolios in our changing views of writing assessment. In R. E. Bennett & W. C. Ward (Eds.), *Construction versus choice in cognitive measurement* (pp. 183–212). Hillsdale, NJ: Erlbaum.

Campbell, M., Carr, J., & Harris, D. (1989). *American School Board Journal, 176*(4), 30–32.

Canter, L. (1989). Assertive discipline—more than names on the board and marbles in a jar. *Phi Delta Kappan, 71,* 57–61.

Carrasquillo, A. L., & London, C. B. G. (1993). *Parents and schools: A source book.* New York: Garland.

Charters, W. W., & Jones, J. (1973). On the risk of appraising non-events in program evaluation. *Educational Researcher, 2*(11), 5–7.

Clandinin, D. J., & Connelly, F. M. (1992). Teacher as curriculum maker. In P. W. Jackson (Ed.), *Handbook of research on curriculum* (pp. 363–401). New York: Macmillan.

Coleman, J. S. (1987). Families and schools. *Educational Researcher,* 32–38.

Coleman, J. S., Campbell, E. Q., Hobson, C. J., McPartland, J., Mood, A. M., Weinfeld, F. D., & York, R. L. (1988). *Equality of educational oppor-*

tunity (reprint ed). Salem, NH: Ayer Company, Publishers.

Coleman, J. S., Hoffer, T., & Kilgore, S. (1982). *High school achievement.* New York: Basic Books.

Collaborative teaching experiences to develop communication skills in elementary school children prekindergarten to grade 5. (1992). (Available from Speech and Language Department, Jackson County Intermediate School District, Jackson, MI 49201)

Combs, A. W. (1982). Affective education or none at all. *Educational Leadership, 39*(7), 495–497.

Combs, A. W., & Snygg, D. (1959). *Individual behavior: A perceptual approach to behavior* (rev. ed.). New York: Harper Row.

Comfort, K. B. (1994). Authentic assessment: A systemic approach in California, *Science and Children, 32*(2), 42–43, 65–66.

Committee of Fifteen. (1895). The report of the sub-committee on the correlation of studies in elementary education. *Educational Review, 9,* 230–303.

Computer education course of study. (1985). (Available from Mandan Public Schools District 1, Mandan, ND 58554.)

Cortes, C. E. (1992). Media literacy: An educational basic for the information age. *Education and Urban Society, 24,* 489–497.

Crandall, D., Eiseman, J., & Louis, K. (1986). Strategic planning issues that bear on the success of school improvement efforts. *Educational Administration Quarterly, 22*(3), 21–53.

Cronin-Jones, L. L. (1991). Science teacher beliefs and their influence on curriculum implementation: Two case studies. *Journal of Research in Science Teaching, 28,* 235–250.

Cuban, L. (1992). Curriculum stability and change. In P. W. Jackson (Ed.), *Handbook of research in curriculum* (pp. 216–247). New York: Macmillan.

Cullinan, D., & Epstein, M. H. (1994). Behavior disorders. In N. G. Haring, L. McCormick, & T. G. Haring (Eds.), *Exceptional children and youth* (6th ed.) (pp. 166–210). Englewood Cliffs, NJ: Merrill/Prentice Hall.

Curry, L. (1990). A critique of the research on learning styles, *Educational Leadership, 48*(2), 50–52, 54–56.

Daman, W. (1991). Adolescent self-concept. In R. M. Lerner, A. C. Petersen, & J. Brooks-Gunn (Eds.), *Encyclopedia of adolescence,* Vol. 2 (pp. 987–991). New York: Garland.

Darling-Hammond, L. (1994). Setting standards for students: The case for authentic assessment, *The Educational Forum, 59*(1), 14–21.

Darling-Hammond, L., & Snyder, J. (1992). Curriculum studies and the traditions of inquiry: The scientific tradition. In P. W. Jackson (Ed.), *Handbook of research on curriculum* (pp. 41–78). New York: Macmillan.

David, J. L. (1994). School-based decision making: Kentucky's test of decentralization, *Phi Delta Kappan, 75,* 706–712.

Davies, I. K. (1976). *Objectives in curriculum design.* Maidenhead, England: McGraw Hill (UK) Limited.

de Charms, R. (1968). *Personal causation.* New York: Academic Press.

de Charms, R. (1984). Motivating enhancement in educational settings. In R. Ames & C. Ames (Eds.), *Research on motivation in education, Vol. 1: Student motivation* (pp. 275–310). New York: Academic Press.

de Landsheere, V. (1991). Taxonomies of educational objectives. In A. Lewy (Ed.), *International encyclopedia of curriculum* (pp. 317–327). New York: Pergamon.

de Vaus, D. A. (1991). *Surveys in social research* (3rd ed.). London: University College London Press.

Deci, E. (1975). *Intrinsic motivation.* New York: Plenum.

Delgado-Gaitan, C., & Trueba, H. (1991). *Crossing cultural borders: Education for immigrant families in America.* London: Falmer.

Dewey, J. (1916). *Democracy and education.* Englewood Cliffs, NJ: Prentice Hall.

Dewey, J. (1933). *How we think: A restatement of the relation of reflective thinking to the educative process* (rev. ed.). Boston: Heath.

Dewey, J. (1938). *Experience and education.* New York: Collier Books.

Dewey, J. (1988). My pedagogic creed. In K. Ryan & J. M. Cooper (Eds.), *Kaleidoscope: Readings in education* (5th ed.) (pp. 401–414). Boston: Houghton Mifflin.

Dolbeare, K. M. (1989). The nature of the economic transformation. In D. S. Eitzen & M. Baca Zinn (Eds.), *The reshaping of America: Social consequences of the changing economy* (pp. 19–23). Englewood Cliffs, NJ: Prentice Hall.

Downey, L. W. (1960). Secondary education: A model for improvement, *School Review, 68*(3), 251–265.

Doyle, W. (1992). Curriculum and pedagogy. In P. W. Jackson (Ed.), *Handbook of research on curriculum* (pp. 486–516). New York: Macmillan.

Edwards, R. C. (1975). The social relations of production in the firm and labor market structure. In R. C. Edwards, M. Reich, & D. M. Gordon (Eds.), *Labor market segmentation* (pp. 3–26). Lexington, MA: D. C. Heath.

Eggen, P., & Kauchak, D. (1994). *Educational psychology: Classroom connections* (2nd ed.). Englewood Cliffs, NJ: Merrill/Prentice Hall.

Eisner, E. W. (1992). Curriculum ideologies. In P. W. Jackson (Ed.), *Handbook for research on curriculum* (pp. 302–326). New York: Macmillan.

Eisner, E. W. (1993). Reshaping assessment in education: Some criteria in search of practice. *Journal of Curriculum Studies, 25,* 219–233.

Eisner, E. W., & Vallance, E. (1974). Introduction: Five conceptions of curriculum: Their roots and implications for curriculum planning. In E. W. Eisner & E. Vallance (Eds.), *Conflicting conceptions of curriculum* (pp. 1–18). Berkeley, CA: McCutchan.

Eitzen, D. S. (1992). Problem students: The sociocultural roots. *Phi Delta Kappan, 73,* 584–588, 590.

Eitzen, D. S., & Baca Zinn, M. (1989). The forces reshaping America. In D. S. Eitzen & M. Baca Zinn (Eds.), *The reshaping of America* (pp. 1–13). Englewood Cliffs, NJ: Prentice-Hall.

Eitzen, D. S., & Baca Zinn, M. (1995). *In conflict and order: Understanding society* (7th ed.). Boston: Allyn and Bacon.

Elam, S. M., Rose, L. C., & Gallup, A. M. (1993). The 25th annual Phi Delta Kappa/Gallup poll of the public's attitudes toward the public schools. *Phi Delta Kappan, 75,* 137–152.

Elam, S. M., Rose, L. C., & Gallup, A. M. (1994). The 26th annual Phi Delta Kappa/Gallup poll of the public's attitudes toward the public schools. *Phi Delta Kappan, 76,* 41–56.

Elkind, D. (1974). *Children and adolescents: Interpretive essays on Jean Piaget.* New York: Oxford University Press.

Elkind, D. (1990). Get ready for the post-modern family. *School Administrator, 6*(8), 8–11, 15.

Elliott, D. L. (1990). Textbooks and the curriculum in the postwar era, 1950–1980. In D. L. Elliott & A. Woodward (Eds.), *Textbooks and schooling in the United States* (pp. 42–55). The Eighty-ninth Yearbook of the National Society for the Study of Education, Part I. Chicago: NSSE.

Elmore, R., & Sykes, G. (1992). Curriculum policy. In P. W. Jackson (Ed.), *Handbook of research on curriculum* (pp. 185–215). New York: Macmillan.

Erikson, E. H. (1963). *Childhood and society* (35th anniversary ed.). 1985. New York: Norton.

Everett, D. (1994, October 30). Jobs boom, on low end. *The Arizona Republic,* pp. D1, D8.

Faunce, R. L., & Bossing, N. L. (1958). *Developing the core curriculum* (2nd ed.). Englewood Cliffs, NJ: Prentice Hall.

Feigelson, J. (1982). Our next war: Who will fight it? *Civil Rights Quarterly, 14*(Spring), 16–21.

Fiske, E. B. (1984). Are they "dumbing down" the textbooks? *Principal, 64*(2), 44–46.

Flammer, A. (1991). Self-regulation. In R. M. Lerner, A. C. Petersen, & J. Brooks-Gunn (Eds.), *Encyclopedia of adolescence, Vol. 2.* (pp. 1001–1003). New York: Garland.

Fullan, M. G. (1985). Change process and strategies at the local level. *The Elementary School Journal, 84*(3), 391–420.

Fullan, M. G., with Stiegelbauer, S. (1991). *The new meaning of educational change* (2nd ed.). New York: Teachers College Press.

Gagné, R. M., & Driscoll, M. P. (1988). *Essentials of learning for instruction* (2nd ed.). Englewood Cliffs, NJ: Prentice Hall.

Gallman, V. (1994, December 4). Welfare mother creature of myth. *The Arizona Republic,* p. A1, A30.

Gardner, H. (1983). *Frames of mind: The theory of multiple intelligences*. New York: Basic Books.

Gitomer, D. H. (1993). Performance assessment and educational measurement. In R. E. Bennett & W. C. Ward (Eds.), *Construction versus choice in cognitive measurement* (pp. 241–263). Hillsdale, NJ: Erlbaum.

Glaser, R. (1984). Education and thinking: The role of knowledge. *American Psychologist, 39,* 93–104.

Goodlad, J. I. (1984). *A place called school: Prospects for the future*. New York: McGraw-Hill.

Goodlad, J. I., & Su, Z. (1992). Organization of the curriculum. In P. W. Jackson (Ed.), *Handbook of research on curriculum* (pp. 327–344). New York: Macmillan.

Goodman, Y. M., Haussler, M. M., & Strickland, D. S. (Eds.). (1981). *Oral and written language development research: Impact on the school* (Proceedings from the 1979 and 1980 Impact Conferences). Urbana, IL: International Reading Association and National Council Teachers of English. (ERIC Document Reproduction Service No. ED 214 184)

Grant, G., with Briggs, J. (1988). Today's children are different. In K. Ryan & J. M. Cooper (Eds.), *Kaleidoscope: Readings in education* (5th ed.) (pp. 94–99). Boston: Houghton Mifflin.

Grossman, P. L. (1989). A study in contrast: Sources of pedagogical content knowledge for secondary English. *Journal of Teacher Education, 40*(5), 24–32.

Gudmundsdottir, S. (1990). Values in pedagogical content knowledge. *Journal of Teacher Education, 41*(3), 44–52.

Gudmundsdottir, S. (1991). Ways of seeing are ways of knowing: The pedagogical content knowledge of an expert English teacher. *Journal of curriculum studies, 23,* 409–421.

Hall, G. E. (1992). The local educational change process and policy implementation. *Journal of Research in Science Teaching, 29,* 877–904.

Hall, G. E., & Hord, S. M. (1986). *Configurations of school-based leadership teams* (Report No. R&DCTE–3223). Austin, TX: University of Texas, Research and Development Center for Teacher Education. (ERIC Document Reproduction Service No. ED 297 415)

Hall, G. E., & Hord, S. M. (1987). *Change in schools: Facilitating the process*. Albany, NY: State University of New York Press.

Hall, G. E., & Loucks, S. (1974). A developmental model for determining whether the treatment is actually implemented. *American Educational Research Journal, 14,* 263–276.

Hall, G. E., Newlove, B. W., George, A. A., Rutherford, W. L., & Hord, S. M. (1993). *Measuring change facilitator stages of concern: A manual for the use of the CFSoC questionnaire*. (ERIC Document Reproduction Service No. ED 353 307)

Haring, N. G. (1994). Overview of special education. In N. G. Haring, L. McCormick, & T. G. Haring (Eds.), *Exceptional children and youth* (6th ed.) (pp. 2–63). Englewood Cliffs, NJ: Merrill/Prentice Hall.

Harrow, A. J. (1972). *A taxonomy of the psychomotor domain: A guide for developing behavioral objectives*. New York: McKay.

Harste, J. C., Short, K. G., with Burke, C. and contributing teacher researchers. (1988). *Creating classrooms for authors: The reading-writing connection*. Portsmouth, NH: Heinemann.

Hart, D. (1994). *Authentic assessment: A handbook for educators*. Menlo Park, CA: Addison Wesley.

Heck, S., Stiegelbauer, S. M., Hall, G. E., & Loucks, S. F. (1981). *Measuring innovation configurations: Procedures and applications*. Austin, TX: University of Texas, Research and Development Center for Teacher Education.

Hein, G. E. (1991). Active assessment for active science. In V. Perrone (Ed.), *Expanding student assessment* (pp. 106–131). Arlington, VA: Association for Supervision and Curriculum Development.

Helser, L. (1994, November 13). Grandparents raising grandkids: Trend widens to mainstream American households. *The Arizona Republic*, pp. H1–H2.

Hersh, R. H. (1994, September 24). The culture of neglect. *Newsweek, 124*(13), 12–13.

Hill, J. C. (1986). *Curriculum evaluation for school improvement*. Springfield, IL: Charles C. Thomas.

Hirsch, E. D., Jr. (1985). Cultural literacy and the schools. *American Educator, 9,* 8–15.

Hirsch, E. D., Jr. (1987). *Cultural literacy: What every American needs to know.* Boston: Houghton Mifflin.

Hord, S. (1987). *Evaluating educational innovation.* London: Croom Helm.

Hord, S. M. (1992). *Facilitative leadership: The imperative for change.* Austin, TX: Southwest Educational Development Laboratory. (ERIC Document Reproduction Service No. ED 370 217)

Hord, S. M., & Hall, G. E. (1986). *Institutionalization of innovations: Knowing when you have it and when you don't* (Report No. R&DCTE-R-3220). Austin, TX: University of Texas, Research and Development Center for Teacher Education. (ERIC Document Reproduction Service No. ED 276 103)

Hord, S. M., & Hall, G. E. (1987). Three images: What principals do in curriculum implementation. *Curriculum Inquiry, 17,* 55–89.

Hord, S. M., Rutherford, W. L., Huling-Austin, L., & Hall, G. E. (1987). *Taking charge of change.* Alexandria VA: Association for Supervision and Curriculum Development.

Hunkins, F. P. (1980). *Curriculum development program improvement.* Englewood Cliffs, NJ: Prentice Hall.

Hunter, L. K. (1991). *Into adolescence: Caring for our planet and our health: A curriculum for grades 5–8.* Santa Cruz, CA: ETR Associates/Network Publications.

Hunter, R., & Scheirer, E. A. (1988). *The organic curriculum: Organizing for learning 7–12.* London: Falmer.

Hymes, D. L., with Chafin, A. E., & Gonder, P. (1991). *The changing face of testing and assessment: Problems and solutions.* Arlington, VA: American Association of School Administrators.

Illinois State Board of Education. (n.d.). *State goals for learning and sample learning objectives.* Springfield, IL: Illinois State Board of Education.

Jackson, P. W. (1992). Conceptions of curriculum and curriculum specialists. In P. W. Jackson (Ed.), *Handbook of research on curriculum* (pp. 3–40). New York: Macmillan.

Jencks, C. (1992). *Rethinking social policy: Race, poverty, and the underclass.* Cambridge, MA: Harvard University Press.

Johnson, M. (1967). Definitions and models in curriculum theory. *Educational Theory, 17*(2), 127–140.

Joint Committee on Standards for Educational Evaluation. (1981). *Standards for evaluations of educational programs, projects, and materials.* New York: McGraw Hill.

Joint Committee on Standards for Educational Evaluation. (1994). *The program evaluation standards: How to assess evaluations of educational programs* (2nd ed.). Thousand Oaks, CA: SAGE Publications.

Kamii, C., Clark, F. B., & Dominick, A. (1994). The six national goals: A road to disappointment. *Phi Delta Kappan, 75,* 672–677.

Kane, M., Berryman, S., Goslin, D., & Meltzer, A. (1990). *The secretary's commission on achieving necessary skills: Identifying and describing the skills required by work.* (Employment and Training Administration, U.S. Department of Labor). Washington, DC: Pelavin Associates.

Kaufman, R., & Herman, J. (1991). *Strategic planning in education: Rethinking, restructuring, revitalizing.* Lancaster, PA: Technomic.

Kaus, C. R., Lonky, E., & Roodin, P. (1984). In R. M. Lerner & N. L. Galambos (Eds.), *Experiencing adolescents: A sourcebook for parents, teachers, and teens* (pp. 231–281). New York: Teachers College Press.

Kelley, E. C. (1962). The fully functioning self. In A. W. Combs, E. C. Kelley, A. H. Maslow, & C. R. Rogers (Eds.), *Perceiving, behaving, becoming* (pp. 9–20). Washington DC: Association for Supervision and Curriculum Development.

Kerr, S. T. (1990). Alternative technologies as textbooks and the social imperatives of educational change. In D. L. Elliott & A. Woodward (Eds.), *Textbooks and schooling in the United States* (pp. 194–221). The Eighty-ninth Yearbook of the National Society for the Study of Education, Part I. Chicago: NSSE.

Kieffer, R. D., & Morrison, L. S. (1994). Changing portfolio process: One journey toward authentic assessment, *Language Arts, 71,* 411–418.

Kilpatrick, W. H. (1918). The project method, *Teachers College Record, 19*(4), 319–335.

Kirsch, I. S., Jungeblut, A., Jenkins, L., & Kolstad, A. (1993, September). *Adult literacy in America: A first look at the results of the National Adult Literacy Survey.* Washington, DC: Office of Educational Research and Improvement, U.S. Department of Education.

Klein, M. F. (1991a). A conceptual framework for curriculum decision making. In M. F. Klein (Ed.), *The politics of curriculum decision-making: Issues in centralizing the curriculum* (pp. 24–41). Albany, NY: State University of New York Press.

Klein, M. F. (1991b). Curriculum design. In A. Lewy (Ed.), *International encyclopedia of curriculum* (pp. 335–342). New York: Pergamon.

Kliebard, H. M. (1992). *Forging the American curriculum: Essays in curriculum history and theory.* New York: Routledge.

Kohlberg, L. (1967). Moral education, religious education, and the public schools: A developmental view. In T. R. Sizer (Ed.), *Religion and public education* (pp. 164–183). Boston: Houghton Mifflin.

Komoski, P. K. (1985). Instructional materials will not improve until we change the system. *Educational Leadership, 42*(7), 31–37.

Krathwohl, D. R., Bloom, B. S., & Masia, B. B. (1964). *Taxonomy of educational objectives. Handbook II: Affective domain.* New York: McKay.

Lauer, R. H. (1992). *Social problems and the quality of life* (5th ed.). Dubuque, IA: William C. Brown.

Leinhardt, G. (1992). What research on learning tells us about teaching. *Educational Leadership, 49*(7), 20–25.

Leithwood, K. A. (1991). Alternative orientations to implementation. In A. Lewy (Ed.), *International encyclopedia of curriculum* (pp. 446–447). New York: Pergamon.

Lenox, M. F., & Walker, M. L. (1994). Information literacy: A challenge for the future. *NASSP Bulletin, 78*(562), 57–72.

Lieberman, A. (1992). Introduction: The changing context of education. In A. Lieberman (Ed.), *The changing contexts of teaching* (pp. 1–10). The Ninety-first Yearbook of the National Society for the Study of Education, Part I. Chicago: NSSE.

Loucks, S. F., Newlove, B. W., & Hall, G. E. (1975). *Measuring levels of use of the innovation: A manual for trainers, interviewers, and raters* (Report No. 3013). Austin, TX: University of Texas, Research and Development Center for Teacher Education.

McCarthy, A. R. (1992). The American family. In L. Kaplan (Ed.), *Education and the family* (pp. 3–26). Boston: Allyn and Bacon.

Maccoby, E. (1984). Middle childhood in the context of the family. In W. A. Collins (Ed.), *Development during middle childhood: The years from six to twelve* (pp. 184–239). Washington, DC: National Academy Press.

Macmillan Literature Series (1991). *English literature with world masterpieces* (signature ed.). Mission Hills, CA: Glencoe/McGraw-Hill.

Macmillan Literature Series (1991). *English literature with world masterpieces, teacher's classroom resources 1.* Mission Hills, CA: Glencoe/McGraw-Hill.

Madaus, G. F., & Kellaghan, T. (1992). Curriculum evaluation and assessment. In P. W. Jackson (Ed.). *Handbook of research on curriculum* (pp. 119–154). New York: Macmillan.

Madaus, G. F., Woods, E. N., & Nuttal, R. L. (1973). A causal model analysis of Bloom's taxonomy. *American Educational Research Journal, 10,* 253–262.

Mahrer, A. R. (1978). *Experiencing: A humanistic theory of psychology and psychiatry.* New York: Brunner/Mazel.

Maslow, A. H. (1968). *Toward a psychology of being* (2nd ed.). Princeton, NJ: Van Nostrand.

Maslow, A. H. (1987). *Motivation and personality* (3rd ed.). New York: Harper Row.

Matczynski, T. J., & Rogus, J. (1985). Needs assessment: A means to clarify the goals of secondary schools. *National Association of Secondary School Principals Bulletin, 69,* 34–40.

Mendez-Morse, S. (1992). Leadership characteristics that facilitate school change. Austin, TX: Southwest Educational Development Laboratory. (ERIC Document Reproduction Service No. ED 370 215)

Mercer, C. D. (1994). Learning disabilities. In N. G. Haring, L. McCormick, & T. G. Haring (Eds.), *Exceptional children and youth* (6th ed.) (pp. 114–164). Englewood Cliffs, NJ: Merrill/Prentice Hall.

Middle school English language arts curriculum guide. (1991). (Available from Horseheads Central School District, Board of Education, Horseheads, NY 14845)

Miller, J. P., & Seller, W. (1985). *Curriculum: Perspectives and practice.* New York: Longman.

Mink, O. G., Esterhuysen, P. W., Mink, B. P., & Owen, K. Q. (1993). *Change at work: A comprehensive management process for transforming organizations.* San Francisco: Jossey-Bass.

Moran, A. (1991). What can learning styles research learn from cognitive psychology? *Educational Psychology, 11*(3–4), 239–245.

Mullis, I. V. S., Dossey, J. A., Foertsch, M. A., Jones, L. R., & Gentile, C. A. (1991). *Trends in academic progress: Achievement of U.S. students in science, 1969–70 to 1990, mathematics, 1973–1990, reading, 1971–1990, writing, 1984–1990.* Washington, DC: U.S. Department of Education.

Multicultural Social Studies Curriculum K–12. (1993). (Available from Tucson Unified School District #1, Tucson, AZ)

Naisbitt, J., & Aburdene, P. (1990). *Megatrends 2000: Ten new directions for the 1990s.* New York: William Morrow.

Nash, A., Cason, A., Rhum, M., McGrail, L., & Gomez–Sanford, R. (1989). *Talking shop: A curriculum sourcebook for participatory adult ESL.* Boston: English Family Literacy Project, University of Massachusetts.

National Assessment Governing Board. (1992). *Reading framework for the 1992 National Assessment of Educational Progress.* Washington, DC: U.S. Government Printing Office.

National Association for the Education of Young Children and the National Association of Early Childhood Specialists in State Departments of Education. (1991). Guidelines for appropriate curriculum content and assessment in programs serving children ages 3 through 8, *Young Children, 46*(3), 21–38.

National Commission on Excellence in Education. (1983). *A nation at risk: The imperative for educational reform.* A report to the nation and the Secretary of Education, United States Department of Education. Washington, DC: U.S. Government Printing Office.

National Council of Social Studies (1994). *Expectations of excellence: Curriculum standards for social studies.* Edison, NJ: NCSS Publishers.

National Council of Teachers of Mathematics (1989). *Curriculum and evaluation standards for school mathematics.* Reston, VA: NCTM.

National Education Association. (1918). *Cardinal principles of secondary education. A report of the commission on the reorganization of secondary education.* Washington, DC: U.S. Government Printing Office.

National Research Council. (1994 November). *National science education standards* (draft). Washington, DC: National Academic Press.

Niemiec, R. P., & Walberg, H. J. (1989). From teaching machines to microcomputers: Some milestones in the history of computer-based instruction, *Journal of Research on Computing in Education, 21,* 263–276.

Oliva, P. F. (1992). *Developing the curriculum* (3rd ed.). New York: HarperCollins.

Pandey, T. (1990). Power items and the alignment of curriculum and assessment. In G. Kulm (Ed.), *Assessing higher order thinking in mathematics* (pp. 39–51). Washington, DC: American Association for the Advancement of Science.

Paradise Valley school district curriculum adoption. (1994). (Available from Paradise Valley Unified School District No. 69, 3012 East Greenway Road, Phoenix, AZ 85032-4499)

Paris, C. L. (1993). *Teacher agency and curriculum making in classrooms.* New York: Teachers College Press.

Parker, J. C., & Rubin, L. J. (1966). *Process as content: Curriculum design and the application of knowledge.* Chicago: Rand McNally.

Patterson, J. L., Purkey, S. C., & Parker, J. V. (1986). *Productive school systems for a nonrational world.* Alexandria, VA: Association for Supervision and Curriculum Development.

Patton, J. R., & Polloway, E. A. (1994). Mild mental retardation. In N. G. Haring, L. McCormick, & T. G. Haring (Eds.), *Exceptional children and youth: An introduction to special education* (6th ed.) (pp. 212–257). Englewood Cliffs, NJ: Merrill/Prentice Hall.

Paulson, F. L., Paulson, P. R., & Meyer, C. A. (1991). What makes a portfolio a portfolio? *Educational Leadership, 48*(5), 60–63.

Personalized education for children: A handbook for early childhood education, K–4. (1982). (Available from Georgia Department of Education, 254 Washington Street NW, Atlanta, GA 30334)

Piaget, J. (1965). *The moral judgment of the child.* New York: Free Press.

Piaget, J. (1970). Piaget's theory. In P. H. Mussen (Ed.), *Carmichael's manual of child psychology, Vol 1* (3rd ed.). (pp. 703–732). New York: Wiley.

Pipho, C. (1991). Centralizing curriculum at the state level. In M. F. Klein (Ed.), *The politics of curriculum decision-making: Issues in centralizing the curriculum* (pp. 67–97). Albany, NY: State University of New York.

Pitch, M. (1994). With students' aid, Clinton signs Goals 2000, *Education Week, 13*(28), 1, 21.

Polya, G. (1957). *How to solve it* (2nd ed.). New York: Wiley.

Presseisen, B. Z. (1988). Avoiding battle at curriculum gulch: Teaching thinking AND content. *Educational Leadership, 45*(7), 7–8.

Probst, R. E. (1987). Adolescent literature and the English curriculum, *English Journal, 76*(3), 26–30.

Raths, L. E., Harmin, M., & Simon, S. B. (1978). *Values and teaching* (2nd ed.). Englewood Cliffs, NJ: Prentice Hall.

Reimer, J., Paolitto, D. P., & Hersh, R. H. (1983). *Promoting moral growth* (2nd ed.). New York: Longman.

Resnick, L. B. (1987). *Education and learning to think.* Washington DC: National Academy Press.

Rivera-Batiz, F. L. (1992). Quantitative literacy and the likelihood of employment among young adults in the United States, *Journal of Human Resources, 27*(2), 313–328.

Rock, I., & Palmer, S. (1990). The legacy of Gestalt psychology, *Scientific American, 263*(6), 84–90.

Romey, W. D. (1988). A person–centered seminar in world geography, *Journal of Geography, 87*(3), 88–95.

Rosenblatt, L. M. (1983). *Literature as exploration* (4th ed.). New York: Modern Language Association.

Rosenthal, R. & Rosnow, R. L. (1991). *Essentials of behavioral research: Methods and data analysis* (2nd ed.). New York: McGraw-Hill.

Ryle, G. (1949). *The concept of mind.* London: Hutchinson.

Sammons, K. B., Kobett, B., Heiss, J., & Fennell, F. (1992). Linking instruction and assessment in the mathematics classroom, *Arithmetic Teacher, 39*(6), 11–16.

Sanders, J. R. (1990). Curriculum evaluation. In H. J. Walberg & G. D. Haertel (Eds.), *International encyclopedia of educational evaluation* (pp. 163–166). New York: Pergamon.

Saylor, J. G., Alexander, W. M., & Lewis, A. J. (1981). *Curriculum planning for better teaching and learning* (4th ed.). New York: Holt, Rinehart & Winston.

Schrag, F. (1992). Conceptions of knowledge. In P. W. Jackson (Ed.), *Handbook of research on curriculum* (pp. 268–301). New York: Macmillan.

Science: A process approach: Commentary for teachers. (1970). Washington, DC: American Association for the Advancement of Science/Xerox Corporation.

Sherraden, M. W. (1988). School dropouts in perspective. In K. Ryan & J. M. Cooper (Eds.), *Kaleidoscope: Readings in education* (5th ed.) (pp. 136–146). Boston: Houghton Mifflin.

Short, E. C. (1986). A historical look at curriculum design, *Theory Into Practice, 25*(1), 3–9.

Short, K. G., & Burke, C. (1991). *Creating curriculum: Teachers and students as a community of learners.* Portsmouth, NH: Heinemann.

Shulman, L. S. (1986). Those who understand: Knowledge growth in teaching. *Educational Researcher, 15*(2), 4–14.

Shulman, L. S. (1987). Knowledge and teaching: Foundations of the new reform. *Harvard Educational Review, 57*(1), 1–22.

Shutes, R., & Petersen, S. (1994). Seven reasons why textbooks cannot make a curriculum. *NASSP Bulletin, 78*(565), 11–20.

Skinner, B. F. (1948). *Walden two*. Englewood Cliffs, NJ: Prentice Hall.

Skinner, B. F. (1968). *The technology of teaching*. Englewood Cliffs, NJ: Prentice Hall.

Slavin, R. (1990). *Cooperative learning: Theory, research, and practice*. Englewood Cliffs, NJ: Prentice Hall.

Smith, B. O. (1983). Curriculum content. In F. W. English (Ed.), *Fundamental curriculum decisions* (pp. 30–39). Alexandria, VA: Association for Supervision and Curriculum Development.

Snyder, J., Bolin, F., & Zumwalt, K. (1992). Curriculum implementation. In P. W. Jackson (Ed.), *Handbook of research on curriculum* (pp. 402–435). New York: Macmillan.

Sosniak, L. A., & Perlman, C. L. (1990). Secondary education by the book. *Journal of Curriculum Studies, 22,* 427–442.

Spanish IV curriculum. (n.d.). (Available from Stoughton Public Schools, 232 Pearl Street, Stoughton, MA 02072-2397)

Sternberg, R. J. (1985). *Beyond IQ: A triarchic theory of human intelligence*. New York: Cambridge University Press.

Stipek, D. J. (1993). *Motivation to learn: From theory to practice* (2nd ed.). Boston: Allyn and Bacon.

Strader, W. H., & Rinker, C. A. (1989). A child centered approach to dinosaurs, *Early Child Development and Care, 43,* 65–76.

Stratemeyer, F. B. (1973). Developing a curriculum for modern living. In R. T. Hyman (Ed.), *Approaches in curriculum* (pp. 53–72). Englewood Cliffs, NJ: Prentice Hall.

Streshly, W. (1992). Staff development in a site-based curriculum development model. *National Association of Secondary Schools Principals Bulletin, 76*(540), 56–63.

Stufflebeam, D. L. (1983). The CIPP model for program evaluation. In G. F. Madaus, M. S. Scriven, & D. L. Stufflebeam (Eds.), *Evaluation models: Viewpoints on educational and human services evaluation* (pp. 117–141). Boston: Kluwer-Nijhoff.

Stufflebeam, D. L. (1991). Professional standards and ethics for evaluators. In M. W. McLaughlin & D. C. Phillips (Eds.), *Evaluation and education:*

At quarter century (pp. 249–282). The Ninetieth Yearbook of the National Society for the Study of Education, Part II. Chicago: NSSE.

Stufflebeam, D. L., Foley, W. J., Gephart, W. J., Guba, E. G., Hammond, R. L., Merriman, H. O., & Provus, M. M. (1971). *Educational evaluation and decision making*. Itasca, IL: F. E. Peacock.

Stufflebeam, D. L., & McCormick, C. H., Brinkerhoff, R. O., & Nelson, C. O. (1985). *Conducting educational needs assessments*. Boston: Kluwer-Nijhoff.

Stufflebeam, D. L., & Shinkfield, A. J. (1985). *Systematic evaluation: A self-instructional guide to theory and practice*. Boston: Kluwer-Nijhoff.

Taba, H. (1962). *Curriculum development*. New York: Harcourt, Brace, & World.

Talwar, R., & Lerner, J. V. (1991). Theories of adolescent development. In R. M. Lerner, A. C. Petersen, & J. Brooks-Gunn (Eds.), *Encyclopedia of adolescence, Vol. 2* (pp. 1141–1147). New York: Garland.

Tanner, D. (1988). The textbook controversies. In L. N. Tanner (Ed.), *Critical issues in curriculum,* (pp. 122–147). The Eighty-seventh Yearbook of the National Society for the Study of Education, Part I. Chicago: NSSE.

Tanner, D. (1993). A nation 'truly' at risk, *Phi Delta Kappan, 75,* 288–297.

Tanner, D., & Tanner, L. (1980). *Curriculum development: Theory into practice* (2nd ed.). Englewood Cliffs, NJ: Merrill/Prentice Hall.

Tanner, D., & Tanner, L. (1990). *History of the school curriculum*. Englewood Cliffs, NJ: Merrill/Prentice Hall.

Tanner, J. M. (1991). Growth spurt, adolescent. I. In R. M. Lerner, A. C. Petersen, & J. Brooks-Gunn (Eds.), *Encyclopedia of adolescence, Vol. 1* (pp. 419–424). New York: Garland.

Thomas, R. M. (1992). *Comparing theories of child development* (3rd ed.). Belmont, CA: Wadsworth.

Trueba, H. T. (1988). English literacy acquisition: From cultural trauma to learning disabilities in minority students, *Linguistics and Education, 1,* 125–152.

Trueba, H. T. (1989). *Raising silent voices: Educating the linguistic minorities for the 21st century*. Cambridge: Newbury House.

Tulley, M. A., & Farr, R. (1990). Textbook evaluation and selection. In D. L. Elliott & A. Woodward (Eds.), *Textbooks and schooling in the United States* (pp. 162–177). The Eighty-ninth Yearbook of the National Society for the Study of Education, Part I. Chicago: NSSE.

Tyler, R. W. (1949). *Basic principles of curriculum and instruction.* Chicago: University of Chicago Press.

Tyree, A. K., Jr. (1993). Examining the evidence: Have states reduced local control of curriculum? *Educational Evaluation and Policy Analysis, 15*(1), 34–50.

U.S. Bureau of the Census. (1993). *Statistical abstract of the United States 1993* (113th ed.). Washington, DC: U.S. Government Printing Office.

U.S. Bureau of the Census. (1994). *Statistical abstract of the United States 1994* (114th ed.). Washington, DC: U.S. Government Printing Office.

U.S. Department of Education. (1991). *America 2000: An education strategy* (rev. ed.). Washington, DC: Author.

U.S. Department of Labor. (1994, May). Tomorrow's jobs. *Occupational outlook handbook: 1994–95.* Bulletin 2450. Washington: DC.

van Geel, T. (1991). Two visions of federalism and the control of the curriculum. In M. F. Klein (Ed.), *The politics of curriculum decision-making: Issues in centralizing the curriculum* (pp. 42–66). Albany, NY: State University of New York.

van Meter, E. J. (1991). The Kentucky mandate: School-based decision making, *National Association of Secondary School Principals Bulletin, 75*(532), 52–62.

Venezky, R. L. (1992). Textbooks in school and society. In P. W. Jackson (Ed.), *Handbook of research on curriculum* (pp. 436–461). New York: Macmillan.

Vygotsky, L. S. (1962). *Thought and language.* Cambridge, MA: MIT Press.

Wadsworth, B. J. (1984). *Piaget's theory of cognitive and affective development* (3rd ed.). New York: Longman.

Ward, S. L. (1991). Moral development in adolescence. In R. M. Lerner, A. Petersen, & J. Brooks-Gunn (Eds.), *Encyclopedia of adolescence, Vol. 2* (pp. 663–668). New York: Garland.

Weber, R. P. (1990). *Basic content analysis* (2nd ed.). Sage University Paper series on Quantitative Applications in the Social Sciences, series no. 07-049. Newbury Park, CA: Sage.

Webster's new world dictionary of American English (3rd. college ed.). (1994). New York: Prentice Hall.

Weinstein, G., & Fantini, M. D. (1970). Identity education. In G. Weinstein & M. D. Fantini (Eds.), *Toward humanistic education: A curriculum of affect* (pp. 66–121). New York: Praeger.

Westbury, I. (1990). Textbooks, textbook publishers, and the quality of schooling. In D. L. Elliott & A. Woodward (Eds.), *Textbooks and schooling in the United States* (pp. 1–22). The Eighty-ninth Yearbook of the National Society for the Study of Education, Part I. Chicago: NSSE.

White, P. A. (1992). Teacher empowerment under "ideal" school-site autonomy. *Educational Evaluation and Policy Analysis, 14*(1), 69–82.

White, R. (1959). Motivation reconsidered: The concept of competence. *Psychological Review, 66,* 297–333.

Wiggins, G. (1993). Assessment: Authenticity, context, and validity. *Phi Delta Kappan, 75,* 200–214.

Wiley, T., & Sikula, J. (1992). Families, schools, literacy, and diversity. In L. Kaplan (Ed.), *Education and the family* (pp. 69–85). Boston: Allyn and Bacon.

Willis, S. (1993, September). Multicultural teaching: Meeting the challenges that arise in practice, *Curriculum Update,* p. 1.

Wiltsey, S. (1975). *The Canterbury Tales* for high-school students. In G. I. Brown (Ed.), *The live classroom through confluent education and Gestalt* (pp. 255–268). New York: Viking.

Wolery, M., & Haring, T. G. (1994). Moderate, severe, and profound disabilities. In N. G. Haring, L. McCormick, & T. G. Haring (Eds.), *Exceptional children and youth* (6th ed.) (pp. 258–299). Englewood Cliffs, NJ: Merrill/Prentice Hall.

Wolf, D. P. (1993). Assessment as an episode of learning. In R. E. Bennett & W. C. Ward (Eds.), *Construction versus choice in cognitive achievement* (pp. 213–240). Hillsdale: NJ: Erlbaum.

Wolf, J. S. (1994). The gifted and talented. In N. G. Haring, L. McCormick, & T. G. Haring (Eds.), *Exceptional children and youth: An introduction to special education* (6th ed.) (pp. 456–500). Englewood Cliffs, NJ: Merrill/Prentice Hall.

Worthen, B. R., Borg, W. R., & White, K. R. (1993). *Measurement and evaluation in the schools.* New York: Longman.

Wyoming Arts Education Curriculum. (1992). (Available from Wyoming Department of Education, Cheyenne, WY)

Zeitlin, M., Lutterman, K. G., & Russell, J. W. (1977). Death in Vietnam: Class, poverty, and the risks of war. In M. Zeitlin (Ed.), *American society, inc.* (pp. 143–155). Chicago: Rand McNally.

Zessoules, R., & Gardner, H. (1991). Authentic assessment: Beyond the buzzword and into the classroom. In V. Perrone (Ed.), *Expanding student assessment* (pp. 47–71). Alexandria, VA: Association for Supervision and Curriculum Development.

Name Index

Subject Index

389

SUGGESTIONS, PLEASE!

The publishers and I would like to know your reactions to this book. Your suggestions will be helpful in planning revisions.

Please answer the following questions, clip, and mail to:

Editor, Curriculum
Prentice Hall/Merrill Publishing Company
445 Hutchinson Avenue
Columbus, OH 43235

Thank you for taking time to respond.

Evelyn J. Sowell

1. In which program are you enrolled for the study of curriculum? (Check all boxes that apply.)

   ☐ doctoral   ☐ C&I
   ☐ masters   ☐ elementary
   ☐ bachelors   ☐ secondary
   ☐ other (specify)   ☐ leadership
   _____   ☐ other (specify)
                              _____

2. What is your previous experience with school curricula? (Check all boxes that apply.)

   ☐ none   ☐ member of curriculum committee
   ☐ as a teacher   ☐ chair/facilitator of curriculum committee
   ☐ as an administrator   ☐ class/team/grade curriculum development
   ☐ as a parent/community member ☐ other _____

3. Identify the single chapter about which you offer suggestions: _____

4. A purpose is indicated in the chapter introduction. Identify any section/information in the chapter that is **unnecessary** or **not pertinent** to this purpose.

5. Identify any section/information that should be **clarified** in order to make the purpose attainable.

6. Describe any information that should be **added** to the chapter to make the purpose clearer.

7. Describe any information that you especially **liked** about this chapter.

8. Describe any suggestions you have concerning the book overall.

THANK YOU.